# Byron and Marginality

for
Michaela, Dana, Swantje and Oliver,
young, dedicated people who have always been more
than colleagues . . .

# Byron and Marginality

Edited by Norbert Lennartz

EDINBURGH
University Press

Edinburgh University Press is one of the leading university presses in the UK. We publish academic books and journals in our selected subject areas across the humanities and social sciences, combining cutting-edge scholarship with high editorial and production values to produce academic works of lasting importance. For more information visit our website: edinburghuniversitypress.com

Edinburgh University Press Ltd
The Tun – Holyrood Road,
12(2f) Jackson's Entry,
Edinburgh EH8 8PJ

Typeset in 11/13 Adobe Sabon by
IDSUK (DataConnection) Ltd, and
printed and bound in Great Britain.

A CIP record for this book is available from the British Library

ISBN 978 1 4744 3941 1 (hardback)
ISBN 978 1 4744 3943 5 (webready PDF)
ISBN 978 1 4744 3944 2 (epub)

# Contents

### III. Cherishing the Marginal – Marginal Genres in Byron

### IV. On the Provocative Margins of Taste

### V. Marginal Affairs – Visual and Paratextual Aspects in Byron

# Foreword

When Professor Norbert Lennartz invited me to open the conference at the University of Vechta, on the subject of Lord Byron and the Margins of Romanticism, I was initially puzzled. How could Byron, more widely read in England than any of the other Romantic poets, and read both in English and in translation across Europe, be at the margins of Romanticism? Yet, as the conference progressed, I began to see the scope for such an approach and started to realise how Byron does not fit so neatly into the traditional Romantic canon.

The papers from that conference have now been brought together in this book, which encourages us to approach Byron in a different and sometimes provocative way. By asking readers to look afresh at aspects of Byron that are familiar – his admiration for Classical poets such as Pope and Dryden, his hostility towards many of his contemporary Romantic poets, the heavy irony and stark realism that characterise so much of his work – we are invited to consider to what extent Byron can be categorised as a 'true' Romantic.

Within the broad scope of this volume, distinguished scholars seek to examine a number of important texts sometimes marginalised in Byron studies, to explore how Byron's own self-created identity as an outsider redefines a form of Romanticism centred on rebelliousness and to reflect on the geographic marginalisation of Byron's own life outside England and his interest in the Orient.

Although I write as someone who is far from being an English literature scholar, I am sure that this volume will make an important contribution to the debate as to whether Byron was indeed marginal to Romanticism, or whether through his rebellious iconoclasm, his humour and irony, and the persona of the marginalised outsider, Byron created a new variant of Romanticism where he takes centre stage.

Robert James (Robin), Lord Byron, 13th Baron Byron

## Acknowledgements

It is open to conjecture whether Byron's marginality (at least in Germany) can be proved by the fact that, after the memorable 1996 Duisburg symposium, it took almost twenty years to organise the next conference on Byron on German soil, and that the conference eventually took place not in one of the places central to German academia (such as Berlin, Munich, Cologne or Bonn, the last of which Byron cheekily rhymed with 'gone' in *Don Juan* X, ll. 489 / 491) but in the marginal site of Vechta, a rural Catholic town in Lower Saxony whose three Piranesian prisons might, however, have piqued Byron's curiosity.

For three days in the June of 2014 Vechta became the centre of Byron studies, a fact that was underlined by the generous funding of the German Research Foundation (DFG) and by the presence of the current Lord Byron, who not only kindly accepted my invitation to come to Vechta but also consented to write a little Foreword for this collection of essays. My heartfelt thanks go to him, but also to the numerous, internationally acclaimed scholars who undertook to explore the paradox between industrial globalisation and rural marginality in Vechta, and to all the top-ranking Byronists who readily sent in their articles to contribute to the book as it is now. One abstract was sadly not followed by the submission of a full-length essay: unable to be present in Vechta, the late Peter Cochran had instantaneously replied to my invitation and sent in a well-argued and pertinent proposal, but his sudden and unexpected death in May 2015 foiled the completion of an essay that would have been a welcome and significant addition to the high quality of the book.

That the title of the book, *Lord Byron and Marginality*, was to assume a new meaning in light of the fact that its publication coincided with the hitherto unthinkable self-incurred marginalisation of Britain in Europe due to Brexit is an additional indication of the fact that the relationship between centrality and marginality has always been a dynamic one and subject to processes of constant negotiation.

What Byron, the most European of all Romantic poets, would have said about Brexit in his poems and to what extent this new aspect of political and economic marginalisation would have whetted his appetite to add lacerating cantos to his *Don Juan* remain in the realm of speculation; that Brexit will have an impact neither on the time-honoured and indispensable cooperation between British and mainland European universities nor on the intellectual exchange among world-wide Byronists goes without saying.

In this respect, it has been a pleasure working with Michelle Houston, Adela Rauchova and Ersev Ersoy from Edinburgh University Press, whose openness to the project and their unbureaucratic way of dealing with it were always deeply appreciated. I express my gratitude to all the participants, who responded to my insistent emails with unwavering kindness and patience and put up with my pestering reminders of deadlines (which, more often than not, ran the whole gamut from dead and deadlier to deadliest).

And, last but not least, I would also like to thank my university for supporting my Byronic projects and, after my spell as a Vice-Principal of the university, for granting me my longed-for sabbatical leave in the winter of 2016/17 to put the finishing touches to the essays. The whole project would never have materialised if my editorial team in the English Department at the University of Vechta – Michaela Hausmann, Dana Jahn MA, Swantje van Mark MA and Oliver Schmidt MA – had not worked so diligently and steadfastly on the project and transformed a bunch of highly individual essays into a homogeneously formatted book. This book is dedicated to these four young Vechta scholars who vicariously stand for all young researchers who daily do such a great and invisible job in reconciling their postgraduate work with the time-consuming projects of their supervisors. My sincerest apologies to you for not expressing my gratitude more often.

Vechta, autumn 2017
Norbert Lennartz

# Editions and Abbreviations

For reasons of standardisation, citations from Byron's primary works will appear in parentheses and refer to the editions below.

BLJ       (1973–94). *Byron's Letters and Journals*, 13 vols, ed. Leslie A. Marchand, London: John Murray. References are given with volume number and page, e.g. (*BLJ*, vol. 1, p. 100).

CCB       (1954). *His Very Self and Voice: Collected Conversations of Lord Byron*, ed. Ernest J. Lovell, Jr, New York: Macmillan.

Childe Harold       George Gordon Byron (1980). *Childe Harold's Pilgrimage* in: *Complete Poetical Works*, vol. 2, ed. Jerome J. McGann, Oxford: Clarendon Press. References are given with regard to the respective Canto (in capitalised Roman numbers) and line numbers, e.g. (*Childe Harold* I, l. 10).

CMP       (1991). *Complete Miscellaneous Prose*, ed. Andrew Nicholson, Oxford: Clarendon Press.

CPW       (1980–93). *Complete Poetical Works*, 7 vols, ed. Jerome J. McGann, Oxford: Clarendon Press.

Don Juan       George Gordon Byron (1986). *Don Juan* in: *Complete Poetical Works*, vol. 5, ed. Jerome J. McGann, Oxford: Clarendon Press. References are given with regard to the respective Canto (in capitalised Roman numbers) and line numbers, e.g. (*Don Juan* I, l. 10).

# Chapter 1

# Lord Byron, Wandering and Wavering between the Centres and Margins of Romanticism: An Attempt at an Introduction

*Norbert Lennartz*

## Romantic pugilism: the fight of the central versus the marginal

A few sporadic efforts have recently been made to write or to document the story of Romantic marginality in British literature,[1] and while some of them concentrate exclusively on the hitherto forgotten and marginalised names of (mostly) female Romantics, others – and in particular this book – succumb to the vortex of the 'big six' and start to look for marginality not so much in the margins, but in the hallowed realms of the canon and its canonised heroes. Here one is immediately struck by the fact that canonicity is a dubious category (see Haekel, Chapter 3), since in Britain there was never – apart from a few fringe movements and associations such as the 'Lake School', the 'Cockney School' or the 'Satanic School'[2] – a tightly knit and cohesive school of Romanticism (to which the German Romantics, with their gravitational centres in Jena, Weimar and Heidelberg, aspired). British 'Romanticism', by contrast, seems to be an academic construction levelled against the splintering of Romanticism into Romanticisms in the wake of Arthur O. Lovejoy, an arbitrary bracket that patches together six male individuals, cranks and nerds, who not only clamoured for singularity but also were eager to relegate their colleagues to the margins of insignificance and dilettantism, and, more often than not, to the edge of lunacy.

Having given up on his friend and interlocutor Coleridge as a hopeless case, William Wordsworth left nobody in any doubt that he was a, not to say *the*, central and canonical figure of a movement that, for want of a better term, later came to be known as Romantic period writing. Through the lenses of his contemporaries and adversaries, the reader, however, learns that Wordsworth, the venerated bard of Grasmere, was anything but a central or even chosen poet. William Hazlitt was rather struck by Wordsworth's provincialism, by his Cumbrian accent and by what he described as his 'gaunt and Don Quixote-like' appearance.[3] Hazlitt's insinuation that Wordsworth resembles a tragicomic figure who, along with Torquato Tasso, became synonymous with the precarious borderline between reason and madness illustrates the relentless and sharp-tongued battle in which Regency writers were fighting for the central position of a movement that was scarcely more than embryonic at that time. Wordsworth's retort seems to be disproportionately vindictive: he not only refused to acknowledge Hazlitt's literary achievement but also played a significant role in the accusations brought against the writer in the unsavoury Keswick rapist affair.[4]

This is the cultural climate in which the greatest slanderer and marginaliser of his contemporaries, Lord Byron, thrived. Never reluctant to reduce his colleagues to marginal non-entities, Byron rejoiced in his position as an aristocrat and European celebrity, and did what his imitator, Heinrich Heine, was to do later on when he 'poured his lye of the most trenchant sarcasm'[5] over the Lakists and the Cockney poet John Keats. In particular, the latter's sensual and mythology-laden poetry was vituperated by Byron as expressions (and oozings) of a misdirected juvenile sexuality: 'a sort of mental masturbation' brought about by the fact that Keats was supposed to be 'always f-gg-g his *Imagination*'.[6] Although he felt sincere remorse when he later learnt of Keats's premature death in Rome, Byron never relented in his efforts to fashion himself as the pop star and genius of Romanticism (see Tuominen-Pope, Chapter 10) and to consign his competitors (and predominantly the turncoats flocking around the Poet Laureate, Robert Southey) to the position of drooling sentimentalists, muddle-brained metaphysicians and intellectually (and sexually) dehydrated dabblers. What these instances of intellectual pugilism or 'aesthetic brawling' (to use and translate August von Kotzebue's idea of an 'ästhetische Prügeley' into English) seem to suggest is that, despite his iconoclastic attitude as a pre-Osbornian Angry Young Man, Byron endorsed a normative (and conservative) understanding of poetry and felt himself to be in a position of intellectual superiority and centrality.

A glance at Byron's poetry and biography makes it sufficiently clear that the envisioned demarcation line between centrality and marginality in his early works, *English Bards and Scotch Reviewers* (1809) or *Hints from Horace* (1811), was a self-willed construction inviting contradiction and quarrel. As if to live up to his position as a scoffer, brawler and challenger of Regency literature from the cultural and topographical outside, Byron, the alleged epitome of canonisation, lives on, deals with and writes from topographical margins (see Minta, Chapter 6). What is even more crucial about his work, however, is that his very poems are deeply moored in marginality, made up of genres, stanzaic forms, themes and characters that are not only outdated and liminal but also paradoxically located within and beyond the chronological margins of the time in which they were penned. The more one focuses on Byron, the more one is compelled to see that he is fascinated by all forms of marginality, especially when he recklessly straddles generic, stylistic and thematic boundaries and fixes on topics that are, even nowadays, considered to be downright scandalous, perverse and morally (if not aesthetically) marginal. Courting marginality and the liminal from a position of self-authorised centrality, Byron vexingly casts himself into and dallies with contradictory roles and identities: on the one hand, he is a pre-Romantic Augustan, on the other, a post- or even anti-Romantic modern who, in the corpus of his heterogeneous poetic works, lets his readers witness a *querelle des anciens et des modernes* reloaded and wonder to what extent the vestiges of his genuine Romantic voice (*Manfred* (1817), *Sardanapalus* (1821) or *Mazeppa* (1819)) are just the spectacle of an elusive and marginal ventriloquism.

## Ex-centric routes to marginal themes

All attempts to chart the trajectory of Byron's turbulent literary career are bound to lead to the insight that Byron's work is, in all respects, ex-centric and, as Jerome J. McGann states, 'marginal' in the sense of being far 'beyond the Romantic framework of reference of say Keats or Wordsworth'.[7] Right from the outset of his career as a writer, Byron reveals himself as a Neoclassicist (see Lessenich, Chapter 4), as an avid reader and staunch supporter of Dryden, Swift and Pope, only to launch from there into an extreme form of Romantic Icarianism in *Manfred* and *Cain* (1821), which runs counter to and turns upside down Pope's axiom of Daedalian contentedness: 'Know then thyself, presume not God to scan / The proper study of Mankind is Man.'[8] This soaring and hyperbolic supernaturalism suddenly tilts into a down-to-earth post-Romantic realism (if not Naturalism),[9] which, in Canto IV of *Don Juan* (1820), is adequately and self-referentially translated into the image of an avian catastrophe: striving Pegasus emulates Icarus and Phaeton, then 'sprains a wing' (*Don Juan* IV, l. 4) and, nose-diving, crashes from the marginal realms of the Romantic sublime into the infernal (and scarcely less marginal) regions of vulgar and 'burlesque' reality:

> And the sad truth which hovers o'er my desk
> Turns what was once romantic to burlesque. (*Don Juan* IV, ll. 23–4)

What Byron seems to imply is that the Romantic mode is neither constant nor sustainable, and is always on the verge of drifting centrifugally into the margins. While the German poet Novalis, in his *Hymns to the Night* (1799), located his visionary poetry on the 'threshold of the world' ('das Grenzgebürge der Welt'), right on the cusp between this and the transcendental world, the 'sad truth' of Byron's poetry is that this equilibrium is fallacious and lost. The Byronic mode inevitably veers into marginal and subterranean regions, thereby accelerating the deconstruction of the myth of the three c's of Romanticism: central, canonical and centripetal, or 'circuitous' in Abrams's terms[10] (a myth that should be added to the list of the thirty myths challenged and dispelled by critics such as Duncan Wu).[11]

Apart from using poetry as an unprecedented rollercoaster that flings its readers from one extreme to the other and deprives them of the illusion of a central resting point, Byron reinforces the marginality of his work by having his popular poems abound in marginal characters and marginal places. While finding himself famous and becoming the star of the literary salons on the publication of the first two Cantos of *Childe Harold's Pilgrimage* in 1812, Byron reverts not only to outcasts and *solitaires* as his literary personae but also, preferentially, to the device of the marginal time traveller. Unlike H. G. Wells's future-bound time traveller in the Victorian science-fiction story *The Time Machine* (1895), Byron's time traveller is a knight errant from the bygone medieval past, or a traveller from the history-obsessed present making a detour into the past, confined to, but also protected by, the firm structures of the Spenserian stanza. Transferred from the time of chivalry (which Byron poignantly deconstructs as 'the most profligate of all possible centuries' in the 'Addition to the Preface') into the Europe of the post-Napoleonic Wars,[12] Childe Harold, 'sore sick at heart' (*Childe Harold* I, l. 46), juxtaposes the grandeur of history and the periods of intense cultural activity with what is left in the dreary present. From the marginal position of a pessimistic and cultural *revenant*, Childe Harold (re-) visits places that look depopulated and deserted, turned into sites that, in the wake of tremendous paradigm shifts, have become forgotten and marginalised. Athens, the centre and hub of Antiquity, is, for Byron (and regrettably for the twenty-first-century reader too), no more than a marginal place, out of touch with the political, cultural and economic centres of a reorganised Europe. Another case in point is Rome in Canto IV: personified as the Niobe of nations, Rome has, in Byron's poem, changed its role from being the magnetic and culturally cornucopian destination of the aristocrats' Grand Tour to a city of sheer absence ('child*less*', 'crown*less*', 'voice*less*', 'tenant*less*').[13] Not only have the ashes of the tombs been desecrated and scattered but also the entire city has been reduced to 'a marble wilderness' (*Childe Harold* IV, l. 710), to a place ransacked for its history, beauty and cultural centrality. From the biased perspective of a cultural malcontent, of a young Byronic man counting himself among the 'orphans of the heart' (*Childe Harold* IV, l. 694), the entire world has lost its ontological centre and has eventually turned into myriads of marginalised fragments, ruins and purposeless cultural citations. When, by the end of the poem, Byron has his persona merge with the 'withered stumps' of his post-Napoleonic wasteland[14] – 'His shadow fades away into Destruction's mass' (*Childe Harold* IV, l. 1484) – the poet's obsession with marginality has reached its peak and been fuelled by the fact that since 1816, in the wake of his disastrous separation from his wife, he had been allocated the role of an exiled writer, a modern Ahasverus roaming the relics of a post-Vienna Congress Europe.

Among the various ex-centric time travellers that move along or beyond the margins of Romanticism in Byron's poems is – along with the Giaour, Tasso or the Corsair – Don Juan. Invented and staged for the first time by the Mercedarian monk Tirso de Molina in 1613, and resuscitated by Molière and Mozart / Da Ponte, Don Juan re-enters the literary universe in Byron's poem as a modern *pícaro*. Flung from the early modern age into an anti-Romantic, absurd and crudely Naturalistic world, Don Juan is no longer a metaphysical rebel, an erotic *homme fatal*, but a boy buffeted around by fate, seduced and harassed by insatiable women and relegated to the margins of slave markets, seraglios and battlefields beyond the pale of Europe. But what is even more different from the poems he had written in the wake of his successful verse epic *Childe Harold's Pilgrimage* is the fact that Byron uses his last major poem to reconnoitre the margins of taste and decorum. Thus, the first (comparatively harmless) breach of decorum lies in the fact that the whole story of Don Juan is narrated not so much as a parabola as in the style of the flashy new gazettes that, so the speaker complains, weekly or monthly cloy their readers with cant, sensational news and trivia. In this context, it is quite fitting that the entire text can no longer be seen as a venerable piece of poetry, but must be regarded as a rich (and indigestible) stew, a journalistic *olla podrida* that the storyteller, a Spanish gentleman, offers to 'a small elderly audience' '*at some distance*'.[15] What the 'small elderly audience' hears is a strange, disenchanting back story about the (or a) modern reincarnation of Don Juan, raised by a domineering mother who – despite her stern regimen of censorship – is not able to keep her son from becoming embroiled in various scandals. Himself haunted by the revelations that Caroline Lamb had made public in her 1816 *roman à clef*, *Glenarvon*, Byron, via his Spanish storyteller, shows how scandals come into being and what a banal 'School for Scandal' it takes to turn a marginal young man into the transitory centre of slander, disparagement, or what people nowadays subsume under the vulgarism of a shit-storm. The 'unseemly plight' of Don Juan's nakedness, the 'pleasant scandal' (*Don Juan* I, l. 1500 / 1501) of being caught *in flagrante* in Donna Julia's Spanish bedroom, are duly unfolded in the medium and style of 'the English newspapers' (*Don Juan* I, l. 1504) – a fact that shows to what extent Don Juan's (Spanish) and Byron's (English) moral *faux-pas* were conflated and eventually ascribed to the topographical marginality of the 'sunburnt nations' (*Don Juan* I, 552) in which both the persona and its creator lived.

A cursory glance at *Don Juan* and other related poems suffices to discern – and this was a far deeper breach of taste and decorum – that Byron had the *enfant terrible*'s fascination with (kinky) sex, crime and perversion of all sorts. The shipwreck in Canto II seems to take a pivotal position both in the poem and in Byron's *œuvre*: the drowning of the Holy Trinity in the form of a ship, the *Trinidada*, entails a long concatenation of absurdities and agonising monstrosities that inexplicably eluded Mario Praz's portrayal of what, in 1933, came to be known as 'the Romantic Agony'. While Praz concentrates exclusively on the 'Beauty of the Medusa' in the very first chapter of his seminal book,[16] he seems to ignore the fact that it was the real shipwreck of the modern *Medusa*, a maritime disaster (monumentalised in Théodore Géricault's 1816 painting *Le Radeau de la Méduse*), that set Byron's (and other dark Romantics') riotous imagination in motion. The conflated end of the *Medusa* / *Trinidada* seems to entail cosmogonic consequences, when the Book of Genesis and its seven-day countdown are blasphemously transformed into an anti-Genesis, a genealogy of cannibalism, with the Romantic focus being suddenly shifted from the central titanic hero, Prometheus, to the marginal gnawing vulture (*Don Juan* II, l. 596). Severe transgressions of the boundaries of taste[17] like these and inroads into the marginal and forbidden realms of the taboo established Byron's reputation as a maniac, as a sufferer from traumatic experience whom Percy Bysshe Shelley monumentalised in the Byronic figure of the Maniac in the poem *Julian and Maddalo* (published posthumously in 1824) – an indelible blemish and mark of Cain that determined Byron's reputation in the Victorian age and led the vanguard of the anti-Byronists around Thomas Carlyle to advise their audiences to shut their Byron in favour of Goethe's later works of Classicist sanity.[18]

## Pubertal manœuvres in the marginal dark

One of Carlyle's objections to Byron was the fact that, as a man of genius, he had failed to reach maturity and to meet the Victorian requirements of adulthood and seriousness.[19] When, in his recent study on *Perverse Romanticism*, Richard C. Sha introduces the baffling category of puberty into the debate in order to elucidate the paradox of Byron's centrality and simultaneous marginality further, one is surprised to see that his provocative hypothesis is basically in line with what conservatives of the Victorian age thought about Byron. What, in Carlyle, is still vaguely polemical is, however, in Sha's book, given a sound and scientific underpinning. Under the title of 'Epic Puberty, and Polymorphous Perversity', Sha reverts to the transitional period of puberty to allow for Byron's insistent use of ambiguities and for the shocking marginality that seems to be at the core of Byron's *Don Juan* and most of his defiant poetry. Focusing on sexual identity, Sha maintains that in puberty the body becomes 'a paradoxical ground of latency' in which – according to physicians and anthropologists of the nineteenth century – 'one feminized sex became two'.[20] While Coleridge occasionally swerves into the marginalised regions of the taboo and, by having recourse to the person from Porlock, ruefully reverts to a self-imposed authority of censorship, Byron refrains from all censorious intervention and, in his poems and other writings, unlocks a Pandora's box of marginal, indecent and devastating topics, such as suicide (see Franklin, Chapter 11), the (good) death (see Mole, Chapter 12), *femmes fatales* (see Bone, Chapter 13) and deviant sex, the last of which, in particular in its burlesque treatment of rape in Canto VIII, elicits bewilderment from critics even today. By putting the emphasis on Don Juan's boyhood, which the 'usual hirsute seasons' (*Don Juan* IX, l. 55) are about to destroy, Byron turns the time-honoured story of the libertine rake into a story of initiation, a rite of passage, which introduces the Spanish youth into the ambiguities and monstrosities of adult life. One of these monstrosities is the fact that the adolescent protagonist has to acknowledge that life is a 'nautical existence' spent on the wide and perilous expanse of women's Brobdingnagian bodies, constantly exposed to the threat of being drowned by genital floods, vaginal eddies and other maelstroms. There are various codified references in the poem to the idea that man's existence is by definition a marginal one, confined to the abdominal *terrae incognitae* of incalculable and freakish women's bodies.

In this context, Sha refers to an interesting example of intertextuality that translates and twists a (much used and abused) quotation from Shakespeare's *Julius Caesar* into a misogynist commentary on what Byron saw as problematic gender constellations.[21] Taking Brutus' well-known lines about the right choice of time – 'There is a tide in the affairs of men / Which taken at the flood leads on to fortune'[22] – as a cue, Byron substitutes women for men and suddenly charges the lines with unforeseen sexual innuendo. Taking into consideration the fact that 'affairs' had been used in puns on vaginas since the early modern age,[23] Byron wittily gives the whole passage such a sexual slant that, to the dismay of his Regency audience, he sees tides no longer in terms of chronology but rather as genital floods that inundate men and cause them to cede the privilege of navigation. While men had been used to colonising the female body and to arrogating the Adamitic right to tag the unknown regions with their names (the Paduan anatomist Gabriele Fallopio leaving the coloniser's flag on the Fallopian tubes), Byron envisages the dawn of a matriarchy in which not only women have taken over the role of the navigators ('Those navigators must be able seamen,' *Don Juan* VI, l. 11) but also the excessive porosity of the female body has nullified, drowned and marginalised its male counterpart. In this respect, Byron's casual remarks about the female body's anti-teleological floods, which lead 'God knows where' (*Don Juan* VI, l. 10), refer back to the central shipwreck scene, where men – bereft of all means of navigation – were shown aimlessly drifting on the watery expanse of the female body of the ocean. Interspersed images of maternity that treacherously relate the ocean to an 'unweaned child' (*Don Juan* II, l. 554) or the rainbow to an airy child 'cradled in vermilion' (*Don Juan* II, l. 731) lend further support to the fact that Byron's poem records a growing process of feminisation that involves Don Juan, and indeed the male sex in general. The witty reference to epicenism in Canto VI, which eventually leads to Don Juan being turned into a Juanna, underscores Sha's definition of puberty as the marginal period *par excellence* that 'cuts across gender lines'[24]; but what it shows even more emphatically is that man's patriarchal self-fashioning, the illusion of the centrality of the male sex, seems to have been superseded by marginal (and liminal) subcategories of gender such as the transgendered or cross-dressed man, the third sex of the eunuch (sexual or intellectual), or the masculine woman.

## Paratextual marginality

Although *Don Juan* is nowadays considered to be Byron's most famous and central work, there is no gainsaying the fact that it is also his most sustained effort to thwart all aspirations to define, fix and categorise it. Anticipating Lord Henry Wotton's *aperçu*, in Oscar Wilde's *The Picture of Dorian Gray* (1891), that 'to define is to limit',[25] Byron sticks to the idea of the poem as an unwieldy and porous receptacle in which central, canonical and marginal (and even downright pubertal) aspects coalesce, spill over from one stanza to another, proliferate and neutralise each other. This typically Byronic approach to literature is visible not only in the metaphors, the rhymes ('Plato' – 'potato' / 'pathetic' – 'emetic') or the vertiginous lists in which he puts priests, sharks, tigers, aldermen and pikes (*Don Juan* II, l. 1256) on the same ontological level, but also in the never-ending digressions that convey the impression of the *ottava rima* being as leaky and oozing as the various (female) bodies in the poem. If one takes Sha's assertions for granted that puberty is 'the material equivalent of improvisation and digression' and that digression is synonymous with deviation,[26] *Don Juan* (and, to a lesser extent, *Beppo* (1818) and *Childe Harold's Pilgrimage*) is a poem celebrating pubertal deviation and anarchy ('I can't help thinking puberty assisted,' the narrator ambiguously says about Don Juan's forays into philosophy).

The poem is thus a dizzying *mélange* of religion and (proto-) Darwinism, of philosophy and journalism, and of epic high culture and pop-cultural vulgarity, and its predominant mode of expression is the meandering digression, the Shandyean *non sequitur*, in which ideas, quotations, associations and marginal allusions seem to be randomly and illogically mixed. The word 'marginalia', in the sense of commentary in the margins, was a Romantic invention, coined by Coleridge,[27] another prolific writer of paratextual annotations in his own and borrowed books, and Byron too was a keen annotator both of his library books (see Gross, Chapter 7) and of his poems, adding (printed) afterthoughts and explanations to the bulky cantos of his *Childe Harold's Pilgrimage*. In *Don Juan*, this distinctive line between annotation and text has been completely lost in a welter of inter- and metatextual references, in footnotes that have been absorbed into the corpus and turned into 'body notes'. In his full-length study, *Romantic Marginality*, Alex Watson addresses the question of the Romantics' preoccupation with footnotes, annotations and other paratextual devices, and shows the extent to which Wordsworth, Southey and Scott saw marginality in terms of geopolitical areas that 'provide[d] an avenue for quasi-colonial editorial interventions'.[28] That this absorption of the marginal by the central and imperial discourse, as Watson reveals in the texts of the self-styled Romantic Establishment, is incompatible with the cosmopolitanism of Byron's lifestyle becomes evident in the poet's texts. Critics such as Francis Jeffrey from the influential *Edinburgh Review* took exception to the fact that Byron's paratextual annotations were written 'in a flippant, lively, trenchant and assuming style – neither very deep nor very witty; though rather entertaining'.[29] In blatant contrast to other Romantic writers and especially to John Cam Hobhouse's idea of paratextuality (as a way of 'espous[ing] national unity at any cost'[30]), Byron was attracted by the possibility of using the margins as a space to give his readers a notion of the teeming and chaotic liveliness of what existed beside the official text and its strait-laced structure. After *Childe Harold's Pilgrimage* and its still neat separation of text and annotation, there is an increase of the marginal in Byron's texts, so that the central discourse is eventually eclipsed by the marginal or by what Jane Stabler identifies as a veritable 'poetics of digression'.[31]

The intrusion of the marginal into the epic mode, of the paratextual into Romantic grandiloquence, is, thus, so deeply interwoven into the text that it is justifiable to talk about Byron's *Don Juan* in terms of a large-scale digression, of an early, pre-Browning dramatic monologue in which the narrator – washing down the *olla podrida* 'with a jug of Malaga or perhaps "right sherries"' and listening to 'the sound of the flute of a Portuguese servant'[32] – lets his thoughts flow freely and without inhibitions. While Wordsworth defined his marginal poetry in the sense of architectural additions to and decorations on a gigantic Gothic cathedral, his central but unwritten kaleidoscopic poem *The Recluse*, Byron's diversified poetry – ranging from marginal(ised) genres such as verse romances (see Camilleri, Chapter 9), eclogues, Hebrew songs and melodies (see O'Neill, Chapter 8) to his 'Oriental Tales' – seems to culminate in his desacralised monumental 'epic of negation'[33]; like James Joyce's experimental novel *Ulysses* (1922), this absorbs everything into a tremendous stream of consciousness (the link between Molly Bloom and the Don Giovanni / Don Juan theme being more than a mere coincidence). As the missing link between Sterne's *Tristram Shandy* (1759–67) and Joyce's iconoclastic novel, the poem dallies with the containedness of the *ottava rima* stanzas, perpetually challenging and undermining them with incoherent quotations, warped references, parentheses, insertions, and protestations of the speaker's inability – 'I can't go on; / I'm almost sorry that I e'er begun' (*Don Juan* I, ll. 919–20). The result is (for early nineteenth-century readers) the disconcerting impression that the marginal seems to have fully encroached on and conquered the central and canonical aspects of the poem. Numerous dashes charged with meaning, sexual *double entendre* but also the aporia of death (see Mole, Chapter 12) are also meant to convey the idea that, beneath the surface of the poem, there are layers of hidden communication that overgrow the text proper and underscore the fact that the image of the poem as a firm textual architecture (with the stanzas as tidy, well-constructed rooms, naves or aisles) is no longer valid and is about to collapse into a semiotic jumble of random characters.

This shift from the central to the marginal, which not only reverses Wordsworth's and Southey's imperial and teleological strategies but also blurs any epistemological difference between what is important and what is ancillary or even parasitical,[34] can also be seen in a genre that paradigmatically caters to Byron's centrifugal approach to texts: his letters, which range from gossip, obscenities, politics and literature to his marginal interest in the fine arts (see Lansdown, Chapter 14). While numerous letters are complemented by paratextual devices such as postscripts and other addenda (see Shears, Chapter 15), there are some that are clearly marked by a significant imbalance caused by the length of the postscripts and the comparative shortness of the letter. The appropriation of the central by the marginal is thus impressively demonstrated and reflects Byron's disinterested attitude towards texts and literature in general. In Canto XIV, he marginalises and almost effaces his poem when he punningly writes, 'these lines should only line portmanteaus' (*Don Juan* XIV, l. 112). Characterised by an ostentatious lack of pattern and relegated to the status of 'scribbling once a week' (*Don Juan* XIV, l. 77), the act of writing is not only marginal and a caprice indulged in *en passant* but also, to a high degree, a carnivalesque process that, on the one hand, shockingly revolves around all sorts of bodily evacuation and porousness, and, on the other, conceives of the textual corpus as something similarly riddled and leaky, as a product over which the writer seems to have lost what Eve Kosofsky Sedgwick calls the volitional 'sphincter'.[35] In this context, it is thus only consistent that the marginality of the poem's textual corpus is related to the sphere of human excrement, to humans' taboo orifices. As a result, in Byron's poem (as in Heinrich Heine's texts), it takes only a little step to change what today is discussed as the high culture of remembrance into the bathetic (and almost Swiftian) horrors of the 'foundation of a closet':

> Some dull MS, oblivion has sank,
> Or graven stone found in a barrack's station
> In digging the foundation of a closet,
> May turn his name up as a rare deposit. (*Don Juan* III, ll. 805–8)

In this respect, Byron not only anticipates Joyce's Leopold Bloom, who is shown sitting on the toilet and using marginal and pop-cultural literature as paper to wipe his bottom with,[36] but also turns literature into an iconoclastic instrument, into a manifesto of a counterculture of Byronism in which predecessors and opponents alike are pilloried, authorities such as King George IV ('Fum, the fourth') ridiculed and values such as the narrative of Christian anthropocentricity disparaged (see Wolfrum, Chapter 5). Seen from this angle, a poet who was held in the highest esteem by Goethe, and who spawned a considerable number of imitators throughout Europe, can paradoxically be labelled as marginal, as a wanderer between margins and centres – between aristocratic supraculture and vulgar pop-, sub- or counterculture – and as a (modernist?) poet, who, from the margins of inter- and paratextuality, created masterpieces outgrowing, reversing and incorporating British Romanticism into a broad and central concept of world literature (see Halmi, Chapter 2).

## Notes

1. See Watson, *Romantic Marginality: Nation and Empire on the Borders of the Page*, as well as the intriguing collection of essays in O'Neill and Sandy, *Romanticism: Critical Concepts*.
2. For a useful overview, see Casaliggi and Fermanis, *Romanticism*, pp. 75–91.

3. Quoted in Wu, *William Hazlitt: The First Modern Man*, p. 11.

4. Ibid., pp. 99, 171.

5. See Heine, 'Ludwig Börne: Eine Denkschrift' III, *Schriften über Deutschland*, in: Schanze (ed.), vol. 4, p. 394.

6. 'Letter to John Murray, 9 November 1820', *BLJ* vol. 7, p. 225.

7. McGann, *Byron and Romanticism*, pp. 134–5.

8. Pope, 'Essay on Man', Epistle II, ll. 1–2, in: *Poetical Works*, p. 251.

9. Lennartz, 'The *bête humaine* and its Food in 19th-century Naturalist Fiction', pp. 255–71.

10. Abrams, *Natural Supernaturalism: Tradition and Revolution in Romantic Literature*, pp. 141–96.

11. Wu, *30 Myths about the Romantics*.

12. Cox, *Romanticism in the Shadow of War: Literary Culture in the Napoleonic War Years*, p. 66.

13. *Childe Harold* IV, l. l. (my italics).

14. Eliot, *The Waste Land* II 'A Game of Chess', l. 104, in: *Collected Poems 1909–1962*, p. 66.

15. 'Preface to Cantos I and II', ll. 77–8 (my italics), *Don Juan*, p. 39. The way the narrator metamorphoses from a Spanish gentleman to a vampire (another marginal figure of the nineteenth century) is discussed in Gigante, *Taste: A Literary History*, p. 133.

16. Praz, *The Romantic Agony*, pp. 25ff.

17. In this context see Gigante, *Taste*, pp. 118–24.

18. Buckley, *The Victorian Temper: A Study in Literary Culture*, p. 36.

19. Ibid., p. 19.

20. Sha, *Perverse Romanticism: Aesthetics and Sexuality in Britain, 1750–1832*, p. 242.

21. Ibid., p. 252.

22. Shakespeare, *Julius Caesar* IV, iii, 216–17.

23. See the entry on 'affair' in Partridge, *Shakespeare's Bawdy*, p. 70. See also Williams, *A Glossary of Shakespeare's Sexual Language*, p. 26.

24. Sha, *Perverse Romanticism*, p. 256.

25. Wilde, *The Picture of Dorian Gray*, p. 161.

26. Sha, *Perverse Romanticism*, p. 243.

27. See the *Oxford English Dictionary* entry for 'marginalia' and its first occurrence in Coleridge's letters in 1832. For this hint, I am indebted to Denise Gigante, who, at the 45th Annual Wordsworth Conference in 2016, gave an intriguing talk on this topic: 'Neither a Borrower Nor a Lender Be, Unless You Lend your Books to S.T.C.'

28. Watson, *Romantic Marginality*, p. 9.

29. Quoted in Watson, *Romantic Marginality*, p. 119.

30. Ibid., p. 136.

31. Stabler, 'Byron's Digressive Journey', pp. 223–39.

32. 'Preface to Cantos I and II', *Don Juan*, p. 38.

33. Wilkie, *Romantic Poets and Epic Tradition*, p. 188.

34. I support Watson's argument that Gérard Genette's definition of the paratext as 'an accessory to the text' is too myopic and in need of reconsideration. See Watson, *Romantic Marginality*, pp. 3, 29.
35. Sedgwick, 'Jane Austen and the Masturbating Girl', p. 831.
36. Joyce, *Ulysses*, p. 67.

## Works cited

Abrams, Meyer H. (1971), *Natural Supernaturalism: Tradition and Revolution in Romantic Literature*, New York / London: Norton.
Buckley, Jerome (1951), *The Victorian Temper: A Study in Literary Culture*, Cambridge: Cambridge University Press.
Casaliggi, Carmen, and Porscha Fermanis (2016), *Romanticism: A Literary and Cultural History*, London / New York: Routledge.
Cox, Jeffrey (2014), *Romanticism in the Shadow of War: Literary Culture in the Napoleonic War Years*, Cambridge: Cambridge University Press.
Eliot, T[homas] S[tearns] (1963), *Collected Poems 1909–1962*, London: Faber & Faber.
Genette, Gérard (1997), *Paratexts: Thresholds of Interpretation*, trans. Jane E. Lewin, Cambridge: Cambridge University Press.
Gigante, Denise (2005), *Taste: A Literary History*, New Haven, CT / London: Yale University Press.
Heine, Heinrich (1968), *Werke*, vol. 4 *Schriften über Deutschland*, ed. Helmut Schanze, Frankfurt: Insel.
Joyce, James (1998), *Ulysses*, ed. Jeri Johnson, Oxford: Oxford University Press.
Lennartz, Norbert (2010), 'The *bête humaine* and its Food in 19th-century Naturalist Fiction', in: Marion Gymnich and Norbert Lennartz (eds), *The Pleasures and Horrors of Eating: The Cultural History of Eating in Literature and the Arts*, Göttingen: Bonn University Press, pp. 255–71.
McGann, Jerome J. (2002), *Byron and Romanticism*, ed. James Søderholm, Cambridge: Cambridge University Press.
O'Neill, Michael, and Mark Sandy (eds) (2005), *Romanticism: Critical Concepts in Literary and Cultural Studies*, vol. 3 *Romanticism and the Margins*, New York: Routledge.
Partridge, Eric (2001), *Shakespeare's Bawdy*, London / New York: Routledge.
Pope, Alexander (1978), *Poetical Works*, ed. Herbert Davies, Oxford: Oxford University Press.
Praz, Mario (1970), *The Romantic Agony*, trans. Angus Davidson, foreword Frank Kermode, Oxford / New York: Oxford University Press.
Sedgwick, Eve Kosofsky (1991), 'Jane Austen and the Masturbating Girl', *Critical Inquiry*, 17, pp. 818–37.
Sha, Richard C. (2009), *Perverse Romanticism: Aesthetics and Sexuality in Britain, 1750–1832*, Baltimore: Johns Hopkins University Press.

Shakespeare, William (2002), *Julius Caesar* (The Arden Shakespeare), ed. David Daniell, London: Thomson Learning.

Stabler, Jane (2000), 'Byron's Digressive Journey', in: Amanda Gilroy (ed.), *Romantic Geographies: The Discourse of Travel in the Romantic Period*, Manchester: Manchester University Press, pp. 223–39.

Watson, Alex (2012), *Romantic Marginality: Nation and Empire on the Borders of the Page*, London: Pickering & Chatto.

Wilde, Oscar (1998), *The Picture of Dorian Gray*, ed. Isobel Murray, Oxford: Oxford University Press.

Wilkie, Brian (1965), *Romantic Poets and Epic Tradition*, Madison: University of Wisconsin Press.

Williams, Gordon (1997), *A Glossary of Shakespeare's Sexual Language*, London: Athlone.

Wu, Duncan (2008), *William Hazlitt: The First Modern Man*, Oxford: Oxford University Press.

— (2015), *30 Myths about the Romantics*, Oxford: Wiley–Blackwell.

# I. Byron's Marginalisation in Romantic World Literature

# Chapter 2

# Byron and *Weltliteratur*

## Nicholas Halmi

If Byron spent much of his life at the geographical margins of the European continent – childhood in Aberdeen, travels in the Spanish Peninsula and the Levant, residence in Venice and the coastal cities of Ravenna, Pisa and Genoa, in voluntary exile from England after 1816 – he none the less occupied a central position in the consciousness of post-Napoleonic Europe. It was the notoriety of his separation from Annabella Milbanke that first brought Byron to Goethe's attention in 1816, and the eminence of his writings and personality that sustained the older poet's interest in him. In late October 1823 – by which time he had read *The Corsair* (1814), *Lara* (1814), *The Siege of Corinth* (1816), *Parisina* (1816), *The Prisoner of Chillon* (1816), *Manfred* (1817), at least the first two cantos of *Don Juan* (1819), *English Bards and Scotch Reviewers* (1809), *Marino Faliero* (1821), *Sardanapalus* (1821), *Cain* (1821) and *The Island* (1823) – Goethe recommended Byron to Johann Peter Eckermann, the Boswell of Weimar, as the most compelling reason to learn English. Although by no means uncritical of Byron, whose apparent misanthropy and licentiousness he regretted, the ennobled privy councillor recognised in the noble lord a profoundly original and spirited writer whom, alone among contemporaries, he thought worthy of comparison with himself: 'Byron allein lasse ich neben mir gelten,' he affirmed to Friedrich von Müller in 1823.[1]

Neglecting *Childe Harold's Pilgrimage* (1812–18) and possibly much of *Don Juan* while overrating the dramas, Goethe's reception of Byron may well seem eccentric, as Eliza Marian Butler concluded in her study of their relationship.[2] Certainly, the writings he praised, particularly the historical dramas, are not the ones on which Byron's reputation now principally rests; but the dramas, like the Eastern tales, do represent the fullness and complexity of human existence through the viewpoints of individuals in conflict with dominant institutions and customs. Fritz Strich's thesis is that Goethe loved Byron like a spiritual son, in whom he recognised the agonies, the errors, the brilliance and the demonic energy of his own youth.[3] It is true that, rather like a proud father, Goethe kept a portfolio in which he preserved documents relating to Byron.[4] But considered in relation to the other authors that he was reading with admiration in the 1820s – Balzac, Manzoni, Scott – and to his complaints, in essays and to visitors, that contemporary German letters were detached from social life, Goethe's enthusiasm for Byron can be understood as deriving from more than a personal identification with the younger poet's *dämonische Natur*. What made Byron an exemplary poet was his attentiveness to the interaction between the *kleine Welt* of private feeling and the *große Welt* of public affairs. Taking an active interest in the languages, cultures and histories of the lands he visited and inhabited in his travels of 1809–11 and post-1816 exile, Byron recognised both the particularity and the generality of conflicts between the private and public worlds: his narrative and dramatic works represent historically specific manifestations of analogous situations. Eulogising him to Eckermann, his companion and unpaid secretary from 1823 to 1832, Goethe remarked in February 1825,

> [h]e is a great talent, a born talent, and I know of no one whose genuinely poetic power [*eigentlich poetische Kraft*] is greater than his. In his perception of the external world [*Auffassung des Äußern*] and his clear view of past conditions he is just as great as Shakespeare. (*GA*, vol. 24, p. 149)

It was only in 1830, a decade after its composition, that Goethe received the manuscript of Byron's suppressed dedication of *Marino Faliero* to him, the postscript to which dismissed the critical differentiation of the Romantic from the Classical as being irrelevant to English literature. Alluding to August Wilhelm Schlegel's *Lectures on Dramatic Art and Literature*, the recently published English translation of which Germaine de Staël is likely to have lent him in Coppet in August 1816, Byron wrote,

> I perceive that in Germany as well as in Italy there is a great struggle about what they call '*Classical and Romantic*' terms which were not subjects of Classification in England – at least when I left it four or five years ago. [. . .] Perhaps there may be something of the sort sprung up lately – but I have not heard much about it, – and it would be such bad taste that I should be very sorry to believe it. (*CPW*, vol. 4, pp. 546–7)[5]

There is no record of the addressee's response to this strangely jocular document, which ridiculed the works of Wordsworth and Southey (in which Goethe had no interest), lamented the unpronounceability of German names (apart from Goethe's own), and referred flippantly to the suicides reported by Madame de Staël (who herself irritated Goethe) to have been occasioned by *Die Leiden des jungen Werthers* (1774). Whatever he may have thought of this dedication, however, Goethe had already declared that the distinction between the Classical and the Romantic was inapplicable to Byron himself. Acknowledging the English poet as the inspiration for Euphorion, the ill-fated son of Faust and Helena in the second part of his tragedy, Goethe had told Eckermann in July 1827,

> I could use no one but him as a representative of the most recent age of poetry [*der neuesten poetischen Zeit*], as he is without question to be reckoned the greatest talent of the century. And then, Byron is not ancient and is not romantic, but is like the present day itself. (*GA*, vol. 24, p. 256)

Goethe usually used the adjectives *klassisch* and *romantisch* not to distinguish historical ages, but as labels for what he considered divergent artistic styles or aesthetic ideologies. More precisely, he tended to classify what he approved of as *klassisch* and what he disapproved of as *romantisch*, as in his notorious remark of April 1829 to Eckermann: 'The classical I call the healthy, and the romantic the sick. And so the *Nibelungen* are classical like Homer, for both are healthy and hearty' (*GA*, vol. 24, p. 332). Gerhard Schulz and Ernst Behler have rightly warned that Goethe's *obiter dicta* of the 1820s, whether published in the journal *Über Kunst und Altertum*, transmitted in letters, or recorded by Eckermann and others, do not amount to a coherent aesthetic theory, but rather reflect the aged writer's concern to shape the perception of his place in literary history.[6] His undoubted distaste for certain tendencies among the German Romantics – such as Joseph Görres's reactionary Catholicism, Zacharias Werner's mystical obscurantism and E. T. A. Hoffmann's fascination with the fantastic and the macabre – lies behind his much-quoted denunciations of Romanticism as unnatural, morbid, formless and escapist. While distancing himself from contemporary German writing, though, he could still use the term *romantisch* in a specifically historical sense to designate medieval literature, and this is what he did in the third act of *Faust II*, first publishing it separately in 1827 under the title 'Helena, klassisch–romantische Phantasmagorie, Zwischenspiel zu Faust'.

Extending chronologically 'from the Sack of Troy to the destruction of Missolonghi', as Goethe observed in a letter of 22 October 1826 to the medievalist Sulpiz Boisserée,[7] the Helena act presents the birth of Euphorion, the modern poet, as the dialectical synthesis of the ancient and the medieval, of the Classical and the vernacular, of southern and northern Europe. While the German Faust is relocated geographically to Troy in the first scene, which imitates the structure and verse forms of Greek tragedy, the Greek Helena is transported temporally to the Middle Ages in the second scene, where she learns to speak rhyming verse and Faust conflates his impending battle with Menelaus with the Dorian invasion of Mycenaean Greece, the Germanic tribes' invasions of the Roman Empire and the medieval Crusaders' invasions of the Peloponnesus (ll. 9442–81) – this last also alluding to Byron's intervention in the Greek War of Independence.[8] In the final scene, a pastoral opera conjured up by Faust in the courtyard of his Trojan palace, Euphorion's brief life is enacted. Likened by Phorkyas (Mephistopheles in disguise) to the young Apollo, creating a golden lyre (l. 9620), and by the chorus first to the kleptomaniac Hermes, relieving the gods of their most emblematic possessions (ll. 9662–78), and then to the hubristic Icarus, falling to his death (l. 9901), Euphorion is a figure to whom Manfred's characterisation of humanity, in the first act of Byron's play, applies: 'half dust, half deity, alike unfit / To sink or soar' (*Manfred* I, ii, 40–1). Warned by his mother that he lacks wings (ll. 9607–8), and assured by his father that (like Antaeus) he derives strength from contact with the earth (ll. 9609–10), Euphorion, after having pursued a maiden from the chorus who turned into a flame, defiantly tries to fly to the land of 'the strong, the free, and the bold' [*zu Starken, Freien, Kühnen*] and lands at his parents' feet (l. 9900), whereupon his lifeless body – in which 'one seems to recognise a well-known figure', as the stage direction says – vanishes, to be followed quickly by Helena.

In one respect, this third scene of the Helena act is the conclusion to the poetic dialogue that had begun, at least in Goethe's eyes, with *Manfred*. Reviewing that play in 1820, the German poet repeated publicly what he had already expressed privately in a letter of October 1817 to his friend Carl Ludwig Knebel: namely, high 'admiration and esteem' for the way that Byron had assimilated and radically transformed *Faust* to suit his own purposes – even if, Goethe conceded, 'the gloomy intensity of a boundlessly deep despair finally becomes tiresome' (*GA*, vol. 24, p. 785). Less than a fortnight after Goethe wrote to Knebel, Byron heard through John Cam Hobhouse that '[a]n American who came the other day from Germany' – identified by E. M. Butler as the scholar George Ticknor – was claiming that 'Manfred was taken from *Goethe's Faust*' (*BLJ*, vol. 5, p. 270).[9] Always defensive about his originality, Byron insisted that his knowledge of Goethe's play was limited to the passages he had heard Matthew Gregory Lewis translate orally in the summer of 1816 and to the quotations in Madame de Staël's *De l'Allemagne* (which he had read in 1813). Repeated to Thomas Medwin, this denial of indebtedness to *Faust* was published a few months after the poet's death in Medwin's *Conversations of Lord Byron* (1824) – along with a eulogy of Byron that Medwin had solicited from Goethe.

But when he read the book, in November 1824, Goethe was evidently not pleased to discover that Byron, while defending himself against the accusation of plagiarism from *Faust*, had questioned the German poet's own originality: 'Goethe has too much sense to pretend that he is not under obligations to authors, ancient and modern; – who is not? You tell me the plot [of *Faust*] is almost entirely Calderon's.'[10] Confronted with a list of his supposed debts to Calderón, Marlowe, Shakespeare and the Book of Job, Goethe irritably proclaimed to Eckermann his ignorance of the works in question (*GA*, vol. 24, p. 139). To Friedrich von Müller, however, he not only admitted his debts but also reproached Byron himself for not having confronted the issue directly:

> How patiently he allows himself to be accused of plagiarism, merely flirting with a defence instead of felling his enemies with the heavy guns [*mit schwerem Geschütze die Gegner niederzudonnern*]. Doesn't everything achieved by the past and the present belong to the poet by right? Why should he be afraid to pluck flowers where he finds them? Only in appropriating others' treasures does a work become great [*entsteht ein Großes*]. Have I not appropriated Job and a Shakespeare song in Mephistopheles? (*GA*, vol. 23, pp. 369–70)[11]

In light of this remark, the identification of Euphorion with the thieving Hermes may be interpreted as both complimenting and settling scores with Byron, while also conveying a general truth about the process of poetic creation.

There was a larger issue at stake here than poetic thievery, however. In the Euphorion opera Goethe effectively appropriated the figure of Byron himself – the boldest form of poetic theft – and I am tempted to say that the cause most advanced by the English poet's death was not the liberation of Greece but the completion of *Faust*. Begun in 1800, the third act of part two remained a fragment – set

entirely in the ancient world, and Helena not yet united with Faust –
until 1825–6, when Goethe was finally able to resume and complete
its composition. Byron's demise in support of the Philhellenist cause
was a gift, Goethe revealed to Eckermann in July 1827:

> He suited me precisely because of his unsatisfied temperament and
> his militant tendency, by which he perished in Missolonghi. [. . .] I'd
> had a very different ending in mind before and had developed it in
> various ways, one of which was quite good [. . .]. Then time brought
> me this with Lord Byron and Missolonghi, and I gladly let the rest
> go. (*GA*, vol. 24, p. 256)

But why was this the case?

As Jane Brown observes, Euphorion seeks a spirit in the flesh
(the chorus girl), and the world in the ether (Greece), and conse-
quently secures neither.[12] If Euphorion's fate is an allegory of the
impossibility of reconciling the ideal and the real outside a work of
art, it is also a commentary on Byron's Philhellenism, about which
Goethe had expressed reservations, according to Friedrich von
Müller's report, in June 1824:

> His Greek endeavour had something impure [*etwas Unreines*] about
> it; it could never have ended well. It is certainly a misfortune that such
> imaginative minds [*ideenreiche Geister*] should be intent on realising
> their ideals and bringing them to life. That won't do, the ideal and
> ordinary reality must remain strictly separated. (*GA*, vol. 23, p. 350)

The Philhellenist project could not succeed, Goethe seems to have
thought, because it was founded on the fantasy of restoring ancient
Greece to its former territory. Had he read Canto II of *Childe Harold's
Pilgrimage*, Goethe would have recognised in Byron's lament for the
disparity between the past and present states of Greece exactly the
fusion of time and timelessness, the ideal and the real, that can be
realised only in literature, and there just fleetingly: 'Fair Greece! sad
relic of departed worth! / Immortal, though no more! though fallen,
great' (*Childe Harold* II, ll. 693–4).

In his essay of 1839 exalting Byron and Goethe as the age's exemplary poets of subjective and objective life, respectively, the Italian
revolutionary Giuseppe Mazzini exclaimed,

> I know of no more beautiful symbol for the destiny of Art in our mod-
> ern times than the death of Byron in Greece. The Holy Alliance of
> Poetry [*Sainte-Alliance de la Poésie*] with the cause of the people – the

union, still so rare today, of Thought with Action, which alone makes the human word [*le verbe humain*] complete, which alone will emancipate the world –.[13]

Such a union is precisely what Goethe thought Byron had not accomplished in Missolonghi. Euphorion can no more realise his imagined Greece historically than Helena, whom Faust has stolen from Menelaus (and, of course, Goethe from Homer), can remain in the modern world poetically. As Helena tells Faust, 'good fortune and beauty are but briefly joined' (*Glück und Schönheit dauerhaft sich nicht vereint, Faust* II, l. 9940). Thus she must follow Euphorion in melting into air, both leaving their clothes behind in 'the memory of the classical past'.[14]

Admittedly, the allegory of Euphorion's death does not do justice to the ambivalence of Byron's Philhellenism. If the description of Greece in the second Canto of *Childe Harold's Pilgrimage* was a major stimulus to the Philhellenist movement, Byron's notes to that Canto betray greater admiration for the Turks as a people than for the Greeks, and an impatience with 'the paradoxes of men who have read superficially of the ancients, and seen nothing of the moderns' (*CPW*, vol. 2, p. 204). In Canto III of *Don Juan*, the interpolated lyric 'The Isles of Greece', commonly read out of context as a Philhellenist anthem, is actually sung by a 'sad trimmer' – associated explicitly with Robert Southey (*Don Juan* III, l. 649) – who changes his tune to suit whatever country he visits.[15] Byron's financial and personal involvement in the Greek War of Independence is likelier to have been motivated by a general antipathy to political oppression and a desire for adventure than by a particular devotion to Greece, a place that he judged to have 'no distinct country and no distinct people', according to William Parry's *Last Days of Lord Byron* (which Goethe read in 1825).[16] Certainly, Byron's recognition of the profound differences between modernity and antiquity reflects something closer to Goethe's own temporalised understanding of history than to Euphorion's idealised misunderstanding of it. It is not poetically that humans dwell on this earth, both poets knew, but historically.

The distinction between subjective and objective emphases, to which Mazzini's essay drew attention, is to be found within each poet more than between them. The shift in focus from the *kleine Welt* in Part 1 of *Faust* to the *große Welt* in Part 2 has a parallel in the last two cantos of *Childe Harold's Pilgrimage*. Canto III is centrally concerned with subjectivity, the various sites visited, from Waterloo to the Jungfrau, serving primarily as occasions for self-reflection – or, in the cases of Waterloo,

Geneva, Verney and Lausanne, for reflection on the psychical states of Napoleon ('antithetically mixt', *Childe Harold* III, l. 317), Rousseau ('self-torturing', *Childe Harold* III, l. 725), Voltaire ('fire and fickleness', *Childe Harold* III, l. 986) and Gibbon ('deep and slow', *Childe Harold* III, l. 995). Canto IV, in contrast, directs our attention continually out-wards from the observing subject to the objective world, the author's narrative journey from Venice to Rome framing a series of reflections on particular historical sites (such as republican Venice, Estese Ferrara, Medicean Florence and imperial Rome) and on general historical pat-terns ('First Freedom, and then Glory – when that fails, / Wealth, vice, corruption, – barbarism at last,' *Childe Harold* IV, l. 108). One may extend, *mutatis mutandis*, to this Canto what Ernst Cassirer wrote of the Helena act of *Faust*:

> Just as Faust's life is here historically contextualised – in that the act implies the basic intellectual tendencies of the Reformation period and, in the conjuring of Helena, symbolises the humanistic striving for a return to antiquity – so Goethe beholds in the image of the Faust poem his own existence against an ever-richer, ever-expanding historical background.[17]

In Byron's case the expanding background results from his immer-sion in foreign lands and their associated languages, cultures and histories. His affirmation, 'I've taught me other tongues – and in strange eyes / Have made me not a stranger' (*Childe Harold* IV, ll. 64–5), confirms the implication of the fourth Canto's epigraph from Ariosto's fourth *Satira*:

> Visto ho Toscana, Lombardia, Romagna,
> Quel Monte che divide, e quel che serra
> Italia, e un mare e l'altro, che la bagna. (*CPW*, vol. 2, p. 120)

What the process of contextualisation reveals, in *Childe Harold* as in *Faust*, is exactly the limits of the assimilability of the past to the pres-ent. Whereas in Canto III Byron, at least in the persona of narrator, tries repeatedly to define the relation of the self to the world, whether harmoniously unified 'in a life intense, / Where not a beam, nor an air, nor leaf is lost, / But hath a part of being' (*Childe Harold* III, ll. 838–40) or defiantly separate as 'fair foes' (*Childe Harold* III, l. 1059), in Canto IV he confronts the evanescence of the individual life and the temporality of history, both of which restrict the appropriative and transformative power of the poetic imagination:

Yet there are things whose strong reality
Outshines our fairy-land. [. . .]
                                [. . .] still teems
My mind with many a form which aptly seems
Such as I sought for, and at moments found;
Let these go too—for waking Reason deems
Such over-weening phantasies unsound,
And other voices speak, and other sights surround. (*Childe Harold*
IV, ll. 50–1, 58–63)

On the one hand, the recognised alterity of the past permits him to define abstract principles of historical behaviour; on the other, it prevents him from appropriating the past *as such* in a purely subjective manner. Though Byron may 'repeople' his poem with the past, as he tells us in stanza 19, doing so serves to emphasise that Venice cannot be repeopled with its own past. Recalling that the Greek sites he saw in 1810 were already ruined when Cicero's friend Servius Sulpicius had seen them in 45 BC – Corinth destroyed in 146 BC, Piraeus in 86 BC – Byron draws a different conclusion from Servius. That great cities could be reduced to such a state reminded Servius, who was seeking to console Cicero on the death of his daughter, of the transience of all human life and works, and hence the relative insignificance of any individual's death.[18] Byron, on the other hand, laments the inexorability of time, observing that Servius' Rome has suffered the same fate as the Greek cities:

For Time hath not rebuilt them, but uprear'd
Barbaric dwellings on their shattered site,
Which only make more mourn'd and more endear'd
The few last rays of their scattered light,
And the crush'd relics of their vanish'd might.
The Roman saw these tombs in his own age,
These sepulchres of cities, which excite
Sad wonder [. . .]
That page is now before me, and on mine
*His* country's ruin added to the mass
Of perish'd states he mourn'd in their decline,
And I in desolation [. . .]. (*Childe Harold* IV, ll. 397–404, 406–9)

'Buried in air' (*Childe Harold* IV, l. 991), the remains of Antiquity constitute a monument to historical temporality – but what of its statuary? In an age instructed aesthetically by Winckelmann and informed archaeologically by researches conducted under the auspices of the Society of Dilettanti and other antiquarian organisations, Byron's Hellenism was no less ambivalent than his Philhellenism. As is well known, he particularly condemned Lord Elgin's removal of the Parthenon's 'Phidian Freaks' because, as he explained in his 'Letter to—[John Murray] on the Rev. W. L. Bowles' of 1821, the treatment of them as purely aesthetic objects violated their historicity and, more importantly, that of their original physical contexts. While acknowledging the aesthetic enhancement of the landscape by artworks left *in situ*, Byron's primary point was not, as one might expect, that the landscape contextualises and helps explicate the art, but rather that the art reveals the historical significance of the landscape:

> There are a thousand rocks and capes – far more picturesque than those of the Acropolis and Cape Sunium [. . .]. But it is the 'Art' – the Columns – the temples – the wrecked vessel – which give them their antique and their modern poetry – and not the spots themselves. – Without them the Spots of earth would be unnoticed and unknown – buried like Babylon and Nineveh in indistinct confusion – without poetry – as without existence [. . .]. – I opposed – and will ever oppose – the robbery of ruins – from Athens to instruct the English in Sculpture – (who are as capable of Sculpture – as the Egyptians are of skating) but why did I do so? – the ruins are as poetical in Piccadilly as they were in the Parthenon – but the Parthenon and it's [*sic*] rock are less so without them. (*CMP*, p. 133)

Regarding the Classicist aesthetic of connoisseurs like Elgin and the Earl of Aberdeen as merely a manifestation of consumer culture – 'their grand saloons a general mart / For all the mutilated blocks of art', as he sneered in *English Bards and Scotch Reviewers* (ll. 1027–32) – Byron remained entirely unmoved by Felicia Hemans's insinuation, in the anonymously published *Modern Greece* (1818), that the Parthenon Marbles belonged in the British Museum because a free Britain was a worthier heir to the artistic patrimony of Periclean Athens than was a subjugated Greece. As the bestselling author of the age, Byron understood very well the intimate connection between taste and the marketplace, and in *Beppo* (1817) even ironised the success of his own Eastern tales as 'samples of the finest Orientalism' (*Beppo*, l. 408); yet he objected specifically to a commodification of Antiquity in the name of aesthetic cultivation. Sent a copy of Hemans's poem by John Murray, he dismissed it as 'good for nothing – written by someone who has never been there' (*BLJ*, vol. 5, pp. 262–3). The author's credentials as a promoter of refined taste were vitiated, in Byron's view, by an ignorance of the historical and architectural contexts of the Parthenon Marbles. To aestheticise Antiquity in the way practised by Elgin and defended by Hemans was to dehistoricise and thus to falsify it.

If he defied 'learned fingers' to describe and understand '[t]he graceful bend, and the voluptuous swell' of Classical sculpture (*Childe Harold* IV, ll. 469, 472), Byron positively enlisted such fingers, specifically Hobhouse's, to annotate his own poem, and indeed to supplement those extensive notes – the 135 pages of which (themselves with footnotes) exceed by 39 pages the length of the poem in the first edition – with a separate volume of nearly 600 pages containing further *Historical Illustrations of the Fourth Canto of Childe Harold* (1818), published simultaneously with the poem and referred to repeatedly in its commentary. Whatever he may have thought of Coleridge's metaphysics, Byron was certainly not averse to explaining explanations. This point deserves emphasis because the original readers' experience of *Childe Harold* IV is not easily reproducible in current editions, which either do not include the authorially solicited commentary in its entirety or (as in Jerome McGann's critical edition) do not make it easy to locate. Present-day readers are assisted by publishers in doing precisely what Byron sought to discourage: namely, to read the poem without regard for its historical references and contexts.

In fact, Byron's personal responses to Classical statues, such as his apostrophe to the Venus (*Childe Harold* IV, ll. 433–50) and ventriloquising of the Dying Gaul (*Childe Harold* IV, ll. 1261–9), are accompanied by deflationary notes that remove the statues from the isolation of subjective experience. The note on the Venus calls attention to James Thomson's description of the same statue in the aestive section of *The Seasons* (1730), while that on the Gaul summarises scholarly debate about whether the figure represented a gladiator, a Greek herald or a Spartan shield-bearer. The notes vindicating such writers as Dante, Boccaccio and Alfieri against the hostility of their contemporaries serve, as McGann has argued, to contextualise both the writers themselves and, by implication, Byron. By explicating the poem's historical references, Hobhouse also insinuates the poet's relation to contemporary European cultural politics. Taken as a whole, then, text and paratexts together, Canto IV of *Childe Harold* is at pains to historicise itself.

To be sure, the ratio of commentary to poem in this Canto is unusually high, but there would be little reason to dwell on its example if it were not broadly representative of Byron's practice. In contrast to Wordsworth, who used prefaces primarily to position his poems critically, Byron used a full array of paratextual apparatus to expose the factual (or at least historically attested) foundations on which his poetic fictions were built. To that extent, his practice is consistent with the dictum expressed in Canto VIII of *Don Juan*:

> 't is the part
> Of a true poet to escape from fiction
> Whene'er he can; for there is little art
> In leaving verse more free from the restriction
> Of truth than prose. (*Don Juan* VIII, ll. 681–5)

Among the works that Goethe is known to have read, *The Corsair* contains topographical notes on the Levant, drawn partly from the author's personal knowledge; *The Siege of Corinth* advertises its derivation from a passage in an eighteenth-century *History of the Turks*, while the notes detail Byron's debts to Coleridge's then-unpublished 'Christabel' and Beckford's *Vathek*; *Parisina* is prefaced by a quotation from Gibbon's 'Antiquities of the House of Brunswick'; *Marino Faliero* begins with a report of Byron's researches on the executed *doge* and concludes with seven appendices of extracts from historical documents and a complaint about being besieged on the Lido by tedious English tourists; and *The Two Foscari* (1821) contains an appendix with long extracts in French from two histories of Venice and a sharply worded personal and political attack on Southey. The characteristic combination of historical and contemporary references in the paratexts to these narratives and dramas serves at once to situate the works' subject matters in the past and their creation, as self-consciously literary works, in the present. Thus it is too reductive to claim that the 'subject (truth) of poetry was not the poetic process itself [. . .] but the human world of men and women in their complex relations with themselves, each other, and their environments'.[19] Excluding poetic form as an object of historical reflection, McGann proves less of a historicist than Byron himself, who constantly calls attention to the historicity of the poetic process and its resultant forms.[20] Exactly that acknowledgement of their own historicity constitutes, I contend, the modernity of Byron's works.

Goethe, for his part, was a little vague about why he considered Byron to be the exemplary poet of the *neueste poetische Zeit*, and his admiration was always qualified (as the Euphorion allegory implies) by disapproval of Byron's personal immoderation. He must, however, have been struck by certain parallels between the English poet's endeavours and his own. I am not referring to *Manfred*, which he praised specifically for transforming *Faust I* so completely that its connection to the earlier drama was almost unrecognisable, or to *The Deformed Transformed* (1824), which Byron acknowledged in a prefatory note to be indebted to *Faust* (and which Goethe read in November 1826). Nor am I referring to the numerous formal, thematic and tonal parallels between *Don Juan* and Goethe's cycle *West-östlicher Divan* (1819).[21]

The parallels I have in mind are at once less specific and more profound. Reviewing Thomas Carlyle's anthology *German Romance* in 1828, Goethe commended the translator's task as one of mediation (*Vermittlung*): communicating the distinctive characteristics of individuals and peoples across linguistic barriers, the translator promotes tolerance by enabling an appreciation of the diversity of humanity in its totality. Translation, however, was for Goethe but one instance of what he considered to be the primary function of art: hence his aphoristic definition, in the *Maximen und Reflexionen* (1833), of art as 'the true mediator [*die wahre Vermittlerin*]' (*HA*, vol. 12, p. 367). Such mediation, which seeks to undermine a simple binary opposition of the native and the foreign by prompting reflection on the constitution of the former through an encounter with the latter, was undertaken precisely in Byron's Eastern tales and historical dramas, as well as – more explicitly, though in works perhaps unknown to Goethe – *Beppo* and the translation of the first Canto of Luigi Pulci's *Morgante Maggiore* (1478).[22] And Byron's sense of Goethe's own dual role as national poet and international mediator is demonstrated in his dedication of *Sardanapalus* to the German poet (published in the second edition of 1823) as 'the first of existing masters; – who has created the literature of his own country – and illustrated that of Europe' (*CPW*, vol. 6, p. 15).[23]

Much of Goethe's literary production in the nineteenth century sought, by affirming the formative value of cross-cultural engagement and itself exhibiting such engagement, to offer an alternative to the reactionary nationalism that had developed in the German lands in response to the Napoleonic invasion. The early books of *Dichtung und Wahrheit*, published in 1811, dwelt on the importance to Goethe's own intellectual development of his polyglot education and the French presence in Frankfurt during the Seven Years' War, and mocked the hollow solemnities of the investiture of the Holy Roman Emperor in 1764. Immersing himself in 1814 in a translation of the fourteenth-century Persian poet Hafez and in scholarship on Turkish, Arabic and Persian poetry, Goethe found both a medium for the rejuvenation of his lyric powers in the *Divan* and, particularly in the extensive *Noten und Abhandlungen zu besserem*

*Verständnis des West-östlichen Divans* [*Notes and Essays for a Better Understanding of the West–Eastern Divan*] (1819), an occasion to instruct his countrymen in the sympathetic appreciation of foreign cultures. Without denying the historical circumstances of its own origin – indeed, the first lines of the first lyric explicitly mention Europe's bursting thrones and shaking kingdoms ('Nord und West und Süd zersplittern, / Throne bersten, Reiche zittern, / Flüchte du, im reinen Osten / Patriarchenluft zu kosten', *HA*, vol. 2, p. 7) – the *Divan* seeks, as Goethe told his publisher in 1815, 'to connect the West and the East, past and present, Persian and German, and to let their morals and mindsets mutually overlap' (*HA*, vol. 2, p. 540). Small wonder, then, that he publicly praised and privately identified, to an extent, with a self-consciously cosmopolitan poet who, alienated from his native land but constantly addressing it, sought to mediate the past to the present, southern to northern Europe, and the East to the West from his 'humbler promontory / Amidst life's infinite variety' (*Don Juan* XV, ll. 145–6).

What Goethe recognised in Byron's works, I suggest, was an affinity with his own efforts, in *Dichtung und Wahrheit*, the *Divan* and his essays on literature from many nations in *Über Kunst und Altertum* (1816–32), towards the development of what he was to call *Weltliteratur*. 'National literature no longer counts for much; the epoch of world literature is at hand, and everyone must now act to accelerate this epoch', he told Eckermann in January 1827 (*GA*, vol. 24, p. 229). In the last two decades of his life, Goethe himself, unsympathetic to the nationalist fervour stimulated by the Napoleonic occupation of the German lands, viewed suspiciously by a younger generation of writers, and less popular with the reading public than in his *Sturm und Drang* years, was displaced from his earlier cultural centrality. As he became, relatively speaking, more culturally marginal within Germany, however, he sought increasingly self-consciously to immerse himself in the literature of other nations, developing from this immersion a more complex conception of national identity – as the *product* of cultural exchange – than he had endorsed in his youth, when, in his 1773 panegyric of Strasbourg Cathedral, he had vindicated Gothic architecture as an autochthonous German phenomenon (*GA*, vol. 13, pp. 16–26). With the rise of *Weltliteratur*, German cultural life might be freed of the parochialism from which (in Goethe's view) it was suffering in the *Biedermeierzeit* – a parochialism that, as we have seen, he labelled *romantisch*. Byron, who continued to enjoy a large readership in Britain even after his permanent departure from the country (despite conservative critics' efforts to marginalise his publications on moral and political grounds), exemplified the possibility of renovating a national literature from without, not in the sense of being self-exiled but by assimilating and adapting 'foreign' literary models and cultural themes. The English poet's international success may well have impressed Goethe as auspicious for the prospects of *Weltliteratur*.

In English the term 'world literature' is now used in three distinct ways: first, to designate an international, transhistorical canon of works, from *Gilgamesh* onwards, which have acquired the status of classics and are represented in pedagogically accessible media such as *The Norton Anthology of World Masterpieces*; second, to designate colonial and postcolonial literature written in or at least translated into English; and third, by Franco Moretti in particular, to designate the literatures of cultures peripheral to Western European consciousness, assimilated through intermediaries and used as the basis for the formulation of so-called 'laws of literary evolution' – that is, a body of theory whose self-professed normative status, and hence predictive power, effectively relieves the critic of the need to read any literature directly.[24] None of these uses coincides with what Goethe, the first to formulate a programmatic concept of *Weltliteratur*, meant by that term, although Moretti presents his proposal for 'distance reading' as fulfilling Goethe's hope. To be sure, both Goethe's concept and Moretti's proceed from a sense of the inadequacy of the cultural horizons afforded by given national literatures; but by disengaging from literature itself in the name of greater inclusiveness and subordinating cultural particularities to the rule of the universalising law, 'distance reading' is more nearly the antipathy than the realisation of Goethe's programme.

Surveying western Europe in the aftermath of the Napoleonic Wars and the restoration of the old monarchies, Goethe conceived *Weltliteratur* not as an established field of data to be analysed by critics, but as an unfolding task to be undertaken by writers and readers, a collective effort to which individual nations would contribute in their individual ways towards the goal of mutual understanding and tolerance. 'What I call world literature', he wrote to Sulpiz Boisserée in 1827, 'will arise when the differences that prevail within a nation are balanced by the outlook and judgement of others' (*HA*, vol. 12, p. 362). Through mutual cultural interchange, nations might become more comprehensible both to others and to themselves, for 'every nation has peculiarities that differentiate it from others and make it feel isolated from, attracted to, or repelled by them. [. . .] Yet a nation's essential character [*Innerlichkeiten*]',

Goethe wrote in November 1829, 'remains unknown and unrecognised not only by others but even by the nation itself' (*GA*, vol. 14, pp. 913–14). Cultural differences were not to be effaced, then, but made more fully visible: 'the idea is not that nations should think alike', Goethe emphasised in *Über Kunst und Altertum* (1828), 'but rather that they should simply become aware of and understand one another and, though they may have no affection for one another, at least learn to tolerate one another' (*HA*, vol. 12, p. 363). To learn about others' existence is to discover the limits of one's own; for just as, in botany, the generality of the genus is definable only in relation to the multiplicity of the species subsumed under it, so the commonalities of humanity become discernible only in relation to the full diversity of human beliefs and practices.

Because, however, 'the literature of another nation cannot be understood and felt [*empfunden*] without an awareness of its general social conditions', as Goethe explained in 1829 to members of a recently formed Berlin society for foreign literature (*GA*, vol. 14, pp. 911–13), the project of cross-cultural engagement from which *Weltliteratur* was supposed to develop demanded not only that foreign literary works be read but also that they be contextualised. Referring to France, Goethe recommended reviews, newspapers and published lecture series as indispensable to acquiring a knowledge of the contemporary literature. English and Italian literature, on the other hand, would have to be approached in their own ways, according to the very different conditions (*ganz andere Verhältnisse*) obtaining in their nations. Whether criticism and scholarship themselves were supposed to form part of *Weltliteratur*, as translations evidently were, or were merely preparations for it, is not clear from Goethe's pronouncements, as Fritz Strich notes (*GA*, vol. 14, p. 1028). But perhaps this is a false distinction anyway, in so far as literary works, after the models of Goethe's and Byron's, could contextualise themselves.[25]

In the last year of his life, Goethe wrote to Wilhelm von Humboldt, 'At my advanced age everything becomes more and more historical to me [. . .], yes, I appear to myself more and more historical.'[26] This observation is attested to by the project of *Weltliteratur*, which was profoundly historicist in two respects. The first was its assumption that nations are shaped by particular socio-historical circumstances and cannot therefore be comprehended in their individuality – which is to say, their difference from other nations – without a knowledge of those circumstances. To that extent, the concept of *Weltliteratur* originated philosophically in Johann Gottfried Herder's nationally

focused historicist theory of culture, particularly as developed in
*Auch eine Philosophie der Geschichte zur Bildung der Menschheit*
(1774), which criticised Enlightenment historiography for neglecting
the empirical diversity of human cultures and remaining blind to its
own historical formation.

Goethe radicalised Herder's critique, however, as a result of the second manifestation of his historicism. This was the recognition that both
the need for and the possibility of *Weltliteratur* were themselves historically conditioned, the need arising from a post-Napoleonic revalua-
tion of national cultures, and the possibility arising from the increasing
efficiency of international communication – such as the postal services
that delivered works by and about Byron to Goethe within a month of
their publication in London. Referring to the Napoleonic occupation
of the German and Italian states, and perhaps also to the French occupation of Frankfurt during his childhood, as recounted in *Dichtung
und Wahrheit*, Goethe insisted, in his introduction to the German edition of Carlyle's *Life of Schiller* (1830), that the very conflict of nations
had entailed cross-cultural encounters that, once peace was restored,
undermined prior assumptions of the self-contained unity of national
identities:

> For the nations, after they had been shaken into confusion and
> mutual conflict by the terrible wars, could not return to their settled
> and independent life without noticing that they had learned many
> foreign ideas and ways, which they had unconsciously adopted, and
> had come to feel here and there previously unrecognised spiritual and
> intellectual needs. Out of this arose the feeling of neighbourly rela-
> tions, and, instead of shutting themselves up as before, they gradually
> came to desire the adoption of some sort of more or less free spiritual
> intercourse. (*HA*, vol. 12, p. 364)

These collective motivations articulated by Goethe for the cultivation
of *Weltliteratur* would have resonated with Byron, who acknowledged
to Medwin, as Goethe was to read in 1825:

> Perhaps, if I had never travelled, – never left my own country young, –
> my views would have been more limited. They extend to the good
> of mankind in general – of the world at large. [. . .] No Italian could
> have rejoiced more than I, to have seen a Constitution established on
> this side of the Alps. I felt for Romagna as if she had been my own
> country, and would have risked my life and fortune for her, as I may
> yet for the Greeks. I am become a citizen of the world.[27]

Medwin himself sought to emphasise the consistency of Byron's political views by juxtaposing with this statement Canto IX, stanza 24, of *Don Juan*, which expresses 'downright detestation / Of every despotism in every nation' (*Don Juan* IX, l. 191–2). Byron's statement may, however, be interpreted more broadly as applying to his literary output from *Childe Harold* onwards, and especially to *Don Juan*, in which he allowed himself the fullest geographical, chronological and national scope for surveying the contingent, complex and often violent intercultural exchanges through which national and individual identities are formed – and he did so in a form that is itself *weltliterarisch* in its use of an Italian stanzaic form, its constant (if ironic) engagement with the epic tradition, its texture of references to a wide range of European literature, and not least its incorporation of quotations from languages other than English into its own fabric. Byron's narrative and dramatic works encouraged British readers to recognise themselves more clearly through the lenses of alterity.

The sociologist Norbert Elias credited the young Goethe with a major role in the late eighteenth-century development of a bourgeois and national *Kultur* as an antithesis to a courtly and cosmopolitan (which is to say, Francophile and Francophone) *Zivilisation*.[28] From that perspective, the project of *Weltliteratur* might appear to represent the mature Goethe's rejection of the cultural impact of *Sturm und Drang* and his anxiousness now to preserve the courtly society into which he was one of the few *Großbürger* to have been, after a fashion, admitted. In so far, however, as a 'gradual shift away from the dominant French cultural style' had already begun within the courts at Mannheim and in Thuringia in the 1770s – a shift that accelerated and extended to other German principalities during the Revolutionary and Napoleonic Wars, resulting in an increasing confluence of cultural values between the courtly élites and the politically excluded *Bürgertum* – Goethe's encouragement of a secular, cosmopolitan literary culture was directed not towards the preservation of a specifically aristocratic aesthetic, but against the ahistorical fantasy of an autonomous, self-enclosed national culture.[29] *Weltliteratur* was an implied antidote to what he perceived as the inclination of 'an entire, not contemptible generation' to pursue 'a false grounding in antiquarianism and nativism [*Vaterländelei*], a debilitating condition in false piety [*Frömmelei*]'.[30] Even if he conceived the German contribution to *Weltliteratur* to be a task for the *Bürgertum*, and he never overcame his own disapproval of Byron's personal conduct, Goethe must have recognised in the exiled aristocrat's works a model of a literature that recognised and embraced historical temporality while rejecting a self-denying monoculturalism.

## Notes

1. Goethe, *Gespräche*, in: *Gedenkausgabe der Werke, Briefe und Gespräche*, vol. 13, p. 308 (this edition hereafter cited parenthetically as *GA*). For details of Goethe's reading of Byron, see Brandl, 'Goethes Verhältnis zu Byron', pp. 3–37.
2. Cf. Butler, *Byron and Goethe: Analysis of a Passion*, pp. 185–6, 190–4.
3. Cf. Strich, *Goethe und die Weltliteratur*, p. 304.
4. Cf. Butler, *Byron and Goethe*, p. 177.
5. On 25 August 1816 Byron thanked Madame de Staël for lending him 'the work of Mr. Schlegel', in: *BLJ*, vol. 5, p. 88.
6. Schulz, *Die deutsche Literatur zwischen französischer Revolution und Restauration*, pp. 292–3; Ernst Behler, 'Romantik', pp. 918–25, at p. 923.
7. Goethe, *Briefe*, vol. 4, p. 205.
8. *Faust* is cited by line numbers from vol. 5 of the *Hamburger Ausgabe* (hereafter *HA*): Goethe, *Werke*, ed. Ernst Trunz.
9. Butler, *Byron and Goethe*, p. 35.
10. Quoted in Medwin, *Conversations of Lord Byron*, p. 142.
11. Butler, *Byron and Goethe*, p. 115, n. 3 surmises that the date of 18 January 1825 given by Eckermann is likely to be incorrect if the conversation with Müller occurred, as the latter recorded, on 17 December 1824.
12. Brown, *Faust: The German Tragedy*, p. 213.
13. Mazzini, 'Byron et Goethe', vol. 11, pp. 187–241, at p. 238. The article was originally published in French.
14. Brown, *Faust*, p. 214.
15. See Saglia, '"Tis Greece!" Byron's (Un)Making of Romantic Hellenism', pp. 199–218, at pp. 204–5.
16. Parry, *The Last Days of Lord Byron*, p. 170; cf. Halmi, 'The Graeco-Roman Revival', in: *The Oxford Handbook of British Romanticism*. For Goethe's knowledge of the book, see *GA* vol. 23, pp. 389, 391–2.
17. Cassirer, *Freiheit und Form: Studien zur deutschen Geistesgeschichte*, p. 403.
18. Cicero, *Epistulae ad familiares*, 4.5.
19. McGann, *Don Juan in Context*, p. 160.
20. Cf. Stabler, *Byron, Poetics and History*; Franklin, 'Byron and History', pp. 81–105.
21. These are analysed fully by Allan, *'Das lebend'ge will ich preisen'. From Ästhetik to Humanität*, pp. 136–211.
22. On the destabilisation of the East / West dichotomy in *The Giaour*, see Bode, 'Byron's Dis-Orientations: *The Giaour*, for Example', pp. 9–25; on the ambiguity of national and linguistic distinctions in the translation of Pulci, see Halmi, 'The Literature of Italy in Byron's Poems of 1817–1820', in: *Byron and Italy*, pp. 39–40.
23. On Byron's reception of Goethe, see Allan, '"The Illustrious Goethe" through Byron's Eyes: A Relationship of Analogy?', pp. 47–63.
24. See Moretti, 'Conjectures on World Literature', pp. 54–68.

25. Cf. Schrimpf, *Goethes Begriff der Weltliteratur*, p. 16: 'Literary criticism, a literature of literature, is for Goethe a wholly integral part of his *oeuvre* [*seines Gesamtwerks*].'
26. Goethe, *Briefe*, vol. 4, p. 463.
27. Medwin, *Conversations of Lord Byron*, p. 229.
28. Elias, *The Civilizing Process: The History of Manners and State Formation and Civilization*, pp. 14–17.
29. Cf. Schrimpf, *Goethes Begriff der Weltliteratur*, pp. 18–30, esp. pp. 22–5; Fink, 'Weltbürgertum und Weltliteratur: Goethes Antwort auf den revolutionären Messianismus und die nationalen Eingrenzungstendenzen seiner Zeit', pp. 173–225, esp. pp. 186–91, 194–6; and Whaley, *Germany and the Holy Roman Empire*, vol. 2, pp. 536–41, 597–601. The quotation is from Whaley, p. 536. As Nicholas Boyle observes, Goethe's 'open detachment from the programme for a courtly Art' began in 1794 and was 'virtually complete' by 1803; see Boyle, *Goethe: The Poet and the Age*, vol. 2, pp. 783–4.
30. 'Goethe to Karl Friedrich Zelter, 24 August 1823', *GA* vol. 21, p. 555; also quoted in Schrimpf, p. 23.

## Works cited

Allan, Shona M. (1999), *'Das lebend'ge will ich preisen'. From Ästhetik to Humanität: A Comparison of Byron and Goethe with Special Reference to Don Juan and the West-östlicher Divan*, unpublished PhD thesis, University of Glasgow.
— (2000), '"The Illustrious Goethe" through Byron's Eyes: A Relationship of Analogy?', in: Paul Bishop and Roger H. Stephenson (eds), *Goethe 2000: Intercultural Readings of His Work*, Leeds: Northern Universities Press, pp. 47–63.
Behler, Ernst (1996–9), 'Romantik', in: Bernd Witte (ed.), *Goethe-Handbuch*, 6 vols, Stuttgart: Metzler, pp. 918–25.
Bode, Christoph (2015), 'Byron's Dis-Orientations: *The Giaour*, for Example', *Romantik*, 4, pp. 9–25.
Boyle, Nicholas (1989–), *Goethe: The Poet and the Age*, 2 vols to date, Oxford: Oxford University Press.
Brandl, Alois (1899), 'Goethes Verhältnis zu Byron', *Goethe Jahrbuch*, 20, pp. 3–37.
Brown, Jane K. (1986), *Faust: The German Tragedy*, Ithaca, NY: Cornell University Press.
Butler, Eliza Marian (1956), *Byron and Goethe: Analysis of a Passion*, London: Bowes.
Cassirer, Ernst (1922), *Freiheit und Form: Studien zur deutschen Geistesgeschichte*, Berlin: Cassirer.
Cicero (2001), *Epistulae ad familiares* 248 (4.5), in: *Letters to Friends*, vol. 2, ed. and trans. D. R. Shackleton-Bailey, Cambridge, MA: Havard University Press, pp. 400–6.

Elias, Norbert (1994), *The Civilizing Process: The History of Manners and State Formation and Civilization*, trans. Edmund Jephcott, Oxford: Blackwell.

Fink, Gonthier-Louis (2003), 'Weltbürgertum und Weltliteratur: Goethes Antwort auf den revolutionären Messianismus und die nationalen Eingrenzungstendenzen seiner Zeit', in: Klaus Manger (ed.), *Goethe und die Weltkultur*, Heidelberg: Winter, pp. 173–225.

Franklin, Caroline (2007), 'Byron and History', in: Jane Stabler (ed.), *Palgrave Advances in Byron Studies*, Basingstoke: Palgrave, pp. 81–105.

Goethe, Johann Wolfgang von (1948–71), *Gespräche*, in: *Gedenkausgabe der Werke, Briefe und Gespräche*, 27 vols, ed. Ernst Beutler, Zürich: Artemis.

— (1968–76), *Briefe*, 4 vols, ed. Karl Robert Mandelkow, Munich: Beck.

— (1994), *Werke*, 14 vols, rev. edn, ed. Ernst Trunz, Munich: Beck.

Halmi, Nicholas (2017), 'The Literature of Italy in Byron's Poems of 1817–20', in: Alan Rawes and Diego Saglia (eds), *Byron and Italy*, Manchester: Manchester University Press, pp. 23–43.

— (forthcoming 2018), 'The Graeco-Roman Revival', in: David Duff (ed.), *The Oxford Handbook of British Romanticism*, Oxford: Oxford University Press.

McGann, Jerome J. (1976), *Don Juan in Context*, London: John Murray.

Mazzini, Giuseppe (1915), 'Byron et Goethe', *Scritti editi ed inediti*, Imola: Galeate, pp. 187–241.

Medwin, Thomas (1966), *Conversations of Lord Byron*, ed. E. J. Lovell, Jr, Princeton: Princeton University Press.

Moretti, Franco (2000), 'Conjectures on World Literature', *New Left Review*, 1, pp. 54–68.

Parry, William (1825), *The Last Days of Lord Byron*, London: Knight & Lacey.

Saglia, Diego (2009), '"Tis Greece!" Byron's (Un)Making of Romantic Hellenism and its European Reinventions', in: Gilbert Hess, Elena Agazzi and Élisabeth Décultot (eds), *Graecomania: Der europäische Philhellenismus*, Berlin: de Gruyter, pp. 199–218.

Schrimpf, Hans Joachim (1968), *Goethes Begriff der Weltliteratur*, Stuttgart: Metzler.

Schulz, Gerhard (1989), *Die deutsche Literatur zwischen französischer Revolution und Restauration*, Munich: Beck.

Stabler, Jane (2002), *Byron, Poetics and History*, Cambridge: Cambridge University Press.

Strich, Fritz (1949), *Goethe und die Weltliteratur*, Bern: Francke.

Whaley, Joachim (2012), *Germany and the Holy Roman Empire*, 2 vols, Oxford: Oxford University Press.

# Chapter 3

# Reshaping the Romantic Canon from the Margins: The Medial Construction of 'Byron' in *Childe Harold's Pilgrimage*

*Ralf Haekel*

## Introduction

It is safe to say that Lord Byron's works, as well as Lord Byron himself, are situated both at the centre and on the margins of British Romanticism. He is at once one of the most famous and most successful poets of the period and at the same time hardly ever treated with the same reverence as, for instance, Wordsworth or Keats. Whilst being one of the most widely read authors of his day, his aesthetics do not conform with typically Romantic ideals: they point to both a Neoclassical past and a modernist future, which turns him into a figure that is paradoxically both ubiquitous and oddly ephemeral, escaping a fixed definition. In this chapter, I will argue that this effect is the result of a medial self-construction of 'Byron' in Lord Byron's own works, securing his status within the Romantic literary canon, as well as establishing the emergence of his celebrity status.[1]

The past three decades have witnessed a dramatic change in the perception of the Romantic canon. The changes in the wake of New Historicist and Gender-Theoretical approaches of the 1980s have led to a fundamental reorganisation of the Romantic canon. Around the turn of the millennium, however, scholars in turn began to question the premises of this general sea change and looked again at the formerly canonical authors. A 1999 conference, organised by the German Society for Romanticism and bearing the title *Re-mapping Romanticism*, investigated and already critically historicised the general revision of the literary canon. In the introduction to the edited collection of the same title, the conference's co-organiser, Christoph

Bode, stated that 'all too often the question of quality, of literary value, was shirked in canon debates',[2] arguing that 'a *serious* debate about why they [hitherto neglected authors] should be included or not has not even begun'.[3]

Within both the traditional canon and the more open approach to Romantic literary history, Lord Byron occupies a position that is hard to define. In the essay 'Re-Mapping Romanticism: Lord Byron – Britain's First Anti-Romantic', published in the same volume, Norbert Lennartz argues:

> The necessity for – or should we say the futility of? – re-mapping this movement, of extending and re-evaluating the traditionally male-dominated canon has nowadays been amply demonstrated by various eminent scholars such as Jerome J. McGann, Duncan Wu and Anne K. Mellor. But while these critics have been vying with each other in unearthing as many female Romantics as possible, a reconsideration of the well-established doyens of Romanticism and, concomitantly, a constructive attempt at redefining Romanticism seems to have fallen into oblivion.[4]

Lord Byron, one of Britain's earliest literary superstars and bestselling authors, predated only by Sir Walter Scott, stands somewhat apart from the canonical Romantics. Although he has always been part of the Romantic literary canon, Byron's position within this canon is hard to pin down. On the one hand, he is undoubtedly considered to be among the most important authors of his time; on the other hand, his poetic and aesthetic notions are at once more conservative and more modern than those of his peers. The marginal position that Byron seems to hold even turns him into the first 'anti-Romantic', as Lennartz claims:

> Lord Byron's heterogeneous work has always frustrated every effort at classification. On the one hand his poems contain numerous echoes of and references to the literature of the Renaissance and Classicism, on the other hand they inaugurate the poetical mode of the modern age, which habitually makes extensive use of the imagery and rhetoric of Romanticism only in order to subject them to bitter and sardonic laughter.[5]

In this chapter, I will argue that Byron not only stands apart from but also has a lot in common with his contemporaries. Looking for similarities within the Romantic canon may lead to surprising insights – and may even heighten striking differences between Byron and the other Romantics.

Recent media-theoretical approaches in literary studies have paved a way for this new perspective, and I will suggest that a focus on the mediality of Romantic poetry opens up the possibility of reading Byronic and Wordsworthian or Shelleyan aesthetics not as contradictory approaches to poetry, but rather as, albeit invariably different, negotiations of similar problems caused by the dawning of modernity. A special case in this context is the medial construction of 'Byron' as Byronic hero in the popular figure of the vampire, first created by John Polidori. From Polidori's novella, the figure wanders off to other media of the Romantic and the Victorian age – drama, opera – and thus sheds a new light on the institutionalised canon from the margins.

## Byron as a medial figure

To speak of Byron and Byron's work from a media-theoretical point of view implies that one has to look at him in the context of other significant Romantic authors – and Romantic topics like the imagination and the sublime. As numerous studies since the 1980s have shown, the Romantic period is not just concerned with nature, subjectivity and the imagination; its aesthetic is also influenced and informed by a fundamental media change in the wake of the Industrial Revolution. The massive expansion of the print market, and new forms of publication, especially periodicals, not only created a new and wider readership but also changed literature as such. Clifford Siskin has argued that this quantitative explosion also had a decisive impact on quality, that 'more is different':

> More of 'literature' became 'Literature', a difference that marks the advent of what we now call Romanticism. [. . .] These decades – the decades of the quantitative sublime – saw Britain's transformation into a print culture – a society saturated by the technology of print.[6]

But whereas the other major Romantic authors, in a more or less hidden manner, inserted a medial self-reflexive element in their works,[7] Byron's medial self-reflexivity took on a decidedly different form. It is therefore expedient to investigate Byron's use of medial self-reflexivity in comparison to his fellow Romantics, especially the use of typical Romantic aesthetic elements such as the imagination and the sublime, especially in light of recent theoretical developments.

In 1983, Jerome McGann published *The Romantic Ideology*, a study that has left its mark on Romantic studies as a whole. Before that, McGann had written an influential study of Byron's poetry, *Fiery Dust* (1968), and had been active as the editor of Byron's *Collected Works* (1980–93). He sees a strict opposition between the traditional Romantic – that is, Wordsworthian and Coleridgean – aesthetic ideal and the Byronic concept of literature and art: 'To be Byronic is precisely not to be laid asleep in body and become a living soul,'[8] to quote a famous line from Wordsworth's 'Tintern Abbey'. In 2002, McGann commented on his initial impulse to go in this direction: 'I wanted to study why Byron, who for nearly a hundred years fairly defined, in the broadest international context, the "meaning" of Romanticism, had all but disappeared from the most serious forms of academic and professional attention.'[9] McGann thus looked at Byron in order to show how literary criticism of the previous decades had systematically marginalised authors and, indeed, alternative 'meanings' of Romanticism. Byron is, of course, an author who was highly critical of exactly those aspects of Romanticism that McGann describes as ideological: an otherworldly conception of the human mind or the imagination. As I want to show, however, in *Childe Harold* (1812–18), Byron takes up the Romantic imagination, as well as the sublime, only to give them his own idiosyncratic twist. Regarding the reflection on the text's mediality, I will argue that the figure of the notorious 'Byronic hero' offers an alternative answer to the problem of how to tackle the relationship between the imagination and the work of art.

This alternative has to be seen in Byron's use of the new possibilities in the wake of the medial paradigm shift occurring around 1800, which, nevertheless, cannot be reduced to the level of medial or textual self-reflexivity. In fact, Byron practises something that can be called a medial self-fashioning. In this context, it is important to take into account the fact that, as Tom Mole has argued, Byron is instrumental in the development of modern celebrity culture. What distinguishes Byron from former famous personalities like the actor David Garrick, however, is his use of an apparatus that comes into being only during the Romantic period: the interplay of an industry, an individual and an audience – 'massive, anonymous, socially diverse, geographically distributed'.[10] This new and anonymous apparatus is, according to Mole, the precondition for the development of a branded identity based on a 'hermeneutics of intimacy',[11] which is a paradox only at first sight because mass culture and anonymity are, in fact, the very preconditions for the medial construction of authenticity and intimacy. Andrew Burkett has described the very same phenomenon: that is, the fact that Byron's works cannot be separated from the construction of the author figure, from a media-theoretical standpoint. He shows how Byronism needs to be seen as a 'phenomenon of mass mediation'[12] and, investigating 'the nature and models of Byronic identity',[13] describes how this identity is consciously created by Byron and his publisher Murray by making use of the print industry whilst also paving the way for new media in the nineteenth century.

In the following reading of *Childe Harold's Pilgrimage*, I want to show how Byronism is indeed based on a medial construction of the figure of 'Byron' in his own work, and that this is indeed a process that unfolds in Lord Byron's critical engagement with the imagination and the sublime. The medial figure of Byron is, I argue, the result of the text's encounter with, and ultimate rejection of, key Romantic characteristics.

## Childe Harold's Pilgrimage

To understand Byron's position within the Romantic canon, the epic *Childe Harold's Pilgrimage* is of key importance. The text is neither as fierce and ferocious a critique of an erstwhile radical Romantic poet turned Tory – Southey – as *The Vision of Judgement* (1822); nor is it a mock-heroic satire like Byron's masterpiece, *Don Juan* (1819–24). Instead, *Childe Harold* is a text that first catapulted Byron to Europe-wide literary fame and that reflects on its own creation, on art and, first and foremost, on the politics of the 1810s. Cantos I and II were published in 1812, and they reflect the political situation of Europe in and after the Napoleonic Wars. The travel narrative traces the voyages of the eponymous hero from Portugal and Spain to Greece, describing the stark contrast between beautiful appearance and corrupted core. The subsequent Cantos III and IV, which are investigated far more extensively by literary scholars than the first two, were published several years later, in 1816 and 1817: that is, after the Congress of Vienna. What is more, Byron spent the summer of 1816 in Switzerland together with the Shelleys, with whom he shared his radical political ideas, thus also coming into immediate contact with the core Romantic ideas he had hitherto despised.

At the heart of the poem is the narrative construction of a deeply melancholic character driven rather aimlessly through Europe. This prototypical Byronic hero is sometimes identified as Harold and sometimes as the narrator, but is always related to the author-figure of Byron himself. One needs to be cautious, however, not to read this as a purely autobiographical narrative, because Byron is very consciously playing with the medial construction of himself as 'Byron'. Christoph Bode remarks:

> On closer inspection, Byron's protagonists, despite their display of melancholy, world-weariness, and their solitariness, are astonishingly abstract and archetypal – hints at their history and motivation are vague, so that one may speak of a striking blank space in this narrative text.[14]

The effect produced by the text is the result of Byron's characteristic use, not to say exploitation, of typically Romantic aesthetic features. The following reading of *Childe Harold* traces Byron's engagement with, and subsequent rejection of, canonical Romantic ideas such as the imagination or the sublime.

### Byron's revision of Romanticism: imagination and the sublime

Byron's work is characterised by a highly idiosyncratic treatment of typically Romantic features. At times he openly rejects elements like the imagination, while at others he embraces them as means to achieve his own ends, which differ fundamentally from those of Wordsworth or Coleridge. His use of the imagination and the sublime is a case in point.

The creative imagination is not among the topics or aesthetic theories generally considered to be at the heart of Byron's works. At the beginning of Canto IV of *Childe Harold's Pilgrimage*, however, Byron makes extensive use of both the language and the imagery of the Romantic creative imagination:

> The Beings of the Mind are not of clay:
> Essentially immortal, they create
> And multiply in us a brighter ray
> And more beloved existence: that which Fate
> Prohibits to dull life in this our state
> Of mortal bondage, by these Spirits supplied,
> First exiles, then replaces what we hate;
> Watering the heart whose early flowers have died,
> And with a fresher growth replenishing the void. (*Childe Harold*
> IV, ll. 37–45)

As products of the imagination and according to the traditional *vita brevis, ars longa*-topos often referred to in Romantic poetry such as in Keats's 'Ode on a Grecian Urn' (1819), artworks transcend the material world; they are 'essentially immortal'. But the imagination in this stanza is described neither as divine nor as transcendental; indeed, the works are the 'Beings of the Mind': the products of the human brain, in other words. Thus, even in this, in terms of Byronic aesthetic standards, very emphatic and Romantic praise of the power of art, the artefacts turn out to be very human and not divine at all. This becomes even clearer in the stanza immediately following:

> Such is the refuge of our youth and age –
> The first from Hope, the last from Vacancy;
> And this wan feeling peoples many a page –
> And, may be, that which grows beneath mine eye:
> Yet there are things whose strong reality
> Outshines our fairy-land; in shape and hues
> More beautiful than our fantastic sky,
> And the strange constellations which the Muse
> O'er her wild universe is skilful to diffuse. (*Childe Harold* IV,
> ll. 46–54)

Here the realm of imaginative art is reduced to 'the refuge of our youth and age', and the speaker opposes it to the empirical 'strong reality' that '[o]utshines our fairy-land' by far – not quite unimportant in a poem belonging to the genre of travel literature. But what is more significant than the sudden sceptical questioning of the Romantic imagination is the fact that it is reduced to an effect of the human brain: 'that which grows beneath mine eye'. In other words, one can read not only Byron's criticism of the core elements of canonical Romanticism as based on a material and rational foundation, but also his praise of the works of art and the imagination as immortal. Hence, in the subsequent lines, the realms of art and reality merge and become indistinguishable as dreams: 'I saw or dreamed of such, – but let them go, – / They came like Truth – and disappeared like dreams' (*Childe Harold* IV, ll. 55–63).

It goes to show that Byron took up traditional elements of Romantic poetry, tested them and rejected them in favour of his idiosyncratic mixture of Neoclassicist ideals and modern scepticism. His poetic endeavour, thus, questions and even blurs the difference between the centre and the margins of Romantic aesthetics.

The Wordsworthian sublime is yet another example. Byron's engagement with canonical Romantic concepts in *Childe Harold* is not restricted to the imagination. In Canto III, there are several passages describing the sublime landscape of the German Rhine and the Alps that Christoph Bode describes as 'purest Wordsworth' – 'reinster Wordsworth':[15]

I live not in myself, but I become
Portion of that around me; and to me
High mountains are a feeling, but the hum
Of human cities torture: I can see
Nothing to loathe in Nature, save to be
A link reluctant in a fleshly chain,
Classed among creatures, when the soul can flee,
And with the sky – the peak – the heaving plain
Of Ocean, or the stars, mingle – and not in vain.

And thus I am absorbed, and this is life: –
I look upon the peopled desert past,
As on a place of agony and strife,
Where, for some sin, to Sorrow I was cast,
To act and suffer, but remount at last
With a fresh pinion; which I feel to spring,
Though young, yet waxing vigorous as the Blast
Which it would cope with, on delighted wing,
Spurning the clay-cold bonds which round our being cling.

And when, at length, the mind shall be all free
From what it hates in this degraded form,
Reft of its carnal life, save what shall be
Existent happier in the fly and worm, –
When Elements to Elements conform,
And dust is as it should be, shall I not
Feel all I see less dazzling but more warm?
The bodiless thought? the Spirit of each spot?
Of which, even now, I share at times the immortal lot?

Are not the mountains, waves, and skies, a part
Of me and of my Soul, as I of them?
Is not the love of these deep in my heart
With a pure passion? should I not contemn
All objects, if compared with these? and stem
A tide of suffering, rather than forego
Such feelings for the hard and worldly phlegm
Of those whose eyes are only turned below,
Gazing upon the ground, with thoughts which dare not glow?
(*Childe Harold* III, ll. 680–715)

In the context of both *Childe Harold* and Byron's other works, this passage is puzzling. It is, however, neither a parody of Romantic pantheism of the Wordsworthian or Coleridgean kind nor a complete turn towards these ideals on Byron's side. Indeed, the passage has a biographical background: while they were staying in Switzerland, Percy Shelley read

Wordsworth to Byron, who, thoroughly impressed, wrote these lines under the influence of this new experience.

In these passages, Byron makes use of one of the most important aesthetic aspects of the late Enlightenment and the Romantic age: the sublime. In order to consider Byron's handling of sublime and awe-inspiring natural landscapes, one needs to go beyond Wordsworth's and other Romantics' use of nature in poetry and look at the political and historical dimension of this discourse from the Classical origins up to the eighteenth century. Byron's very critical treatment of the sublime in *The Vision of Judgment* has to be seen in this context, as Alexandra Böhm explains:

> With his treatise *Peri Hypsous*, Pseudo-Longinus aimed at a critique of his age, which he considered to be a period of political and moral decline. Opposed to this, the ideal of sublime grandeur embodied Classical Greece with its political autonomy. While these aspects are true for Byron as well, the literary-theoretical dimension of the sublime in Pseudo-Longinus already points towards the differences from the English Romantics, as Byron explicates in his 'Letter to Murray'. *Peri Hypsous* turns away from the Hellenistic ideal of literature as characterized by elegance, transparency and urbanity, and stresses magnitude, passion, and the overwhelming. Byron defends in Pope exactly those qualities of harmony, clarity and the urbane, evoking openness, tolerance and variability, already depreciated by Pseudo-Longinus.[16]

At the same time it cannot be denied that Byron made extensive use of the sublime in the entire poem. As far as the description of the natural and cultural landscape in Cantos I and II is concerned, the sublime fulfils two functions: one is to illustrate the 'cyclic philosophy of history highlighting devastation',[17] which is central to an understanding of the first half of the poem: that is, to see history and human works as subject to eternal change and devastation. Here, as Michael R. Edson explains, the main obstacle lies in the 'difficulty of distinguishing the sublime from the mock-sublime'.[18] The other function lies in the construction of the hero, who, fraught with some nameless and thus even more horrifying guilt, is forced to wander in order to escape his past.

What Byron does not, however, do – with the exception of those stanzas quoted above – is create a pantheistic bond between sublime landscape and the hero's / narrator's melancholy selfhood. To speak of an aesthetic crisis in this context would surely go too far. What is more likely is that Byron was playing a game with identity when he was writing in the manner of Wordsworth: he was merely trying on the mask to see if it fits.[19] To use Tom Mole's term, he used these elements to create a branded identity. What can be said is that Byron was, at the time he wrote the third Canto, on the threshold of a new form of poetry that he would only fully embrace three years later, in *Don Juan*, which satirises Byron's own medial creation: his aesthetic alter ego, the Byronic hero.

### Narrative and medial self-construction in Childe Harold

The great success of Byron's poetry, as well as of the Byronic hero, is based on the fact that his contemporary readers tended to identify the torn and melancholy characters with Byron's own personality. The poems make such an identification possible exactly because they do not give away too many biographical details but rather leave enough blank spaces to be filled by the readers. This, in turn, led to a paradox: the invention of the biographical Byron as the source of the texts he had penned in the first place:

> Byron's life appeared as a reality for his readers once he had stretched representation to the point where an absence of origins made it impossible for his characters to be read as fiction. The real Byron had to be invented as the absent cause of what was inexplicable within the poems themselves.[20]

I will try to explore this thought in further detail.

Byron differs from other Romantic authors in his stark rejection of essentialist concepts of identity, selfhood and subjectivity. The imagination does not serve to explore the depths of the human mind but is a means to create the self continually in the narrative medium – which implies that the self vanishes as soon as the narrative ceases to be. Vincent Newey argues:

> *Childe Harold* III and IV is pervaded by this sense of the self as that which is constantly being brought into existence in the mind and through language – and which is therefore also always provisional and on the point of dissolution.[21]

Jerome McGann describes this performative and strangely fleeting character of Byronic self-fashioning in the following terms:

> the texts rise to unbuild themselves repeatedly. In the process they cast not dark shadows but a kind of invigorated negative textual space. So here 'meaning' slips free of every conclusion, including the idea of conclusiveness, and fuses its eventuality.[22]

Unlike Shelley, for instance, Byron does not reflect on the text of the poem as the ultimately self-reflexive medium that eventually, because access to transcendence is eternally barred, can refer only to its own materiality.[23] On the contrary, the text creates a persona that is both its effect and considered to be its source. In the opening passages of Canto III, the speaker describes the protagonist in the following terms:

> In my youth's summer I did sing of One,
> The wandering outlaw of his own dark mind;
> Again I seize the theme, then but begun,
> And bear it with me, as the rushing wind
> Bears the cloud onwards: in that Tale I find
> The furrows of long thought, and dried-up tears,
> Which, ebbing, leave a sterile track behind,
> O'er which all heavily the journeying years
> Plod the last sands of life, – where not a flower appears.
> (*Childe Harold* III, ll. 19–27)

In the course of this Byronic self-fashioning process, the text – in the following famous passage – makes use of the traditional imagination but reflects that this imagination creates only an anti-essentialist form of selfhood:

> 'Tis to create, and in creating live
> A being more intense that we endow
> With form our fancy, gaining as we give
> The life we image, even as I do now –
> What am I? Nothing: but not so art thou,
> Soul of my thought! with whom I traverse earth,
> Invisible but gazing, as I glow
> Mixed with thy spirit, blended with thy birth,
> And feeling still with thee in my crushed feelings' dearth.
> (*Childe Harold* III, ll. 46–54)

If the Byronic self is a void – that is, something that must be created over and over again, it is at the same time reduced to only a medial effect. In this passage, Byron brilliantly reflects on the way his literary fame worked, which was initiated by the publication of the first two Cantos of *Childe Harold* in 1812, and immediately reinforced by the first of the Byronic tales, *The Giaour*, in 1813. Byron constructs an artificial version of himself in his own work that is performative, theatrical, rhetorical and illusory, and the immediate success of his works reflects the fact that his readership followed him in identifying the characters with the author as an effect of the medium of literature. This worked despite the fact that Byron's *œuvre* is not a typically Romantic exploration of the subjective self as in, say, Wordsworth's *Prelude* or 'The Immortality Ode'. The Byronic hero is so very significant not because he resembles the egotistical Wordsworthian self or the Gothic villains, but because he is an elusive figure – and at the same time identified by the readership as a version of Byron himself: he is both the source of the work and its product. In other words, the text does not reflect Byron's or his speakers' subjectivity, but therefore it can become the space of a perpetual yet fleeting self-fashioning in and through the imagination of the readership.

It is important in this context for both Harold and the speaker to be fashioned as melancholy characters. In one passage, the Childe is described in the following terms:

> He, who grown aged in this world of woe,
> In deeds, not years, piercing the depths of life,
> So that no wonder waits him. (*Childe Harold* III, ll. 37–9)

The dark, brooding and also visionary hero finds his counterpart in the speaker who fears falling prey to the dangers of his melancholy disease:

> Yet must I think less wildly: – I *have* thought
> Too long and darkly, till my brain became,
> In its own eddy boiling and o'erwrought,
> A whirling gulf of phantasy and flame:
> And thus, untaught in youth my heart to tame,
> My springs of life were poison'd. (*Childe Harold* III, ll. 55–60)

Again, this is remarkable not because of the association with the dark and sexualised Gothic villain but rather because of the long tradition of melancholy as the necessary predisposition for creative ingenuity, a line of thought that goes back to Classical Antiquity but which became a key cultural paradigm only in the Renaissance. In their classic study *Saturn and Melancholy* of 1964, Raymond Klibansky, Erwin Panofsky and Fritz Saxl convincingly show that the birth of the modern concept of the original genius in the early modern period is closely linked with the concept of melancholy. Byron consciously used the Spenserian stanza and also early modern psychology to conjure up and reflect upon the origin of the creative genius. This is all the more important since melancholy, as it is based on the doctrine of the four humours, is a very physical explanation of the human mind. At the turn of the nineteenth century, a humoral explanation of the soul had been utterly replaced by a neuronal explanation of the mind and the brain, which is, however, also a very bodily and material theory.

The key passage quoted above may indicate that Byron is indeed reflecting here on the workings of the mind and the brain:

> 'Tis to create, and in creating live
> A being more intense that we endow
> With form our fancy, gaining as we give
> The life we imagine, even as I do now. (*Childe Harold* III, ll. 46–9)

This passage suggests a train of thought; it implies that reality – indeed, the self in the world, one of the key Romantic problems – is created as an act of the thinking brain, and that it ceases to exist as soon as the train of thought ends.

In a word, Byron's anti-Romantic Romanticism is challenging the dominant aesthetics and poetics while simultaneously negotiating the same key problems and phenomena at the dawning of modernity. To read Byron in this way is to merge marginalised as well as central Romantic concepts. Byron is and will remain both a paradigmatic and a paradoxical figure of British and European Romanticism, in that he builds a bridge between early modern and modernist literature.

## Medial *revenants* of the Byronic hero

It is striking that, unlike his fellow Romantics, Byron does not focus on the *text* as a medium but rather on the *author* and the *hero* as medial effects. These medial effects became remarkably adaptable in later literary, theatrical and film history. With his novella *The Vampyre* (1819), John Polidori, Lord Byron's physician, who accompanied him through Europe for some time, created not only the first vampire story in the English tongue but also the first modern vampire story in general. Polidori's novelty lies not so much in the form of the story but rather in the conception of the evil protagonist, Lord Ruthven. The vampire, who is modelled on both Lord Byron and the contemporary popular and literary image of him, is a monster of a new kind, in that he is a melancholy and highly eroticised *revenant* with an aristocratic social background and, hence, differs from the plebeian ghouls of popular rural folklore. Additionally, the Byronic vampire is the prototype of the transmedial monster that is not restricted to literature but is, of course, even more famous for his appearance on the movie screen.

Why is it that the Byronic vampire had such an appeal for later writers, from Sheridan le Fanu via Bram Stoker to Ann Rice? John Polidori's story was originally published on 1 April 1819 in the *New Monthly Magazine*. Partly because of its novelty and partly because the story was considered to have been written by Byron himself, *The Vampyre* created a craze all over Europe. Not only did the nineteenth century produce numerous fictitious works with an aristocratic or Byronic vampire, but also *The Vampyre* almost immediately transcended its generic and medial boundaries. In 1820, Charles Nodier published a sequel to Polidori's story called *Lord Ruthwen ou les vampires*, allegedly co-written by Cyprien Bérard, which, in turn, was almost immediately adapted for the stage by John Robinson Planché in his play *The Vampyre, or, The Bride of the Isles*. There were numerous stage adaptations at the time, in England and on the Continent: a French melodrama written by Nodier together with Achille Jouffroy and Carmouche music by Alexandre Piccini, which premiered in June 1820; Heinrich August Marschner's opera *Der Vampyr*, with a libretto by Wilhelm August Wohlbrück, performed in Leipzig in 1828; and in the same year, the first performance of another German opera (in Stuttgart) based on Polidori's story, and this time composed by Peter Joseph von Lindpaintner with a libretto by Cäsar Max Heigl.[24] The Byronic vampire, it seems, was prone to adaptation in other media.

Lord Ruthven's appeal lies in the fact that he is able to extract his supernatural power from other human beings, which presupposes that this power is material and immanent. As a vampire, he is someone 'who, apparently, had nothing in common with other men',[25] but, then again, depends on other humans' vital energy; in other words, he is a biological monster who has to transgress his bodily boundaries in order to feed parasitically on other bodies. Thus, the vampire reduplicates what Polidori himself does with the Byronic hero. In creating a vampire that is modelled on Byron's own creations as well as Byron's public persona, Polidori's novella parasitically depends on the public figure of Byron just as Ruthven depends on the blood of the innocent. The medial effect of the Byronic hero is thus perpetuated and serialised. Not only does the hero need to be created over and over again, as reflected in *Childe Harold*, but also his re-creation can be prolonged beyond his author's physical death, as one can see in the lasting appeal of the figure of the vampire and other Byronic villains and heroes.

## Conclusion

The example of the Byronic vampire shows not only that Byron's work challenged – and still challenges – the Romantic canon from the margins, but also that, by transgressing its generic and medial boundaries, the very modernity of Byron's approach to the medium of literature keeps on testing the way we discuss the concept of the literary canon in general. Depending on time and aesthetic stance, the centre and the margins of a literary canon may appear interchangeable. What is more, a cursory look at the concepts of the imagination and the sublime, as well as identity formation, shows both differences between Byron and his contemporaries, and striking resemblances. The treatment of the imagination betrays a focus on the material basis of the mind, a thought that also fascinated Shelley and Keats, among others. Byron condemned the theory of the sublime – yet made extensive use of it in *Childe Harold's Pilgrimage*; whether this was done ironically or not is hard to say. Finally, the construction of identity in Byron's poetry betrays a fascination with the concept of the medium and mediality. However, he does not focus on the literary text but on its effect: the medial amalgam of author, narrator and character. The fascination of the Byronic hero was so great that it even transcended the boundaries of Byron's own work, thus creating such a figure as the modern transmedial vampire.

In his approach to material and medial concerns, Lord Byron breaks down the barriers between central and marginalised aspects of Romanticism. It becomes apparent that he was absorbed by the same aesthetic problems that characterise many of the works of his peers – imagination, the sublime and the medium of poetry; he differs only in that he provided strikingly different, but in no way less fascinating, answers. Thus, Byron's early works enable us to see that the marginalisation of key Romantic concepts is an aspect not only of literary criticism but also of a given aesthetic point of view. His own approach fundamentally questions and thus breaks down the opposition between margins and centre, and helps us to see similarities where formerly there were only differences.

## Notes

1. See Mole, *Byron's Romantic Celebrity*.
2. Bode, 'By Way of Introduction: Re-Mapping Romanticism', p. 13.
3. Ibid., p. 14 (italics in the original).
4. Lennartz, 'Re-Mapping Romanticism', p. 101.
5. Ibid., p. 103.

6.  Siskin, 'More is Different: Literary Change in the Mid and Late Eighteenth Century', pp. 819, 822.
7.  See Haekel, *The Soul in British Romanticism*.
8.  McGann, *Byron and Romanticism*, p. 12.
9.  Ibid., p. 1.
10. Mole, *Byron's Romantic Celebrity*, p. 3.
11. Ibid., pp. 22–7.
12. Burkett, *Romantic Mediations*, p. 37.
13. Ibid., p. 21.
14. 'Byrons Protagonisten sind nämlich bei genauerem Hinsehen trotz der zur Schau gestellten Melancholie, des Weltschmerzes und ihres Einzelgänger-tums erstaunlich abstrakt und typenhaft – Hinweise auf ihre Geschichte und Motivation bleiben vage, so dass man von auffälligen Leerstellen in diesem Erzähltext sprechen kann.' Bode, *Selbst-Begründungen*, p. 122 (my translation).
15. Ibid., p. 129.
16. 'Mit seiner Schrift *Peri Hypsos* zielte Pseudo-Longinus auf eine Kritik der eigenen Gegenwart, die er als Epoche des politischen und moralischen Ver-falls empfand. Das Ideal erhabener Größe dagegen verkörperte für ihn das klassische Griechenland mit seiner politischen Selbstbestimmung. Während diese Aspekte auch auf Byron zutreffen, verweist die literaturtheoretische Dimension des Sublimen bei Pseudo-Longinus schon auf die Differenz zu den englischen Romantikern, die Byron in seinem 'Letter to Murray' expliziert. Denn die Schrift *Peri Hypsos* wendet sich vom hellenistischen Literaturideal ab, das sich durch Anmut, Transparenz und Urbanität auszeichnet, und akzentuiert dagegen Größe, Leidenschaft und Überwäl-tigungskraft. Byron verteidigt an Pope genau die vom Sublimen schon bei Pseudo-Longinus abgewerteten Eigenschaften des Harmonischen, Verständlichen und des Urbanen, das Offenheit, Toleranz und Wandel-barkeit assoziiert.' Böhm, *Heine und Byron*, p. 205 (my translation).
17. Kostadinova, 'The Rise of the Sublime and the Fall of History', p. 197.
18. Edson, 'Soil and Sublimity in *Childe Harold's Pilgrimage*', p. 178.
19. See Bode, *Selbst-Begründungen*, p. 130.
20. Elfenbein, *Byron and the Victorians*, p. 20.
21. Newey, 'Authoring the Self: *Childe Harold* III and IV', p. 149.
22. McGann, *Byron and Romanticism*, p. 13.
23. See Haekel, 'Towards the Soul: Percy Bysshe Shelley's *Epipsychidion*', pp. 667–84.
24. See Summers, *The Vampire: His Kith and Kin*.
25. Polidori, *The Vampyre*, p. 5.

## Works cited

Bode, Christoph (2001), 'By Way of Introduction: Re-Mapping Romanti-cism', in: Christoph Bode and Fritz-Wilhelm Neumann (eds), *Re-Mapping Romanticism: Gender – Text – Context*, Essen: Die Blaue Eule, pp. 9–18.

— (2008), *Selbst-Begründungen: Diskursive Konstruktion von Identität in der britischen Romantik I: Subjektive Identität*, Trier: WVT.

Böhm, Alexandra (2012), *Heine und Byron: Poetik eingreifender Kunst am Beginn der Moderne*, Berlin: de Gruyter.

Burkett, Andrew (2016), *Romantic Mediations: Media Theory and British Romanticism*, New York: SUNY.

Edson, Michael R. (2005), 'Soil and Sublimity in *Childe Harold's Pilgrimage'*, *Revue de l'Université de Moncton* (special issue: Byron and the Romantic Sublime), pp. 177–87.

Elfenbein, Andrew (1996), *Byron and the Victorians*, Cambridge: Cambridge University Press.

Haekel, Ralf (2011), 'Towards the Soul: Percy Bysshe Shelley's *Epipsychidion'*, *European Romantic Review*, 22, pp. 667–84.

— (2014), *The Soul in British Romanticism: Negotiating Human Nature in Philosophy, Science and Poetry*, Trier: WVT.

Klibansky, Raymond, Erwin Panofsky and Fritz Saxl (1964), *Saturn and Melancholy: Studies in the History of Natural Philosophy, Religion and Art*, London: Nelson.

Kostadinova, Vitana (2005), 'The Rise of the Sublime and the Fall of History', *Revue de l'Université de Moncton* (special issue: Byron and the Romantic Sublime*)*, pp. 189–202.

Lennartz, Norbert (2001), 'Re-Mapping Romanticism: Lord Byron – Britain's First Anti-Romantic', in: Christoph Bode and Fritz-Wilhelm Neumann (eds), *Re-Mapping Romanticism: Gender – Text – Context*, Essen: Die Blaue Eule, pp. 101–12.

McGann, Jerome J. (2002), *Byron and Romanticism*, ed. James Søderholm, Cambridge: Cambridge University Press.

Mole, Tom (2007), *Byron's Romantic Celebrity: Industrial Culture and the Hermeneutic of Intimacy*, Basingstoke: Palgrave Macmillan.

Newey, Vincent (1988), 'Authoring the Self: *Childe Harold* III and IV', in: Bernard Beatty and Vincent Newey (eds), *Byron and the Limits of Fiction*, Liverpool: Liverpool University Press, pp. 148–90.

Polidori, John ([1819] 2008), *The Vampyre, and other Tales of the Macabre*, ed. Chris Baldick, Oxford: Oxford University Press.

Siskin, Clifford (2005), 'More is Different: Literary Change in the Mid and Late Eighteenth Century', in: John Richetti (ed.), *The Cambridge History of English Literature, 1660–1780*, Cambridge: Cambridge University Press, pp. 797–823.

Summers, Montague (1928), *The Vampire: His Kith and Kin*, London: K. Paul.

# Chapter 4

# Byron and Romantic Period Neoclassicism

*Rolf Lessenich*

In the Romantic period, the margins or borderlines separating Romanticism from Neoclassicism were not clearly defined, any more than the margins defining Christianity against Paganism in the fourth century AD. There was a medley of voices, with authors repeatedly changing positions, until, after decades of heated debates, they were *post festum* summarised under two opposed groups, whose margins or borderlines of inclusion and exclusion were nevertheless broad and permeable. Analogously, Romantic period poets could change and even mix modes, as did, for instance, Percy Bysshe Shelley's sometime friend and sometime adversary Thomas Love Peacock, the famous Greek scholar and Neoclassicist who, in his verse tale *Rhododaphne* (1818), mixed Classical legend with Romantic magic. He was a chameleon and border-crosser who obviously enjoyed his repeated changes of role, and was fascinated by Classical Greek and Roman tales and legends featuring changes (such as Ovid's *Metamorphoses* and Apuleius' *Golden Ass*).

In accordance with David Hume's sceptical philosophy of identity, Byron was also a chameleon – so called by Lady Blessington – in many respects.[1] Radical Whig in the House of Lords and Cambridge, yet a Tory in Albemarle Street and fine society, a writer alternately in the Romantic and Neoclassical modes, he created a Byronic hero who was, in turn, alternately noble and criminal, rational and sensitive. In a letter to his young confidante, Elizabeth Pigot, in which he implicitly admitted his penchant for adolescent boys, the nineteen-year-old lord honestly confessed his '(in general) changeable Disposition'.[2] The characters of Arnold and Caesar, from Byron's unfinished *doppelgänger* drama *The Deformed Transformed* (1824), in which he modelled Caesar on Goethe's Mephistopheles, represent the ever-changing sides of Byron's personality, alternating roles played seriously. Numerous biographical and psychoanalytical studies have tried to account for this bewildering complexity, especially in view of his central theme of the fall of man and expulsion from Paradise. Byron's Romantic disillusionism has been related to his early experience with his mother, who alternately loved and hated him as she both loved and hated his runaway father. Illusions of Paradise were inevitably followed by the reality of Paradise Lost. The dialectical synthesis of Paradise Regained then proved to be just another illusion followed by another experience of loss, constituting an absurd circle rather than a spiral ascent. Byron's friend and first biographer, Thomas Moore, aligned the emotional inconsistency of the poet's childhood with an inconstant mother 'without judgment or self-command',[3] though he failed to mention Byron's sexual inconsistency in his alternating choice of women and adolescent boys.[4] In his novel *Venetia* (1837), Benjamin Disraeli then created a combined portrait of Byron's mother and wife in the destructive Lady Annabel Herbert, and Charles Dickens may have even used this as the model for the equally destructive Miss Havisham in *Great Expectations* (1861).[5] Disraeli's Plantagenet Cadurcis, modelled on Byron, is both an ingenious 'spoiler'[6] and the unhappy victim of his character, moulded by the intolerable education bestowed upon him by his mother, Lady Herbert, who alternately soothes him as her 'dear boy' and insults him as her 'little brat'.[7] In the view of Marxist Romantic scholars, especially Jerome J. McGann, the Romantic disillusionist Byron was the outstanding social realist in a company of neo-Platonic dreamers and *soi-disant* visionaries.[8]

Byron was not the only Romantic disillusionist of his age, however. Almost all of the male Romantic poets and numerous female ones were literary chameleons, commuting between the progressivist Augustan Neoclassicism of the 'old [orthodox] school' with which they were acquainted on the one hand, and the Romanticism of the 'new [heretical] schools' on the other; their interest in the unconscious included dreams and madness, a preference for night over daylight and for the individual, feeling heart over general reason, and associated cults of primitivism, naturalism, childhood, non-erudition and originality.[9] Although he refused to adopt the terminology of the 'Classical–Romantic' divide, sparked by the Schlegel brothers in Germany and continued by Madame de Staël and Stendhal in France,[10] Byron was both involved in and torn between the dispute throughout his poetic career. He knew of the existence of some such movement as Romanticism, which defined itself against the established Augustan tradition.[11] When he took the side of the tradition of the 'old school', he lashed out against 'the trashy Jingle of the crowd of "Schools and upstarts'": namely, the Romantics.[12] What we now call Romanticism (in all its various forms) was under constant attack by the Romantic-period Neoclassicists of the Augustan tradition, including William Gifford, Thomas James Mathias, Richard Mant, Lady Anne Hamilton, George Canning and sometimes Byron himself. These (mostly) Tories, who took pride in their knowledge of the Classical tradition and their mastery of Greek and Latin, marshalled Horace and the rules of reason against the 'dissent' of the Wartons, Gray, Collins, Cowper, Walpole, Radcliffe, Blake, Hayley, Wordsworth, Coleridge, Keats and, again, sometimes Byron himself. There was, however, a good reason why many Whigs, too, highly esteemed the Classical tradition, and Horace in particular: sexual liberation, including the model of Greek and Latin homosexuality. Byron's Whig friends in his Cambridge student days, John Cam Hobhouse, Scrope Berdmore Davies and Charles Skinner Matthews, were, like Byron himself, fiercely contemptuous of moral cant and showed a keen interest in same-sex love, on the nebulous margins of lawfulness and illegality.[13] Byron's first collection of poems, *Hours of Idleness* (1807), with its rule-despising pose of originality and a diction inspired by Thomas Gray, was scathingly reviewed in the Scottish Enlightenment *Edinburgh Review*, awakening both his need for revenge and his admiration for the satires of Juvenal, Dryden, Pope and Gifford. Changing sides, Byron wrote a formal verse satire, *English Bards and Scotch Reviewers* (1809), in the Neoclassical style of Gifford's *Baviad* (1791) and *Maeviad* (1795), followed by a Neoclassical *ars poetica* in the same didactic heroic couplets, *Hints from Horace* (MS 1811). A close examination of *Hints from Horace*, however, and of its digressions in particular, reveals how Byron strove to transgress the narrow limits of Horatian rule and decorum, as he could no longer share Pope's faith in a pre-established cosmic order.[14] Pleading 'variety' versus 'cant', he distrusted whatever confined the poet to excessive restraint – the reason why he rejected Erasmus Darwin's hermetically closed heroic couplets as too pompous.[15] Byron's virulent attacks against the 'apostates from poetic rule', such as Scott, Wordsworth, Coleridge and the Gothic and Della Cruscan authors, polemically ignored how deeply these authors of the 'new schools' were indebted to James Thomson, Thomas Gray and James Beattie, his chief models for *Hours of Idleness*:

> Truth! rouse some genuine Bard, and guide his hand
> To drive this pestilence from out the land.[16]

In *Hours of Idleness*, however, Byron's borrowing from Pope, whom he admired all his life, along with Horace and Gifford, was just as explicit as his echoing of Thomson, Gray and Beattie.[17] Byron's imagery in *English Bards and Scotch Reviewers* resounds with biblical allusions. An apostate is a heretic from eternal truth, a plague on mankind to be exterminated from the earth, a 'fallen' angel expelled from Paradise. By implication, Byron then regarded his writing in the pre-Romantic tradition of literary dissent as a *lapsus*, a repetition of the fall of man in art. This repentance also found expression as Byron turned away from the Romantic drama type of *Manfred* (1817) to the Neoclassical model of the tragedies of Vittorio Alfieri in his later dramas of 1821–2, with their observances of the Aristotelian unities, in an aristocratic reaction against the rule-despising popular culture of the London stage, and the illegitimate theatres in particular.[18] In *The Deformed Transformed*, then, Byron repeated his 'fall' into heresy, writing a lyrical Romantic drama of the same type as *Manfred*, without respecting the unities and with a magical plot revolving around the motif of the Romantic *doppelgänger*.

In the raging Pope–Bowles controversy of 1821, the year of publication of *Marino Faliero* and *The Two Foscari*, Byron elaborated on the biblical imagery of heresy and the fall into sin. William Lisle Bowles's ten-volume edition of *The Works of Alexander Pope* (1806), with its strictures on Pope's poetry, brought Bowles into conflict with Thomas Campbell and other advocates of Neoclassicism.[19] As an admirer of Pope and Gifford, Byron, again in Neoclassical mood,[20] entered the lists in favour of Pope, in his long 'Letter to—[John Murray] on the Rev. W. L. Bowles', dated 7 February 1821, Ravenna.[21] Byron reproached Bowles, who ranked nature above art and sensibility above reason, charging him with sentimental imposture, facile writing, and prostitution of literature to the low taste of the populace – major sins in Horace's *ars poetica*. Mapping Classical Antiquity on to his own age, Byron paralleled the degeneration of poetry from the Classical Antiquity of Horace to the late Antiquity of Claudian with the decline from the Age of Pope to the Age of the French Revolution: 'we [of the lower Empire] are upon a wrong revolutionary poetical system – or systems – not worth a damn in itself'.[22] His aristocratic disdain of poets of low origin and their alleged ignorance of the Classical tradition prompted him to include the 'Cockney Poets' in his attack, notably John Keats, summarising them together with the 'Lake Poets' as rebels against the valid Augustan model,[23] and thus paving the way for the later construction of a 'Romantic School'. Thus, he called Keats 'a tadpole of the lakes, a young disciple of the six or seven new Schools'.[24] What united these 'Schools' was their 'erroneous [anti-Augustan] System'[25] – a term that invariably carried negative associations in Byron's philosophy, as when, for example, he chided 'the founders of sects and systems' in *Childe Harold's Pilgrimage* (1812–18).[26] Byron had to confess that in his Romantic poetry he had been, and still was, 'amongst the builders of this Babel attended by a confusion of tongues', erecting an Oriental 'Mosque' and a 'grotesque edifice' inadequately and unfittingly 'by the side of a Grecian temple of the purest Architecture'.[27] This same self-reproach is found in an earlier letter, written before the controversy, in which Byron disavowed the many sectarian schools of his time as comprising the heterogeneous mass of deranged modern poets united by their enmity towards Pope:

> These three personages Southey – Wordsworth, and Coleridge had all of them a very natural antipathy to Pope [. . .]. But they have been joined in it by those who have joined them in nothing else, – by the Edinburgh Reviewers, by the whole heterogeneous Mass of living English Poets – excepting Crabbe, Rogers, Gifford and Campbell [. . .] and by me, – who have shamefully deviated in practice – but have ever loved and honoured Pope's Poetry with my whole soul, and hope to do so till my dying day.[28]

Byron's imputation to the Lake Poets of the charges of insanity, drug and alcohol addiction, and psychopathy – the standard Neoclassical charges against the Romantics – had already appeared in the first Canto of his satire *Don Juan* (1819), conveyed with intertextual reference to the Ten Commandments:

> Thou shalt believe in Milton, Dryden, Pope;
> Thou shalt not set up Wordsworth, Coleridge, Southey;
> Because the first is crazed beyond all hope,
> The second drunk, the third so quaint and mouthy. (*Don Juan* I, ll. 1633–6)[29]

The vocabulary of sin (adoring false gods and committing adultery with false muses) again indicates a temporary conversion from heretical Romanticism (or rather Romanticisms) to the one saving Classical tradition, though undercut by parodic humour.

Byron's siding with Pope against Bowles and Keats in the Pope–Bowles controversy coincided with his writing of the first Cantos of *Don Juan*, 'a *satire* on *abuses* of the present *states* of Society',[30] which was preceded by an epigraph from Horace's *Epistula ad Pisones*: 'Difficile est proprie communia dicere' ('It is hard to treat in your own way what is common').[31] It also coincided with his plans to publish *Hints from Horace*, a hitherto unpublished sequel to *English Bards and Scotch Reviewers*, his *Dunciad*. He had written it in Athens in 1811, and now, after nine years, it was time to release it to the reading public, according to Horace's rule of 'nonum prematur in annum'[32]. He thus endorsed Neoclassical reproaches of the Romantic speed of release and the immaturity of mass production. 'I wrote better then than now,' he told John Murray, 'but that comes from my having fallen into the atrocious bad state of the times – partly.'[33] Byron admitted to wavering between two schools of writing, never constant to one thing. In *Hints from Horace*, he had argued, against Romantic reproaches of obsolescence, that the Classical tradition was not a dead, mummified body kept for display but a living, dynamic tradition, adapting itself to every age.[34] He was obviously 'prepared to make the necessary cultural and historical adjustments'.[35] And now, in *Don Juan*, he realigned himself with this tradition in a startlingly original and updated way, setting out with a variation on the beginning of Virgil's *Aeneid*, replacing 'arma virumque cano' with a modern 'arma virumque careo' and pointing out the fast-moving nature of nineteenth-century life and the vanity of glory:

> I WANT a hero: an uncommon want,
> When every year and month sends forth a new one. (*Don Juan* I,
> ll. 1–2)

The classical rules, such as to 'plunge in *medias res*' and 'rend'ring general that which is especial', are called up and examined for their validity in modern times, in the liberal English (as opposed to the strict French) tradition of John Dryden.[36] References to Classical literature and poetics in *Don Juan* are legion, though Virgil and Horace are inconsistently blended with the licentiousness and digressions of Sterne's *Tristram Shandy* (1759–67), though Byron broke the Neoclassical rules in a comic demonstration of his view of the indomitability of human passions and in the sense of his Pyrrhonism. A recent study has competently demonstrated the connection between Byron's sceptical view of systems, including the Horatian one, and the freely rambling style and reflexive images of his poetry and prose, and of *Don Juan* in particular.[37] With an allusion to Virgil's *Aeneid*, Byron defends his Pyrrhonic reluctance to commit himself to one 'truth' only, '[i]mpartial between Tyrian and Trojan' (*Don Juan* XV, l. 731).[38]

His insistence on 'life's infinite variety' (*Don Juan* XV, l. 146)[39] was irreconcilable with old-type literary orthodoxy. In fact, *Don Juan* is Horatian, but in a modern sceptical way that eschews unwavering positions, aware that there are no clear-cut and impervious margins defining the territories of opposed groups. The reviews of *Don Juan* understood that Byron had relinquished the sentimental Romantic in favour of the Neoclassical and Enlightenment tradition, and Neoclassically minded reviewers expressed their approval of Byron's anti-Romantic mode, secretly relishing his heresies and obscenities as witty offences against the Classical rule of decorum. John Gibson Lockhart's eulogy of *Don Juan* in his anonymously published *John Bull's Letter to Lord Byron* (1821), which Byron enjoyed immensely when John Murray sent it to him in Italy, is the most obvious case in point. Alluding to Byron's part in the Pope–Bowles controversy, Lockhart dismissed Byron's Bowles-inspired Romantic poems such as *Childe Harold's Pilgrimage* as humbug, works fortunately given up in favour of Pope-inspired comedy and satire:

> they are the triumphs of humbug; but you are not a Bowles: you ought to be (as you might well afford to be) ashamed of them. [. . .] You say you admire Pope, and I believe you: [. . .] Stick to Don Juan: it is the only sincere thing you have ever written; and it will live many years after all your humbug Harolds have ceased to be, in your own words, 'A school-*girl's* tale – the wonder of an hour'.[40]

Lockhart's pamphlet reads like a digest of all the strictures that Neoclassical critics of Romanticism advanced against the Romantics. Romantic poets are denigrated as primitive and childish, snivelling idiots or sentimental impostors interested only in short-term sales figures, serving short-lived fashions and producing their ephemeral works in a state of madness or alcohol- or drug-induced intoxication. Lockhart imagined Byron laughing up his sleeve at his commercial success in making a credulous public (especially women) mistake his melancholic, histrionic, Hamlet-like mask for the true suffering man. Byron's 'humbug' (Byron himself would call it 'cant') was at present 'a very saleable article':

> The whole of your misanthropy, for example, is humbug. You do not hate men, 'no, nor woman neither', but you thought it would be a fine interesting thing for a handsome young Lord to depict himself as a dark-souled, melancholy, morbid being [. . .]. In spite of all your pranks (Beppo, &c. Don Juan included,) every boarding-school

in the empire still contains many devout believers in the amazing misery of the black-haired, high-browed, blue-eyed, bare-throated, Lord Byron. How melancholy you look in the prints![41]

Under the cloak of anonymity Lockhart can afford not to be a humbug and can express his admiration at a work so full of filth and heresy. The identification of his name as a favourable reviewer in this periodical would have forced Lockhart to find fault publicly with what he enjoyed privately. The *Quarterly*'s editor and reviewers, who raved at Percy Shelley's heresies and Thomas Moore's obscenities, have a secret predilection for *Don Juan*.

> Old [William] Gifford's brow relaxed as he gloated over it; Mr. [John Wilson] Croker chuckled; Dr. [Thomas Dunham] Whitaker smirked; Mr. [Henry Hart] Milman sighed; Mr. [John Taylor] Coleridge (I mean not the madman, but the madman's idiot nephew) took it to bed with him.[42]

> They could not speak of it without praising it, and that would have been doing something against themselves – it would have amounted to little less than coming in as accessories to the crime of *lèse majesté* against the liege Lord of the Quarterly Reviewers, and of all other reviewers who print their Reviews – Humbug.[43]

It was not until 1822 that the *Quarterly Review* ended its silence over Byron's *Don Juan*, publishing a harsh critique of the work's religious and moral outlook in a review of Byron's dramas written by Reginald Heber.[44]

In his satire on literary humbug, Lockhart did not spare the editor William Blackwood nor the Tory *Blackwood's Edinburgh Magazine*, on whose board he had sat from the setting up of the periodical in 1817. In 1825 Lockhart took over editorship of the *Quarterly Review*, following William Gifford and John Taylor Coleridge, and again acted the humbug he indicted in *John Bull's Letter to Lord Byron*. Lockhart could quickly change literary allegiances, like both Byron himself and Lockhart's father-in-law, Walter Scott, who wavered between *Marmion* and his edition of John Dryden, Whiggism and Toryism, and who had repeatedly praised Byron's *Childe Harold's Pilgrimage* for its courageous honesty and originality in the *Quarterly Review* in 1816–18. The first publication of Lockhart's *Ancient Spanish Ballads, Historical and Romantic*, for instance, was in 1823. Some of his reviews are also Romantic-friendly, such as his praise for Samuel Coleridge's mysteriousness and qualities of poetic diction in *Blackwood's Edinburgh Magazine* (1819)[45] and his defence of William Wordsworth in *Peter's Letters to his Kinsfolk* (1819).[46] And even in *John Bull's Letter* he implicitly admits his Romantic sympathies by parading his Prometheanism as 'a real son of the Japeti genus', challenging the literary establishment of which he himself was a member.[47]

Thomas Campbell and Samuel Rogers, whom Byron eulogised along with Dryden, Pope and Gifford in *Don Juan* against Wordsworth, Coleridge and Southey, are other examples of poets changing literary loyalties, sometimes in one and the same poem. Campbell's *The Pleasures of Hope* (1799) is a Popean didactic poem in heroic couplets, which nevertheless sympathised with the ideals of the French Revolution and with the Poles against the division of Poland. His *Gertrude of Wyoming* (1809), by contrast, written in the style of the 'new schools', is a Romantic poem lamenting the massacre of hundreds of American Revolutionaries by British Loyalists in the Wyoming Valley in 1778. When Byron praised Campbell at the expense of the Lake School poets, he thought of *The Pleasures of Hope* and not of the sentimental primitivism of *Gertrude of Wyoming*, which pervades the Romantic narrative from its beginning:

> ON Susquehanna's side, fair Wyoming!
> Although the wild-flower of thy ruined wall
> And roofless homes a sad remembrance bring
> Of what thy gentle people did befall,
> Yet thou wert once the loveliest of all
> That see the Atlantic wave their morn restore.[48]

Rogers's Popean *The Pleasures of Memory* (1792), on which Campbell's *The Pleasures of Hope* was modelled, carried eighteenth-century Augustan diction (as attacked by Wordsworth) to the extreme. Byron admired it for this, at least in his Neoclassical mood. In his 'Letter to—[John Murray] on the Rev. W. L. Bowles' (1821), quoted above, Byron polemically eulogised Rogers's alleged Horatian excellence over a crowd of modern poetasters, calling him 'the last Argonaut of Classic English poetry – and the Nestor of our inferior race of living poets'.[49] Nevertheless, the banker Rogers was a Holland House Whig like Campbell, and a close friend of Wordsworth, Coleridge and Henry Fuseli. When Byron praised *The Pleasures of Memory* for its adherence to the rules, he repressed the fact that Rogers's Romantic narrative poem *Jacqueline*, written in the diction and metre of the 'new schools', was published in the same volume as his own *Lara* (1814):

> [. . .] from the Convent's neighbouring tower
> The clock had tolled the midnight hour,
> When Jacqueline came forth alone,
> Her kerchief o'er her tresses thrown;
> A guilty thing and full of fears,
> Yet ah, how lovely in her tears![50]

When Byron saw some of Robert Burns's unpublished letters, Byron's view of Burns betrayed not only his awareness of his own antithetically mixed nature but also the paradox of his own poetics. The Neoclassicist Byron objected to Burns's prostitution to the vulgar taste of the populace and pretended ignorance of the Classical tradition, yet the Romantic Byron welcomed his sensibility and literary, as well as moral, rebellion:

> They are full of oaths and obscene songs. What an antithetical mind! – tenderness, roughness – delicacy, coarseness – sentiment, sensuality – soaring and grovelling, dirt and deity – all mixed up in that one compound of inspired clay![51]

Burns was not only the Romantic radical and primitive ploughman poet that he acted out. He knew very well that to live on his literary art, as was his plan following the failure of his farm in Ayrshire, he needed Augustan culture, a knowledge of the Classical tradition and access to the fine literary circles of Edinburgh. An avid reader, he taught himself both Classical and English literature and a smattering of Classical languages – a little Latin and less Greek, enough to be of serviceable use in the fine society of authors who cultivated primitivism yet would not deny their progressivist education and their learning. Burns was a notorious code-switcher, on the margin between roughness and politeness, a border-crosser without being marginal in a negative sense.[52] After the successful publication of the Kilmarnock volume of his *Poems Chiefly in the Scottish Dialect* (1786), the 27-year-old anti-aristocrat Burns went to Edinburgh, where he persuaded an aristocrat, the Earl of Glencairn, to introduce him to Henry Mackenzie, Hugh Blair, Lord Monboddo, Adam Ferguson and other figures of the literary establishment. A historicist painting by William Borthwick Johnstone, *Sibbald's Circulating Library 1786* (1856), shows him clothed extremely elegantly rather than boorishly and placed in the centre of a group of these famous Scotsmen. When he declared that the only Latin he knew was 'Amor vincit omnia', this was the same kind of self-fashioning as demonstrated by Fra Lippo Lippi in Robert Browning's famous dramatic monologue, 'All the Latin I know is Amo, I love.'[53] Not all the 1786 poems 'chiefly' in the Scottish dialect were, in fact, in Scots. Burns, who had studied Dryden and Pope, could also write in polished Augustan English. The first volume of the new *Oxford Edition of the Works of Robert Burns* (2014), edited by Nigel Leask and containing Burns's commonplace books, tour journals and miscellaneous prose, proves that he also wrote a most accomplished and studied Augustan prose.

The case of James Hogg, the self-styled Ettrick Shepherd who saw his life's work as becoming Burns's poetic successor, makes that double identity of Romantic primitivist and Augustan Neoclassicist even clearer. Hogg persuaded himself to buy into the false belief that he was born on the same day as his idol Burns, 25 January, wore a shepherd's plaid, spoke broad Scots, and loved being the fêted guest of honour on Burns Nights.[54] However, he was also a cultivated Augustan Neoclassicist with a supreme command of literary and spoken English, as well as being a member of the editorial board of the Tory *Blackwood's Edinburgh Magazine*, which satirised the 'Cockney School' poets for their alleged boorishness and ignorance of the Classical tradition. As a boy, he read translations of Greek and Latin classics in the circulating library in Peebles,[55] and his precocious *Scottish Pastorals* (1801) contained imitations of Thomas Gray and Edward Young,[56] foreshadowing Byron's precocious *Hours of Idleness* (1807). The magazine's *Noctes Ambrosianae*, named on the Classical model of Aulus Gellius' *Noctes Atticae*, poked fun at this cultivated Tory's paradoxical self-fashioning as the ignorant Scottish country lout that he himself simultaneously ridiculed, featuring him as the Ettrick Shepherd. Hogg's parody of Wordsworth's simple diction and of the Cockney poet William Hazlitt's breaking of the rule of decorum is a brilliantly marginal satire on primitivist Romantic writing composed in rude, self-parodic Augustan couplets meant to betray their histrionic code switching:

> Delicious creature, with sweet gladsome *hair*,
> And belly polished round like *welwet* fair!
> Thy balmy *hudder* (pressed by maiden fingers
> Not half so soft) where creamy beauty lingers.[57]

Like Byron, Hogg owed his popularity to effective literary self-staging, and especially to his role as the Ettrick Shepherd in *Noctes*

*Ambrosianae*. This series of satirical dialogues epitomises the Scottish update of the Classical tradition of the aristocratic Greek symposium in *Blackwood's Edinburgh Magazine*, focusing on hard drinking, gluttony, rough satire and noisy conviviality. There, Hogg is characterised in parallel with Byron, both actors of popular Romantic roles in the view of Lockhart, who co-authored the satires with John Wilson and William Maginn. In fact, Hogg was actually more rather than less self-educated and sophisticated than Burns, the self-styled Ploughman Poet.[58] Though conscious of being a working-class poet like Burns, he was a diehard Tory, opposed to working-class politics and reform bills – quite unlike the radical Burns – and aspired to full social acceptance in polite, university-educated literary circles in Edinburgh as well as London.[59] His publisher's assertion that, after the age of seven, he had 'never received any education whatever' only served to increase a Romantic public's interest in the allegedly heaven-taught author of 'The Queen's Wake' (1813).[60] In his works, Hogg's knowledge of Classical literature and mythology is astonishing. Though occasionally annoyed at being represented as the simple boor among erudite men of letters at Ambrose's Tavern, Hogg tolerated and even encouraged Lockhart's and Wilson's portrayals of him, just as Byron relished Lockhart's construction of him as the effective impostor and humbug.

In his lyric on the role play of a Romantic actor and artist, forced by reason and sanity to divest himself of his sensitive medieval knight costume and face reality, Heinrich Heine commented on Byron's and his own role switching as typical of the Romantic period, denying a difference between mask and identity:

> Nun ist es Zeit, daß ich mit Verstand
> Mich aller Torheit entledge;
> Ich hab so lang als ein Komödiant
> Mit dir gespielt die Komödie.
>
> Die prächtgen Kulissen, sie waren bemalt
> Im hochromantischen Stile,
> Mein Rittermantel hat goldig gestrahlt,
> Ich fühlte die feinsten Gefühle.
>
> Und nun ich mich gar säuberlich
> Des tollen Tands entledge,
> Noch immer elend fühl ich mich,
> Als spielt ich noch immer Komödie.

Ach Gott! im Scherz und unbewusst
Sprach ich was ich gefühlet;
Ich hab mit dem Tod in der eignen Brust
Den sterbenden Fechter gespielet.[61]

The broad margins of Romanticism nowhere show themselves more permeable than in these instances of Romantic irony (in the sense of Friedrich Schlegel),[62] assuming a most deeply felt Romantic pose and simultaneously or subsequently disavowing it with Horace, Virgil, Boileau, Molière, Dryden, Pope and Alfieri. One of Byron's ideals was *mobilité*, connected to his variable poetic skill (*metis*) in interplay with his physical vitality (*bie*) and the Homeric resourceful Ulysses (*polumetis Odysseus*), who travelled far and wide.[63] This may serve as an alternative explanation for Byron's histrionic love of and posing in various dresses, especially military uniforms, often interpreted psychoanalytically as a search for his father, the handsome Captain John Byron, a similarly chameleon-like poseur and brash officer, whom he had never come to know. Byron was a role player who acted all his biographical and literary roles seriously.

## Notes

1. Townsend, *Lord Byron as Literary Chameleon: A Study in Literary Influence*.
2. 'Letter to Elizabeth Bridget Pigot, 5 July 1807', *BLJ*, vol. 1, p. 125.
3. Byron, *The Life, Letters and Journals of Lord Byron*, ed. Thomas Moore, p. 13.
4. Cf. MacCarthy, *Byron: Life and Legend*.
5. Nickerson, 'Byron, Shelley and Miss Havisham', pp. 14–15.
6. West, *Byron and the Spoiler's Art*.
7. Disraeli, *Venetia*, in: *The Bradenham Edition of the Novels and Tales of Benjamin Disraeli*, vol. 7, pp. 23–33.
8. McGann, *The Romantic Ideology*.
9. This was the favourite binary terminology in English critical writings of the Romantic period, especially in the Tory *Anti-Jacobin* (1797–8) and the *Anti-Jacobin Review and Magazine* (1798–1821).
10. See Byron's rejected dedication of *Marino Faliero* (1821) to Goethe, *CPW*, vol. 6, pp. 546–7.
11. Lansdown, 'The Romantic Movement', in: *The Cambridge Introduction to Byron*, p. 37.
12. 'Letter to John Murray, 7 February 1821', in: *CMP*, p. 149.

13. Crompton, *Byron and Greek Love: Homophobia in 19th-century England*, p. 107.
14. Stabler, *Byron, Poetics and History*, pp. 73–105.
15. Priestman, *The Poetry of Erasmus Darwin*, pp. 240–1.
16. *English Bards and Scotch Reviewers*, ll. 687–8, CPW, vol. 1, p. 250.
17. Townsend, *Lord Byron as Literary Chameleon*, pp. 53–70.
18. Englemann, 'Alfieri and Byron', pp. 35–6.
19. A chronological list of publications implicated in the controversy is provided by van Rennes, *Bowles, Byron and the Pope Controversy*, pp. 166–8, and in *CMP*, pp. 408–10.
20. Possible reasons for Byron's return to Pope's poetics (though not Pope's world view) in the early 1820s are discussed by Stabler in *Byron, Poetics and History*, pp. 172–97.
21. The first edition of the long *Letter* was published in London in 1821, the second and third edition in Paris in 1821.
22. 'Letter to John Murray, 15 September 1817', *BLJ*, vol. 5, p. 265. See also Sachs, *Romantic Antiquity: Rome in the British Imagination, 1789–1832*, pp. 116–31.
23. Keach, 'Byron Reads Keats', p. 204.
24. 'Some Observations upon an Article in Blackwood's Edinburgh Magazine, 15 March 1820', in: *CMP*, p. 116.
25. Ibid., p. 107.
26. Ibid., p. 116, and *Childe Harold's Pilgrimage* III, l. 381, CPW, vol. 2, p. 92.
27. 'Letter to John Murray, 7 February 1821', in: *CMP*, p. 148.
28. 'Some Observations upon an Article in Blackwood's Edinburgh Magazine, 15 March 1820', in: *CMP*, p. 106.
29. Also see van Rennes, *Bowles, Byron and the Pope Controversy*, pp. 53–6.
30. 'Letter to John Murray, 25 December 1822', *BLJ*, vol. 10, p. 68.
31. Horace, 'Epistula ad Pisones', l. 128, p. 460.
32. Ibid., l. 388, p. 482.
33. 'Letter to John Murray, 23 September 1820', *BLJ*, vol. 7, p. 179. See Marchand, *Byron: A Portrait*, p. 332.
34. Lessenich, *Neoclassical Satire and the Romantic School 1780–1830*, pp. 167–8.
35. Webb, 'The Unexpected Latinist: Byron and the Roman Muse', p. 406.
36. *Don Juan* I, l. 41 and XV, l. 200, in: CPW, vol. 5, pp. 10, 596.
37. Howe, *Byron and the Forms of Thought*, pp. 158–71.
38. Virgil, 'Aeneid', in: *Eclogues, Georgics, Aeneid*, I. 574, vol. 1, p. 280.
39. Byron here quotes Shakespeare, *Antony and Cleopatra*, II, ii, 241 (Cleopatra's 'infinite variety').
40. [Lockhart], *John Bull's Letter to Lord Byron*, pp. 81–2.
41. Ibid., p. 80.
42. Ibid., pp. 82–3.
43. Ibid., p. 84.

44. *Quarterly Review*, 27 July 1822, pp. 476–524.
45. *Blackwood's Edinburgh Magazine*, 6 (October 1819), pp. 3–12.
46. Lockhart, *Peter's Letters to his Kinsfolk*, vol. 1, pp. 122–3.
47. [Lockhart], *John Bull's Letter to Lord Byron*, p. 4.
48. Campbell, *Gertrude of Wyoming*, ll. 1–6, in: *Complete Poetical Works*, p. 45.
49. 'Letter to — [John Murray] on the Rev. W. L. Bowles', *CMP*, p. 121.
50. [Byron], *Lara: A Tale*, and [Rogers], *Jacqueline, A Tale*, ll. 5–10, p. 81.
51. 13 December 1813, *BLJ*, vol. 2, p. 376. See also Marchand, *Byron: A Portrait*, p. 157.
52. For Burns's code switching between Standard English, Scots and French as multiple identity construction see Broadhead, *The Language of Robert Burns*, p. 91.
53. For Burns's acquaintance with the Classical authors, without sufficient knowledge of Greek and Latin, see Currie, *Life of Burns*, prefixed to vol. 1 of *The Works of Robert Burns: Style, Ideology, and Identity*, pp. 259–60.
54. Hughes, *James Hogg: A Life*, pp. 245–7.
55. Ibid., p. 25.
56. Ibid., p. 40.
57. Hogg, *A New Poetic Mirror*, 'Hamatory Verses to a Cow', ll. 1–4, in: Groves (ed.), *Poetic Mirrors*, p. 114.
58. Lessenich (2012), '"Noctes Ambrosianae" (1822–35): A Comic Symposium of the Romantic Period', p. 198.
59. Alker and Nelson, 'Hogg and Working-Class Writing', pp. 55–63.
60. *Oxford Dictionary of National Biography*, online version.
61. Heine, 'Buch der Lieder, Die Heimreise, XLIV, 1823–24', in: *Sämtliche Schriften*, vol. 1, p. 130. See the editor's comment on Romantic role playing in Heine's poetry. The poem was congenially translated by Untermeyer in *Poems of Heinrich Heine*, p. 117:

Now is it time that I should start
And leave all folly behind me.
As comic actor I've played my part
In a comedy that was assigned me.

The settings were painted brilliant and bold
In the latest romantic fashions;
My knightly mantle was splendid with gold;
I thrilled with the noblest passions.

And now at last I must say good-bye
To speeches once distracting . . .
But I am wretched and I sigh
As though I still were acting.

Oh God! unknown I spoke in jest
The things I felt most deeply;
I've acted, with death in my very breast,
The dying hero, cheaply.

62. Handwerk, 'Romantic Irony', p. 203.
63. Camilleri, 'Byron's Cunning Poetics', pp. 221–41.

## Works cited

Alker, Sharon and Holly Faith Nelson (2012), 'Hogg and Working-Class Writing', in: Ian Duncan and Douglas S. Mack (eds), *The Edinburgh Companion to James Hogg*, Edinburgh: Edinburgh University Press, pp. 55–63.

Broadhead, Alex (2014), *The Language of Robert Burns: Style, Ideology, and Identity*, Lewisberg: Bucknell University Press.

Byron, Lord George Gordon ([1830] 1932), *The Life, Letters and Journals of Lord Byron*, ed. Thomas Moore, London: John Murray.

[Byron], *Lara: A Tale*, and [Rogers] (1814), *Jacqueline, A Tale*, London: John Murray.

Camilleri, Anna (2016), 'Byron's Cunning Poetics', *Essays in Criticism*, vol. 6, pp. 221–41.

Campbell, Thomas (1907), *Complete Poetical Works*, ed. J. Logie Robertson, London: Oxford University Press.

Crompton, Louis (1985), *Byron and Greek Love: Homophobia in 19th-century England*, London: Faber & Faber.

Currie, James (1820), *Life of Burns*, in: *The Works of Robert Burns*, vol. 1, London: T. Cadell / W. Davies.

Disraeli, Benjamin ([1837] 1926–7), *The Bradenham Edition of the Novels and Tales of Benjamin Disraeli*, vol. 7, ed. Philip Guedalla, London: Peter Davies.

Englemann, Diana (1999), 'Alfieri and Byron', in: *Carte Italiane: A Journal of Italian Studies*, 16, pp. 31–53.

Groves, David (ed.) (1990), *Poetic Mirrors, Comprising the 'Poetic Mirror' (1816) and 'New Poetic Mirror' (1829–1831)*, Frankfurt am Main: Peter Lang.

Handwerk, Gary (2000), 'Romantic Irony', in: Marshall Brown (ed.), *The Cambridge History of Literary Criticism*, vol. 5, 'Romanticism', Cambridge: Cambridge University Press, pp. 203–25.

Heine, Heinrich (1975), *Sämtliche Schriften*, ed. Klaus Briegleb, Munich: Hanser.

Horace (1966), 'Epistula ad Pisones', in: *Satires, Epistles and Ars Poetica*, trans. H. Rushton Fairclough, Loeb Classical Library, Cambridge, MA: Harvard University Press.

Howe, Anthony (2013), *Byron and the Forms of Thought*, Liverpool: Liverpool University Press.

Hughes, Gillian (2007), *James Hogg: A Life*, Edinburgh: Edinburgh University Press.

Keach, William C. (2001), 'Byron Reads Keats', in: Susan J. Wolfson (ed.), *The Cambridge Companion to Keats*, Cambridge: Cambridge University Press, pp. 203–13.

Lansdown, Richard (2012), *The Cambridge Introduction to Byron*, Cambridge: Cambridge University Press.

Lessenich, Rolf (2010), '"Noctes Ambrosianae" (1822–35): A Comic Symposium of the Romantic Period', in: Marion Gymnich and Norbert Lennartz (eds), *The Pleasures and Horrors of Eating: The Cultural History of Eating in Literature and the Arts*, Göttingen: Bonn University Press, pp. 187–203.

— (2012), *Neoclassical Satire and the Romantic School 1780–1830*, Göttingen: Bonn University Press.

Lockhart, John Gibson (1819), *Peter's Letters to his Kinsfolk*, vol. 1, Edinburgh, London and Glasgow.

[—] (1947), *John Bull's Letter to Lord Byron*, ed. Alan Lang Strout, Norman: University of Oklahoma Press.

MacCarthy, Fiona (2002), *Byron: Life and Legend*, London: John Murray.

McGann, Jerome J. (1983), *The Romantic Ideology*, Chicago: University of Chicago Press.

Marchand, Leslie A. (1971), *Byron: A Portrait*, London: John Murray.

Nickerson, Charles C. (2008), 'Byron, Shelley and Miss Havisham', *Times Literary Supplement*, 5478, pp. 14–15.

*Oxford Dictionary of National Biography*, online version, available at <http://oxforddnb.com/> (last accessed 18 January 2016).

Priestman, Martin (2013), *The Poetry of Erasmus Darwin*, Farnham: Ashgate.

Rennes, Jacob Johan van (1927), *Bowles, Byron and the Pope Controversy*, Amsterdam: H. J. Paris.

Sachs, Jonathan (2010), *Romantic Antiquity: Rome in the British Imagination, 1789–1832*, Oxford: Oxford University Press.

Stabler, Jane (2002), *Byron, Poetics and History*, Cambridge: Cambridge University Press.

Townsend, Richard Lee (1971), *Lord Byron as Literary Chameleon: A Study in Literary Influence*, Ann Arbor: University of Michigan Press.

Untermeyer, Louis (1923), *Poems of Heinrich Heine*, London: Routledge.

Virgil (1967), *Eclogues, Georgics, Aeneid I–VI*, trans. H. Rushton Fairclough, Loeb Classical Library: Cambridge, MA: Harvard University Press.

Webb, Timothy (2015), 'The Unexpected Latinist: Byron and the Roman Muse', in: Norman Vance and Jennifer Wallace (eds), *The Oxford History of Classical Reception in English Literature*, vol. 4 (1790–1880), Oxford / New York: Oxford University Press, pp. 385–411.

West, Paul (1960), *Byron and the Spoiler's Art*, London: Chatto & Windus.

# II. Byron's Marginal Identities and Places

# Chapter 5

# 'When a man talks of system, his case is hopeless': Byron at the Margins of Romantic Counterculture

*Friederike Wolfrum*

## The structure of Romanticism

When we talk about Byron and the margins of Romanticism, this is a question of positioning Byron and, thus, first of all of defining the construct of Romanticism(s) to which we are referring. In this chapter, I will selectively focus on a conceptualisation of Romanticism as a countercultural movement in order to examine Byron's marginal status as a countercultural agent via his involvement with Leigh Hunt and *The Liberal*.

This volume's title hints at a critical re-examination of the Wellekian view of Byron as, in Jerome McGann's words, 'the debased margin of a complex cultural center',[1] a position that, for a long time, rendered Byron's position within studies of Romanticism problematic. The necessary theoretical groundwork for a reinterpretation is found in some recent proposals, such as Michael Ferber's or Christoph Bode's, to define (European) Romanticism through a set of Wittgensteinian family resemblances:[2] by relying on a network of entities that are interrelated through a number of partially shared characteristics rather than, as Classical theory has it, a limited number of necessary and sufficient conditions for a poet or work being styled as Romantic, these approaches allow for a framework that is sufficiently complex and open-ended not only to affirm Byron's position within Romanticism but also to map it out in detail. Where the Wittgensteinian model, however, is undecided concerning the internal structure within a category – each member is defined exclusively by its interrelations with other members rather than being mapped on to a general structure characteristic of the overall category – this is clearly not how most scholars perceive the structure of 'Romanticism': while the idea of strict hierarchies and canons is debatable, we do want to be able to say that, for instance, William Wordsworth may be more representative of Romanticism than John Hamilton Reynolds, or, to take two examples from Ferber's list of distinctive traits of Romanticism, that 'imagination for the view of poetry' may be more central than the characteristic 'volcano as a theme'.[3]

This possibility is provided by prototype theory, an important development building on Wittgenstein, which was pioneered by the experimental psychologist Eleanor Rosch and significantly extended as a general theory of categorisation by the cognitive linguist George Lakoff.[4] Lakoff posits that through experience humans acquire individual but culturally conditioned *idealised cognitive models* (ICMs); the ICM for 'bachelor' within Western civilisation, for instance, is built around the ideal case of a young, unmarried and male person. Single instances are measured against this ideal case, resulting in prototype effects: an old bachelor is less representative within the category than a young one, while 'the Pope' will result in a mismatch with the underlying model. Several ICMs can furthermore combine to make up more complex *cluster models*: thus, for the concept 'mother', different degrees of membership in underlying ICMs – 'woman who gives birth'; 'genetic mother'; 'female who nurtures a baby'; 'wife of father'; 'closest female ancestor' – determine overall graded membership.[5]

The benefit of this model is that, according to Lakoff's research, ICMs and cluster models are usually structured radially, 'where there is a central case and conventionalised variations of it which cannot be predicted by general rules'.[6] Analysing Romanticism as a prototype category accordingly enables us to conceptualise it in terms of (overlapping combinations of) radially graded memberships and characteristics, where more or less representative cases are measured against an abstract prototypical ideal. At the same time, it allows for 'fuzzy' category boundaries (instead of ontologically stable ones) where cases of unclear membership can be equally rendered as inside or outside the category.

In this context, I would like to apply prototype theory to the study of Romanticism by deliberately selecting 'Romantic counterculture' – referring, in this context, to a belief in and active deployment of the cultural power of writings in negating the dominant culture – as one of a number of relevant ICMs that make up the cluster model 'Romanticism', and centre my argument around it, without any claim to exclusivity, predominance or absolute generalisability of this trait. This will allow me to analyse Byron's stance towards and involvement in countercultural agency as indicative of his positioning within the category as compared to his – arguably more prototypical – contemporaries.

## Countercultural Romanticism

Numerous studies across the disciplines have acknowledged the connection between Romanticism and counterculture since the study of the latter was initiated in response to the youth movements of the 1960s.[7] Where Lionel Trilling's *The Opposing Self* (1955) was subtitled 'The Romantic Image of the Self', Theodore Roszak's *The Making of a Counter Culture* (1968) was prefixed by a quotation from William Blake, and Frank Musgrove's *Ecstasy and Holiness* (1974) introduced two scales of countercultural values denominated 'the Ruskin–Southey scale' and 'the Godwin–Shelley scale', claiming:

> Nineteenth-century Romanticism was strikingly like the contemporary counter culture in its explicit attack on technology, work, pollution, boundaries, authority, the unauthentic, rationality and the family. It had the same interest in altered states of mind, in drugs, in sensuousness and sensuality.[8]

This continuity between European Romanticism and later countercultures was put into focus again as recently as in 2012 in Thomas Tripold's study *Die Kontinuität romantischer Ideen: Zu den Überzeugungen gegenkultureller Bewegungen*, which identifies a Romantic network of convictions – the idea of the authentic self and the idea of the metaphysical and holistic pathos, supplemented by sensibility, Romantic love and sociability, originality, opposition to instrumental reason, natural philosophy and the unconscious, and enchantment – that recur within both the 1960s counterculture and the New Age movement.[9]

While the idea of cultural power in the forms of writing and system-making may be claimed as a historically specific product of the Enlightenment, the strong focus on Romanticism within these studies overstates the case, probably as a result of their origins in the 1960s: Romantic writers conceptualised themselves as part of a long tradition going back all the way to Classical Antiquity (witness, for example, Hunt's identification with the Neoterics). J. Milton Yinger's seminal sociological study (1982, but based on research begun in the 1960s), accordingly, takes a more moderate stance by locating the first culmination, but not the beginning of countercultural writing in English literature in the Romantic period:[10]

> There is no obvious beginning [to countercultural literature in Western culture]. One might refer to Swift, Richardson, and Blake in English literature, but Blake was strongly influenced by Milton. [. . .] One can say that by the time the great hopes for social change aroused by the French Revolution had been frustrated, [. . .] the strength of criticism had mounted. [. . .] Among the Romantics, of whom Wordsworth was the central writer, the sense of dismay was profound.[11]

Still, European Romanticism does inhabit a privileged place within this tradition, one that Tripold interprets as the birth of modern-day conceptions of counterculture. Tripold employs concepts authored by Victor Turner in order to identify Romanticism as a spontaneous, socially unstructured grouping (*communitas*) in opposition to a structured and normative society that reacts to an unsettling period of social change (*liminality*), in this particular case to the phase that Reinhart Koselleck has termed *Sattelzeit*.[12] Christoph Bode works along similar lines in suggesting a reconceptualisation of polymorphism not as the problem but as the solution to defining Romanticism: Romantic writings answer the challenges of the rapid functional diversification of modern society. According to his proposal, 'the unity of European Romanticism would consist exactly in its irreducible heterogeneity and self-contradiction',[13] and the movement's variform output, Bode claims, may function like the trial-and-error logarithm of a present-day supercomputer. This potential for (seemingly non-consequential) trial and error, I would like to argue, may be claimed for literature in general as a virtual testing ground for new ideas, and is the primary mechanism behind the countercultural potential of many literary works. Recent studies in cognitive poetics that seek to define fiction's evolutionary function for individual and society have come to similar conclusions.[14] This may be exactly the difference between counterculture and political activism, if one looks at Timothy Leary's description of counterculture:

> [T]he focus of counterculture is the power of ideas, images, and artistic expression, not the acquisition of personal and political power. [. . .] the seizure and maintenance of political power requires adherence to structures too inflexible to accommodate the innovation and exploration that are basic to the countercultural raison d'être.[15]

Yet what distinguishes countercultural writings from the more general conceptualisation of fiction as trial and error is its pervasive use of negation, as evident in Yinger's definition:

> The term counterculture is appropriately used whenever the normative system of a group contains, as a primary element, a theme of conflict with the dominant values of society, where the tendencies, needs, and perceptions of the members of that group are directly involved in the development and maintenance of its values, and wherever its norms can be understood only by reference to the relationship of the group to the surrounding dominant society and its culture.[16]

Hans Ulrich Gumbrecht, in an analysis of literary carnivalesque countercultures that I will return to at the end of this chapter, similarly employs systems theory in order to define the relationship between a society and its carnivalesque elements as a relation of negations.[17] Trilling, again, goes so far as to claim the adversary mode as characteristic of most modern literature, but defines it as an act of subversion with the aim of detaching and alienating readers rather than advertising alternatives:

> Any historian of the literature of the modern age will take virtually for granted the adversary intention, the actually subversive intention, that characterizes modern writing – he will perceive its clear purpose of detaching the reader from the habits of thought and feeling that the larger culture imposes, of giving him a ground and a vantage point from which to judge and condemn, and perhaps revise, the culture that produced him.[18]

## The question of countercultural agency

Looking at Romanticism as a countercultural movement and attempting to position Byron against this background, we need to address the question of Byron's own stance towards countercultural agency. Two central characteristics of Romantic counterculture as discussed above, polymorphism and negation, are prominently mentioned in Richard Lansdown's interpretation of Byron's lines on Classicism and Romanticism in the rejected dedication of *Marino Faliero* (1821) to Goethe:

> [Byron] knew that some such movement [as Romanticism] existed. But, as his comment implies, the nature of Romanticism is difficult to establish because it is so diverse. That diversity itself suggests that

the movement is a negative reaction, taking many forms: a broad rejection of an existing state of affairs, rather than a development in harmonious accord with it.[19]

Byron explicitly discusses the existence of a countercultural grouping surrounding Leigh Hunt in an 1818 letter to John Murray, where he comments on a *Quarterly* review of Hunt's volume *Foliage*:

> Southey would have attacked me, too, there, if he durst, further than by hints about Hunt's friends in general; and [by] some outcry about his 'Epicurean system', carried on by men of the most opposite habits, tastes, and opinions in life and poetry (I believe), that ever had their names in the same volume – Moore, Byron, Shelley, Hazlitt, Haydon, Leigh Hunt, Lamb – what resemblance do ye find among all or any of these men? and how could any sort of system or plan be carried on, or attempted amongst them?[20]

Acknowledging the polymorphism that Bode sees as characteristic of Romanticism, Byron refutes the existence of a united group or the practicability of any such attempt. The rejection in the context of Hunt's *Foliage* is poignant; Jeffrey Cox has identified the 'Cockney School' not just as the most concerted effort within Byron's generation to unite the different strands of negative reaction, but also specifically as a countercultural movement with a strong belief in the power of cultural agency:[21]

> It is not so much that they engaged in a 'shift to spiritual and moral revolution' over social and political revolt as it is that they found that they could best contribute to the struggle to change their society through cultural acts: this is a shift or an escape only if one believes cultural acts stand wholly apart from politics, while the Hunt circle clearly believed not only that politics shape poetics but that poetry can alter ideology. [. . .] The Cockney School did exist, as both a community and as an educational project, the goal of which was nothing less than a radical reform of England brought on not by violence but by poetical and political instruction.[22]

*Foliage*, in particular, is designed to declare the allegiances and shared commitments of the Cockney School; the volume constitutes an elaborate attempt, by way of personal addresses within sonnets, public epistles and its programmatic preface, to recreate textually the group that Hunt had succeeded in gathering in the wake of his 1813–15 imprisonment.[23] Positing Hunt as the group's social, political and poetic leader, the volume promotes a certain way of life as well as mode of writing: 'Hunt's poems [. . .] seek to provoke us into new practice, to argue we should adopt what we might see as a counter-cultural lifestyle devoted to free nature, a liberated community and imaginative freedom.'[24] Addressing Byron in *Foliage* can thus be seen as an attempt to appropriate Byron's cultural authority; this makes Byron's attitudes towards Hunt's poetics and the ultimate breakdown of their cooperation crucial to addressing the question of Byron's marginality via a reconstruction of his affinities and discontents with countercultural late Romanticism.

The vehemence of Byron's charge – 'how could any sort of system or plan be carried on, or attempted' – may mirror his frustration with prior experiences of discord and inefficiency within the Hampden Club and the Whig Party.[25] That Byron, within the historical context of post-Napoleonic Europe, is an apparently unlikely countercultural agent has been thoroughly demonstrated by Malcolm Kelsall.[26] Aristocratic bias and a deep-seated affinity with the Whig tradition combine to alienate him equally from radically democratic loyalties and a strong belief in effective agency, as expressed in the appendix to *The Two Foscari* (1821):

> I look upon [revolutions] as inevitable, though no revolutionist: I wish to see the English constitution restored and not destroyed. Born an aristocrat, and naturally one by temper, with the greater part of my present property in the funds, what have I to gain by a revolution?[27]

Kelsall interprets Byron's political outlook (here, in the Venetian plays) as essentially futile:

> The choice is between class revolution or the continuation, *sine die*, of 'corruption' in the form of a reactionary oligarchy opposed by a party which has lost all guts for reform. Whig constitutionalism is a dead letter; joining the radicals will bring in [Henry] Hunt and Cobbett, worse than Robespierre or Marat. [. . .] There is nothing to be done.[28]

He goes on to regard this disbelief in effective agency as a major difference between Byron and Hunt:

> [*The Vision of Judgment*] [. . .] presents an order which is in constitutional stasis between opposed patrician forces. Just as in the Venetian plays there is no way in which this oligarchical system can evolve. This is one in a number of important distinctions between Byron and his fellow 'progressive' editors of *The Liberal* (Shelley and Hunt in particular), and may help to explain why the opposition journal so swiftly disintegrated.[29]

On top of this, Byron claims not to share his contemporaries' belief in the power of (countercultural) writing:

> Mr. Southey [. . .] calls upon the 'legislature to look to it', as the toleration of such writings led to the French Revolution [. . .]. This is not true, and Mr. Southey knows it to be not true. Every French writer of any freedom was persecuted; Voltaire and Rousseau were exiles, Marmontel and Diderot were sent to the Bastille, and a perpetual war was waged with the whole class by the existing despotism. In the next place, the French Revolution was *not* occasioned by any writings whatsoever, but must have occurred had no such writers ever existed. It is the fashion to attribute every thing to the French Revolution, and the French Revolution to every thing but its real cause. That cause is obvious – the government exacted too much, and the people could neither *give* nor *bear more*. Without this, the Encyclopedists might have written their fingers off without the occurrence of a single alteration. And the *English* revolution – (the first, I mean) – what was it occasioned by? The *puritans* were surely as pious and moral as Wesley or his biographer? Acts – acts on the part of government, and *not* writings against them, have caused the past convulsions, and are tending to the future. (*CPW*, vol. 6, p. 223)

The extent of Byron's statement should, however, be taken with a grain of salt: written as a reaction to Robert Southey's 'Satanic School' attacks and his demand for censorship, at a time when Byron was under the impression left by Percy Bysshe Shelley's *Adonais* (1821) and the idea that 'Southey [. . .] should be perhaps the killer of Keats' (*BLJ*, vol. 8, p. 163),[30] Byron had cause to be strategic when it came to discussions of his own radical tendencies and the freedom of the press. If one reads closely, Byron does not exert the absolute futility of all countercultural writings, but only what we can also find in Yinger's theory: that revolutionary social change does not arise *ex nihilo*: 'a counterculture [. . .] develops out of conflict with the dominant tradition'.[31]

Still, Byron's preference for action and philosophical materialism is well known – as, for instance, evidenced in his discussion with Hunt over the constitution of poets. Here, Byron insists that 'an addiction to poetry is very generally the result of "an uneasy mind in an uneasy body"',[32] thus agreeing with William Hazlitt's *Round Table* assertion that 'those who are dissatisfied with themselves will seek to go out of themselves into an ideal world', while '[p]ersons in strong health and spirits [. . .] seldom devote themselves in despair to religion or the Muses'.[33] Hunt, who holds the opposite position – that poets tend to develop an unhealthy physique and subsequent mental instability in consequence of their occupation – insists on misreading Byron: 'I conceive, in fact, notwithstanding what you said in your last, that you & I think alike on the subject.'[34]

## The problem with system

During the years of their acquaintance in London, Byron and Hunt seem to have been on good terms both professionally and personally. Byron criticised Hunt's poetics when proofreading *The Story of Rimini*, but simultaneously encouraged him in the composition: 'you have 2 excellent points in that poem – originality – & Italianism – I will back you as a bard against half the fellows on whom you throw away much good criticism & eulogy'.[35] It seems that Byron started distancing himself from Hunt only in the wake of the critical reception of *Rimini* in 1816 and, more decisively, with the publication of *Foliage* in 1818, a copy of which Hunt sent through Shelley. I take the title of this paper from a letter that Byron wrote to Thomas Moore after he had received the volume:

> When I saw Rimini in MS., I told [Hunt] that I deemd it good poetry at bottom, disfigured only by a strange style. His answer was, that his style was a system, or upon system, or some such cant; and, when a man talks of system, his case is hopeless: so I said no more to him, and very little to any one else. ('Letter to Thomas Moore, 1 June, 1818', *BLJ*, vol. 4, p. 237)

This well-known aversion to system is clearly central to Byron's change of heart. Byron refers to an 1815 letter to Hunt, where he curtly attempts to end a discussion about Hunt's programmatic invention of neologisms and colloquialisms in *Rimini*: 'I have not time nor paper to attack your system – which ought to be done – were it only because it is a system.'[36] Hunt's reaction demonstrates a fundamental difference in their philosophies:

> As to my 'system', [. . .] you must know that, Hibernically speaking, I will not allow my system to be a system; neither am I disposed, as you may think I am, to decry or undervalue a certain artificial dignity in poetry where it is suitable; – Shakespeare himself uses it, and most nobly. I only prefer the more natural way in general, & on subjects that most decidedly demand it.[37]

In conceptualising his own poetic diction as 'more natural', Hunt fails to see what is crucial to Byron's understanding: that any programmatic innovation upon an existing (systematic) tradition of language use constitutes a new (artificial) system.

Byron's critique of system, as best illustrated in the following description of his future wife's behaviour, is reminiscent of Francis Bacon's warning of deductive reasoning anticipating nature[38]: 'the least word – or alteration of tone – has some inference drawn from it – sometimes we are too much alike – & then again too unlike – this comes of *system* – & squaring her notions to the Devil knows what'.[39] This position is in line with the British tradition of empiricism and distrust of generalised systems of thought, and is politically meaningful as a critical response to the *philosophes* and a rationality that, many felt, led to and characterised the French Revolution.[40]

The notion of system as a new Enlightenment means of producing comprehensive knowledge is important to discursive (self-)definitions within Romanticism, as demonstrated by Clifford Siskin.[41] Siskin argues that system as an Enlightenment genre became progressively problematic as the number of new systems increased and master systems were introduced that tried but could only fail to reconcile existing ones. As a result, system proliferated into other genres, as exemplified in both David Hume and William Godwin's moves away from treatise to essay and novel, respectively.[42] In poetry, the most salient example of this was Wordsworth's professed aim to enclose a philosophical system within poetry; this is what Hunt was emulating. The shift from system-as-genre to system-within-genre not only was a move away from hermetically closed systems towards more open-ended (essayistic) ones, but also it shifted the focus from the general / objective to the personal / subjective, as expressed by William Blake's Los – 'I must Create a System, or be enslav'd by another Mans'[43] – and by Wordsworth's Wanderer:

> If tired with systems, each in its degree
> Substantial, and all crumbling in their turn,
> Let him build systems of his own, and smile
> At the fond work, demolished with a touch.[44]

Wordsworth's lines include an awareness of the ephemerality of systems that is further developed into the realisation that personal systems lose their claim to absolute truth, which we find expressed in Byron's *Don Juan* (1819–24):

> One system eats another up, and this
> Much as old Saturn ate his progeny;
> For when his pious consort gave him stones
> In lieu of sons, of these he made no bones.

> But System doth reverse the Titan's breakfast,
> And eats her parents, albeit the digestion
> Is difficult. Pray tell me, can you make fast,
> After due search, your faith to any question?
> Look back o'er ages, ere unto the stake fast
> You bind yourself, and call some mode the best one.
> Nothing more true than *not* to trust your senses;
> And yet what are your other evidences? (*Don Juan* XIV, ll. 5–16)

Where Blake and Wordsworth advocate personal systems, Byron recedes into a sceptical relativism that distances his notion of system even further from the original Enlightenment ideal.

The establishment of personal systems within poetry, again, was counteracted by the critics' own act of system-making in sorting contemporary poets into 'schools', which Byron tried to but could not completely escape. The disadvantage of being perceived as part of a system in the context of *The Liberal* was realised by Thomas Moore, who urged, 'Alone you may do any thing [. . .]. You are, single-handed, a match for the world [. . .] but, to be so, you must stand alone.'[45]

Byron's affinity with sceptical thought has been thoroughly analysed in studies by M. G. Cooke (1969), Terence Hoagwood (1993), Emily Bernhard Jackson (2010) and, most recently, Anthony Howe (2013).[46] As Howe points out, however, Byron is at least as interested in ethical as in epistemological implications and thus rejects the epistemic deadlock that he (mistakenly) associates with Pyrrhonic scepticism as ethically unsound:[47] 'As Byron was acutely aware, sceptical thought is always vulnerable to its own energies. [. . .] "System" thus cannot be dismissed without thought and must, in some cases, be embraced.'[48] That Byron did not completely exempt himself from being implicated in systematic activity can be gleaned from a letter to John Murray of 15 September 1817:

> With regard to poetry in general I am convinced the more I think of it – that [Moore] and *all* of us – Scott – Southey – Wordsworth – Moore – Campbell – I – are all in the wrong – one as much as another – that we are upon a wrong revolutionary poetical system – or systems – not worth a damn in itself. ('Letter to John Murray, September 15, 1817', *BLJ*, vol. 5, p. 265)

Where Byron carefully acknowledges the need for system, however, Hunt's poetics display a pragmatic concept of knowledge that vehemently embraces this need and looks almost like a caricature of Byron's:

> We should consider ourselves as what we really are, – creatures made to enjoy more than to know, to know infinitely nevertheless in

proportion as we enjoy kindly, and finally, to put our own shoulders to the wheel and get out of the mud upon the green sward again [. . .] my creed, I confess, is not only hopeful, but cheerful; and I would pick the best parts out of other creeds too, sure that I was right in what I believed or chose to fancy, in proportion as I did honour to the beauty of nature, and spread cheerfulness and a sense of justice among my fellow-creatures.[49]

Hunt's programme is similarly projected into his criticism of Shakespeare:

Shakespeare, may or may not have believed in destiny; I believe he did, just about as much as he believed in the contrary. But whatever he might have thought of it's [sic] use in a play or so [. . .] he knew well, that utility of some sort or other, was the only test of truth within the limits of the human understanding.[50]

The difference here is not necessarily one in (political) opinion, but one in different understandings of the role of poetry and counter-cultural agency. Byron draws a line between life and art, between (counter)culture and activism, where Hunt does not: if '[o]ne system eats another up', this is exactly what art should make us aware of, thus fulfilling the functions that Leary and Trilling ascribe to counter-culture and literature, mobility and detachment. This does not necessarily hold true for life, where, as Roderick Beaton has demonstrated, Byron could act quite strategically and pragmatically in the best interest of 'the Cause'.[51] This attitude strongly reflects Byron's view of the capacities and functions of language, which for him does not carry meaning but destabilises and distorts it. As Howe notes, to Byron language is not a tool of epistemological progress, aiding societal and cultural development towards an ultimate truth, but is itself to be treated as an object of sceptical analysis: 'it is precisely in breaking free from the assumptions of philosophy that poetic writing finds its epistemological value'.[52] Hunt's utilitarian attitude towards language in this sense aims at the domain that, in Byron's view, needs to be most vigilantly guarded against – ideological recruitment, irre-spective of the underlying motives or goals:

Byron's critique of 'system' is more complex and sympathetic than is sometimes thought. Where it often seems most aggressively direct is in the poet's attacks on some of his prominent literary contempo-raries. If 'system' lays claim to the unique grounds of poetic meaning,

he concluded, then we risk losing one of our most profound challenges to the narrowing of apprehension in which modernity is busily
involved.[53]

Mary Shelley, unlike Hunt himself, seems to have recognised this and
interpreted the clash between Byron and Hunt in terms of poetics
rather than class difference:

> [Hunt] sees this somewhat differently & talks about your being a
> Lord, he is quite in the wrong – it is Rimini-pimini – & follage & all
> that, which makes you dislike entering into the journal, although his
> talents of another kind have caused you to enter into it.[54]

With all this in mind, it is rather surprising that, by 1821, Byron
agreed to enter on, or even proposed, a common literary project
with Hunt and Shelley, and in addition one that had the potential
of recreating a coterie similar to the Hampstead / Marlow circle.
A number of external necessities seem to have conspired in prompting Byron to search for both a new political role and a new poetic
voice: changes in the political landscape after 1819, particularly
through William Cobbett and Henry Hunt's success in wresting the
radical cause from Sir Francis Burdett in the Westminster elections
of 1818 and 1820, had forced Byron into a 'recognition that [. . .]
his own political identity, as aristocratic champion of the people, as
gentlemanly radical, as the classically educated spokesman for an
inarticulate populace, ha[d] been erased'.[55] Along with this came a
discernible drop in sales, increasing irritation with Murray's inter-
ferences as his publisher, and, thus, the need for experimentation
and new alliances. At the same time, Byron seems to have been
impatient for some kind of agency, as noted by Kelsall: 'the boiler
sounds as if it is about to explode because the energy is not being
translated into progressive motion'.[56] *The Liberal* was an attempt
at that. Jane Stabler sees Byron's formal experiments in *The Age of
Bronze* and *The Island* (both 1823) in this vein: 'In his last poems
using heroic couplets [. . .] classical allusions and digressive couplets
are detached [. . .] from their aristocratic milieu and take on shifting
alliance with the radicalism of Leigh Hunt and Douglas Kinnaird.'[57]
Given the political situation, it is not surprising, then, that Byron's
involvement with Hunt and Shelley drew an unprecedented amount
of hostility from friends and foes alike before Hunt even reached
Italy, nor that *The Liberal* failed. In the event, Byron never quite

committed himself to the journal and his countercultural involvement soon gave way to activism in Greece; it is a matter of debate
what would have happened, had *The Liberal* had the chance to
develop unimpeded.

## Modes of negation

In an attempt to distinguish different literary modes of countercultural writing in Byron and Hunt, I will now, in a last step, turn to
Hans Ulrich Gumbrecht's analysis of countercultural modes. In his
investigation of the literature of the late Middle Ages as part of a
transition phase from a medieval to a Renaissance society, Gumbrecht
develops Mikhail Bakhtin's concept of the carnivalesque by employ-
ing Niklas Luhmann's systems theory to define what he terms 'literary
counter-worlds' as negative and heterogeneous reactions characterised by 'relations of negation'.[58] Gumbrecht differentiates between
three modes of countercultural writings:[59]

> asymmetrical negation: positions within movements of historical
>    renewal that highlight differences against the background of
>    shared identity with the official culture
> symmetrical negation: complete reversals of official culture in alter-
>    native, often carnivalesque worlds that exaggerate differences
>    and conceal common ground ('anti-cultures')
> strictly recursive negation: transgressions of taboos and accepted
>    boundaries of experience in a negation of all negations that can
>    lead to disorder and anarchy ('uncultures')

Of these three modes, according to Gumbrecht, only asymmetrical
negation is likely to play a formative role in the cultural evolution
of a society; implementing the visions offered by symmetrical negation would entail a complete reversal of a society's identity, while
strictly recursive negation would lead to disorientation.[60] Rather, the
exaggerated conflict scenarios depicted in symmetrical negation tend
to provoke laughter and relieve tension, thus, ultimately, promoting
acceptance and stability in a time of social change.[61]

    If we try to apply this model to Hunt's writings, it appears that
they favour constellations of asymmetrical negation. The conflict
within *The Story of Rimini*, for example, echoes that of the texts of
the late Middle Ages that are the focus of Gumbrecht's study: a feudal

society is confronted with the alternative ideals of courtly love and chivalry. Throughout, the text is clearly sympathetic with the lovers' ideals, but it does end on a conciliatory note that acknowledges common ground within a society united in grief. Byron, in comparison, tends towards variations of the strictly recursive mode: where both Southey's *A Vision of Judgement* (1821) and Shelley's *Adonais* display partisan sympathies, *The Vision of Judgment* (1822) contrasts two different systems – God's and Sathan's, Tory and Whig – without strictly endorsing or rejecting either one of them, and ends in conciliatory tolerance of both.[62] In *The Island*, again, official culture and counterculture are displayed with equal amounts of sympathy and censure, and the poem offers a solution with the third option of 'going native' (something that Maria Schoina claims Byron, unlike Hunt, could do).[63] This third option, however, is ephemeral and thus not a sustainable counterproposal: it is a personal solution that will in time need to be replaced. *Don Juan*, finally, is a constant exercise in strictly recursive negation, where the narrator subverts himself as creator of meaning, inciting his readers to perform their own never-ending acts of meaning construction:

> But if I had been at Timbuctoo, there
> No doubt I should be told that black is fair.
>
> It is. I will not swear that black is white;
> But I suspect in fact that white is black,
> And the whole matter rests upon eyesight.
> Ask a blind man, the best judge. You'll attack
> Perhaps this new position – but I'm right;
> Or if I'm wrong, I'll not be ta'en aback: –
> He hath no morn nor night, but all is dark
> Within; and what seest thou? A dubious spark. (*Don Juan* XII, ll. 559–68)

As there is no absolute truth and no objectively superior perspective, solutions can only be individual, biographically and historically contingent, and can never be generalised. This realisation lies behind Lamartine's line: 'Tous les systèmes sont faux; le génie seul est vrai.'[64]

Byron and Hunt thus react to the same problematic historical situation and are united by a common motivation, but their understanding of literature's role within counterculture differs too much, as does their idea of the general epistemological implications. Byron may be more conservative in his use of Pyrrhonism, but also more perceptive in his awareness and suspicion of ideology. If we selectively posit countercultural agency as the centre of our definition of Romanticism, we can see how Hunt operates primarily through asymmetrical negation, aiming at an improved alternative version of the current social and political reality, where Byron prefers modes of strictly recursive negation that question both the current state and any particular alternative offered. From this perspective, the representatives of Romanticism are strongly linked by their countercultural involvement, with Hunt at the centre of a concerted effort encompassing both politics and poetry. Against this backdrop, Byron's own ambiguous stance towards such system building and divergent mode of countercultural writing explains how, even as an active member, he remains marginal to this circle.

## Notes

1. McGann, *Byron and Romanticism*, p. 238.
2. See Ferber, 'Introduction', in: Ferber (ed.), *A Companion to European Romanticism*, pp. 6–7, and Bode, 'Romantik – Europäische Antwort auf die Herausforderung der Moderne? Versuch einer Rekonzeptualisierung', pp. 86–8.
3. Ferber's proposal presupposes a similar internal structure: 'A definition based on this idea would amount to a list of distinctive traits, with some ranking as to importance and generality, but no one trait, maybe not even two or three, would be decisive.' Ferber, 'Introduction', p. 6.
4. Cf. Lakoff, *Women, Fire, and Dangerous Things: What Categories Reveal about the Mind*.
5. Ibid., ch. 4 ('Idealized Cognitive Models'), pp. 68–76.
6. Ibid., p. 84.
7. I follow J. Milton Yinger, who first suggested the term 'contra-culture' (later changed to 'counterculture') to refer to the general sociological concept of a recurring phenomenon that, directly or indirectly, participates in (non-teleological) evolutionary social change, as opposed to any specific manifestation. Cf. Yinger, 'Contraculture and Subculture', p. 627: 'The term subculture, when used in the third way described here, raises to a position of prominence one particular kind of dynamic linkage between norms and personality: the creation of a series of inverse or counter values (opposed to those of the surrounding society) in face of serious frustration or conflict. To call attention to the special aspects of this kind of normative system, I suggest the term contra-culture.'
8. Musgrove, *Ecstasy and Holiness: Counter Culture and the Open Society*, p. 65.

9. Tripold, *Die Kontinuität romantischer Ideen: Zu den Überzeugungen gegenkultureller Bewegungen*. '[Ein] Überzeugungsnetz der Romantik', p. 57. Crucially, Tripold modifies Arthur O. Lovejoy's history of ideas approach by defining ideas as convictions embodied within social practices, pp. 45–9.

10. Cf. Trilling, *The Opposing Self: Nine Essays in Criticism*; Roszak, *The Making of a Counter Culture: Reflections on the Technocratic Society and its Youthful Opposition*; and Yinger, *Countercultures: The Promise and Peril of a World Turned Upside Down*.

11. Yinger, *Countercultures*, p. 135.

12. Tripold, *Die Kontinuität romantischer Ideen*, pp. 40–5.

13. My translation; 'die Einheit der europäischen Romantik bestünde gerade in ihrer irreduziblen Heterogenität und Selbstwidersprüchlichkeit'. Bode, 'Romantik', p. 90.

14. Cf., for example, Boyd, *On the Origin of Stories: Evolution, Cognition, and Fiction*; and Turner, *The Literary Mind: The Origins of Thought and Language*. Boyd describes art as 'cognitive play' and sees, besides social functions, the 'ability to imagine the world as other than it is' (p. 197) as a central function of fictional narrative, arguing that because 'fiction extends to our imaginative reach, we are not confined to our here and now or dominated by automatic responses', p. 198.

15. Leary, 'Foreword', in: *Counterculture through the Ages: From Abraham to Acid House*, p. x.

16. Yinger, *Countercultures*, pp. 22–3.

17. Gumbrecht, 'Literarische Gegenwelten, Karnevalskultur und Epochenschwelle vom Spätmittelalter zur Renaissance', p. 98: 'Wir wollen die verschiedenen Modi der Beziehung zwischen Alltagswelten und Karnevalskultur als Negationsverhältnisse beschreiben.'

18. Trilling, *Beyond Culture: Essays on Literature and Learning*, pp. 12–13.

19. Lansdown, *The Cambridge Introduction to Byron*, p. 37.

20. 'Letter to John Murray, November 24, 1818', *BLJ*, vol. 6, p. 83. Byron mistakenly attributes the review, written by John Wilson Croker, to Southey.

21. Cf. Cox, *Poetry and Poetics in the Cockney School: Keats, Shelley, Hunt and Their Circle*, in particular ch. 2 ('The Hunt Era').

22. Ibid., p. 62.

23. See Cox, 'Leigh Hunt's *Foliage*: A Cockney Manifesto', pp. 58–77.

24. Ibid., p. 63.

25. See Erdman, 'Byron and the Genteel Reformers', pp. 1065–94.

26. See Kelsall, *Byron's Politics*.

27. Appendix to *The Two Foscari*, *CPW*, vol. 6, p. 223.

28. Kelsall, *Byron's Politics*, p. 116.

29. Ibid., p. 130.

30. Cf. also Cochran, 'Byron and Shelley: Radical Incompatibles', pp. 63–86.

31. Yinger, *Countercultures*, p. 187.

32. 'Letter to Leigh Hunt, 4–6 November 1815', *BLJ*, vol. 4, p. 332.
33. X.Y.Z. [William Hazlitt], 'The Round Table: No. 22', *The Examiner*, 22 October.
34. 'Letter to Byron, November 7, 1815', in: Cochran (ed.), 'Byron's Correspondence and Journals 06', *Peter Cochran's Website*, p. 85.
35. 'Letter to Leigh Hunt, 30 October 1815', *BLJ*, vol. 4, p. 326.
36. 'Letter to Leigh Hunt, 4–6 November 1815', *BLJ*, vol. 4, p. 332.
37. 'Letter to Byron, 7 November 1815', in: Cochran (ed.), 'Byron's Correspondence and Journals 06', p. 85.
38. See Siskin, 'The Problem of Periodization: Enlightenment, Romanticism and the Fate of System', p. 106.
39. 'Letter to Lady Melbourne, 13 November 1814', *BLJ*, vol. 4, p. 231.
40. See Howe, *Byron and the Forms of Thought*, pp. 29–31.
41. See Siskin, 'The Problem of Periodization'.
42. Ibid., pp. 108–14, at p. 118.
43. Blake, *Jerusalem: The Emanation of The Giant Albion*, p. 10:21.
44. Wordsworth, *The Excursion* IV, ll. 603–6, in: *Poetical Works*, vol. 5, p. 128.
45. 'Letter to Byron, January 1822', in: Cochran (ed.), 'Byron's Correspondence and Journals 14', pp. 24–5.
46. Cooke, *The Blind Man Traces the Circle: On the Patterns and Philosophy of Byron's Poetry*; Hoagwood, *Byron's Dialectic: Skepticism and the Critique of Culture*; Bernhard Jackson, *The Development of Byron's Philosophy of Knowledge: Certain in Uncertainty*; Howe, *Byron and the Forms of Thought*.
47. See Howe, *Byron and the Forms of Thought*, pp. 21–3.
48. Ibid., pp. 31–2.
49. Hunt, 'Preface, Including Cursory Observations on Poetry and Cheerfulness', in: *Foliage, or Poems Original and Translated*, pp. 16f.
50. Ibid., pp. 37–8.
51. Beaton, *Byron's War: Romantic Rebellion, Greek Revolution*.
52. Howe, *Byron and the Forms of Thought*, p. 33.
53. Ibid., p. 33.
54. 'Letter to Byron, 16 November, 1822', in: Cochran (ed.), 'Byron's Correspondence and Journals 15', p. 29.
55. Cronin, *The Politics of Romantic Poetry: In Search of the Pure Commonwealth*, p. 172.
56. Kelsall, *Byron's Politics*, p. 151.
57. Stabler, *Byron, Poetics and History*, p. 179.
58. Gumbrecht, 'Literarische Gegenwelten', pp. 97–8.
59. For two different definitions of these three modes, see Gumbrecht, 'Gegenkultur', pp. 671–3, and Gumbrecht, 'Literarische Gegenwelten', pp. 100–1.
60. Gumbrecht, 'Literarische Gegenwelten', p. 101.
61. Gumbrecht, 'Gegenkultur', p. 673.

62. Cf. Cochran, 'Byron and Shelley: Radical Incompatibles', p. 85.
63. Cf. Schoina, 'Leigh Hunt's "Letters from Abroad" and the "Anglo-Italian" Discourse of *The Liberal*', pp. 115–25, and Schoina, '"To engraft ourselves on foreign stocks": Byron's Poetics of Acculturation'.
64. Lamartine, 'Discours de réception', in: *Œuvres de Lamartine de l'Académie Française*, p. 764.

## Works cited

Beaton, Roderick (2013), *Byron's War: Romantic Rebellion, Greek Revolution*, Cambridge: Cambridge University Press.
Bernhard Jackson, Emily (2010), *The Development of Byron's Philosophy of Knowledge: Certain in Uncertainty*, Basingstoke: Palgrave Macmillan.
Blake, William (1821), *Jerusalem: The Emanation of The Giant Albion, The William Blake Archive*, available at <http://www.blakearchive.org/exist/blake/archive/work.xq?workid=jerusalem&java=no> (last accessed 30 March 2015).
Bode, Christoph (2010), 'Romantik – Europäische Antwort auf die Herausforderung der Moderne? Versuch einer Rekonzeptualisierung', in: Anja Ernst and Paul Geyer (eds), *Die Romantik: Ein Gründungsmythos der Europäischen Moderne*, Göttingen: V&R unipress, pp. 85–96.
Boyd, Brian (2009), *On the Origin of Stories: Evolution, Cognition, and Fiction*, Cambridge, MA: Belknap Press of Harvard University Press.
Cochran, Peter (2006), 'Byron and Shelley: Radical Incompatibles', *Romanticism on the Net*, 43, pp. 63–86.
— , ed. (2009) 'Byron's Correspondence and Journals 06: From London and Other Places in England, January 1815–April 1816', *Peter Cochran's Website*, available at <https://peter cochran.files.wordpress.com/2009/02/06-london-1815–18168.pdf> (last accessed 30 March 2015).
— , ed. (2009), 'Byron's Correspondence and Journals 14: From Pisa, October 1821–October 1822', *Peter Cochran's Website*, available at <https://petercochran.files.wordpress.com/2009/02/14-pisa-1821–18225.pdf> (last accessed 30 March 2015).
— , ed. (2009), 'Byron's Correspondence and Journals 15: From Genoa, October 1822–July 1823', *Peter Cochran's Website*, available at <https://petercochran.files.wordpress.com/2009/02/15-genoa-1822–182312.pdf> (last accessed 30 March 2015).
Cooke, Michael G. (1969), *The Blind Man Traces the Circle: On the Patterns and Philosophy of Byron's Poetry*, Princeton: Princeton University Press.
Cox, Jeffrey N. (1998), *Poetry and Poetics in the Cockney School: Keats, Shelley, Hunt and Their Circle*, Cambridge: Cambridge University Press.
— (2003), 'Leigh Hunt's *Foliage*: A Cockney Manifesto', in: Nicholas Roe (ed.), *Leigh Hunt: Life, Poetics, Politics*, London / New York: Routledge, pp. 58–77.

Cronin, Richard (2000), *The Politics of Romantic Poetry: In Search of the Pure Commonwealth*, Basingstoke: Macmillan.

Erdman, David V. (1941), 'Byron and the Genteel Reformers', *PMLA*, 56, pp. 1065–94.

Ferber, Michael (2005), 'Introduction', in: Michael Ferber (ed.), *A Companion to European Romanticism*, Oxford: Blackwell, pp. 1–9.

Gumbrecht, Hans Ulrich (1980), 'Literarische Gegenwelten, Karnevalskultur und Epochenschwelle vom Spätmittelalter zur Renaissance', in: Hans Ulrich Gumbrecht (ed.), *Literatur in der Gesellschaft des Spätmittelalters*, Heidelberg: Carl Winter, pp. 95–144.

— (1997–2003), 'Gegenkultur', in: Klaus Weimar, Harald Fricke and Jan-Dirk Müller (eds), *Reallexikon der deutschen Literaturwissenschaft: Neubearbeitung des Reallexikons der deutschen Literaturgeschichte*, 3 vols, Berlin / New York: de Gruyter.

Hoagwood, Terence Allan (1993), *Byron's Dialectic: Skepticism and the Critique of Culture*, London / Toronto: Associated University Presses.

Howe, Anthony (2013), *Byron and the Forms of Thought*, Liverpool: Liverpool University Press.

Hunt, Leigh (1818), 'Preface, Including Cursory Observations on Poetry and Cheerfulness', in: *Foliage, or Poems Original and Translated*, London: C. and J. Ollier, pp. 9–39.

Kelsall, Malcolm (1987), *Byron's Politics*, Sussex: Harvester Press.

Lakoff, George (1987), *Women, Fire, and Dangerous Things: What Categories Reveal about the Mind*, Chicago / London: University of Chicago Press.

Lamartine, Alphonse de (1840), *Œuvres de Lamartine de l'Académie Française*, Brussels: Société Belge de Librairie.

Lansdown, Richard (2012), *The Cambridge Introduction to Byron*, Cambridge: Cambridge University Press.

Leary, Timothy (2005), 'Foreword', in: Ken Goffman and Dan Joy (eds), *Counterculture Through the Ages: From Abraham to Acid House*, New York: Villard, pp. ix–xi.

McGann, Jerome J. (2002), *Byron and Romanticism*, ed. James Søderholm, Cambridge: Cambridge University Press, pp. 236–55.

Musgrove, Frank (1974), *Ecstasy and Holiness: Counter Culture and the Open Society*, Bloomington: Indiana University Press.

Roszak, Theodore (1968), *The Making of a Counter Culture: Reflections on the Technocratic Society and its Youthful Opposition*, New York: Doubleday & Comp.

Schoina, Maria (2006), 'Leigh Hunt's "Letters from Abroad" and the "Anglo-Italian" Discourse of *The Liberal*', *Romanticism*, 12, pp. 115–25.

— (2006), '"To engraft ourselves on foreign stocks": Byron's Poetics of Acculturation', *Romanticism on the Net*, 43, available at <http://dx.doi.org/10.7202/013593ar> (last accessed 18 January 2016).

Siskin, Clifford (2009), 'The Problem of Periodization: Enlightenment, Romanticism and the Fate of System', in: James Chandler (ed.), *The Cambridge History of English Romantic Literature*, Cambridge: Cambridge University Press, pp. 101–26.

Stabler, Jane (2002), *Byron, Poetics and History*, Cambridge: Cambridge University Press.

Trilling, Lionel (1955), *The Opposing Self: Nine Essays in Criticism*, New York: Viking Press.

— (1965), *Beyond Culture: Essays on Literature and Learning*, New York: Viking Press.

Tripold, Thomas (2012), *Die Kontinuität romantischer Ideen: Zu den Überzeugungen gegenkultureller Bewegungen. Eine Ideengeschichte*, Bielefeld: transcript.

Turner, Mark (1996), *The Literary Mind: The Origins of Thought and Language*, Oxford: Oxford University Press.

Wordsworth, William (1940–9), *The Poetical Works of William Wordsworth*, ed. Ernest de Selincourt and Helen Darbishire, 5 vols, Oxford: Clarendon Press.

X.Y.Z. [William Hazlitt] (1815), 'The Round Table: No. 22', *The Examiner*, 22 October, 408, p. 684.

Yinger, J. Milton (1960), 'Contraculture and Subculture', *American Sociological Review*, 25, pp. 625–35.

— (1982), *Countercultures: The Promise and Peril of a World Turned Upside Down*, New York: Free Press.

# Chapter 6

# At the Margins of Europe: Byron's East Revisited and *The Giaour*

*Stephen Minta*

Byron's East is an anomalous composite. It is framed by at least four elements. Firstly, it is framed by the power of the Ottoman Empire, which for Europeans had long been synonymous with the exotic, the unreadable and the systemically cruel. By Byron's time, the Empire had been in long decline,[1] but it still retained a formidable residue of influence over a wide range of subject peoples.[2] In the second place, there is the framing presence of a distant past, in the form of the complex associations attached to an 'ancient Greece', a Greece that was far more familiar to educated Europeans than any of the contemporary elements in the picture. Thirdly, there is a loosely defined Albanian dimension, formally part of the Ottoman Empire, though, with the rise to power of Ali Pasha from the 1780s, increasingly resistant to it.[3] Fourthly, there is what might be described as 'modern Greece', though its identity and limits in the early nineteenth century are not always clearly definable. For many visitors, 'modern Greece' was, in any case, always a defused entity, sometimes completely overwhelmed by the knowledge of what Greece once had been.

Byron's youthful experience of this Eastern complex began in September 1809, when he and John Cam Hobhouse first arrived on Greek soil, and it ended in April 1811, when he left Greece to return to England. During this time away from home, Byron travelled to Tepelena in southern Albania, to meet with Ali Pasha (October 1809), settled in Athens (December 1809 to March 1810, July 1810 to April 1811) and visited Turkey, including Constantinople (March 1810 to July 1810). His immediate response to this early experience made him famous overnight, with the publication, in March 1812, of the first two Cantos of *Childe Harold*. Sometime after, probably in late 1812, he began the composition of *The Giaour*, which he subtitled

'A Fragment of a Turkish Tale'; originally a poem of 344 lines, it progressively lengthened in subsequent versions, ending with the seventh edition of 1,334 lines in December 1813. Despite Byron's fears, the poem proved highly popular, with fourteen editions by 1815.[4]

Clearly, the direct experience of the East, in however transitory a form, was crucial to Byron's literary success. At the same time, direct experience is invariably linked to anticipation and, thus, to the fact of prior acquaintance by other means. A characteristic mode of *Childe Harold* I and II promotes a happy coming together of bookish memory and topical discovery. It is only by this process that some random stream in Greece can become the 'vaunted rill' of the Hippocrene Fountain, for example (*Childe Harold* I, l. 5). So, thinking about what may lie behind *The Giaour*, I begin by looking at Byron's reading of Turkish history and customs before he left for the East. In a very long list of books that he compiled during his last month at Trinity College, Cambridge (1807), and which represented his reading up to that point, he includes entries for 'Arabia', where he praises the Koran for its 'most sublime poetical passages far surpassing European Poetry', for 'Persia', 'Greece' (no writer later than Apollonius Rhodius) and 'Turkey', where, in connection with the history of the Ottoman Empire, he claims to have read 'Knolles [Richard Knolles, 1550?–1610], Sir Paul Rycaut [1628–1700] and Prince Cantemir [Dimitrie Cantemir, 1673–1723]'.[5]

The historical works of these three writers are unlikely to have left specific traces in Byron's poetry. Knolles and Cantemir are long versions of narrative history, highly detailed.[6] Rycaut's *Present State of the Ottoman Empire*, his best-known work on Turkey, is also long and detailed, though, as its title suggests, it is more concerned with the current state of things than with historical narrative. For readers of Byron, the interest of these works is not, then, concerned with specific borrowings, but is rather a matter of general impressions; and while it is inevitably over-simplifying to try to summarise these impressions, what follows is an attempt.

All three writers provide plenty of support for traditionally held views about the Ottoman Empire.[7] Their writings are full of the violence of imperial power; so Cantemir notes of the Emperor Mehmed III (1595–1603) that he 'stains the beginning of his reign with the blood of his nineteen brothers' and that 'Christian Writers' assert that he 'threw ten of his Father's concubines, that were with child, into the sea'.[8] Throughout these historical accounts, there is a fascination with the relationship between absolute power and concealed sexual extravagance, the forbidden theatre of the seraglio, with its mutes, dwarves and eunuchs black and white. At the same time, of the three writers, only Rycaut regularly frames the descriptions in a way that is culturally comparative or competitive. Addressing the reader, Rycaut says,

> If the Tyranny, Oppression and Cruelty of [the Ottoman State] . . . seem strange to thy Liberty and Happiness, thank God that thou art born in a Countrey the most free and just in all the World [. . .]. And thus learn to know and prize thy own freedom, by comparison with Foreign Servitude' ('To the Reader').

Knolles and Cantemir do not talk in this way. They can sound remarkably accepting of the accounts they give, almost matter of fact; and, what is important for our reading of *The Giaour*, they are well aware that Ottoman culture has no monopoly on the cruel and the barbarous. So, for example, in Knolles we find the story of a Turkish galley, returning to Constantinople from Tripoli. The ship is driven off course by a storm and a 'Noble *Venetian*' who hears of the incident takes the Turks captive, 'committing great Cruelties without the least distinction of Age, Quality or Sex, the Women [. . .] being barbarously us'd, and afterwards thrown into the Sea'. Among them is 'a certain Beautiful Virgin' who begs for protection because she was born a Christian. 'But neither her Beauty nor Persuasions would prevail on the *Venetian*, who after he had ravish'd her, cast her with the rest into the Sea.'[9]

Cantemir is the writer who may have attracted Byron most. Although he died only twenty years or so after Rycaut, his perspective on the Ottoman Empire is very different. Rycaut still fears the Empire and is a little in awe of the discipline of its soldiery. Cantemir resolutely entitles his work a history of the 'Growth and Decay' of the Ottomans. This sense of the fragility of Empire plays to a very Byronic fascination. The passage from *The Giaour* that may owe something to Cantemir directly has an interesting relation to this theme. Here are the relevant lines, describing the desolation of Hassan's house after his death:

> The steed is vanished from the stall,
> No serf is seen in Hassan's hall;
> The lonely Spider's thin grey pall
> Waves slowly widening o'er the wall;
> The Bat builds in his Haram bower;
> And in the fortress of his power
> The Owl usurps the beacon-tower. (*The Giaour*, ll. 288–94)

Here is the possible source in Cantemir: 'The Spider has wove her Web in the Imperial Palace, the Owl has sung her watch Song upon the Towers, of *Efrasiyab*.'[10] It is the historical context that makes this an interesting moment. Cantemir quotes the words in connection with the surrender of the Greeks, after the Ottoman conquest of Constantinople (1453) under the Emperor Mehmed II. The Emperor, he says, went in a triumphal procession to Hagia Sophia, the Greek Orthodox cathedral. He then ordered the *ezan*[11] to be sung, after which 'he goes to the Imperial Palace, and as he is entering, being addicted to Poetry, he is reported to say an extempore Distich in the *Persian* language'. These lines of Persian poetry are then quoted by Cantemir as above ('The Spider has wove [. . .]').[12] Cantemir continues:

> as we see Spiders throw their Webs over ruinous and deserted Houses; in like manner, the *Grecian* Empire, subverted and wrested from its ancient Possessors, is likely to become as the Palaces of *Efrasiyab*, in which, instead of Guards, Owls make their Nests, and scream out their direful Notes. A true Prediction, and fulfilled in every Circumstance!

This context, if it is in Byron's mind, is resonant. It connects the almost anonymous fate of Hassan to the pageant of the fall of empires: firstly, the Turkish Empire, now in decline, its defeat already foreshadowed by the fall of Byzantium; behind it, the legendary world of Afrasiab, the Turanian king, archenemy of Iran.[13] There is a receding pattern, endlessly, inescapably repeated. The effect achieved, of loss on a huge scale, is a little like that of Baudelaire in 'Le Cygne' (1861), the great poem of exile that he dedicated to Victor Hugo. Starting from a specific memory of Andromache in the first line, the poem eventually opens out on to the universality of the experience of loss, as the poet thinks of

> A quiconque a perdu ce qui ne se retrouve
> Jamais, jamais![14]

Cantemir is also instructive in the way that he offers a context for the use of the term *Giaour*. This was a word Byron much favoured: it appears in *Childe Harold* II, *The Bride of Abydos* (1813), *The Corsair* (1814) and *Don Juan* (1819–24).[15] The term had long been in the English language.[16] The first use recorded by the *Oxford English Dictionary* (OED) is from 1589, in an essay by Anthonie Jenkinson, in Richard Hakluyt's *The Principall Navigations, Voiages and Discoveries of the English Nation*, where its pejorative sense in Turkish speech is already clearly understood: 'being a Christian, and called amongst them [i.e. the Turks] Gower, that is, unbeleever, and uncleane'.[17] *Giaour* comes from Persian *gaur*. The French / English spelling (*giaour*) represents the Turkish pronunciation of the Persian word; in Turkish the spelling is *gâvur*. The term designates, in Turkish, a non-Muslim, especially a Christian.[18] The most obvious source for the term in Byron is William Beckford's *Vathek: An Arabian Tale* of 1786, where *giaour* is extensively used.

What is interesting about Cantemir's discussion is the way he gives the word *giaour* a broad social context, noting that the Turks 'gave Nicknames to almost every Nation that comes to their knowledge'. He gives a range of examples:

> They use to call the *Jews* [. . .] Dogs: the *Persians* [. . .] Red-heads: the *Armenians* [. . .] Turd-eaters: the *Georgians* [. . .] Lice-eaters [. . .] those that are subject to them, especially the *Greeks* [. . .] Sheep without Horns [. . .] the *Albanians* [. . .] Sellers of Lungs [. . .] the *Polanders*, *Fodul Gaur* [*giaour*], boasting, arrogant Infidels [. . .] the *Italians* and all the *Franks* [. . .] of a thousand colours, that is, deceitful: the *French* [. . .] crafty: the *Dutch* [. . .] Cheese-mongers: the *English* [. . .] Clothiers: the *Spaniards* [. . .] idle.[19]

Such cultural stereotyping might seem to confirm the absolute otherness of Ottoman attitudes, whereas it actually flattens our sense of cultural difference. If the Europeans thought of the Turks as cruel, religious fanatics, mired in deceit,[20] the Turks thought the same of Europeans, and had long done so.[21] Byron prefaces *Childe Harold* with a quotation from *Le Cosmopolite, ou le citoyen du monde* (1753) that begins: 'L'univers est une espèce de livre, dont on n'a lu que la première page quand on n'a vu que son pays.'[22] This is usually taken as an illustration, or confirmation, of what is to follow in the poem – travel broadens the mind – but the French quotation might also serve as a challenge, and what follows might be a working out of that challenge. Perhaps travel only confirms that it is simply the superficial things that vary, however much the exoticism of the locale or the apparent otherness of the people you encounter may suggest otherwise. As Byron famously noted:

> I see not much difference between ourselves & the Turks, save that we have foreskins and they none, that they have long dresses and we short, and that we talk much and they little. – In England the vices in fashion are whoring & drinking, in Turkey, Sodomy & smoking, we prefer a girl and a bottle, they a pipe and pathic. (*BLJ*, vol. 1, p. 238)

I turn now to look at a number of early responses to Byron's *Giaour*, before concluding with a discussion of some more recent accounts.

The early reviewers of *The Giaour*, with few exceptions, knew that they were in the presence of an important poem. At the same time, many of them struggled with it, at the level of plot, form, setting or interpretation. The plot by now has become reasonably clear to us: Leila is a beautiful slave in the harem of the Turkish Muslim Hassan. Hassan is referred to as an 'Emir' at line 357.[23] Leila is seduced by a young Venetian, who is the Giaour of the title. Hassan has Leila drowned at sea for her sexual infidelity. The Giaour takes revenge, kills Hassan and then, overcome with a wild mix of emotions, seeks out a Christian monastery in which to make an unrepentant confession and end his days.

As to the form of the poem, it is a collection of fragments, which, in the fictional world of the tale, have been put together by an editor. Different, unidentified voices contribute their share of the story and then vanish from the reader's presence. The fictional editor attaches some footnotes, of varying degrees of seriousness or light-heartedness, and, occasionally, these are to be identified with Byron himself.

The poem is set in what Colin Jager describes as a 'homogenized eastern location'; the location of the Christian monastery is, he says, similarly 'indeterminate'.[24] This is not quite accurate. The poem begins clearly enough in Greece, with a memory of the approach by sea to Piraeus. There is a mention of Cape Sounion and the Greek islands, and rhetorical gestures in the direction of Thermopylae and Salamis, in the context of the 'Greece is not what it once was' theme. There is also reference to the legendary pirates of the Mani Peninsula. This is all very general but, at line 528, the place where the Giaour and Hassan finally meet is clearly located:

> The chief before, as deck'd for war,
> Bears in his belt the scimitar
> Stain'd with the best of Arnaut blood,
> When in the pass the rebels stood,
> And few return'd to tell the tale
> Of what befell in Parne's vale. (*The Giaour*, ll. 523–8)

Hassan ('The chief') appears here as a Turkish leader who has fought successfully against the Albanians (Arnauts),[25] the irregular forces who had terrorised the Peloponnese in the 1770s (see below). The Giaour has taken up with a group of these rebel Albanians, in order to pursue his revenge.[26] He now wears Albanian clothing (*The Giaour*, l. 615). Hassan and his men are ambushed somewhere in a pass through the mountain range that separates Attica from Boeotia (Mount Parnes / modern Greek Párnitha).[27] Nowhere does the poem suggest that any of the actions in *The Giaour* takes place outside Greece, except for the episode in the Christian monastery. To reach this, we are told, the Giaour had to cross the sea 'from Paynim land' (*The Giaour*, l. 808),[28] so – though it is of no importance – Byron probably imagined the Giaour as going to Italy or, just possibly, to the Ionian islands, which had long been in Venetian hands.

The temporal setting of the poem is the period after the ending of the Russo-Turkish War of 1768–74. Having called in Albanian irregular forces for assistance in the war, the Ottomans were subsequently unable to control them; finally, in 1779, they were expelled from the Peloponnese.[29] The action of *The Giaour*, Byron says, took place 'soon after' this expulsion (*CPW*, vol. 3, p. 40).

It is important not to lose sight of how difficult many of the early reviewers found the poem, since the difficulty is an essential aspect of whatever sense may be gained from it. The various elements that make up the tale 'place a tremendous burden upon the reader: it is difficult enough to figure out the plot, let alone who speaks, whom to trust, and whom, in the end, to believe'.[30] This begs the question of what a 'belief' in any aspect of the poem might entail and whether, indeed, belief is relevant at all, but the reminder that this is a difficult poem is valuable.

The early reviewers often acknowledged that *The Giaour* has moments of great beauty and power, and that these speak to the reader, whether the reader is fully clear about the overall direction of the tale or not. Naturally, praise is not universal. The reviewer for *The British Review* of October 1813 is uncompromising; he says that the character of the Giaour presents the reader with the same problems as the Childe Harold, of whom the reviewer writes: 'his name, character, and office occasioned us considerable perplexity, and our impatience to advance to the interior was checked by a sort of sphynx which embarrassed us at the entrance'. This reviewer finds almost nothing to admire in *The Giaour*. He rails against the darkness of the poem, noting the use and abuse of the adjectives 'black' and 'dark' throughout the tale. Hassan is black; so is the Giaour's horse and so is his beard; then we have Leila's eyes, the cypress tree, Hassan's brow, not to mention the dark in soul and the dark in spirit.[31]

In contrast to *The British Review*, we have the simplicity of Francis Jeffrey's opening to his account of *The Giaour* in *The Edinburgh Review*: 'This, we think, is very beautiful [. . .].'[32] But if the majority of the reviewers could see greatness in *The Giaour*, very few were able to approve of the poem. The two main concerns have to do with its form, on the one hand, and the troubling nature of the character of the Giaour himself, on the other. I take these two issues in turn.

Jeffrey is one of the few to defend the fragmentary nature of the poem and his witty contextualisation has frequently been quoted. He notes that the reading public of his time has grown impatient 'of the long stories that used to delight our ancestors', so that 'the taste for fragments, we suspect, has become very general; and the greater part of polite readers would now no more think of sitting down to a whole Epic than to a whole ox' (p. 299). Byron, in his preface (or advertisement) to the poem, immediately notes that it is composed of 'disjointed fragments', and in the penultimate line we are told of '[t]his broken tale',[33] but he does not carry most of the reviewers with him. The reviewer for *The British Review* says that real fragments are not a problem, where time has erased the greater part of a text, but where a writer seeks 'to plan imperfection, and to pre-arrange confusion', that is unacceptable (p. 133).[34] With a fine sense of the uncompromising, he says: 'We shall continue to require a beginning, middle, and end [. . .]. Both nature and art in all their designs and arrangements abhor mutilation, and delight in the correspondence and union of parts' (p. 134).

As far as the character of the Giaour is concerned, there was widespread alarm amongst the early reviewers. The writer for *The British Review* once again sets the tone:

> The character of his Giaour is of a cast which we cannot approve [. . .]. The Giaour is evidently one of those persons whom modern poetry and the German drama have [. . .] so frequently introduced to us – a being, whose tumultuous passions, mixed with a sort of blustering humanity and turbid sentiment, assume the right of trampling upon the rights of others, of breaking the bands of society, and of treating honest men and their wives 'living peaceably in their habitations' as creatures of a lower world, designed for their pastime. (p. 144)

The writer is keen to stress the dangers of the poem:

> There is a sort of morbid, sentimental hue thrown over the stormy character of the Giaour, which is likely to beget a feeling in which too much of admiration enters, for a reader not well grounded in good principles to be safe under its influence. (p. 144)

The formulation now sounds extreme but, as we shall see, modern criticism that is unwilling to engage with this aspect of the poem risks losing an important dimension of it.

What is in question here, of course, is Byron's apparent lack of a moral compass.[35] *The Anti-Jacobin Review* confirms this sense: 'we may express our concern [. . .] and also regret, that [Byron] failed to point the moral, which the tale, even in its present imperfect state, obviously presented'.[36] However, part of what the poem disturbingly reveals is that the 'obvious' moral of the tale is much less interesting than its darker aspects. As Nellist puts it, in *The Giaour* 'Blame for what happens becomes secondary to the sheer fact of suffering' (p. 51). The danger, as the early reviewers were well aware, is of morality easily eclipsed by the fascination with pain. The reader is simply left to confront the darkness, in the face of horrors that can be glimpsed and yet never fully confronted by the imagination. What *might* it be like to be the Giaour, to know the extraordinary price of sexual guilt? – 'What felt *he* then . . . ?' (*The Giaour*, l. 267). Here is a challenge to the reader's imagination that never lets up.

Almost all the early reviewers were troubled by what they felt they were being drawn towards: the appeal of horror, where an intimation of suffering surpasses in its power the mind's capacity to provide a moral commentary on it. The writer in *The Eclectic Review* says that, in *The Giaour*, 'the poetry, like the glare of lightning on a dark night, just serves to shew, and to exaggerate, the darkness around',[37] while *The Anti-Jacobin Review* underlines the writer's sense of fundamental unease at the apparent nihilism of the poem. Very early on, at line 70, the poet talks about the immediate aftermath of death and refers to 'The first dark day of nothingness' (*The Giaour*, l. 70).

It is easy now to overlook the implications of the line. The *Anti-Jacobin*'s reviewer, though, can scarcely believe what he reads: the line suggests, he says, the impact of 'the revolutionary philosophists of modern France'. Here is a suggestion of the total annihilation of the human spirit. He goes on, 'surely a Christian nobleman could have no such meaning' (p. 130), but clearly Byron was at least tempted by the idea. The *OED* picks up this use of *nothingness* – although its definition (under 1.c) fails to bring out the full force of the line: it gives merely 'absence or cessation of consciousness or life', when it is apparent that the line suggests much more than simply 'the first dark day of the cessation of consciousness'. The *OED* does recognise, though, that this is the first recorded English use of the word in its specialised sense.

I look now at the responses of some modern critics to the two objections that the early reviewers raised in their discussion of *The Giaour*. A good deal of modern criticism deals with the objections by seeking to neutralise their force. As before, I take the two issues in turn.

First of all, there is the question of form. Many of the early reviewers, as we have seen, found the fragmentary nature of the poem problematic, whether in terms of the artistic integrity of the 'finished' poem or simple ease of comprehension. The kind of neutralisation process to which I refer is well evidenced in Robert F. Gleckner's account of *The Giaour*. Gleckner argues that a 'sense of the whole' is possible,[38] that the fragments can be made to yield a coherence beyond the effect of their simple accumulation. While the individual voices we hear through the poem are always limited in their knowledge and sentiments, the poet, he suggests, is able 'to maneuver us into the position of seeing all the points of view represented at once'.[39] But even if this is the case, there is no whole to which the different points of view can be subordinated. These 'disjointed fragments' of a 'broken tale' have no relation to anything outside or beyond them. In that sense, they are not the literary equivalent of the Parthenon Marbles that Lord Elgin brought back from the East. The reviewer from *The British Review*, who sought to distinguish 'real' fragments from invented ones, had a point. Where real fragments hint at a possibility of cultural wholeness, pre-arranged 'confusion', as the reviewer terms it, risks precisely that.

Sophie Thomas, in some suggestive comments on the Romantic fragment, writes that fragments

> are, by definition, disturbing entities. They play upon the imagination by promising or suggesting more than what they are, while reminding the viewer or reader that what they promise can never be recovered or fully experienced. Fragments simultaneously raise and disavow the possibility of totality and wholeness, thus becoming suitable figures for all manner of disruption and discontinuity. (p. 502)[40]

This is even more the case with the 'counterfeit' fragment. Byron himself wrote to Murray about the lengthening *Giaour* on 26 August 1813 (*BLJ*, vol. 3, p. 100): 'I have but with some difficulty *not* added any more to this snake of a poem.' Byron might have carried on adding fragments but, given that he chose so obviously to let the form reflect the uncertainty of what is being described or evoked, no number of further additions would necessarily have brought us closer to wholeness, or even coherence. For all that, critical attempts to redefine the structure of *The Giaour*, in favour of a recoverable sense of order, continue on a regular basis. For example, Marilyn Butler, in an interesting essay, still insists on the 'two halves of the poem' and the symmetry that allegedly operates within the manner of the tale's telling.[41]

If the desire to neutralise disturbing aspects of form is characteristic of a number of critical accounts, a corresponding urge to
resolve the psychological chaos of *The Giaour* is even more noticeable. Most of these efforts come down to a desire to domesticate the
chaos, by making the key figures (notably Hassan and the Giaour)
represent something culturally significant that transcends the supposed anarchy of their individual selves, whereas, I would suggest,
these figures have no deep cultural significance and stand for nothing
more than the appalling aloneness that they inhabit. Jager sees the
collision between the two as 'a face-off between modernity and tradition' or as 'tradition's rage *at* modernity'.[42] He suggests that 'Hassan
kills Leila because she is his property,' opening up a cultural opposition, in which love 'is linked to a freedom that orthodox tyrants like
Hassan cannot understand',[43] but we know almost nothing about
Hassan, whether he was an 'orthodox tyrant' or not. Nothing in
the poem suggests that he was not in love with Leila; he might have
killed her for that reason (*The Giaour*, ll. 677–8). To infer that he
did not love her because he owned her is an unwise step – we can
think of Achilles and his Briseis (*Iliad*, 9, ll. 340–3) – but, in any case,
*The Giaour* deliberately withholds the information that would make
a discussion here in any way meaningful.

Speculation about the nature of character in *The Giaour* has been
particularly problematic in the wake of the West's preoccupation with
Muslim culture since the 1990s. Eric Meyer says forcefully that the
poem 'is too plainly a paean to militant Hellenism and to the hegemony
of West over East'.[44] Shahidha Bari suggests that 'The Giaour's apostatic
Christianity posits a Western religious scepticism in the face of the strict
sexual morality of Hassan's Islamic theocracy.'[45] A lot of current work
still shows the influence, however indirect, of Samuel Huntington's
'The Clash of Civilizations?' essay of 1993. That essay argued that, in
future, the source of world conflict would not be primarily ideological or economic, but cultural: 'The clash of civilizations will dominate
global politics. The fault lines between civilizations will be the battle
lines of the future.'[46] Reading poems like *The Giaour* in this feverish
context is inevitably distorting, as critics look for evidence within the
text to support large cultural identifications. Moreover, 'clash of civilizations' readings open up much larger issues about the constructions
we place on individual lives and the circumstances in which groups
engage with others.[47]

Had Byron sought to promote a poem about cultural difference, he
would, no doubt, have chosen a more iconic figure than the Giaour.

As Jager notes, the Giaour 'is a stateless and nameless man who operates on the borderlands of cultures, traditions, and beliefs'.[48] There is nothing to learn from the poem about the clash of cultures. The landscape of a moribund Greece is the theatre for emotions and actions that could be played out between two men anywhere at any time, regardless of cultural affiliation. As the Giaour says, in Hassan's place he would have done the same thing (*The Giaour*, ll. 1062–3). The parallelism works against any attempt at cultural differentiation.[49] The religious and social colouring of the tale is part of the landscape, not fundamental to the story.[50] The finest moments in *The Giaour* are often not time-bound or culture-bound. Here, for example, we hear one of the narrators of the poem, a Muslim fisherman, recalling the moment when Leila is drowned at sea:

> Sullen it plunged, and slowly sank,
> The calm wave rippled to the bank;
> I watch'd it as it sank, methought
> Some motion from the current caught
> Bestirr'd it more, – 'twas but the beam
> That chequer'd o'er the living stream –
> I gaz'd, till vanishing from view,
> Like lessening pebble it withdrew . . . (*The Giaour*, ll. 374–81)

This is consciousness in fascinating play with the indeterminate. The 'it' in the first line has no immediate referent. We watch and fear; in a second we know that 'it' is a body struggling to be free, but we are sure of this only because Byron has already told us in his preface what is going to happen. Otherwise, we might be tempted, like the narrator, to avoid the dawning horror, by telling ourselves that the vague intuition is a simple trick of the light.

But beyond the horror of the events that *The Giaour* portrays or suggests is a greater challenge: the fascination with the darkness from which we struggle to escape. Most of the early reviewers sensed this and were troubled by it. Baudelaire, in the final poem of *Les Fleurs du mal* (1857), summarises the issue in a single line. Travel, he says, offers only a bitter wisdom; for the world endlessly reflects back to us an image of the self, a self that offers '[u]ne oasis d'horreur dans un désert d'ennui!'[51]

This is why the Giaour can find no repentance; he still craves the oasis, even, or especially, with the thoughts of impending death: 'And I shall sleep without the dream / Of what I was, and would be still'

(*The Giaour*, ll. 997–8). He chooses the pain of experience over the nothingness of 'dull, unvarying days' (*The Giaour*, l. 992):

> Yet still in hours of love or strife,
> I've scap'd the weariness of life;
> Now leagu'd with friends, now girt by foes,
> I loath'd the languor of repose. . . . (*The Giaour*, ll. 984–7)

There is no moral, no sense of binary satisfaction, available in *The Giaour*. It recounts a struggle between men, not between cultures. It suggests that life is not very different at the margins from anywhere else; indeed, that the whole idea of margin and centrality is a convenient illusion that blurs the quality of sameness. *The Giaour* illustrates what Mallarmé, in a very different context, calls 'tout l'essaim éternel du désir' ('all the eternal swarm of desire');[52] and, whether true or false, Byron's own nonchalant, distancing, account of the context of the story remains one of the best reflections on it:

> I heard it by accident recited by one of the coffee-house story-tellers who abound in the Levant, and sing or recite their narratives [. . .]. I regret that my memory has retained so few fragments of the original. (*CPW*, vol. 3, p. 423)

### Notes

1. The Ottoman Empire reached its greatest territorial extension in the 1670s. Some Turkish writers from as early as the late fifteenth century engaged with the theme of decline, but it was generally recognised as a definitive tendency from the 1680s onwards. Inalcik and Quataert, *An Economic and Social History of the Ottoman Empire*, pp. 413, 420.
2. In Wallachia, Moldavia, Serbia, Bosnia, Bulgaria, Macedonia, Albania, Greece, Anatolia, Iraq, Syria, Egypt and North Africa.
3. Fleming, *The Muslim Bonaparte: Diplomacy and Orientalism in Ali Pasha's Greece*. Fleming draws the important distinction between Ali Pasha's world view and conventional Ottoman attitudes: 'Ali represented not traditional Ottoman despotism but rather a new breed of Ottoman governor who looked to the West rather than to the Ottoman bureaucracy for aggrandizement and political gain', pp. 23–4.
4. On the publishing history, see *CPW*, vol. 3, p. 413.
5. *CMP*, pp. 1–4. I have used the following editions for these writers: (1) *The Turkish History . . . Comprehending the Origin of that Nation, and the Growth of the Othoman Empire, . . . Written by Mr. Knolls, Continued by Sir Paul Rycaut to . . . 1699 . . . The Second Edition . . .*

*Brought down to this Present Year, 1704* (1704), 2 vols, London: Robert Clavell. Hereafter Knolles. (2) P. Rycaut (1686), *The History of the Present State of the Ottoman Empire. In Three Books*, 6th edn, London: C. Brome. Hereafter Rycaut. (*The Present State* went through at least fifteen editions between 1667 and 1704. For a list, see Anderson, *An English Consul in Turkey*, pp. 294–7.) (3) Dimitrie Cantemir (1756), *The History of the Growth and Decay of the Othman Empire ... Written Originally in Latin ... Translated into English ... by N. Tindal*, London: A. Millar. Hereafter Cantemir.

6. McGann has identified one possible borrowing from Cantemir, to which I shall return.

7. As the *Oxford English Dictionary* (OED) notes, under 'Turk, 4.a.', the name suggests a person who is cruel or tyrannical, who behaves savagely; or, indeed, who treats his wife harshly. The first example of this extended use of the term is 1536. The mysteriousness of Ottoman Turkey was another commonplace. Knolles begins his history by saying 'The Rise of the *Turks* is so very obscure, that neither they themselves, nor their best Historians, know well whence to deduce it.' Knolles, *The Turkish History*, I, p. 1. The OED notes that the name *Turk* is of unknown origin.

8. Cantemir, *Growth and Decay of the Othman Empire*, Book III, ch. VII, p. 236.

9. Knolles, *The Turkish History*, I, p. 1.

10. Cantemir, *Growth and Decay of the Othman Empire*, Book III, ch. I, p. 102.

11. The call to prayer by a muezzin.

12. There is a variant quoted in Jones, *A Grammar of the Persian Language*, vol. 5, in: *The Works of Sir William Jones*: 'The spider holds the veil *in* the palace of Caesar; the owl stands sentinel *on* the watch-tower of Afrasiab,' p. 289.

13. See the entry, by Ehsan Yarshater, under *Afrasiab*, in the *Encyclopaedia Iranica*, I, 6, pp. 570–6. Afrasiab 'symbolizes the opposition between Iran and Turan, which constitutes the main theme of the Iranian national saga'. The article notes that the Turks cultivated the legends of Afrasiab as a Turkish hero, after they came into contact with the Iranians in the sixth century.

14. Baudelaire, *Œuvres complètes*, p. 83. 'Of whoever has lost what can never, never be found again!'

15. It is clear how Byron pronounced the word, from its use at the rhyme with 'tower', 'lower', 'power', 'bower' and 'hour'.

16. There are many varied forms of the word in English: *gower, gaur, gour, giaur, giaour* and so on.

17. Hakluyt, *The Principall Navigations, Voiages and Discoveries of the English Nation*, p. 370. Following the ending of the Greco-Turkish War of 1919–1922, 500,000 Muslims who were living in Greece at the time were expelled to Turkey. These refugees were frequently referred to by the inhabitants of Turkey as *giaours* because they spoke Greek.

18. Interestingly, from the point of view of the present discussion, *gâvur* used in Turkish with a verb means 'to waste utterly', 'to ruin', while the noun *gâvurluk* indicates, besides the 'quality of being a non-Muslim', 'Christian fanaticism' or 'cruelty'.

19. Cantemir, *Growth and Decay of the Othman Empire*, Book III, ch. VI, p. 230.

20. Ibid., Book III, ch. IV, p. 197: 'It is universally known how artfully the *Othmans* can dissemble.'

21. See Cobb, *The Race for Paradise: An Islamic History of the Crusades*. For Muslims, the Crusades were an indicator of the inherently aggressive nature of the Franks. Even before the First Crusade, the tenth-century Baghdadi man of letters Mas'udi commented that the Franks tended towards brutishness, being dull-witted, sluggish and corpulent; and that religious fanaticism was characteristic of all inhabitants of the western quadrant of the world, the Franks included (p. 17). Compare Ibn al-Athir's account of the behaviour of the Franks during the conquest of Constantinople in 1204, in: El-Cheikh, *Byzantium Viewed by the Arabs*, p. 202. On the question of deceit, Sevket Pamuk quotes a twentieth-century Turkish writer who was not alone in arguing that European merchants in the seventeenth century, through the use of debased coins, had robbed unsuspecting Ottomans in what he called the 'biggest counterfeiting scheme in history'. Pamuk, *A Monetary History of the Ottoman Empire*, p. 150. Pamuk challenges this interpretation of the seventeenth-century situation.

22. 'The Universe is a kind of book, of which one has only read the first page when one has only seen one's own country' (*CPW*, vol. 2, p. 3). Byron noted that *Le Cosmopolite* was 'an amusing little vol. & full of French flippancy' (*BLJ*, vol. 2, p. 105).

23. This, as the *OED* notes, is a title of honour borne by the descendants of the prophet Mohammed. Byron's note to the line says that the emirs are 'the worst of a very indifferent brood' (*CPW*, vol. 3, p. 418), a reputation that was long-standing. Rycaut says they were 'the most abominable *Sodomites* and abusers of Masculine youth in the World', p. 211.

24. Jager, 'Byron and Romantic Occidentalism', *Romantic Circles: Praxis Series*, in a volume entitled 'Secularism, Cosmopolitanism, and Romanticism', §3. There is no pagination. References are to the numbered paragraphs.

25. *Arnaut* derives from the Turkish word for an Albanian (*arnavud*), which itself derives from Byzantine and Modern Greek.

26. 'I watch'd my time, I leagu'd ['banded together'] with these, / The traitor in his turn to seize'; *The Giaour*, ll. 685–6.

27. Byron and Hobhouse crossed the range on their way from Thebes to Athens in late 1809. In *Childe Harold* II, l. 702, Byron records passing the fort at Phyle, which, in Classical times, controlled one of the major routes across Mount Parnes ('Spirit of Freedom! when on Phyle's brow

[. . .]'). In Byron's time, the area was home to a number of Albanian villagers; see Stoneman, *A Traveller's History of Athens*, p. 227. The mountain is visible from the Acropolis in Athens. McGann wrongly glosses *Parne* as 'Parnassus' (*CPW*, vol. 3, p. 419).

28. Until the Greeks began to achieve their independence in 1830, the whole country was formally part of the Ottoman Empire, and so in 'pagan' (*paynim*) hands, from a Christian perspective. Greece retained an important Turkish minority until the ethnic cleansing that followed the Asia Minor disaster of 1922.

29. Dakin, *The Unification of Greece, 1770–1923*, p. 17. Byron's preface underlines the horrors of this period: he writes of the desolation of the Peloponnese and of the 'unparalleled' nature of 'the cruelty exercised on all sides' (*CPW*, vol. 3, p. 40). Between 30,000 and 60,000 residents of the Peloponnese died or fled during 'the dark days of reprisal', in: Inalcik and Quataert, *An Economic and Social History of the Ottoman Empire*, vol. 2, p. 654.

30. Jager, 'Byron and Romantic Occidentalism', §3.

31. [Anon.], *The British Review, and London Critical Journal*, pp. 132–45, at pp. 132, 141.

32. [Francis Jeffrey], *The Edinburgh Review*, pp. 299–309, at p. 299.

33. The *OED* glosses *broken* here as meaning 'incomplete', 'fragmentary' or 'imperfect'.

34. 'For our parts, we should as soon think of contracting with a builder to construct us a house in a finished state of dilapidation, as to accept at the hand of an author a heap of fragments as a poem,' *The British Review*, p. 133.

35. Compare Nellist, 'Lyric Presence in Byron from the *Tales* to *Don Juan*', pp. 39–77: 'the spectacular and exotic landscapes [of the *Tales*], by removing familiar circumstance, set the stay-at-home imagination free from its moral moorings, no less than later the locations chosen by Conrad and Kipling', p. 47. There is more to the anxiety prompted by *The Giaour* than can be explained by the simple removal of the familiar, however.

36. [Anon.], *The Anti-Jacobin Review*, pp. 127–38, at p. 129.

37. [Anon.], *The Eclectic Review*, pp. 523–31, at p. 523. The reviewer says later: 'the moral tendency of this fragment [*The Giaour* . . .] we are convinced, is exceedingly pernicious', p. 531.

38. Gleckner, *Byron and the Ruins of Paradise*, p. 116.

39. Ibid., p. 116.

40. Thomas, 'The Fragment', pp. 502–20, at p. 502.

41. Butler, 'The Orientalism of Byron's *Giaour*', pp. 78–96.

42. Jager, 'Byron and Romantic Occidentalism', §27.

43. Ibid., §5.

44. Meyer, '"I Know Thee not, I loathe Thy Race": Romantic Orientalism in the Eye of the Other', pp. 657–99, at p. 664.

45. Bari, 'Listening for Leila: The Re-direction of Desire in Byron's *The Giaour*', pp. 699–721, at p. 707.

46. Huntington, 'The Clash of Civilizations?', pp. 22–49, at p. 22. The essay provoked much controversy. Akeel Bilgrami, for instance, wrote of 'the vast, generalizing terms of Huntington's [. . .] portentous claims', Bilgrami, 'Occidentalism, the Very Idea: An Essay on Enlightenment and Enchantment', pp. 381–411, at p. 383.
47. So Cobb, for example, wonders at 'the pervasive modern use of the Crusades as an analogy or birth moment for some allegedly epochal clash between "Islam and Christianity" [. . .]. This was not a clash of Islam versus Christianity. It was at best a clash of specific Frankish polities warring with specific Muslim ones, where universal claims to religious truth or holy war almost always took a backseat to specific regional and political interests.' Cobb, *The Race for Paradise*, p. 278.
48. Jager, 'Byron and Romantic Occidentalism', §3.
49. When the writer in *The British Review* scathingly says that the Giaour 'debauches a lady of the harem of a Turkish emir' and then adds 'it would have been the same to him had it been an honest citizen's wife' (p. 144), his position is curiously not as absurd as may first appear.
50. The same could be said for Byron's use of Turkish or Greek words in the poem. Some (like 'Bairam', 'caloyer', 'chiaus' and 'giaour') had long been in the English language. In the case of a few others ('ataghan', 'tophaike', 'bi'smillah'), Byron appears to have been the first to introduce them into English.
51. Baudelaire, 'Le Voyage', in: *Œuvres completes*, p. 126: 'An oasis of horror in a desert of tedium'.
52. Mallarmé, 'L'Après-midi d'un faune', in: *Œuvres complètes*, vol. 1, p. 25.

## Works cited

Anderson, S. P. (1989), *An English Consul in Turkey: Paul Rycaut at Smyrna, 1667–1678*, Oxford: Clarendon.

[Anon.] (August 1813), *The Anti-Jacobin Review*, 45, pp. 127–38.

[Anon.] (October 1813), *The British Review, and London Critical Journal*, 5, pp. 132–45.

[Anon.] (November 1813), *The Eclectic Review*, 10, pp. 523–31.

Bari, Shahidha (2013), 'Listening for Leila: The Re-direction of Desire in Byron's *The Giaour*', *European Romantic Review*, 24, pp. 699–721.

Baudelaire, Charles (1961), *Œuvres complètes*, ed. Yves-Gérard Le Dantec and Claude Pichois, Paris: Gallimard.

Bilgrami, Akeel (2006), 'Occidentalism, the Very Idea: An Essay on Enlightenment and Enchantment', *Critical Enquiry*, 32, pp. 381–411.

Butler, Marilyn (1988), 'The Orientalism of Byron's *Giaour*', in: Bernard Beatty and Vincent Newey (eds), *Byron and the Limits of Fiction*, Liverpool: Liverpool University Press, pp. 78–96.

Cantemir, Dimitrie (1756), *The History of the Growth and Decay of the Othman Empire . . . Written Originally in Latin . . . Translated into English . . . by N. Tindal*, London: A. Millar.

Cobb, Paul M. (2014), *The Race for Paradise: An Islamic History of the Crusades*, Oxford: Oxford University Press.

Dakin, Douglas (1972), *The Unification of Greece, 1770–1923*, London: Benn.

El-Cheikh, Nadia Maria (2004), *Byzantium Viewed by the Arabs*, Cambridge, MA: Harvard University Press.

Fleming, Katherine E. (1999), *The Muslim Bonaparte: Diplomacy and Orientalism in Ali Pasha's Greece*, Princeton: Princeton University Press.

Gleckner, Robert F. (1967), *Byron and the Ruins of Paradise*, Baltimore: Johns Hopkins University Press.

Hakluyt, Richard (1589), *The Principall Navigations, Voiages and Discoveries of the English Nation*, 3 parts, London: George Bishop and Ralph Newberie.

Huntington, Samuel P. (1993), 'The Clash of Civilizations?', *Foreign Affairs*, 72, pp. 22–49.

Inalcik, Halil and Donald Quataert (1997), *An Economic and Social History of the Ottoman Empire*, 2 vols, Cambridge: Cambridge University Press.

Jager, Colin (2008), 'Byron and Romantic Occidentalism', *Romantic Circles: Praxis Series*, no pagination.

[Jeffrey, Francis] (July 1813), *The Edinburgh Review*, 21, pp. 299–309.

Jones, Sir William (1807), *A Grammar of the Persian Language*, vol. 5, in: *The Works of Sir William Jones*, 13 vols, London: Stockdale.

Knolles, Richard (1704), *The Turkish History . . . Comprehending the Origin of that Nation, and the Growth of the Othoman Empire, . . . Written by Mr. Knolls, Continued by Sir Paul Rycaut to . . . 1699 . . . The Second Edition . . . Brought down to this Present Year, 1704*, 2 vols, London: Robert Clavell.

Mallarmé, Stéphane (1998–2003), *Œuvres complètes*, ed. Bertrand Marchal, 2 vols, Paris: Gallimard.

Meyer, Eric (1991), '"I Know Thee not, I loathe Thy Race": Romantic Orientalism in the Eye of the Other', *ELH*, 58, pp. 657–99.

Nellist, Brian (1988), 'Lyric Presence in Byron from the *Tales* to *Don Juan*', in: Bernard Beatty and Vincent Newey (eds), *Byron and the Limits of Fiction*, Liverpool: Liverpool University Press, pp. 39–77.

Pamuk, Sevket (2000), *A Monetary History of the Ottoman Empire*, Cambridge: Cambridge University Press.

Rycaut, Paul (1686), *The History of the Present State of the Ottoman Empire. In Three Books*, 6th edn, London: C. Brome.

Stoneman, Richard (2004), *A Traveller's History of Athens*, London: Phoenix.

Thomas, Sophie (2005), 'The Fragment', in: Nicholas Roe (ed.), *Romanticism*, Oxford: Oxford University Press, pp. 502–20.

Yarshater, Ehsan, '*Afrasiab*', in: *Encyclopaedia Iranica*, I, 6, pp. 570–6.

# Chapter 7

# Literary Forefathers: Byron's Marginalia in Isaac D'Israeli's *Literary Character of Men of Genius*

*Jonathan Gross*

Lord Byron's most significant marginalia occur in Isaac D'Israeli's *The Literary Character of Men of Genius*. This is not surprising, for Byron read D'Israeli's book twice, in 1810 and 1811, as a young man in Athens. 'I have read [D'Israeli's works] oftener perhaps than those of any English author whatever – except such as treat of Turkey,' he wrote.[1] With every new edition, D'Israeli incorporated Byron's marginalia. '*The Literary Character, Illustrated by the History of Men of Genius, Drawn from their own Feelings and Confessions* spanned almost the entire career of Isaac D'Israeli,' Spevack notes, 'appearing first as an *Essay on the Manners and Genius of the Literary Character* in 1795 and in four further editions.'[2] 'I don't know a living man's books I take up so often, or lay down more reluctantly, as Israeli's,' Byron wrote on 24 November 1818.[3] When he received a copy of the third edition on 10 June 1822, Byron confessed that 'the *Literary Character* has often been to me a consolation, and always a pleasure'.[4]

Two points bear emphasis. First, Byron read D'Israeli's book twice in Athens (1810) and at least once in Venice (1818), both before and after he became famous. D'Israeli's 1795 edition 'of *An Essay on the Literary Character*, with ms. Notes, was obtained by John Murray, who showed it to the author'. Murray obtained the book 'probably in Nov. 1815 when he bought Byron's library', and incorporated Byron's marginalia into the second and third editions, often without notifying him.[5] On 4 November 1818, Byron complained in two long paragraphs about Murray's 'breach of confidence to do this without my leave'.[6] Secondly, the annotations themselves are more numerous than originally thought. Though Andrew Nicholson transcribed the majority of Byron's penned marginalia, he did not include pencilled annotations, fifty-seven of which were made by either Captain Thomas Fyler (the English captain who returned D'Israeli's book to Murray), Anna Jameson (England's first female art historian, who borrowed Byron's annotated copy of D'Israeli from Fyler) or Lord Byron. My argument is that they are primarily Byron's, with the exception of two that may well be by Anna Jameson.[7] John Murray shared Byron's annotations with D'Israeli to encourage the latter to produce a second edition[8] and to promote Byron's poetry at a time when sales were flagging.

In engaging in this important correspondence with D'Israeli, John Murray II shaped Byron's celebrity and reputation to such an extent that it is hard to determine the true genius in this act of literary self-promotion: Byron, Murray or the behind-the-scenes advisor Isaac D'Israeli. Isaac D'Israeli was friends with two generations of Murrays, John Murray I and John Murray II. Benjamin D'Israeli was the son of Isaac and both were very close to the Murray family. By reviewing John Murray II's correspondence, one can see how important Isaac D'Israeli was as a literary forefather in shaping Murray's publishing plans, the acceptance of *Childe Harold* for publication, and the promotion of Byron's poetic works, especially *The Siege of Corinth* (1816). I use the expression 'literary forefather' in a literal, figurative and plural sense, arguing that John Murray's father, and Benjamin Disraeli's, cast important light on the relationship between Murray and Byron. In a third sense, Murray, D'Israeli and even Walter Scott in his review of *Childe Harold*, Canto III, played a role in guiding Byron's literary career as he entered and abandoned the *haut ton* of the English literary world, literally without a father to guide him. Writing, unlike dialectic, exists perpetually in such an orphaned state, for writing can neither defend itself nor come to its own support. Plato's observation in *Phaedrus* (275e) concerning what Guinn Batten has called the orphaned imagination is even more true of a published yet orphaned author such as Byron as he re-emerged on the literary scene in Regency England in 1812 with the publication of *Childe Harold*.

## 1.

Isaac D'Israeli was John Murray's 'close intimate and literary advisor' at the time John Murray II was expanding his father's publishing firm.[9] 'When young John Murray started in business on his own account', Samuel Smiles notes,

> his acquaintance with D'Israeli, who was twelve years his senior, soon ripened into an intimate friendship. A very large mass of letters, notes, and scraps of memoranda testify to the constant, almost daily

communication which was kept up between them, for D'Israeli, in addition to his own work, very soon became the literary adviser to his friend.[10]

D'Israeli visited the British Museum every day, compiling *Calamities of Authors* (1812), *Quarrels of Authors* (1814) and *Curiosities of Literature* (1791–1823), among other works, so while it is an exaggeration to claim that Murray provided 'virtually the only connection' between D'Israeli and the outside world,[11] D'Israeli did serve as a father figure to John Murray II. 'It cannot now be ascertained what was the origin of the acquaintance between the D'Israeli and Murray families,' Samuel Smiles notes:

> The first John Murray published the first volumes of Isaac D'Israeli's 'Curiosities of Literature', and though no correspondence between them has been preserved, we find frequent mention of the founder of the house in Isaac D'Israeli's letters to John Murray the Second.[12]

John Murray II published several editions of 'Narrative Poems' and *Flim Flams* (1804), favouring Isaac D'Israeli's work as a writer and compiler of anecdotes.[13] Isaac and John Murray II also vacationed together in Margate and discussed literary matters frequently. 'Mrs. D'Israeli will receive particular gratification from the interesting note you have sent us on the birth of our boy – when she shall have read it,' Isaac wrote to John Murray on 22 December 1804. Benjamin Disraeli, who considered *Literary Character* 'the most perfect' of his father's compositions,[14] went on to write three novels with Byronic characters, including *Vivian Grey* (1826), which parodied John Murray and ended the two-decade friendship with the family. Byron remained an important influence in Isaac D'Israeli's home, where 'the name of Byron was always held in reverence'.[15] Benjamin Disraeli found Byron's gondolier in Venice, Giovanni Battista Falcieri, and hired him to serve as his father's personal valet in London;[16] literary forefatherdom thus extended in many different directions, over literal and literary genealogies.

These facts are worth reiterating because the modern version of John Murray II's letters lists Isaac D'Israeli simply as a 'poet, man of letters and father of the prime minister and novelist, Benjamin Disraeli' without acknowledging his essential role as advisor to Murray. Isaac D'Israeli hoped to be John Murray II's guide over the Alps, as it were, of literary authorship: '[H]e thinks all belles lettres are nonsense, and denies the existence of taste,' D'Israeli wrote of one author, 'but it exists! and I flatter myself you will profit under that divinity. I have much to say on this subject and on him when we meet.'[17] They met so often that it is surprising Murray's friendship with Isaac D'Israeli, and the latter's role in fostering Byron's fame, have been so overlooked.[18] Perhaps one reason is confidentiality. 'It is a most disagreeable office to give opinions on MSS,' D'Israeli wrote in 1804, and

> one reads them at a moment when one has other things in one's head – then one is obliged to fatigue the brain with thinking; but if I can occasionally hinder you from publishing nugatory works, I do not grudge the pains. At the same time I surely need not add, how very confidential such communications ought to be.[19]

Murray was happy to rely upon D'Israeli as a literary forefather, in large part because Isaac knew Murray's actual father, John Murray I. In short, D'Israeli was a man whose eighteenth-century tastes influenced Byron and Murray in equal measure.

By the time Robert Charles Dallas presented Byron's manuscript of *Childe Harold* to Murray, D'Israeli had shaped Murray's tastes so that he might 'profit under [the] divinity' of Byron's genius.[20] Murray acknowledges this on 7 September 1812, when he quotes D'Israeli to encourage Byron to complete *Childe Harold*: 'Indeed my Lord [Lord Byron], I hope that you will cut the tugging strings of care and allow your mind to soar into its congenial element of Poesy':

> From a delirious Earth avert thine eyes
> And dry thy fruitless tears, and seek fictitious Skies
> D'Israeli[21]

D'Israeli's behind-the-scenes involvement in that poem's publication is made manifest in Murray's letter, only his second to Byron (the first was in 1811). Perhaps he deserves a more prominent place in Nicholson's appendix, 'How Murray Became Byron's Publisher'. D'Israeli was a great fan. He loved 'the Corsair', as he noted on 3 February 1814. He attended a dramatic performance of the poem with Murray and wrote, in 1815:

> I am anxious to tell you, that I find myself, this morning, so strangely affected by the perusal of the poem [*Siege of Corinth*] last night, that I feel that it is one which stands quite by itself. I know of nothing of the kind which is worthy of comparison with it.[22]

He compared the poem favourably to the work of Homer and preferred some passages of *Marino Faliero* (1821) to Shakespeare.[23]

D'Israeli claims that he came upon a copy of Byron's marginalia in *Literary Character* accidentally ('a copy accidentally fell into my hands', he says of the 1795 edition; 'a gentleman from Italy shared his copy with me', D'Israeli states, regarding the 1818 edition, though the gentleman was the British Captain Fyler). Murray was clearly responsible for both accidental discoveries. Murray and D'Israeli were in touch almost every day. No doubt Murray had begun the game of anonymity at his periodical, the *Quarterly Review*, which William Gifford found so essential: 'Be active and secret!' Gifford wrote.[24] Murray encouraged D'Israeli to expand *Literary Character* into a second edition in order to promote Byron. D'Israeli appears in the illustration where Walter Scott and Byron converse at 50 Albemarle Street, Murray's publishing house, and Ogden asserts he 'was probably present at the famous first meeting',[25] though Murray does not mention D'Israeli as being present on that occasion.[26] 'It was not fair of you to show my copy,' Byron complained to Murray of the 1795 edition,[27] but Murray's brilliant marketing move, in 1813 and 1818, helped to increase the author's sales. Murray's fostering of Walter Scott's friendly relations with the poet prove that Murray could be relied upon to employ such behind-the-scenes tactics, without which he never would have been so spectacularly successful.[28] In the most justly famous example, Murray asked Scott to review *Childe Harold* III for the *Quarterly Review*.

As the recipient of such literary favours, Byron informed Murray that he had 'twice read' Isaac D'Israeli's work, according to the latter's preface in the 1818 edition:

> a copy which has accidentally fallen in to my hands formerly belonged to the great poetical genius of our times, and the singular fact that it was twice read by him in two subsequent years, at Athens, in 1810 and 1811, instantly convinced me that the volume deserved my attention [. . .]. The marginal notes of the noble writer convey no flattery – but amidst their pungency and sometimes their truth, the circumstance that a man of genius could, and did read, this slight effusion at two different periods of his life was a sufficient authority, at least for an author, to return it once more to the anvil.

D'Israeli allows readers to peep behind the covers of the 1795 edition of his work, lent to him by Murray: '*The defects of great men are the consolation of the dunces*' appears underlined in D'Israeli's volume. Byron responded to D'Israeli's comment in the 1818 edition by writing on page iv (Fig. 1)[29] that

> I was wrong, but I was young and petulant, & probably wrote down any thing little thinking that those observations would be betrayed to the Author whose abilities I have always respected & whose works in general I have read oftener than perhaps those of any English author whatever – except such as treat of Turkey, –

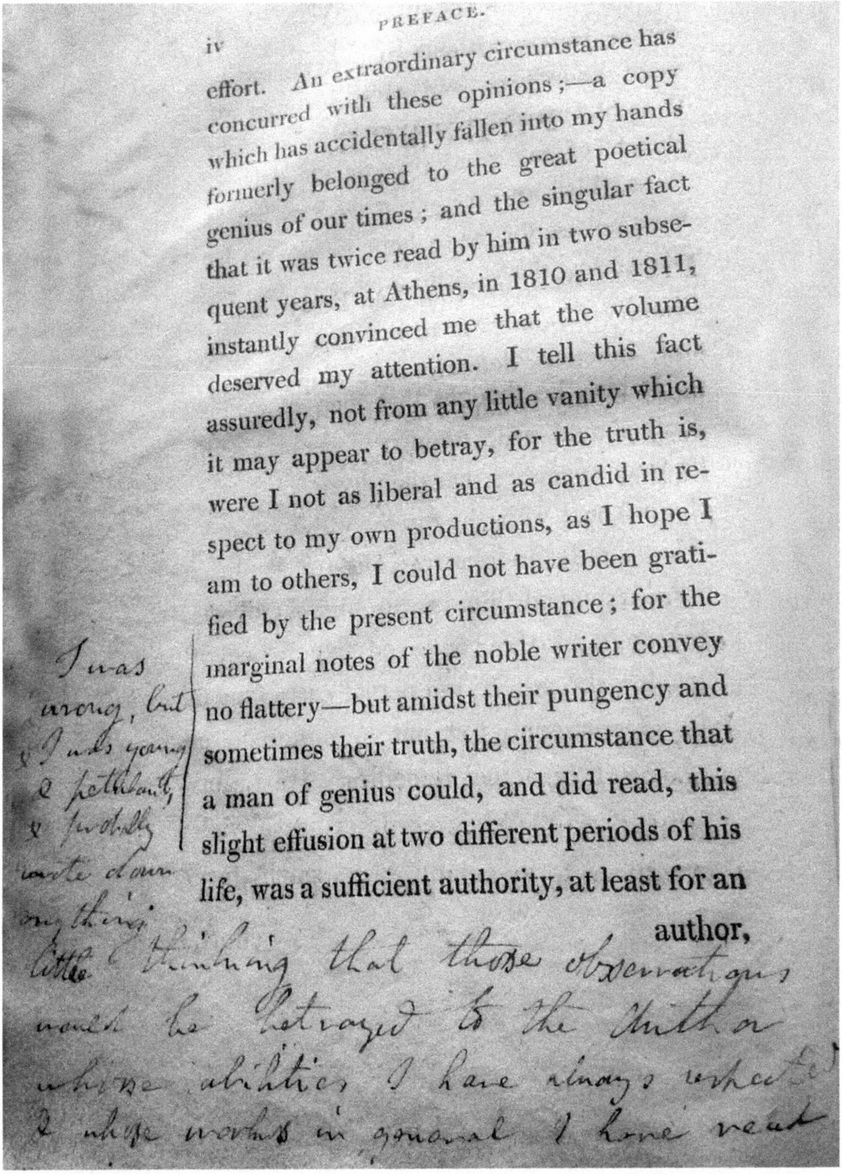

iv

PREFACE.

effort. An extraordinary circumstance has concurred with these opinions;—a copy which has accidentally fallen into my hands formerly belonged to the great poetical genius of our times; and the singular fact that it was twice read by him in two subsequent years, at Athens, in 1810 and 1811, instantly convinced me that the volume deserved my attention. I tell this fact assuredly, not from any little vanity which it may appear to betray, for the truth is, were I not as liberal and as candid in respect to my own productions, as I hope I am to others, I could not have been gratified by the present circumstance; for the marginal notes of the noble writer convey no flattery—but amidst their pungency and sometimes their truth, the circumstance that a man of genius could, and did read, this slight effusion at two different periods of his life, was a sufficient authority, at least for an author,

*I was wrong, but I was young & petulant, & probably wrote down anything. little thinking that those observations would be betrayed to the author whose abilities I have always respected & whose works in general I have read*

Figure 1  From Isaac D'Israeli's *Literary Character of Men of Genius* (1818, 2nd edition); courtesy of Kislak Center for Special Collections, University of Pennsylvania, Preface iv.

By 1818, when Byron's popularity was waning, the poet realised just how valuable D'Israeli could be.[30] Byron thus took the initiative of sharing his marginalia with Captain Fyler, who gave it to Anna Jameson in Venice; she returned the book to D'Israeli, through Murray,

for further circulation. As we have seen, Murray never failed to follow up on a lead that would help Byron, or a friendship that pro-
moted sales. 'Thus they prop one another's rickety heads at M –'s
shop, and a spurious reputation, like a false argument, runs in a cir-
cle,' Hazlitt complained. 'Cr-k-r affirms that G-ff-rd is sprightly, and
G-ff-rd that Cr-k-r is genteel: D'I – that J-c-b is wise, and J-c-b that
D'I – is good natured.'[31] When Benjamin Disraeli rudely satirised
Murray in *Vivian Grey* (1826) – after both men lost money in South
American mines and in a political newspaper, *The Representative* –
Isaac's close friendship with Murray was briefly interrupted. Isaac's
last contribution to the *Quarterly Review* was a review of *Spence's
Anecdotes*, for which he was paid 50 pounds in 1820.[32]

In the mean time, D'Israeli assisted Murray in promoting Byron's
fame. 'From the perusal of Rycaut's folio of Turkish history in childhood, the noble and impassioned bard of our times retained those
indelible impressions, which gave life and motion to the "Giaour",
the "Corsair", and "Alp",' D'Israeli wrote in *Literary Character*.
Byron not only read Rycaut but also breathed life into him. 'Without
this Turkish history', according to D'Israeli, 'we should still have
had our poet'. Though he ridicules his earlier work as the product of
haste, Byron now uses D'Israeli's book to revisit his career. Aristocratic *jeux d'esprit* that took 'a week each' to write[33] are now refash-
ioned by Byron as the product of lifelong study.

> Knolles. Cantemir. De Tott. Lady Mary Wortley Me. Hawkins's
> translation from Mignot's History of the Turks – the Arabian Nights
> all travels or histories or books upon the East I could meet with I had
> read as well as Rycaut before I was ten years old (p. 51)

Byron writes in the margins of the 1818 copy of D'Israeli's book. One
is not incompatible with the other, but where Byron once represented
himself as a careless dandy, 'noble and impassioned', he now markets himself as a child prodigy, formidably learned. This, of course,
fits D'Israeli's own formula for men of genius. If Byron's reading
does not impress, then his outrageous comments will. 'I was oftener
tempted to turn Mussulman than poet,' he scribbles in the 1818 edition of D'Israeli's *Literary Character*, twisting the book sideways
and separating his notes with lines, to make his comments legible
(Fig. 2). He even shows his irritability, providing direct evidence for
D'Israeli's chapter title, 'On the Irritability of Genius'.

D'Israeli disagrees with Byron only to make his praise more genuine, in a sham travesty of anonymity. 'The great poetical genius of

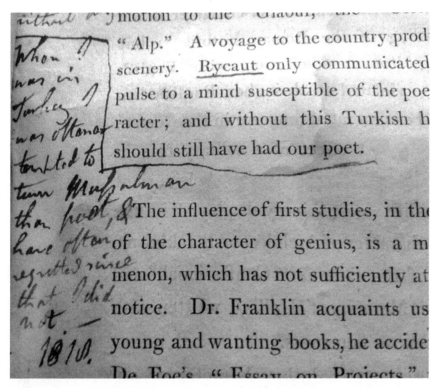

Figure 2 From Isaac D'Israeli's *Literary Character of Men of Genius* (1818, 2nd edition); courtesy of Kislak Center for Special Collections, University of Pennsylvania, p. 51.

our times has openly alienated himself from the land of his brothers,' D'Israeli wrote in *Literary Character*:

> He becomes immortal in the language of a people whom he would contemn; he accepts with ingratitude the fame he loves more than life, and he is only truly great on that spot of earth, whose genius, when he is no more, will contemplate (on) his shade in anger and in sorrow.

Byron provided a footnote for 'land of his brothers' ('Cains'), and D'Israeli may well have prompted Byron to think of himself as an exile. 'What was rumoured of me in that Language?' Byron wrote in the margins of D'Israeli's *Literary Character* (Fig. 3):

> – if true – I was unfit for England – If false – England was unfit for me. – 'there is a World Elsewhere'; I have never regretted for a moment that country – but often that I ever returned to it at all. It is

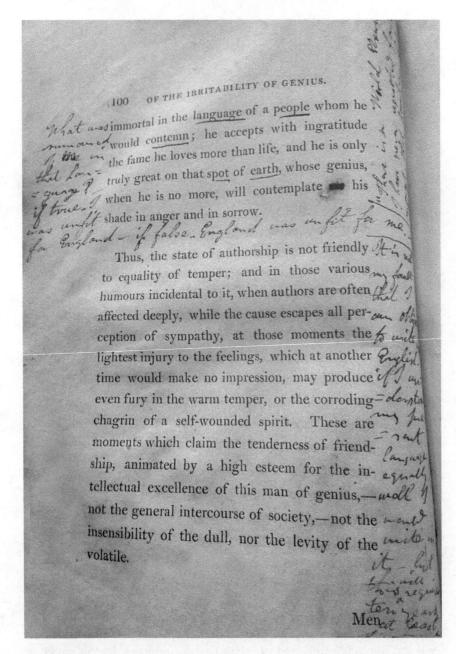

What was immortal in the language of a people whom he would contemn; he accepts with ingratitude the fame he loves more than life, and he is only truly great on that spot of earth, whose genius, when he is no more, will contemplate his shade in anger and in sorrow.

Thus, the state of authorship is not friendly to equality of temper; and in those various humours incidental to it, when authors are often affected deeply, while the cause escapes all perception of sympathy, at those moments the lightest injury to the feelings, which at another time would make no impression, may produce even fury in the warm temper, or the corroding chagrin of a self-wounded spirit. These are moments which claim the tenderness of friendship, animated by a high esteem for the intellectual excellence of this man of genius,—will not the general intercourse of society,—not the insensibility of the dull, nor the levity of the volatile.

Figure 3  From Isaac D'Israeli's *Literary Character of Men of Genius* (1818, 2nd edition); courtesy of Kislak Center for Special Collections, University of Pennsylvania, p. 100.

not my fault that I am obliged to write in English – if I understand my present language equally well I would rather write in it – but this will require ten years at least to form a Style, no tongue so easy to acquire a little of, or so difficult to master thoroughly as Italian . . . .[34]

Both *Cain* (1821) and *Don Juan* reflect D'Israeli's influence on Byron's imagination, as does D'Israeli's translation of such poems as 'Mejnoun and Leila', a possible source for Byron's Leila in *The Giaour* and *Don Juan* (1819–24).[35] Byron imagined his exile as comparable to the Hebrew exodus, continuing the marginal relationship to mores in Regency England by collaborating with Isaac Nathan on *The Hebrew Melodies* against the objections of John Cam Hobhouse and John Murray.

Byron's next entry in D'Israeli's 1818 edition concerns Vittorio Alfieri, 'a brother-spirit in our own noble poet', of whom D'Israeli writes

[they] were rarely seen amidst the brilliant circle in which they were born; (1) the workings of their imagination were perpetually emancipating them, and one deep loneliness of feeling (2) proudly insulated them, among the impassioned triflers of their rank.

Byron added two notes and underscored Disraeli's poignant phrase, 'deep loneliness of feeling'. Those notes read as follows:

1. I fear this was not the case – I have been but too much in that circle, especially in 1812–13–14.
2. true.

Byron was caught between acknowledging his dandyism and recognising he was a lonely spirit. He conformed to D'Israeli's portrait, fascinated by the latter's astute insights:

Genius contracts those peculiarities of which it is so loudly accused in its solitary occupations – that loftiness of spirit, those quick jealousies, those excessive affections and aversions which view everything as it passes in its own ideal world, and rarely as it exists in the mediocrity of reality [. . .]. The great poetical genius of our own times has openly alienated himself from the land of his brothers [footnoted as 'Cains' by Byron]. He becomes immortal in the language of a people whom he would contemn. Does he accept with ingratitude the fame he loves more than life?[36]

D'Israeli edited the passage as follows:

> I shall preserve a manuscript note of Lord Byron on this passage;
> not without a hope that we shall never receive from him the genius
> of Italian poetry, otherwise than in the language of his 'father land':
> an expressive term which I adopted from the Dutch language some
> years past and which I have seen since sanctioned by the pens of Lord
> Byron and of Mr. Southey. His lordship has here observed, 'It is not
> my fault that I am obliged to write in English. If I understand my
> present language equally well, I would rather write in it – but this will
> require ten years at least to form a Style, no tongue so easy to acquire
> a little of, or so difficult to master thoroughly as Italian.'[37]

D'Israeli defines the term 'father land' with regard to Byron and England, even as he emphasises Byron's foreignness. Although Byron's
relationship to Scotland and to the Scottish-born Walter Scott and
John Murray might qualify as another fatherland (*Don Juan* X, ll.
129–36),[38] D'Israeli adapts this term from the Dutch in a way that
reminds us of how vexed this question was for D'Israeli. Benjamin
Disraeli claimed his family was descended from the Spanish 'Laras',
concealing their origins in Cento in the province of Ferrara, Italy, as
Portuguese exiles escaping the Spanish Inquisition.[39] Isaac's son was
able to become Prime Minister only by converting as a young boy.[40]

Even if the Jews counted as forefathers of another sort, Byron's final
notation in D'Israeli's *Literary Character of Men of Genius* shows him
to be influenced by the latter's observations of 1795[41] and 1818:

> When the heads of the town, unawares to Petrarch, conducted him
> to the house where the poet was born, and informed him that the
> proprietor had often wished to make alterations, but that the towns-
> people had risen to insist that the house which was consecrated by
> the birth of Petrarch should be preserved unchanged; this was a tri-
> umph more affecting to Petrarch than his coronation at Rome.

Byron scribbled in the margins of D'Israeli's book:

> It would have pained me more that the proprietor should have 'often'
> wished to make alterations than (that) it could give pleasure that the
> rest of Arezzo rose against his right (for right he had)[;] the deprecia-
> tion of the lowest of mankind is more painful than the applause of
> the highest is pleasing[;] the sting of a Scorpion is (far) more a torture
> than the possession of anything short of Venus could be in rapture.[42]

Byron's last marginal comment in D'Israeli's 1818 edition thus anticipates themes that recurred in *Childe Harold* IV, *Don Juan* and 'The

Lament of Tasso' (1817): disgraced fatherlands, neglected tombs and genius persecuted by dunces.

By the time D'Israeli published his 1818 edition, Byron was already an unwitting subject, contributor and collaborator. When the poet died, however, D'Israeli dedicated the fourth edition to Robert Southey.[43] 'Knowing each other primarily through their books,' he wrote in the dedication, 'they had long enjoyed "an intimacy, without the inconvenience, often resulting from a personal acquaintance"'.[44] The irony of sharing a book with Byron's most public literary enemy may never have occurred to D'Israeli. In fact, he barely knew Southey personally, and D'Israeli's biographer speculates that Byron's meetings with D'Israeli were few and far between, as we shall see. Such was the literary *character* of men of genius, however. They were most sociable when least present.

## 2.

D'Israeli met Byron a few years before he travelled abroad. 'Such a fantastic and effeminate thing I never saw,' D'Israeli wrote.

> It was all rings and curls and lace. I was ashamed to speak to him; he looked more like a girl than a boy. I remember his shirt collar was all thrown over from his neck, and I observed him, while he spoke to some one, fence with a light cane in a very affected manner.

On a second meeting, Byron seemed transformed.[45] 'Shortly after the publication of the second Canto of Childe Harold I met his Lordship again and viewed him with a very different interest,' D'Israeli writes. 'He was entirely changed. I never met a man with a more modest, gentlemanly, and perfectly unaffected manner. He was now in full fame, and until he left England I often met him.'[46] The fencing, 'with a light cane', confirms Murray III's anecdote, though Nicholson dismisses it as 'profoundly questionable'.[47]

On 22 May 1813, Byron wrote to Murray to return D'Israeli's *Curiosities of Literature* and to ask for a copy of Thomas Moore's *Twopenny Postbag* (1813), offering to review the latter. Byron strikes a less respectful tone in a letter to Moore. 'I must tell you a story,' Byron writes on 25 July 1813:

> [Morris] (of indifferent memory) was dining out the other day, and complaining of the P[rince]'s coldness to his old wassailers. D*** (a learned Jew) bored him with questions – why this? And why that?

'Why did the P[rince] act thus?' – 'Why, sir, on account of Lord **
who ought to be ashamed of himself.' – 'And why ought Lord ** to
be ashamed of himself?' – 'Because the P[rince], sir, *******' 'And
why, sir, did the P[rince] cut *you?*' – 'Because, G–d d–mme, sir, I stuck
to my principles.' – 'And *why* did you stick to your principles?' Is not
this last question the best that was ever put, when you consider to
whom? It nearly killed M**[Morris].[48]

D'Israeli's naïveté was a ruse, according to Benjamin, and Byron
concurred.[49] 'I have been sparring with Jackson for exercise this
morning,' Byron wrote on 17 March 1814,

> and mean to continue and renew my acquaintance with the muffles.
> My chest, and arms, and wind are in very good plight, and I am
> not in flesh. [. . .] Redde the 'Quarrels of Author' (another sort of
> *sparring*) – a new work, by that most entertaining and researching
> writer, Israeli. They seem to be an irritable sect, and I wish myself
> well out of it. (*BLJ*, vol. 3, p. 251)

Byron distinguishes D'Israeli as 'entertaining and researching',
distinct from the 'irritable set' he wished himself 'well out of'. '"I'll
not march through Coventry with them, that's flat,"' he wrote,
quoting *Henry IV*. 'What the devil had I to do with scribbling? It
is too late to inquire, and all regret is useless' (*BLJ*, vol. 3, p. 252).
Byron worried that continuing down the path that he had chosen
was not only effeminate but also isolating (*BLJ*, vol. 3, p. 252). He
wrote of D'Israeli again on 12 June 1815, adopting a tone of facetious disregard.

> Murray, the bookseller, has been cruelly cudgelled of misbegotten
> knaves, 'in Kendal Green', at Newington Butts, in his way home
> from a purlieu dinner – and robbed, – would you believe it? – of
> three or four bonds of forty pounds a piece, and a seal-ring of his
> grandfather's, worth a million! This is his version, – but others opine
> that D'Israeli, with whom he dined, knocked him down with his last
> publication, 'the Quarrels of Authors', in a dispute about copyright.
> Be that as it may, the newspapers have teemed with his 'injuria for-
> mae', and he has been embrocated and invisible to all but the apoth-
> ecary ever since. (*BLJ*, vol. 4, p. 297)[50]

About this same time, in 1815, George Ticknor also mocked the
bibliophile[51] as the butt of many jokes, though the young Harvard

graduate may have misread ridicule for envy, an effort to dislodge D'Israeli from his cherished position as Murray's confidant. We have no record of Murray and D'Israeli's numerous intimate dinner conversations but a plan to visit Waterloo was foiled by Murray's ill health. Instead, Murray was accompanied by D'Israeli's nephew on 17 July 1815, and joined the author of *Literary Character* after.[52] Byron wrote to D'Israeli for a final time in 1823, encouraging him to inspect his 'Memoir'.

## 3.

My third section summarises Byron's encounters with D'Israeli,[53] though their literary encounters, through marginalia, were more circuitous. Anna Jameson's *Diary of an Ennuyée* (1826) partially transcribes Byron's marginalia in the third edition of D'Israeli's book (1818). Jameson read Fyler's copy of Byron's marginalia in *Literary Character* in Venice, before Fyler returned to England. 'A little while ago Captain F. lent me D'Israeli's *Essays on the Literary Character*,' she wrote, 'which had once belonged to Lord Byron; and contained marginal notes in his hand-writing.' She adds that

> Mr. F. told us at Venice, that on entering the states subject to Austria, he had his Johnson's Dictionary taken from him, and could never recover it; so jealous is the government of English principles and English literature, that *all* English books are prohibited until examined by the police.[54]

If he read Johnson, Fyler may also have marked up sections of D'Israeli's book; he was not averse to writing his address, 19 Dover Street, on the back flap, or annotating references to several pages.[55] On the other hand, Fyler most likely preserved Byron's pencil marks, knowing their value, and shared Byron's marginalia with Jameson and, eventually, D'Israeli. The auctioneer's letter claims that Byron gave the book to Fyler. 'The book is given additional melancholy interest from the fact that Byron presented it, ten days before his death, to his dear friend and companion, Mr. Fyler,' this letter claims,

> whose book-stamp and initials appear on the flyleaf facing title-page, at the top of which is written in the poet-chieftain's hand: 'this book belonged to Lord Byron and was given by him to Mr. Fyler when he parted from him at Athens. – Byron/'.[56]

William Marshall disproves this and raises an important question.

> The fact that Byron was not in Athens during his final Greek journey
> presents a problem [. . .]. The signature appears quite certainly to be
> Byron's, while the inscription would seem to be that of another, one
> who did not know the details of Byron's last journey, perhaps a later
> member of the Fyler family who was trying to reconstruct for poster-
> ity the provenance of the book.[57]

Marshall's conjecture is magnanimous, since forgery is also possible,
perhaps by Captain Byron. Evidence for a forged note includes the
following: the note is historically inaccurate, as Lord Byron gave the
book to Fyler in 1818, not 1824; 'this book' is scrawled in darker
ink than the poet's signature, which it in part obscures; and a boxy
'r' of Lord Byron's signature is written tentatively, as if to resemble or
imitate the poet's own signature.[58] Finally, and perhaps most importantly, auctioneers would consider Lord Byron's bequeathing of a
book to Fyler ten days before he died far more valuable, because
marked by pathos, than one merely handed to a captain between
1818 and 1824.

Most of the pencil marks are written in the same hand, though
two may be by Anna Jameson. Four lines from Byron's *The Giaour*
appear at the bottom of one page, in response to Akenside's 'Ode
to Study' in D'Israeli's book: 'the keenest pang the wretched feel / is
rapture to the dreary void / That fearless Desert of the mind / That
waste of feelings unemployed – Byron' (Fig. 4).

Another pencilled note appears next to allegations of Roman
immodesty ('because we are Christians'; Fig. 5), which seems to be
written in a feminine hand that differs from the penned annotations;
the phrase is possibly Jameson's, and some of the passages regarding
art may well be hers as well, including the allusion to *The Giaour*.
She possessed the book in Venice, long enough to have marked it
up, and she may not have been as careful as Fyler. She certainly read
all of Byron's annotations in pen well enough to summarise them. If
Byron's, then the poet would have been suggesting a further poem for
inclusion by D'Israeli, whose book would be returned by Fyler. The
other fifty-seven annotations tally with Byron's interests: solitude,
exile, genius, and what became known as the Pope–Bowles controversy, with Byron following D'Israeli's lead.[59] If all of the remaining
pencil marks are, in fact, his, then Byron finished reading the second edition of *Literary Character* by November of 1818. He marked
passages on Moses Mendelsohn (9), Isaac Newton (1), Galileo (1),

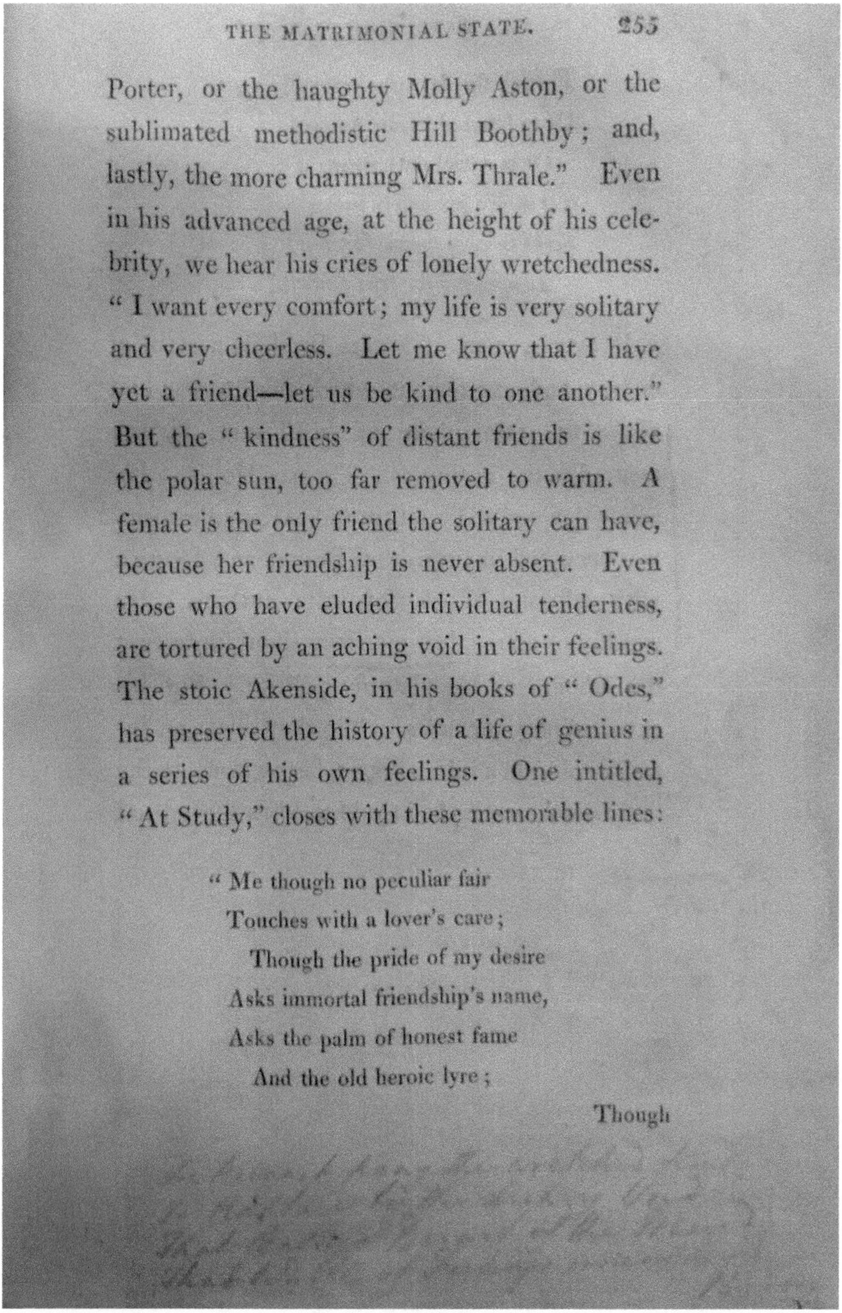

THE MATRIMONIAL STATE.   255

Porter, or the haughty Molly Aston, or the
sublimated methodistic Hill Boothby; and,
lastly, the more charming Mrs. Thrale." Even
in his advanced age, at the height of his celebrity, we hear his cries of lonely wretchedness.
" I want every comfort; my life is very solitary
and very cheerless. Let me know that I have
yet a friend—let us be kind to one another."
But the " kindness" of distant friends is like
the polar sun, too far removed to warm. A
female is the only friend the solitary can have,
because her friendship is never absent. Even
those who have eluded individual tenderness,
are tortured by an aching void in their feelings.
The stoic Akenside, in his books of " Odes,"
has preserved the history of a life of genius in
a series of his own feelings. One intitled,
" At Study," closes with these memorable lines:

> " Me though no peculiar fair
> Touches with a lover's care;
>   Though the pride of my desire
> Asks immortal friendship's name,
> Asks the palm of honest fame
>   And the old heroic lyre;
>
>                       Though

Figure 4  From Isaac D'Israeli's *Literary Character of Men of Genius*
(1818, 2nd edition); courtesy of Kislak Center for Special Collections,
University of Pennsylvania, p. 255.

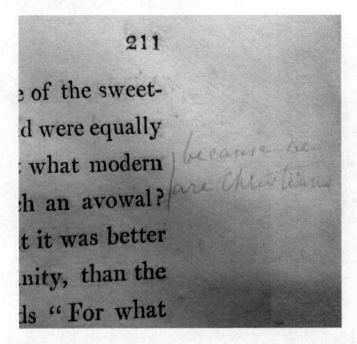

Figure 5  From Isaac D'Israeli's *Literary Character of Men of Genius*
(1818, 2nd edition); courtesy of Kislak Center for Special Collections,
University of Pennsylvania, p. 211.

Euclid, Benjamin Franklin (2), Racine (1) and Corneille (1). Below I
have placed a slanted line next to the first word in a passage presumably marked by Byron in D'Israeli's book:

> 1. Mendelsohn . . . was a / Polish Jew, expelled from the communion of
> the / Orthodox, and the calumniated student was now a vagrant, with
> more sensibility than fortitude. But this vagrant was a philosopher,
> a poet, a naturalist, and a mathematician. Mendelsohn, at a distant
> day, never alluded to him / without tears . . . . / Then was seen one of
> the most extraordinary spectacles in the history of modern literature.
> Two houseless Hebrew youths might be dis / covered in the moonlight
> streets of Berlin, sitting in, retired corners, or on the steps of some /
> porch, the one instructing the other, with an Euclid in his hand, what
> was more extraord / inary, it was a Hebrew version, composed by /
> himself, for one who knew no other language. Who could then have
> imagined that the future / Plato of Germany was sitting on those steps!
>   The Polander, whose deep melancholy had settled on his heart, died –
> yet he had not lived in vain, since the electric spark that lighted up / the
> soul of Mendelsohn had fallen from his own. (p. 65)

2. When we reflect on the magnitude of the labours of Cicero, Erasmus, Gesner, Baronious, Lord Bacon, Usher, and Bayle, we seem asleep at the base of these monuments of study, and scarcely awaken to admire. Such / are the laborious instructors of mankind! (p. 149)

3. To this habit of continuity of attention [Byron's X in margin here] tracing the first simple idea / through its remoter consequences, Galileo and Newton owed many of their discoveries. It was one evening in the cathedral of Pisa that Galileo observed the vibrations of a brass lustre pendant from the vaulted roof. (p. 157)

4. After D'Israeli cites *English Bards*: / Thus comes the shadow of death among those who are existing with more than life about them. Yet there is no celebrity for the artist [. . .]. (p. 190)

5. / In substituting fortune for the object of his designs, the man of genius deprives himself of the / inspirations of him who lives for himself; that is, for his Art. If he bends to the public taste, not daring to raise it to his own, he has not the choice of his subjects, / which itself is a sort of invention. (p. 244)

6. At the moment the poet Rousseau was giving versions of the Psalms, full of unction, as our neighbours say, he was profaning the same pen with the most infamous of epigrams. We have heard of an erotic poet of our times composing sacred poetry, or night-hymns in churchyards. The pathetic genius / of Sterne played about his head, but never reached his heart (p. 283)

7. After comments on the sensual Corneille and the 'tender Racine', D'Israeli argues that 'It is not therefore surprising if we are often erroneous in the conception we form of the personal character of a distant author. Klopstock was / an enthusiast for retirement only when writing verses' (286).

8. In proving that the character of the man may be very opposite to that of his writings, we / must recollect that the habits of life may be / contrary to the habits of the mind [see #13]. (p. 292)

9. Though there may be no identity between the book and the man, still for us, an author is ever an abstract being, and, as one of the Fathers said, 'a / dead man may sin dead, leaving books that make others sin'. An author's wisdom or his folly does not die with / him. The volume, not the author, is our companion, and is for us a real personage, performing before us, whatever it inspires; 'he being dead, / yet speaketh'. Such is the vitality of a book! (p. 294)

10. The people are a vast body, of which / men of genius are the eyes and the hands; and the public mind is the creation of the philosophical writer; these are axioms as demonstrable as / any in Euclid, and as sure in their operation, as any principle in mechanics. (p. 352)

11. How, therefore, can the character of an author be considered as politicians do not secretly think so, at the moment they are proclaiming to the world; nor do they fancy, as they would have us imagine, / that

paper and pens are only rags and feathers; whatever they affect, the truth is, that they consider the worst actions of men as of far less / consequence than the propagation of their opinions. They well know, as Sophocles declared, that 'opinion is ever stronger than truth'. (p. 354)

12. Observe the influence of authors in forming the character of men, where the solitary man of genius stamps his own on a people. The / parsimonious habits, the money-getting precepts, the wary cunning, and not the most scru / pulous means to obtain the end, of Dr. Franklin, imprinted themselves on his Americans; loftier feelings could not elevate a man of genius, who became the founder of a trading people. (p. 355)

13. Beccaria abolished torture [. . .] Locke and Voltaire on 'Toleration' have long made us tolerant, but the principles of many works of this stamp have become so incorporated in our / minds and feelings, that we can scarcely at this day conceive the fervour they excited at the / time, or the magnanimity of their authors in the decision of their opinions. (p. 360)

14. Feyjoo, the first popular authors of their nations who taught England, France, and Spain to become a reading people; while their fugitive page imbues with intelligent sweetness and an un / cultivated mind, like the perfumed mould which the swimmer in the Persian Sadi took up; it was a piece of common earth, but astonished at its fragrance, he asked whether it was musk / or amber? 'I am nothing but earth, but roses were planted on my soil, and their odorous virtues have deliciously penetrated through all my / pores.' (p. 362)

Forty more pencilled marks appear, touching on various themes. In D'Israeli's book, Byron read that authors were honoured in medieval and Renaissance Europe. 'Petrarch was at once invited by the city of Rome and the court of France, to receive the crown of laurel.'[60] In England, by contrast, '[m]en of letters, in our country resemble "houseless wanderers" scattered and solitary, disunited and languid'.[61] The cynical, worldly and ironic tone of the book, with its mention of John Moore's *Zeluco*,[62] makes it easy to see what Byron admired. Anticipating Byron's *The Vision of Judgment* (1822), for example, D'Israeli skewered Wilkes as an unprincipled fellow who gave up the 'fervours of literary and patriotic glory' to become a 'domestic voluptuary'.[63] D'Israeli also satirised prolific authors who ruined their publishers with unwelcome trash that made even the bookshelves groan, anticipating Byron's comic portrait of George III begging off from Southey's fatuous verses.[64]

At a time when there was simply too much literature to digest fully in a single year, D'Israeli distinguished 'men of letters' from the 'man of genius'. Soon the distinction fell apart. Though he once argued that genius was innate (1795), he now came to believe it was acquired (1818, 1823), perhaps inspired by his own increasing fame. Citing D'Israeli as the predecessor for his own book entitled *Genius* (2002), Harold Bloom distinguishes two ancient Roman meanings in ways that are helpful to my analysis of forefathers in this essay:

> One is to beget, cause to be born, that is to be a paterfamilias. The other is to be an attendant spirit for each person or place: to be either a good or evil genius, and so to be someone who, for better or for worse, strongly influences someone else.

For Bloom, to be a literary genius is to be a forefather or 'paterfamilias' (women authors of powerful imagination also qualify, and D'Israeli cites Clairon, a French actress 'before she saw a theatre').[65] Bloom notes that 'We all learn to distinguish, firmly and definitively, between genius and talent. A "talent" classically was a weight or sum of money, and as such, however large, was necessarily limited. But "genius", even in its linguistic origins, has no limits.'[66] Competing in the trade of bookselling, John Murray conflates 'genius' and celebrity ('fame'). 'The fame of Byron's genius is invaluable to me,' he writes.[67] Applying Bloom's distinction, we could say that Murray begat Byron's genius[68] through clever marketing of his 'talent'.

Had D'Israeli not encouraged Murray II to publish a man of genius and to use D'Israeli to vet manuscripts, Murray II might never have published *Childe Harold*. Had John Murray II not encouraged Byron to 'marginalise' in Isaac D'Israeli's book by sending him a copy, and then shared this annotated copy with D'Israeli, who was a close friend, Byron's own reputation would not have received a 'puff' when Fyler, Jameson and D'Israeli read his marginalia that were included in the third edition.[69] D'Israeli developed a new genre for bibliophiles of the Romantic age that drew on the anecdote, a strategy he no doubt gleaned from his extensive research on Jean-Jacques Rousseau.[70] D'Israeli negotiated the terms of Byron's genius. Byron was fully aware of D'Israeli's role in the poet's status as celebrity author and responded with perfect irony and poise in 1823 to the new edition of D'Israeli's *Literary Character*: 'I really cannot know whether I am, or am not, the genius you are pleased to call me, – but I am very willing to put up with the mistake, if it be one.' 'Byron was always haunted with the fear and the necessity of plagiarism,' D'Israeli concluded. 'He need not have been alarmed. He is one of the most original of writers.'[71] Murray exhibited Romantic sociability,[72] helping D'Israeli appreciate his own value.

> The fact is my works being all about the feelings of literary men were exceedingly interesting to him [Byron]. They contained knowledge which he could get nowhere else. It was all new to him. He told me he had read my works over and over again. I thought this of course a compliment, but some years afterwards found it to be true.[73]

## Notes

1. *CMP*, p. 219.
2. Spevack, *Curiosities Revisited: The Works of Isaac D'Israeli*, p. 103. On Byron's copy of the second edition, see Marshall, 'The Byron Collection in Memory of Meyer Davis, Jr.', pp. 9–10.
3. See Felluga, *Perversity of Poetry: The Romantic Ideology and the Popular Male Poet of Genius*, pp. 105–42; and Cafarelli, 'Byron and the Pathology of Genius', pp. 205–21.
4. *BLJ*, vol. 9, p. 171. D'Israeli dedicated the fourth edition to Robert Southey; Spevack, *Curiosities Revisited: The Works of Isaac D'Israeli*, p. 105.
5. Ogden, *D'Israeli*, p. 107; *CMP*, p. 546; *BLJ*, vol. 5, p. 42. Ogden and Nicholson's formulation differs from that of Donald Reiman, who asserts that 'Captain Fyler showed the book to D'Israeli himself, who included Byron's notes in the Preface to the third edition,' Reiman and Fischer, *Shelley and His Circle, 1773–1822*, vol. 10, p. 561.
6. *BLJ*, vol. 6, p. 84.
7. Stabler, *The Artistry of Exile*, p. 47, n. 30.
8. Smiles, *A Publisher and His Friends: Memoir and Correspondence of the Late John Murray, with an Account of the Origin and Progress of the House, 1768–1843*, vol. 1, p. 270.
9. Nicholson, *Letters of John Murray*, p. 14.
10. Smiles, *A Publisher and His Friends*, vol. 1, p. 41.
11. Cline, 'Unpublished Notes on the Romantic Poets by Isaac D'Israeli', p. 139.
12. Smiles, *A Publisher and His Friends*, vol. 1, p. 41.
13. D'Israeli, *Flim-Flams! Or the Life and Errors of my Uncle, and the Amours of my Aunt, with Illustrations and Obscurities, by Messrs. Tag, Rag, and Bobtail*, p. 43. Zachs, *The First John Murray*, pp. 239, 247.
14. Monypenny, *The Life of Benjamin Disraeli, Earl of Beaconsfield*, vol. 1, p. 13.
15. Ibid., p. 15. Maurois, *Disraeli: A Picture of the Victorian Age*, p. 9.
16. Ogden, *D'Israeli*, p. 120.

17. Smiles, vol. 1, p. 49.
18. Ibid., vol. 1, pp. 41–55.
19. Ibid., vol. 1, p. 50.
20. Nicholson, *Letters of John Murray*, p. 471, Appendix A.
21. Smiles, vol. 1, p. 9.
22. Ibid., vol. 1, pp. 223, 358.
23. Ogden, *D'Israeli*, p. 119.
24. Smiles, *A Publisher and His Friends*, vol. 1, p. 123.
25. Ogden, *D'Israeli*, p. 122.
26. Smiles, *A Publisher and His Friends*, vol. 1, p. 267.
27. Ogden, *D'Israeli*, p. 107.
28. Smiles, *A Publisher and His Friends*, vol. 1, pp. 374, 376.
29. D'Israeli, *Literary Character*, Meyer Davis copy, p. 4. (The volume that Byron annotated is now in the Meyer Davis collection in the University of Pennsylvania Library); Rare Book Collection. Byron PN150.D52 1818.) All references are to the 1818 edition, unless marked 1795. D'Israeli, *An Essay on the Manners and Genius of the Literary Character* (1795); D'Israeli, *The Literary Character, Illustrated by the History of Men of Genius, Drawn from their own Feelings and Confessions* (1818).
30. *CMP*, p. 219.
31. Ogden, *D'Israeli*, p. 136.
32. Ibid., p. 136.
33. Smiles, *A Publisher and His Friends*, vol. 1, p. 222; Jameson, *Diary of an Ennuyée*.
34. D'Israeli, *The Literary Character*, p. 100.
35. D'Israeli, *Romances*; Cardonne outlines 'Mejnoun and Leila', and D'Israeli versifies it.
36. D'Israeli, *The Literary Character*, p. 122.
37. Ibid., p. 122.
38. Clubbe, 'Byron and Scott', p. 85.
39. Monypenny, *The Life of Benjamin Disraeli*, p. 5.
40. Ibid., p. 23.
41. Disraeli, *The Literary Character*, p. ix.
42. Ibid., p. 221.
43. Cline, 'Unpublished Notes', p. 139, n. 5.
44. Ogden, *D'Israeli*, p. 126. Southey thought D'Israeli 'thoroughly good-natured', with a mixture of 'information and ignorance, cleverness and folly'. Southey, *Selections from the Letters of Robert Southey*, vol. 3, p. 352. Cited in Ogden, 'D'Israeli, Isaac (1766–1848)'.
45. Cline contradicts himself: 'It is not known exactly when or where D'Israeli and Byron met, though it is possible that the meeting occurred at the home of John Murray, publisher to both Byron and D'Israeli, who provided virtually the only connection between D'Israeli and the outside world,' 'Unpublished Notes', p. 137. D'Israeli was not such a recluse and he notes that he met Byron well before the latter became famous.

46. Cline, 'Unpublished Notes', p. 142.
47. Nicholson, *Letters of John Murray*, p. xvii. Nicholson may have other reasons for this assertion.
48. *BLJ*, vol. 3, p. 79.
49. Ogden, *D'Israeli*, p. 107.
50. Also quoted in Smiles, *A Publisher and His Friends*, vol. 1, p. 268.
51. Ibid., vol. 1, p. 271.
52. Ibid., vol. 1, pp. 273, 277.
53. Stabler, *The Artistry of Exile: Romantic and Victorian Writers in Italy*, p. 47.
54. Jameson, *Diary of an Ennuyée*, p. 85.
55. Flyleaf, Meyer Davis Collection, pp. 134, 168, 192.
56. Auctioneer's Letter, Meyer Davis Collection, copy.
57. Marshall, 'The Byron Collection in Memory of Meyer Davis, Jr.', p. 10. See also Nicholson, *Letters of John Murray*, pp. 73–4; and *CMP*, pp. 219–21, 546–49; Quennell, *Byron: A Self-Portrait*, vol. 2, p. 467; Marshall, 'The Byron Collection', pp. 9–10. Reiman mentions 'Thomas Fyler', see Reiman, *Shelley and His Circle 1773–1822*, vols 7 and 8, p. 561. While Thomas Bycliffe Fyler did live on 19 Dover Street, his bookplate does not match the JBF insignia. Perhaps the bookplate belonged to his brother, James, who acquired the work subsequently; Stabler, *The Artistry of Exile*, states that 'the Rowles party saw Byron's original marginal annotation in the copy he gave to Captain Fyler', p. 47.
58. Title page, D'Israeli, Meyer Davis Collection. See Ehrsam, *Captain Byron Major Byron – The Incredible Career of a Literary Forger*.
59. Byron meditated on the subject as early as 15 February 1817 (*BLJ*, vol. 5, p. 174), publishing in 1821.
60. D'Israeli, *The Literary Character*, p. xii.
61. Ibid., p. 4.
62. Ibid., p. 288.
63. Ibid., p. 109.
64. Ibid., 1795 preface, p. ix.
65. Ibid., pp. 45–7, at p. 47.
66. Bloom, *Genius: A Mosaic of One Hundred Exemplary Creative Minds*, p. 7.
67. Nicholson, *Letters of John Murray*, pp. 73–4.
68. Malek, 'Isaac D'Israeli, William Godwin, and the Eighteenth-Century Controversy Over Innate and Acquired Genius', pp. 47–64.
69. Connell, 'Bibliomania: Book Collecting, Cultural Politics, and the Rise of Literary Heritage in Romantic Britain', see p. 45, n. 33.
70. [Anon.], *Historical and Literary Memoirs and Anecdotes, Selected from the Correspondence of Baron de Grimm and Diderot with The Duke of Saxe-Gotha, And Many Other Distinguished Persons, Between the Years 1753 and 1790; Translated from the French* (1815), 4 vols.
71. Cline, 'Unpublished Notes', p. 141.

72. Tuite and Russell, *Romantic Sociability: Social Networks and Literary Culture in Britain, 1770–1840.*
73. Cline, 'Unpublished Notes', p. 141.

## Works cited

[Anon.] (1815) *Historical and Literary Memoirs and Anecdotes, selected from the Correspondence of Baron de Grimm and Diderot with The Duke of Saxe-Gotha, And Many Other Distinguished Persons, Between the Years 1753 and 1790; Translated from the French*, 4 vols, London: Henry Colburn.

Batten, Guinn (1998), *The Orphaned Imagination: Melancholy and Commodity Culture in English Romanticism*, Durham, NC: Duke University Press.

Bloom, Harold (2003), *Genius: A Mosaic of One Hundred Exemplary Creative Minds*, New York: Warner.

Cafarelli, Annette Wheeler (1993), 'Byron and the Pathology of Genius', in: Alice Levine and Robert N. Keane (eds), *Re-Reading Byron: Essays Selected from the Hofstra University's Byron Bicentennial Conference*, New York: Garland, pp. 205–21.

Cline, Clarence Lee (1941), 'Unpublished Notes on the Romantic Poets by Isaac D'Israeli', *Studies in English*, 21, pp. 138–46.

Clubbe, John (1973), 'Byron and Scott', *Texas Studies in Literature and Language*, 15, pp. 67–91.

Connell, Philip (2000), 'Bibliomania: Book Collecting, Cultural Politics, and the Rise of Literary Heritage in Romantic Britain', *Representations*, 71, pp. 24–47.

D'Israeli, Isaac (1795), *An Essay on the Manners and Genius of the Literary Character*, London: T. Cadell and W. Davies.

— (1799/1805), *Romances*, London: Cadell.

— (1806), *Flim-Flams! Or the Life and Errors of my Uncle, and the Amours of my Aunt, with Illustrations and Obscurities, by Messrs. Tag, Rag, and Bobtail*, London: John Murray.

— (1818), *The Literary Character, Illustrated by the History of Men of Genius, Drawn from Their Own Feelings and Confessions*, 2nd edn (with Byron's marginalia), London: John Murray.

— (1822), *The Literary Character, or the History of Men of Genius, Drawn from Their Own Feelings and Confessions*, London: John Murray.

Ehrsam, Theodore G. (1951), *Captain Byron Major Byron – The Incredible Career of a Literary Forger*, London: John Murray.

Felluga, Dino (2005), *Perversity of Poetry: The Romantic Ideology and the Popular Male Poet of Genius*, New York: SUNY.

Jameson, Anna (1826), *Diary of an Ennuyée*, London: Henry Colburn.

Malek, James (1980), 'Isaac D'Israeli, William Godwin, and the Eighteenth-Century Controversy Over Innate and Acquired Genius', *Rocky Mountain Review of Language and Literature*, 34, pp. 47–64.

Marshall, William H. (1967), 'The Byron Collection in Memory of Meyer Davis, Jr.', *Library Chronicle*, 33, pp. 8–29.

Maurois, André (1964), *Disraeli: A Picture of the Victorian Age*, Upper Saddle River, NJ: Prentice-Hall.

Monypenny, William Flavelle (1913), *The Life of Benjamin Disraeli, Earl of Beaconsfield*, 2 vols, New York: Macmillan.

Nicholson, Andrew, ed. (2007), *Letters of John Murray*, Liverpool: Liverpool University Press.

Ogden, James (1969), *D'Israeli*, Oxford: Oxford University Press.

— (2004), 'D'Israeli, Isaac (1766–1848)', in: H. C. G. Matthew and Brian Harrison (eds), *Oxford Dictionary of National Biography*, Oxford: Oxford University Press; online edition, ed. Lawrence Goldman, May 2008, available at http://www.oxforddnb.com.ezproxy.depaul.edu/view/article/7690 (last accessed 9 December 2015).

Plato (1999), *Euthyphro, Apology, Crito, Phaedo, Phaedrus*, trans. Harold North Fowler, Loeb Classical Library, Cambridge, MA: Harvard University Press.

Quennell, Peter (1950), *Byron: A Self-Portrait, Letters and Diaries, 1798–1824*, 2 vols, New York: Charles Scribner's Sons.

Reiman, Donald H. (1986), *Shelley and His Circle 1773–1822*, vols 7 and 8, Cambridge, MA: Harvard University Press.

Reiman, Donald H. and Doucet Devin Fischer, eds (2005), *Shelley and His Circle, 1773–1822*, vols 9 and 10, Cambridge, MA: Harvard University Press.

Smiles, Samuel (1891), *A Publisher and His Friends: Memoir and Correspondence of the Late John Murray, with an Account of the Origin and Progress of the House, 1768–1843*, 2 vols, London: John Murray.

Spevack, Marvin (2007), *Curiosities Revisited: The Works of Isaac D'Israeli*, Hildesheim / New York: Olms.

Stabler, Jane (2011), *The Artistry of Exile: Romantic and Victorian Writers in Italy*, Oxford: Oxford University Press.

Tuite, Clara (2015), *Lord Byron and Scandalous Celebrity*, Cambridge: Cambridge University Press.

Tuite, Clara and Gillian Russell, eds (2006), *Romantic Sociability: Social Networks and Literary Culture in Britain, 1770–1840*, Cambridge: Cambridge University Press.

Zachs, William (1998), *The First John Murray and the Late Eighteenth-century London Book Trade, with a Checklist of his Publications*, Oxford: Oxford University Press.

# III. Cherishing the Marginal – Marginal Genres in Byron

# Chapter 8

# 'Like a Flash of Inspiration': Byron's Marginalised Lyricism in *Hebrew Melodies*

## Michael O'Neill

### 1.

Despite distinguished critical work, often of a contextual kind, in recent decades by critics such as Frederick Burwick and Paul Douglass, Kurt Heinzelman, Sheila A. Spector, Stuart Peterfreund, Toby Benis, Tom Mole, Jeremy Davies and others,[1] Byron's *Hebrew Melodies* (1815) tend to be marginalised in accounts of his work. Two poems – 'She Walks in Beauty' and 'The Destruction of Sennacherib' – receive the dutiful homage exacted by their status as anthology pieces but, for the most part, the rest of the volume languishes in relative obscurity. There is an evident irony in this marginalisation, partly the result of the downgrading of Byron's lyrical verse in favour of his more ambitious longer poems and tales, since *Hebrew Melodies* is a volume that deals with the historical experience of the Jewish people, a race marginalised and worse in Western Christian culture. Byron is capable of anti-Semitic gibes at the expense of his musical associate, Isaac Nathan, or at least of ventriloquising such gibes: 'why do you always twit me with his vile Ebrew nasalities' (*BLJ*, vol. 4, p. 280), an insult made, one presumes, to placate his addressee, Thomas Moore, who felt Byron was treading on his patch in the volume.[2] Yet he displays what Nathan describes as 'a peculiar feeling of commiseration towards the Jews'.[3] In this respect, Benis comments on the way in which biographers of the poet 'have linked the poet's awareness of his own moral isolation from British society to his compassion for the idea of the Jews as a people in Diaspora, scattered across a hostile, Christian Europe'.[4] Moreover,

Nathan is clear that in the portraiture of the Jewish cause, Byron saw an image of 'the truly distressed state of Ireland'.[5]

Whether these perceptions result in appropriation of Jewish experience of an invalid or presumptuous kind is one critical issue that the poetry raises. Siding with the marginalised evidently risked transgression of orthodox Christian norms, as the response of some conservative contemporary reviewers reveals. Jeremy Davies, for example, quotes the reviewer for the *British Review* of August 1815 as remarking that 'a young Lord is seldom the better for meddling with Jews'.[6] But in their sometimes conflicted tonalities, Byron's melodies are not necessarily going to satisfy, either, what Benis postulates as 'a Regency-era Hebrew scholar'.[7] Nor in the same critic's words does the volume 'resemble any other kind of "national air" produced at the time'.[8] Nor, finally, is it clear that the volume takes solace in the idea of creating 'another metaphorical homeland: the artistic pursuit of beauty expressed through musical tropes and heritage'.[9]

This is not to deny that the volume undertakes an 'artistic pursuit of beauty' or that 'musical tropes and heritage' matter greatly to it. Its fineness, however, has much to do with its refusal to accept standard cultural attitudes, including the satisfactions of aesthetic self-delight. It eludes contemporary or subsequent frameworks for the understanding of Romantic lyric. Cannily, it appeals to the reader wishing to consume it uncritically, yet its creative energies question and scrutinise their own purposes. In this respect, when Frederick W. Shilstone describes the volume as 'Byron's discourse on art, an examination of how his poetry takes the materials of a transient world of process and lends them the grace of immortality',[10] a word to emphasise is 'examination'. It is an unstable, fascinating volume, oscillating between the personal and historical, the Jewish and Christian, the losses of history and the recompense of song, the raw and the cooked, at once a 'discourse on art' and, in places, a critique of its ultimate insufficiency, the lyrical and the meta-lyrical.

## 2.

The volume's complex achievement is the subject of the present essay, which takes its title from Byron's reported comment to Nathan about 'My Soul Is Dark' and focuses in this section on analyses of five poems, two strongly Hebraic, three less evidently so, in keeping with Byron's decision to include poems only indirectly related to the overt theme of the volume, but linked to it in their concern with feeling, music, song and mood.[11] Of 'My Soul Is Dark' Nathan writes:

> It was generally conceived, that Lord Byron's reported singularities, approached on some occasions to derangement, and at one period indeed, it was very currently asserted, that his intellects were actually impaired. The report only served to amuse his Lordship. He referred to the circumstance, and declared, that he would try how a *Madman* could write; seizing the pen with eagerness, he for a moment fixed his eyes in majestic wildness on vacancy; when like a flash of inspiration, without erasing a single word, the above verses were the result, which he put into my possession with this remark: 'if I am mad who write, be certain that you are so who compose!' There were occasions, nevertheless, on which his Lordship seemed grieved at the misrepresentations that were made of him: they were however transitory, and became afterwards the subject of his jocularity and wit.[12]

There is a great deal of art in Byron's lyrics, yet they often have an effect of 'a flash of inspiration'. Nathan's account brings out the blend of posturing and power evident in much of Byron's work. The poet simulates, one suspects, the onset of the *furor poeticus* but, in so doing, attains it too. Byron adopts what Maureen N. McLane calls 'a longstanding topos of charismatic and traditional authority' and asks whether such 'authority' is still available to the contemporary poet.[13] Byron's lyrics take on the perspectives of Old Testament figures and model these perspectives in the light of the poet's own lyric needs, desires and energies. Re-examining the lyric art and imaginative force of poems frequently marginalised in accounts of Byron's poetic career, this section will offer brief comparisons with the lyricism of other Romantic poets, including Wordsworth, Shelley and Moore.

To turn to the poem Byron produced for Nathan in 'a flash of inspiration':

> 1.
> My soul is dark – Oh! quickly string
> The harp I yet can brook to hear;
> And let thy gentle fingers fling
> Its melting murmurs o'er mine ear.
> If in this heart a hope be dear,
> That sound shall charm it forth again –
> If in these eyes there lurk a tear,
> 'Twill flow – and cease to burn my brain:

2.

But bid the strain be wild and deep,
Nor let thy notes of joy be first:
I tell thee, minstrel, I must weep,
Or else this heavy heart will burst;
For it hath been by sorrow nurst,
And ach'd in sleepless silence long;
And now 'tis doomed to know the worst,
And break at once – or yield to song. ('My Soul Is Dark', ll. 1–16)

Byron occupies a subtly mobile position in the poem, both Saul demanding song and David, the 'minstrel', supplying it, almost as though David were wording Saul's wish to hear David's song. He deploys stylistic techniques that interweave the gnomic authority of the Old Testament and the syntactical subtlety of the modern lyrical poet. The overall impression of 'a flash of inspiration', if we grant Byron's poem the effect its composition excited in Nathan, is partly the effect of a short opening sentence full of suggestiveness: 'My soul is dark.' Lyrical, speaking from the centre of a self, not exactly confessional, the poem is an act of verbal contrivance serving an ideal of the authentic; it contrives, that is, to suggest a purity of feeling, a whole-souled knowledge and communication of the soul's despondency. In so doing it artfully recalls, as E. H. Coleridge notes, an Ossianic turn of phrase, 'My soul is dark' from 'Oina-Morul'.[14] In turn, this state is at one with and passes into the desire to hear a flow of sound. The result is to make the poem itself seem like an answer to the poet's wish for a sound that both answers to and, in some sense, offsets his soul's darkness.

The poet-speaker asks for sounds from '[t]he harp I yet can brook to hear', where the stress on 'yet' implies the speaker's closeness to a state in which he could not 'brook to hear' any sounds. That wish relates to the distracting, calming effect of listening to song, a synecdoche for poetry itself, an effect brought out in the 'If' clauses of the last four lines of this opening stanza. Poetry will, the speaker hopes, work cathartically, and allow him to entertain again 'hope' and grief (in the form of the, as yet unshed, 'tear'). The act of speech or song will contribute to a process of recovery and expression, and save the speaker from two intertwined conditions: lack of knowledge of his true condition (the song will serve as a litmus test to determine whether 'in this heart a hope be dear') and escape from overwrought feeling (the tear, once shed, will 'cease to burn my brain'). Yet the poem 'knows' more than the speaker; in its condition of achieved lyric, it supplies a model for the blend of outcry and solace that the speaker desires. This achievement comes at a price, however, in that the poem's life consists in its mimicry of unstable, conflicted feelings; their continued rehearsal is the condition of its artistic existence: an existence that answers in its own way to the Hegelian account of lyric as paraphrased by Jonathan Culler: namely, that its 'distinguishing feature is the centrality of subjectivity coming to consciousness of itself through experience and reflection'.[15]

At the start of the second stanza, 'But', Byron's signature conjunction, implies a shift, as if the first stanza had seemed escapist in its apparent desire for an anodyne music made up of 'melting murmurs'. Now Byron / Saul demands that the 'strain be wild and deep'; his 'dark soul' is at once beyond words and in sympathy with his 'heavy heart'. Peremptory, almost morbid, ache and longing determine the abruptness of the close. When the speaker asserts that his heart is 'doomed to know the worst' he implies that song may ensure he confronts 'the worst', as though song possessed prophetic knowledge of futurity; in this respect, the final phrase, 'or yield to song', is an alternative and sequel to knowing the worst as it phrasally chimes syntactically across the poem with 'My soul is dark.' In yielding to song, the soul can express and, to a degree, bring light to its darkness.

The poem uses two devices that Byron employs in other *Hebrew Melodies*: firstly, that of clipped, suggestive abstraction, the use of words such as 'joy' and 'sorrow' in tetrameter rhythms that oblige diction to work vigorously; secondly, that of repeated rhyme. Although the immediate impression is of alternating quatrain rhymes, the sustaining of the *b* rhyme in each stanza's first quatrain so that it becomes the *a* rhyme of each stanza's second quatrain creates a sense of retardation, of a turning back, as though the prospect of knowledge of and escape from gloom were questioning as well as articulating itself. Especially when line 5 recurs in its sound to line 4, the speaker seems unable to let go of a feeling; in stanza 1 the feeling is associated with appeals to the 'ear' of what is 'dear' and might provoke a welcome 'tear'; in stanza 2 there is a stress on inner pent-up emotion as a result of which the 'heart will burst, / For it hath been by sorrow nurst'; 'nurst', there, has a quietly sardonic force, as in Shelley's use of a comparable word and device in lines that his Byron figure, Maddalo, speaks in *Julian and Maddalo* (1824): 'Most wretched men / Are cradled into poetry by wrong, / They learn in suffering what they teach in song' (ll. 544–6). The two words 'nurst' and 'cradled' are wrenched out of their usual context in jarringly eloquent ways.[16] Lyric poetry for both writers is a 'natural' activity nurtured by complex processes of emotional exclusion.

In 'I Saw Thee Weep', a different rhyme scheme serves a different emotion:

> 1.
> I saw thee weep – the big bright tear
> Came o'er that eye of blue;
> And then methought it did appear
> A violet dropping dew:
> I saw thee smile – the sapphire's blaze
> Beside thee ceased to shine:
> It could not match the living rays
> That fill'd that glance of thine.
>
> 2.
> As clouds from yonder sun receive
> A deep and mellow dye,
> Which scarce the shade of coming eve
> Can banish from the sky,
> Those smiles unto the moodiest mind
> Their own pure joy impart;
> Their sunshine leaves a glow behind
> That lightens o'er the heart. ('I Saw Thee Weep', ll. 1–16)

For Giorgio Agamben, an important way of understanding a poem is Paul Valéry's definition of poetry as 'a prolonged hesitation between sound and sense (*hésitation, prolongée entre le son et le sens*)'.[17] This poem stages such a 'hesitation' through its pausing over its own sense of its meanings. It, too, is also concerned, initially, with weeping, but the weeping is a point of departure for a contrast with the smiles that take over the poem. Yet the contrast is also a parallel, and Nathan himself comments finely when he describes the poem as exhibiting 'a fine distinction between opposite feelings'.[18] Both tears and smiles offer the self a mode of emotional and aesthetic pleasure, almost disconcertingly annihilating, in so doing, the difference between weeping and laughter. Both states are grist to the mill of the poem's subjective use of emotional spectacle. Yet the hint of appropriating relish in the poem concedes its personal nature ('methought' betrays this awareness) and contends with a recognition of the addressee's alterity.

The poem's form of configuring its 'thee' acknowledges descent from Wordsworth's portrayal of Lucy in 'She dwelt among th' untrodden ways', though the singularity of Lucy, who calls forth startlingly divergent comparisons, both '[a] Violet by a mossy stone / Half-hidden from the Eye!'[19] and '[f]air, as a star when only one / Is shining in the sky!' (ll. 7–8),[20] passes in Byron's poem into a more socially available viewability. As '[a] violet dropping dew' the addressee is heir to Wordsworth's Lucy and the source of a new freshness of feeling. If Wordsworth prizes the fact that Lucy is '[h]alf-hidden', Byron shapes the woman's identity as open to transformative viewing. If this approach suggests a reading of the woman as available for poetic commodification, Byron complicates matters by allowing for the inadequacy of his subsequent simile; 'the sapphire's blaze / Beside thee ceased to shine', since the woman outshines the brilliant precious stone, an extinguishing caught in the sonic passage from 'blaze' to 'cease', before 'living rays' picks up the rhyme with 'blaze' and establishes, as though restoring, a recomposed awareness of the woman's otherness. The effect of the final lines of the stanza is almost circular, absorbed: 'living rays' offer the promise of a life-bestowing 'glance' and yet they also compose the nature of what Byron calls, with deictic precision, 'that glance'. It is the glance, so to speak, rather than the person who is receiving the glance (the speaker) that finally takes primary position in the stanza. And that glance takes in the workings of the poem itself.

Ernest Hartley Coleridge and Rosemary Ashton, McGann tells us in his edition, 'associate the poem with Lady Frances Wedderburn Webster, largely because of the "eye of blue" in line 2' (*CPW*, vol. 3, p. 469). Like a number of poems in *Hebrew Melodies*, the poem has enough specificity to invite biographical interest and enough lyric generality to absorb such specificity into its own poetic space. It does not require the reader to bring in any biblical or Judaic contexts, though the poem links with others that project Byron as soothing harpist to his own Saul-like gloom and, indeed, with the topos of weeping in the volume, the cumulative effect of which is to suggest lamentation as a near-permanent feature of culture. The long sentence that takes up the whole of the elegant second stanza recalls, in an even more minor key, the elegiac 'sober colouring'[21] of the minor key close of Wordsworth's 'Ode: Intimations of Immortality' (1815).

Again, Byron, for all the generalised lyric idiom in which he is working, seeks to tether his observations to particular experience, referring to 'clouds from yonder sun', by contrast with Wordsworth who speaks with grand impressiveness to '[t]he Clouds that gather round the setting sun',[22] clouds that are endlessly recurrent. The effect in Byron is to imply a shifting location of thought and feeling, and thus to reinforce the impression of an abiding preoccupation. Gathering and letting fall its implications, the sentence downplays and highlights interlocking opposites: the stanza's opening simile behaves as though the 'deep and mellow dye' is able to resist 'the shade of evening sky', while knowing that this shade '[c]an banish' the dye 'from the sky'. The stanza illustrates Byron's ability to create suggestions that go beyond the obvious or hackneyed, leaving the reader not only with '[a] deep and mellow dye, / Which scarce the shade of coming eve / Can banish from the sky', but also with a fugitive, steadfast glimpse of 'the moodiest mind' and its need for solace. It is a supple, poised lyric, halfway between sunshine and coming eve, and the lithe rhyming (only once does Byron pair the same part of speech – and that is when he talks of the dye that the sky retains) does much to give the poem its tilting balance and measured lilt.

Moore is an important forerunner of *Hebrew Melodies* and Shelley a major inheritor of the collection. Yet the poets work in different ways. Moore's 'The Harp That Once Through Tara's Halls' (1808) is cited as an influence by Peter Cochran in his website edition of the volume on Byron's 'Oh! Weep for Those'.[23] The two poems are given in succession:

*Oh! Weep for Those*
   1.
Oh! weep for those that wept by Babel's stream,
Whose shrines are desolate, whose land a dream;
Weep for the harp of Judah's broken shell;
Mourn – where their God hath dwelt, the Godless dwell!

   2.
And where shall Israel lave her bleeding feet?
And when shall Zion's songs again seem sweet?
And Judah's melody once more rejoice
The hearts that leap'd before its heavenly voice?

   3.
Tribes of the wandering foot and weary breast!
How shall ye flee away and be at rest?
The wild-dove hath her nest, the fox his cave –
Mankind their Country – Israel but the grave. (ll. 1–12)

*The Harp that Once Through Tara's Halls*
The harp that once through Tara's halls
The soul of music shed,
Now hangs as mute on Tara's walls
As if that soul were fled. –
So sleeps the pride of former days,

So glory's thrill is o'er,
And hearts, that once beat high for praise,
Now feel that pulse no more.

No more to chiefs and ladies bright
The harp of Tara swells;
The chord alone, that breaks at night,
Its tale of ruin tells.
Thus Freedom now so seldom wakes,
The only throb she gives
Is when some heart indignant breaks,
To show that still she lives.[24]

Moore's poem has a sharply defined clarity as it sets then against now, and is able to introduce clever nuances, as in the double meaning of 'shed': 'The soul of music' was both lavished on Tara's halls and discarded there, too, almost as though Moore were implying the possible futility of his own task as professional cultural elegist. Shelley surely remembered that effect in his late lyric, 'When the Lamp Is Shattered' in the line '[t]he rainbow's glory is shed'.[25] The rainbow's glory is projected and lost in a redeployment of Moore's double meaning. In both cases, lyric creates the music whose vanishing it laments and establishes a role for itself as personal or cultural memorialist.

Moore's poem grows more intricate, as he imagines a 'chord' surviving, participant in a movement towards extinction that cries out against its inevitable going. Cochran is right to detect its influence on Byron's poem, yet Byron wears his rue and remembrance with a difference; his relationship to the cultural subject matter of Jewish diasporic lament is less easy to read from or into the poem than is Moore's relationship with Ireland's wrongs and losses.[26] There are connections and parallels made by both Moore and Byron between Jewish and Irish sufferings. Stuart Peterfreund points out that 'Moore himself takes note of the similarities to be observed in the lots of the Irish and the Jews in an Irish melody entitled "The Parallel".'[27] Yet Moore's relations with Ireland are evident; Byron's with Jewish suffering are less so, except that in his act of virtuosic empathy he can summon up biblical cadences and imply, with that subtly flattering indirection that is his trademark, an obscure but deep link between apparently remote subject matter and private feeling, as well as feeling about public themes. Moore's example, had, at the very least, encouraged Byron, as Jeffrey W. Vail puts it, 'to indulge his penchant both for melancholy poetry and for the advocacy of the downtrodden'.[28]

Metrical tact is key to the success of 'Oh! Weep for Those', as, indeed, is the poem's modes of address to 'those' and, in the final stanza, 'ye'. In Thomas Ashton's words, 'Byron does not disappoint those who expect Hebrew Melodies about music to be richly musical.'[29] The ear waits for something more anapaestic, more rollicking from the first word that feels like a call to incantation. But the poem settles into an iambic rhythm with strong substitutions in the first feet of lines 3 and 4 and line 9; the result is that a tearless drive is given to the poem's call to the listener to duplicate the weeping of those 'who wept by Babel's streams'. The poet's exhortation to 'weep' is self-addressed, too, as though demanding an appropriate affective response of himself – with the implication that he is having to rise to the heights of a demandingly self-chosen theme; revealingly, McGann sees the poem 'as probably the first of the series which B[yron] wrote specifically as a "Hebrew Melody"' (*CPW*, vol. 3, p. 468). The impression of momentum, sustained in the questions of stanza 2 and the couplet rhymes, exists alongside a dignity of attitude. The final stanza makes evident Byron's sympathy for, rather than identity with, 'those that wept by Babel's stream'.

Like Moore's lyric, the poem proposes no answer to the displacements and losses that it bewails. Byron's speaker affectingly asserts in his poem's last line the exilic condition endured by Israel: 'Mankind' has its 'Country' – all people, that is, have their own country, all but the only country mentioned in the poem, Israel, which has only 'its grave'. 'We that look on but laugh in tragic joy', Yeats will write in 'The Gyres' (1938) of viewing the spectacle of recurrent cultural and historical losses.[30] Byron recommends, with dry-eyed intensity, that we should '[w]eep for the harp of Judah's broken shell; / Mourn – where their God hath dwelt the Godless dwell'. Only the poet's own implicit reconstruction of 'Judah's broken shell' through his poetic singing offers a possible source of consolation.

'Our sweetest songs are those that tell of saddest thought,' Shelley will write in 'To a Skylark' (1820),[31] and it is noticeable that a number of Byron's poems leave their traces on his lyrics. The confessional late poem, 'The Serpent Is Shut Out from Paradise' (1822), is, as William Keach has brought out, full of Byron, from Shelley's self-mocking use of Byron's 'favorite nickname' for him, the Snake, to the modified *ottava rima* in which it is written.[32] Both Shelley and Byron have recourse to an image in Matthew 8: 20, the Authorised Version at its barest and most majestic: 'The foxes have holes, and the birds of the air have nests, but the Son of man hath not where to lay his head.' Shelley writes:

The crane o'er seas and forests seeks her home.
No bird so wild, but has its quiet nest
When it no more would roam.
The sleepless billows on the Ocean's breast
Break like a bursting heart, and die in foam
And thus, at length, find rest.
Doubtless there is a place of peace
Where *my* weak heart and all its throbs will cease.[33]

Shelley's 'place of peace' sounds like a calculated euphemism for Byron's 'grave'; it is suggestive of the influence exercised by *Hebrew Melodies* that a cadence or allusion, adapted by Shelley to poignant personal ends, should stay in the mind of one of the period's greatest lyric poets. Shelley's resourcefulness shows in the way in which the lyric chord is sustained, the swept string kept vibrating, throughout the stanza. Many of his later lyric poems appear to announce an end, yet they persist in evoking the aftermath or prolongation of the end. In this case, the onward life of a breaking heart propels the lines, as though a series of afterthoughts maintained the poetry's life: thus in the lines, '[b]reak like a bursting heart, and die in foam, / And thus, at length, find rest', the long-vowelled assonance of 'length' and 'rest', along with the throbbing stress on monosyllabic words, does much to suggest a condition of imagined endurance and longed-for, scarcely attainable 'rest'.

Byron's rhythms in 'Oh! Weep for Those' are sturdier, brisker, sweeping up paradox as they go, at once emphatic and careering. The second stanza's series of questions beat against the walls of historical grievance and indifference, demanding a reply, knowing they will receive none. At the same time, the stanza serves a performative function, as is the case with much Romantic lyricism. It conjures up a simulacrum of the state it implicitly sees as impossible to attain, its final three lines imagining a revival, not simply of 'Zion's songs' and 'Judah's melody', but of their capacity to 'again seem sweet' and 'rejoice / The hearts that leap'd before its heavenly voice'. There, the movement across the line ending confirms that 'rejoice' is a transitive verb, corresponding to the hope embodied in the poem that the collection as a whole might affect the reader.

The couplet rhymes serve to express the poem's rising and falling of hope and despair, regathered energy and exhaustion. In the final stanza, the lines '[t]ribes of the wandering foot and weary breast, / How shall ye flee away and be at rest' demonstrate admirably an effect of 'speeding and slowing' that Yeats located in the lyrics of

Robert Bridges, in whose work he often found 'words often common-place made unforgettable by some trick of speeding and slowing'.[34] Yeats's example from Bridges is '[a] glitter of pleasure / And dark tomb', where the second line slows after the haste of the first. Comparably, in the third stanza of Byron's poem the first line exhibits a fine semantic tension between 'wandering' and 'weary', compulsive movement and inescapable fatigue, and the second line manages to 'flee' through the triple internal rhyme of 'ye', 'flee' and 'be', as if to deny the possibility glanced at by the rhyme word.

When, in one of the two most famous poems in *Hebrew Melodies*, 'She Walks in Beauty', Byron writes, '[o]ne shade the more, one ray the less / Had half impair'd the nameless grace / Which waves in every raven tress, / Or softly lightens o'er her face', his words might be applied as much to his own tonalities and nuances in his poem as to his 'cousin, the beautiful Mrs. Wilmot' (*CPW*, vol. 3, p. 467). Indeed, as Robert F. Gleckner has maintained, the poem's '"She" is not merely Lady Wilmot [. . .], but rather Woman – or mankind.'[35] It is at once, that is, a graceful, gendered tribute and a meditation on a transcendent quality of goodness:

> 1.
> She walks in beauty, like the night
> Of cloudless climes and starry skies;
> And all that's best of dark and bright
> Meet in her aspect and her eyes;
> Thus mellow'd to that tender light
> Which heaven to gaudy day denies.
>
> 2.
> One shade the more, one ray the less
> Had half impair'd the nameless grace
> Which waves in every raven tress,
> Or softly lightens o'er her face;
> Where thoughts serenely sweet express
> How pure, how dear their dwelling place.
>
> 3.
> And on that cheek, and o'er that brow,
> So soft, so calm, yet eloquent,
> The smiles that win, the tints that glow,
> But tell of days in goodness spent,
> A mind at peace with all below,
> A heart whose love is innocent! ('She Walks in Beauty', ll. 1–18)

James Wedderburn Webster's account of Byron's response to seeing the lady goes like this:

> When we returned to his rooms in Albany, he said little, but desired Fletcher to give him a *tumbler* of *Brandy*, which he drank at once to Mrs. Wilmot's health, then retired to rest, and was, I heard afterwards, in a sad state all night.

'Mrs. Wilmot [. . .] is a swan, and might frequent a purer stream,' Byron also wrote of the lady, a comment relevant to the poem's peculiar grace; it suggests the thin but absolute line between the woman's beauty and anything flirtatious or coquettish (*CPW*, vol. 3, p. 467). The poem places the woman in a space of her own, allowing her to swim down a 'purer stream' by suggesting how the 'smiles' and tints speak 'only' (the force of 'But' in line 16) 'of days in goodness spent'. She may 'walk in beauty, like the night / Of cloudless climes and starry night', but she is not in danger of wandering astray. Central to Byron's poetic ensnaring of the woman's *je ne sais quoi* is his celebration of a beauty that harmonises potential opposites: 'And all that's best of dark and bright / Meet in her aspect and eyes: / Thus mellow'd to that tender light / Which heaven to gaudy day denies.' Subtly associating the night in which the woman walks with the 'tender light' of 'heaven', Byron expels the 'gaudy day' in another anticipation of a Shelleyan motif: the superiority of starlight to daylight, a trope used throughout *The Triumph of Life* (1824). The poem's balance has to do with its interest in subtle shadings and rebalancings, enacted through the even rocking to and fro of the iambic octosyllabics and the alternating rhymes. Each stanza contains two rhymes only as Byron gives us access to '[a] mind at peace with all below, / A heart whose love is innocent', the more eloquently because we suspect that the onlooker, the poet, is not so 'at peace' or so 'innocent', where 'innocent' recovers its full meaning of not causing harm. The poem succeeds in avoiding blandness by an alertness to its own linguistic conduct; resourcefully, for example, the last stanza's *a* and *b* rhymes rhyme, firstly, noun, verb and preposition, and, secondly, adjective, verb and then, again, adjective – the two adjectives both trisyllabic words ('eloquent' and 'innocent') that imply the onlooker's work of observation and understanding.

The poem contains little that is explicitly Hebraic but the hymning of goodness earns the lyric its place in the collection. In the other best-known poem in *Hebrew Melodies*, the Hebraic context is starkly evident. This is 'The Destruction of Sennacherib:'

1.

The Assyrian came down like the wolf on the fold,
And his cohorts were gleaming in purple and gold;
And the sheen of their spears was like stars on the sea,
When the blue wave rolls nightly on deep Galilee.

2.

Like the leaves of the forest when Summer is green,
That host with their banners at sunset were seen;
Like the leaves of the forest when Autumn hath blown,
That host on the morrow lay withered and strown.

3.

For the Angel of Death spread his wings on the blast,
And breathed in the face of the foe as he pass'd;
And the eyes of the sleepers wax'd deadly and chill,
And their hearts but once heaved, and for ever grew still!

4.

And there lay the steed with his nostril all wide,
But through it there roll'd not the breath of his pride:
And the foam of his gasping lay white on the turf,
And cold as the spray of the rock-beating surf.

5.

And there lay the rider distorted and pale,
With the dew on his brow, and the rust on his mail;
And the tents were all silent, the banners alone,
The lances unlifted, the trumpets unblown.

6.

And the widows of Ashur are loud in their wail,
And the idols are broke in the temple of Baal;
And the might of the Gentile, unsmote by the sword,
Hath melted like snow in the glance of the Lord! (ll. 1–24)

The poem is one of a destructive power destroyed by a far greater power. Byron may obliquely be thinking of Napoleon,[36] though no straightforward parallels suggest themselves, and it is unclear whether Byron would have regarded Wellington as the vehicle of the Lord's workings. The poem captures the 'gleaming' menace of the Assyrian as he (both singular and collective) 'came down', the 'wolf on the fold' image suggesting his brutal energy and the curiously satisfying shimmer of power that is extended in line 2 to 'his cohorts [. . .] gleaming in purple and gold'. Byron strips the poetry of adjectives (only 'blue' and 'deep' serve as modifiers in this stanza, 'purple and gold' leading an absolute life of their own), and sets the scene with a flurry of nouns and verbs, organised into musical, energetic anapaests. There is a beauty in 'like stars on the sea, / When the blue wave rolls nightly on deep Galilee' that conjures up a world in concert with and yet wholly opposed to the warlike intent of those with shining spears.

Byron's source, 2 Kings 19: 33–6, reads as follows (Authorised Version):

> Therefore thus saith the LORD concerning the king of Assyria, He shall not come into this city, nor shoot an arrow there, nor come before it with shields, nor cast a bank against it. By the way that he came, by the same shall he return, and shall not come into this city, saith the LORD. For I will defend this city, to save it, for mine own sake, and for my servant David's sake. And it came to pass that night, that the angel of the LORD went out, and smote in the camp of the Assyrians an hundred fourscore and five thousand: and when they arose early in the morning, behold, they were all dead corpses. So Sennacherib king of Assyria departed, and went and returned, and dwelt at Nineveh.

Byron does a lot with his biblical source, making his poem more biblical than the Bible itself, albeit by means of 'the kind of visual opulence that would have delighted Cecil B. De Mille',[37] showing himself alert to the inexorable, even unimaginable will and ability to enforce of the Lord. He heightens the effect of Psalm-like parallelism through his use of anapaestic couplets and counterbalancing image sets that suggest power and its arrest by a greater power, as in the second stanza. Again the very smoothness of the rhyming couplets captures the overriding dominance of the Lord that brings about the destruction of the host, or as the poem's close has it: 'And the might of the Gentile, unsmote by the sword, / Hath melted like snow in the glance of the Lord.' It takes the reader a while to hear in full the deadly menace of the phrase 'unsmote by the sword', which suggests both its opposite, that they were sword-smitten, as though Byron has coined a new word for smiting with the sword, and the limits of mere human 'might'.

The poem seems to mimic in its movement the terrifying capacity to annihilate possessed by 'the glance of the Lord'. It structures itself out of opposites. An example that offers itself is the use of the word 'roll' or its cognates. At the close of the first stanza it implies a glossy recurrence: 'And the sheen of their spears was like stars on the sea, / When the blue wave rolls nightly on deep Galilee.' This nightly 'rolling' is contrasted with the fourth stanza's depiction of the horse's synecdochical death: 'But through it there roll'd not the breath of his pride.' That not rolling has the greater force for the implied contrast with the first stanza and through the work done by the word 'not'; we intuit the pride of the rolling breath even as we experience its cessation.

Moreover, the Lord's fiat of destruction is likened to seasonal change, so that the fallen host is '[l]ike the leaves of the forest when Autumn hath blown'. The simile suggests that the Lord's capacity for destruction has something of the regularity of the turning seasons, even as its singularity is stressed. Thus, there is a sense, in the comparison, of similitude and dissimilitude. Again, as result of the host being blown away, a situation is created in which 'the tents were all silent, the banners alone, / The lances unlifted, the trumpet unblown'. Tennyson will rework Byron's word 'unlifted' in a passage from 'Mariana' (1830): 'Unlifted was the clinking latch.'[38] Christopher Ricks points out that '[w]e strain our ears for the unforthcoming sound, for "uplifted", not "unlifted"', as we wait with Mariana for the lover who will never come.[39] Byron too, in the lances 'unlifted', brings the opposed activity to mind, only to assert its non-happening.

The same effect occurs with 'the trumpets unblown', which reminds us of the blowing of autumn earlier in the poem. Something similar happens when the Angel of Death 'breathed in the face of the foe as he pass'd', creating an effect exactly contrary to that of Genesis, and the account of Adam's creation, when God 'breathed into his nostrils the breath of life' (Genesis 2: 7). The breathlessness consequent upon the Angel's death-laden breathing in Byron's poem is asphyxiatingly dwelt on in two stanzas, and the poem, like the collection as a whole, fuses antitheses: the poet's breathing animates, almost parodically, the breathless corpses smitten by the Angel of the Lord, responding to the strangely uncanny blend of arising and dying in verse 35: 'and when they arose early in the morning, behold, they were all dead corpses'. The poem is no straightforward celebration of righteous power. As Benis points out, it 'ends with a sombre retreat from the battlefield to those left behind':[40] 'And the widows of Ashur', we learn, 'are loud in their wail.' Suffering is by no means restricted to the Jewish people.

3.

Is Byron in *Hebrew Melodies* proposing song, art, poetry and their 'redemptive harmony'[41] as the ultimate refuge against the devastations of history and culture? One's answer, I shall suggest, is at best mixed. It is striking how often song links itself, in the volume, less with certitude or assurance than with yearning. In 'If That High World', Byron opens with a conditional gesture that suffuses the poem, leading Nathan to comment to the poet 'that the monosyllable (if) with which it commenced, would doubtless form the ground of very grave condemnation'.[42] The wrap-around rhymes of lines 4 and 5 in each stanza suggest a persistence of hope, but also a concomitant doubt:

> If that high world, which lies beyond
> Our own, surviving Love endears;
> If there the cherish'd heart be fond,
> The eye the same, except in tears –
> How welcome those untrodden spheres!
> How sweet this very hour to die!
> To soar from earth and find all fears
> Lost in thy light – Eternity!
>
> It must be so: 'tis not for self
> That we so tremble on the brink;
> And striving to o'erleap the gulph,
> Yet cling to Being's severing link.
> Oh! in that future let us think
> To hold each heart the heart that shares;
> With them the immortal waters drink,
> And soul in soul grow deathless theirs! ('If That High World', ll.
> 1–16)

The poem expresses an impassioned feeling that love should survive death in the afterlife, but it is full of complications. It hopes for a state, in itself rendered with expressive obscureness, in which hearts and souls mingle after death, yet retain their unique capacity to love as they love on earth and to 'grow deathless'. But that post-mortal hope – of growing deathless – betrays a lack of trust that the post-mortal state in itself will be one of deathlessness, as though deathlessness might, at best, be the reward for continued striving after life is over. Indeed, the poem is more about the essential nobility of striving to 'o'erleap the gulph', a felicitously awry off-rhyme with the 'self' that would so 'o'erleap', than it is about any assurance that the 'high world' will be one which 'surviving Love endears'.

'It must be so' is an affecting phrase because it reveals the element of inescapable wish-fulfilment present in the poem. Poetry is the vehicle for such wish-fulfilment and a mode through which critique of wish-fulfilment can be made. But only when burdened by awareness that it can only express hope, which implies a state of incomplete knowledge, does the poetry seem a form of truth-telling. Such truth-telling, rather than any glorification of the capacity of poetry to confer immortality, is a salvageable value to emerge from the volume's treatment of song. It is a poem whose strongest tie is to '[b]eing's severing link', to the tearing but still existing bond that ties us to Being. Emily Brontë will refocus the intensity of Byron's line when, in 'Remembrance' (1845), the speaker imagines being cut off from memory of her beloved by '[t]ime's all-severing wave', her rhythms and wording a protest against such severing.[43]

In 'The Harp the Monarch Minstrel Swept' (1815), affirmation of the power of 'David's lyre' (l. 10) builds to a crescendo in the rhyme-supported last few lines of stanza 1, but in the comparable position in the second and final stanza, affirmation passes into a more self-qualifying mode:

> Since then, though heard on earth no more,
> Devotion and her daughter Love
> Still bid the bursting spirit soar
> To sounds that seem as from above,
> In dreams that day's broad light can not remove.
> ('The Harp the Monarch Minstrel Swept', ll. 16–20)

This hauntingly turned and tuned single sentence, among the most memorable moments in the volume, subjects prophetic claims for song to steadfast 'examination', to use Shilstone's word. Subjective desire and ardent hope are apparent in the lines, which pay eloquent tribute to '[d]evotion and her daughter Love', and their impact on 'the bursting spirit'. But the sounds of David's lyre are 'heard on earth no more', unavailable to the modern poet, who can at best imagine 'sounds that seem as from above', where 'seem' demands we attend to its suggestion of possible illusion, and who does so in possibly insubstantial 'dreams that day's broad light cannot remove'. Byron captures the pathos of the modern poet who cannot but pursue dreams that may be misleading.

He implies this pathos in his witty remark to Nathan, who needed the extra lines that are quoted above (ll. 16–20) to 'complete the verse': Nathan records Byron as saying, 'Here, Nathan, I have brought you down again,' having 'sent' him 'to Heaven'.[44] The joke disguises yet charts the poem's trajectory. The poem brings us down in the very act of suggesting 'sounds that seem as from above'. The rhyming of 'love' with 'above' and 'remove' may seem conventional, but the way in which the absolute abstraction, 'Love', seeks to link itself with what lies, it is hoped, 'above' and with 'dreams that day's broad light can not remove' shows Byron as a fine lyric poet of what might be called heart-broken longing for transcendence.

It is no accident that one of the most plangent songs about singing in the volume, 'By the Rivers of Babylon We Sat Down and Wept', presents a singer (or chorus of singers) singing of a virtuous refusal to sing. Aware of the corrupt uses of art enjoined by conquering power, the poem's 'we' assert:

> They demanded the song: but, oh never
> That triumph the stranger shall know!
> May this right hand be wither'd for ever,
> Ere it string our high harp for the foe!
> ('By the Rivers of Babylon We Sat Down and Wept', ll. 9–12)

Of course, the singer sings of the refusal to sing, but the defiance registered in these lines, curt in their very cantabile lilt, protects the 'high harp' from forced tribute and implies Byron's wariness of the purposes of art, song, music. It is a vigilance that serves him well in *Hebrew Melodies*.

Yet that vigilance is not incompatible with a drive, quite different in force from Moore's laments, towards a compacted violence of feeling, ultimately reactive, defiant and utopian in character, that keeps open a gaze towards what lies 'above' and articulates a stance of resistance to tyranny. That stance can be mocked, often by Byron himself, but it carries through his poetry until his great 'Missolonghi Melody', 'On This Day I Complete My Thirty-Sixth Year' (1824). That poem, weary, exhausted at its outset, a monument to heroic courage and fortitude by its end, is recognisably the product of the poet who composed 'On the Day of the Destruction of Jerusalem by Titus'. There, the captive speaker, about to be led in fetters to Rome, looks at the burning city; he thinks of the many times he has watched the sun declining but wishes, on this occasion, 'that the lightning had glared in its stead, / And the thunderbolt burst on its conqueror's head' ('On the Day of the Destruction of Jerusalem by Titus', ll. 15–16). Vail offers a fine comparison between this poem and Moore's 'Though the Last Glimpse of Erin with Sorrow I See'.[45] Strong as the connection between the poems is, what Moore's poem lacks is the vibrant protest, just quoted, that bursts from the speaker of Byron's poetry. Song may be a form of self-critiquing, sentimental rhetoric in Byron's hands, but it raises itself above mere self-deconstruction in *Hebrew Melodies*. It bears witness to longings, feelings and nobilities of hope that sustain a determination to speak for the victims of history, present and past, doing so, paradoxically, from the perspective of one who put himself at the centre of English literary culture through his empathy with what it means to live on a culture's margins.

## Notes

This essay grew out of a talk delivered at Seaham Hall on 25 October 2014 to a joint meeting of the Newstead Abbey Byron Society and the Irish Byron Society. I am grateful to Ken Purslow and Allan Gregory for inviting me to speak on this occasion and for suggesting I took *Hebrew Melodies* as my topic. For their kind and helpful attention to a draft of the essay, I am grateful to Dr Madeleine Callaghan and Dr Oliver Clarkson.

1. See Byron, *A Selection of Hebrew Melodies*; Heinzelman, 'Politics, Memory, and the Lyric: Collaboration as Style in Byron's *Hebrew Melodies*', pp. 515–27; Spector, *Byron and the Jews*; essays by Peterfreund and Benis (both 2011) in: Sheila A. Spector (ed.), *Romanticism / Judaica: A Convergence of Cultures*; Mole, 'The Handling of *Hebrew Melodies*', pp. 18–33; Davies, 'Jewish Tunes, or *Hebrew Melodies*: Byron and the Biblical Orient', in: *Byron and Orientalism*. See also the typically witty notes in Peter Cochran's invaluable online edition and discussions in Gross, *Byron: The Erotic Liberal* and Hoagwood, *From Song to Print: Romantic Pseudo-Songs*.
2. For a discussion of the interaction between Byron and Moore in relation to *Hebrew Melodies* see Vail, *The Literary Relationship of Lord Byron and Thomas Moore*, pp. 81–102.
3. Nathan, *Fugitive Pieces and Reminiscences of Lord Byron*, p. 24.
4. Benis, 'Byron's *Hebrew Melodies* and the Musical Nation', p. 33.
5. Nathan, *Fugitive Pieces*, p. 25.
6. Quoted from Davies, 'Jewish Tunes, or *Hebrew Melodies*', p. 197.
7. Benis, 'Byron's *Hebrew Melodies* and the Musical Nation', p. 36.
8. Ibid., p. 32.
9. Ibid., p. 40.
10. Shilstone, *Byron and the Myth of Tradition*, p. 112.

11. For compositional details of three poems ('I Speak Not – I Trace Not – I Breathe Not', 'She Walks in Beauty' and 'Son of the Sleepless') that 'can definitely be assigned to the months immediately preceding Byron's work on the Hebrew Melodies', see Ashton, *Byron's Hebrew Melodies*, pp. 22–3.
12. Nathan, *Fugitive Pieces*, p. 37.
13. McLane, *Balladeering, Minstrelsy, and the Making of British Romantic Poetry*, p. 184.
14. See Ashton, *Byron's Hebrew Melodies*, p. 157.
15. Culler, 'Lyric, History, and Genre', pp. 63–77, at p. 66.
16. Quoted from *Percy Bysshe Shelley: The Major Works*.
17. Agamben, 'The End of the Poem', pp. 430–4, at p. 430.
18. Nathan, *Fugitive Pieces*, p. 35.
19. Wordsworth, 'She dwelt among th' untrodden ways', ll. 5–6. The edition is taken from O'Neill and Mahoney, eds, *Romantic Poetry: An Annotated Anthology*. Wordsworth's 'Ode: Intimations of Immortality' is taken from the same anthology.
20. Ibid., ll. 7–8.
21. Wordsworth, 'Ode: Intimations of Immortality', l. 200.
22. Ibid., l. 199.
23. McGann (*CPW*, vol. 3, p. 468) associates the first line of 'The Harp the Monarch Minstrel Swept' with the first line of the same poem by Moore.
24. Quoted from Moore, *The Poetical Works of Thomas Moore*.
25. Shelley, 'When the Lamp Is Shattered', *Percy Bysshe Shelley*, l. 4.
26. For further discussion, see Benis, 'Byron's *Hebrew Melodies* and the Musical Nation', p. 32.
27. Peterfreund, 'Enactments of Exile and Diaspora in English Romantic Literature', in *Romanticism / Judaica*, p. 17. See also Vail, *Lord Byron and Thomas Moore*, p. 92.
28. Vail, *Lord Byron and Thomas Moore*, p. 92.
29. Ashton, *Byron's Hebrew Melodies*, p. 85.
30. Yeats, 'The Gyres', l. 8, *Poems*.
31. Shelley, 'To a Skylark', *Percy Bysshe Shelley*, l. 90.
32. Keach, *Shelley's Style*, p. 218.
33. Shelley, 'The Serpent Is Shut Out from Paradise', *Percy Bysshe Shelley*, ll. 41–8.
34. Yeats, 'Introduction', in: *The Oxford Book of Modern Verse, 1892–1935*, p. xviii.
35. Gleckner, *Byron and the Ruins of Paradise*, p. 205.
36. See Ashton, *Byron's Hebrew Melodies*, p. 80n.
37. Byron, *A Selection of Hebrew Melodies*, p. 20.
38. Quoted from Tennyson, 'Mariana', l. 6, *The Poems of Tennyson*.
39. Ricks, *Tennyson*, p. 48.
40. Benis, 'Byron's *Hebrew Melodies* and the Musical Nation', p. 39.

41. Ashton, *Byron's Hebrew Melodies*, p. 85.
42. Nathan, *Fugitive Pieces*, p. 5.
43. Quoted from Emily Brontë, *The Complete Poems*, l. 4.
44. Nathan, *Fugitive Pieces*, p. 33.
45. Vail, *Lord Byron and Thomas Moore*, p. 93.

## Works cited

Agamben, Giorgio (2014), 'The End of the Poem', in: Virginia Jackson and Yopie Prins (eds), *The Lyric Theory Reader: A Critical Anthology*, Baltimore: Johns Hopkins University Press, pp. 430–4.

Ashton, Thomas L. (1972), *Byron's Hebrew Melodies*, London: Routledge and Kegan Paul.

Benis, Toby R. (2011), 'Byron's *Hebrew Melodies* and the Musical Nation', in: Sheila A. Spector (ed.), *Romanticism / Judaica: A Convergence of Cultures*, Farnham: Ashgate, pp. 31–44.

Brontë, Emily (1992), *The Complete Poems*, ed. Janet Gezari, London: Penguin.

Byron, Lord George Gordon (1988), *A Selection of Hebrew Melodies*, ed. Frederick Burwick and Paul Douglass, Tuscaloosa: University of Alabama Press.

Cochran, Peter, ed. (2009), 'Hebrew Melodies', *Peter Cochran's Website*, available at http://peter cochran.files.wordpress.com/2009/03/hebrew_melodies.pdf (last accessed 2 September 2016).

Culler, Jonathan (2014), 'Lyric, History, and Genre', in: Virginia Jackson and Yopie Prins (eds), *The Lyric Theory Reader: A Critical Anthology*, Baltimore: Johns Hopkins University Press, pp. 63–77.

Davies, Jeremy (2006), 'Jewish Tunes, or *Hebrew Melodies*: Byron and the Biblical Orient', in: Peter Cochran (ed.), *Byron and Orientalism*, Newcastle upon Tyne: Cambridge Scholars Press, pp. 197–214.

Gleckner, Robert F. (1967), *Byron and the Ruins of Paradise*, Baltimore: Johns Hopkins University Press.

Gross, Jonathan D. (2000), *Byron: The Erotic Liberal*, Lanham, MD: Rowman and Littlefield.

Heinzelman, Kurt (1988), 'Politics, Memory, and the Lyric: Collaboration as Style in Byron's *Hebrew Melodies*', *Studies in Romanticism*, 27, pp. 515–27.

Hoagwood, Terence (2010), *From Song to Print: Romantic Pseudo-Songs*, New York: Palgrave Macmillan.

Keach, William (1984), *Shelley's Style*, New York: Methuen.

McLane, Maureen N. (2008), *Balladeering, Minstrelsy, and the Making of British Romantic Poetry*, Cambridge: Cambridge University Press.

Mole, Tom (2002), 'The Handling of *Hebrew Melodies*', *Romanticism*, 8, pp. 18–33.

Moore, Thomas (1910), *The Poetical Works of Thomas Moore*, ed. A. D. Godley, London: Oxford University Press.

Nathan, Isaac (1829), *Fugitive Pieces and Reminiscences of Lord Byron*, London: Whittaker, Treacher, and Co.

O'Neill, Michael and Charles Mahoney, eds (2008), *Romantic Poetry: An Annotated Anthology*, Malden, MA: Blackwell.

Peterfreund, Stuart (2011), 'Enactments of Exile and Diaspora in English Romantic Literature', in: Sheila A. Spector (ed.), *Romanticism / Judaica: A Convergence of Cultures*, Farnham: Ashgate, pp. 13–30.

Ricks, Christopher ([1972] 1978), *Tennyson*, London: Macmillan.

Shelley, Percy Bysshe (2003), *Percy Bysshe Shelley: The Major Works*, ed. Michael O'Neill and Zachary Leader, Oxford: Oxford University Press.

Shilstone, Frederick W. (1988), *Byron and the Myth of Tradition*, Lincoln: University of Nebraska Press.

Spector, Sheila A. (2010), *Byron and the Jews*, Detroit: Wayne State University Press.

—, ed. (2011), *Romanticism / Judaica: A Convergence of Cultures*, Farnham: Ashgate.

Tennyson, Lord Alfred (1969), *The Poems of Tennyson*, ed. Christopher Ricks, London: Longmans.

Vail, Jeffrey W. (2002), *The Literary Relationship of Lord Byron and Thomas Moore*, Baltimore: Johns Hopkins University Press, pp. 81–102.

Yeats, William B. (1936), 'Introduction', in: W. B. Yeats (ed.), *The Oxford Book of Modern Verse, 1892–1935*, Oxford: Clarendon Press.

— (1990), *Poems*, ed. Daniel Albright, London: Dent.

# Chapter 9

# Out of Romanticism: Byron and Romance

*Anna Camilleri*

That Byron's poetry is often considered to stand at the margins of Romanticism is in part the result of generic association. Byron excelled at satire. His *magnum opus, Don Juan* (1819–24), while perilous to categorise (epic, mock-epic, anti-epic, novel?), is safe to read as a satirical poem. Satire relies upon the sociability of the poet and the reader. From Juvenal and Horace, to Dryden and Pope, and thence to Byron, satire manages at once to be gregarious in tone whilst antisocial in its antagonistic content. In such comic (anti) sociability, satire – and Byron – can be seen to stand at odds with the serious and solitary genre of lyric, and it is that which has come to be seen as the defining genre of what modern scholars and university syllabi now confidently label 'Romanticism'. Lyric, like the Romantic poet-hero, emerges from the private, the contemplative and the confessional state. With the lyric mode standing preeminent in the dominant critical narrative of Romanticism, the satirically minded Byron has been understandably marginalised, yet there are fundamental inaccuracies with this popular story. Most obviously, sidelining Byron in discussions of Romantic lyricism overlooks Byron's considerable lyric output. All four of his Juvenalian collections are comprised exclusively of lyric poetry (with the exceptions of various school-translation exercises from Greek and Latin). At the height of his fame, Byron published the *Hebrew Melodies* (1815), the contents of which were not simply lyric in form but intended to be sung, being initially bound with musical settings by Isaac Nathan. Byron's lyric practice was central to his eventual success in the *ottava rima*, a stanza form with which he first experiments in his lyric 'Epistle to Augusta' (1816), and this poetic debt to lyric is evident in both of his long poems. *Childe Harold's Pilgrimage* (1812–18) and *Don*

*Juan* (1819–24) each offer instances of lyric interruption.[1] One way of underscoring the erroneous marginalisation of Byron from what may be deemed Wordsworthian Romanticism is to explore Byron's little attended-to lyrics. Another way, however, is to challenge the relatively narrow generic classification with which we have tended to conceptualise Romanticism. This essay seeks to contend Byron's centrality for current understandings of Romanticism, by the recovery of contemporary notions of what it was to be 'Romantic'. Although 'Romantic' is an anachronistic term, on the rare occasions it was used within the period it denoted those narratives of adventure and peril that had been attributed to past writers (the 'old Romances'), but also to those writers who participated in the recovery of the Romance as part of a wider programme of Medieval Revival. In the less told, competing version of Romanticism, it is not the lyric Wordsworth, Shelley or Keats that are foregrounded, but Walter Scott, Thomas Moore and Byron. The closest contemporary reviewers come to identifying a Romantic 'school' is in their alignment of these three latter figures, who are considered as examples of Romantic practice until at least the 1870s.[2] Predating what William St Clair has termed the 'unifying' concept of Romanticism, it is Romance, and not lyric, that determines Romantic identity.[3]

To suggest the centrality of Romance to contemporary and current critical conceptions of Romanticism is by no means a novel critical stance. Stuart Curran reminds us of the etymological connection between Romance and the period we term Romanticism.[4] Similarly, Michael O'Neill persuasively elaborates the etymological proximity of the terms as articulating a plausible meta-connectedness, arguing that they are 'decisively twinned', and that each 'yokes together the dissimilar, fusing or holding in tension the ancient and the novel, the marvellous and the ordinary'.[5] Equally, Diego Saglia has perceptively indicated that verse Romances can be read as the 'discursive embodiment' of a literary period that is at once 'a cultural threshold' as well as being 'a culture of thresholds'.[6] While reading Romanticism alongside Romance might not be new, it is also a not *un*problematic pairing. Each of these terms resists definition. Definitions of 'Romanticism' are either confounded by historical and intellectual expansiveness (arguments could, for instance, be made for an open-ended Romanticism or Romanticisms from the Enlightenment to postmodernism), or undermined by exclusivity. The university concept of Romanticism, for example, is not only too frequently entirely white, male and middle-class, but also often so narrow as to exclude a figure who embodies all three of these things. As Seamus

Perry points out, '[w]hatever generalization I make from the canon of "Romantics" I have in mind, you can always reply, "But now, what about Byron?"'[7] It is similarly difficult to determine identifying features of Romance – certainly more difficult than with lyric, which at least offers formal parameters. Even within the brief period from the 1790s to the 1830s that we deem Romantic, the label of 'Romance' was applied to poetry and prose of varying lengths with no recognisable features other than a connection with the past. This essay, along with others in the volume, will assume that there is such a thing as Romanticism, and that it is largely understood to be dominated by a small collection of work by an even smaller collection of poets who were, on the whole, very little read in the period in which they lived and published.

One of the curious ironies of Romantic studies is that it currently marginalises those very figures that gave rise to the appellation of the period. Scott, Byron and Moore, whose poems dominate contemporary sales figures, were all predominantly writers of 'Tales' – or Romances. Print culture testifies to the centrality of the Romance as the dominant popular mode in the period. The Medieval Revival prompted the publication of a significant number of medieval metrical verse Romances.[8] Although the second half of the eighteenth century can be considered the start of this programme of resuscitation with the publication of Thomas Warton's *Observations on the Fairy Queen* (1754), Richard Hurd's *Letters on Chivalry and Romance* (1762) and Thomas Percy's *Reliques of Ancient English Poetry* (1765), it is the opening decade of the nineteenth century that witnesses an escalation in Romance revival.[9] Following hot on each other's three-volume heels were Joseph Ritson's *Ancient English Metrical Romances* (1802), George Ellis's *Specimens of Early English Metrical Romances* (1805) and Henry Weber's *Metrical Romances* (1810). This programme of metrical verse romance resuscitation had an evident effect on how English poetry was conceived and conceived of. Walter Scott's first attempt at his own Metrical Romance, *The Lay of the Last Minstrel* (1805), followed from his compilation *Minstrelsy of the Scottish Border* (1802–3) and his edited version of *Sir Tristrem: A Metrical Romance of the 15th Century* (1804). That he wrote the *Lay* to pay for a horse gives some indication in his confidence of the poem's commercial success.[10] Certainly, Byron's romances were produced in numbers that imply a staggeringly large readership. Print runs for *Childe Harold* and the various Turkish Tales reached 100,000 copies (*The Corsair* (1814) famously sold out of its initial 10,000 copies on the first day of publication) – this in contrast to the entirety of Wordsworth's poems, which numbered 13,000.[11] As St Clair matter-of-factly observes, 'Scott and Byron sold more poems in a normal afternoon than Shelley and Keats did during the whole of their lives.'[12] It is for good reason, then, that George Saintsbury labels the period from Wordsworth to Keats 'The Triumph of Romance'.[13]

It is, of course, Byron's publisher, Murray, that we might credit with Byron's centrality within the Romance revival. It had been Byron's intention to publish another satire on his return from Greece, but Murray was suitably alert to public taste to know that what readers craved was not the wit and repartee of *Hints from Horace* (1811) but a Romance. The poem from whose publication Byron awoke to find himself famous advertised its allegiance to the spirit of Romance in its title, even if the content did not quite live up to expectations. The secondary title of the first two Cantos of *Childe Harold's Pilgrimage: A Romaunt* gave readers a clear specification as to the identity of the poem,[14] which the opening stanzas reinforce, being conducted in a measure all too familiar to contemporary audiences. Greg Kucich has discussed at length the 'simple and unrestrained facility' of the stanza's use throughout the eighteenth century.[15] The twelve-line stanza had been revived by James Thomson in *The Castle of Indolence* (1748), and became an immensely popular verse-vehicle for long narrative poems, James Beattie's *The Minstrel* (1771) perhaps being the most famous, along with Thomas Campbell's *Gertrude of Wyoming* (1809) and Mary Tighe's *Psyche* (1805), poems proximal to Byron's own. Yet doubts were raised as to how Spenserian the stanza was when executed by Byron, Wordsworth famously grumbling that Byron had 'spoiled' Spenser's stanza.[16] Kucich, however, has suggested that Byron's spoiled stanza is in fact 'acting out poetically the kind of revisionary Spenserian criticism beginning to appear in the second decade of the nineteenth century'.[17] We might extend Kucich's formal observations to suggest that Byron is actively and deliberately engaged in a process of participation and revision with Romance as it was understood in 1812 – a process that we might even consider a form of self-marginalisation.

Throughout Canto I of *Childe Harold*, Byron engages in simultaneous practice and critique of the possibilities of Romance. This complex compositional strategy, where he defects even as he enlists, is initially evident through the archaisms that appeared initially as a resounding declaration of Romancing. The Spenserian skeleton of Byron's Romance is initially fleshed out with the additional markers of Romance: archaic diction and the purported prominence of English heritage and history. The use of archaisms is particularly intense in the opening six stanzas, as if in justification of the subtitle: 'whilome' (*Childe Harold* I, l. 10); 'wight' (I, l. 14); 'Sore' (I, ll. 15 and 46); and 'hight' (I, l. 19). In these opening stanzas Byron does not merely proffer a sprinkling of archaic terminology. His concern to establish medieval verisimilitude extends to the syntax, in, for instance, our initial encounter with the protagonist: 'Childe Harold bask'd him in the noon-tide sun' (*Childe Harold* I, l. 28). Yet contemporary readers were unconvinced by Byron's protestations of fidelity to Romance, the *Anti-Jacobin Review* declaring that the poem was 'whimsically, and improperly, denominated'.[18] Indeed, the poet's lexical fidelity to Romance is relinquished in the poem almost as soon as Childe Harold relinquishes 'his father's hall' (*Childe Harold* I, l. 55). While language becomes the initial indicator of Byron's unstable identification with Romance, a more elaborate sidelining occurs in the relocation to Spain, that 'renown'd, romantic land!' (*Childe Harold* I, l. 387). Having abandoned the language of the English Romance tradition, it becomes evident that even the supposed birthplace of Romance cannot sustain Byron's Romantic endeavour. The narrator begins by accusing modern Spain of having lost her historic affiliation with chivalry:

> Where are those bloody banners which of yore
> Wav'd o'er thy sons, victorious to the gale,
> And drove at last the spoilers to their shore?
> Red gleam'd the cross, and wan'd the crescent pale,
> While Afric's echoes thrill'd with Moorish matrons' wail. (*Childe Harold* I, ll. 391–5)

While Spain was considered the likely birthplace of literary Romance, in these lines Byron appears more concerned to establish historical rather than literary veracity.[19] In his recollection of the crusading emblems of cross and crescent, Byron's initially reaches for a factual rather than fictional account to lament the demise of chivalry. Although, as Saglia asserts, 'late eighteenth-century cultural theorists often accused Spanish culture of having decreed the end of chivalric literature with the publication of *Don Quixote*',[20] it is not until Canto XIII of *Don Juan* (1823) that Byron connects literary degeneration with actual heroic decay:

> Cervantes smiled Spain's Chivalry away;
> A single laugh demolished the right arm
> Of his own country; – seldom since that day
> Had Spain had heroes. (*Don Juan* XIII, ll. 81–4)

Establishing historical precedent for Spanish heroic endeavour enables Byron to critique 'the fall of Spain' all the more keenly (*Childe Harold* I, l. 552). The birthplace of Romance has succeeded in marginalising the heroic. The appearance of the Maid of Saragossa suggests the sustenance of Spain's glorious past from unlikely quarters. Like Joan of Arc before her, the Spanish Maid appears as a nation's only hope:

> Who can appease like her a lover's ghost?
> Who can avenge so well a leader's fall?
> What maid retrieve when man's flush'd hope is lost?
> Who hang so fiercely on the flying Gaul,
> Foil'd by a woman's hand, before a batter'd wall? (*Childe Harold* I, ll. 580–4)

The amplified rhetoric of these lines is, once again, revealed to participate in Byron's poetic process of identification and departure. The note appended by Byron undermines the celebration of contemporary heroism in the stanza itself: 'Such were the exploits of the Maid of Saragoza. When the author was at Seville she walked daily in the Prado, decorated with medals and orders, by command of the Junta' (*CPW*, vol. 2, p. 189). The ironising force of this historical commentary on the futility of the ideals of Romance is amplified by the belatedness of the note, being marginalised in an appendix rather than footnoted.[21] The note itself offers a double instance of heroic deflation. It initially appears to reinforce poetic claims of extraordinary exploit through historical fact – the poet has seen this heroine with his own eyes, celebrating her heroic achievements. Yet having flirted with the image of patriotic commemoration of heroic exploit, this is then revealed to be routine procedure: merely a cheap publicity stunt by the controlling élite. Far from the Minerva-like figure that stalks the battlefields of the Peninsula War, Agustina of Aragón emerges as an emblem of heroic decay. Canto I of *Childe Harold*, then, provides an ironically detached commentary on the impossibility of adhering to the demands of Romance. Modern European culture has forced Romance to the margins. To produce a modern 'Romaunt' requires a new poetic strategy.

By the publication of Canto III of the poem, Byron not only had ditched the erroneous subtitle but also had modernised Romance by bringing it into contact with what we now deem 'Romanticism'. Canto III of *Childe Harold* is the one that both contemporary and modern critics identify as the most 'Wordsworthian'. Most explicit are Walter Scott and Francis Jeffrey. Scott discerns a general poetic

sympathy with the Lakers, pointing to the Wordsworthian nature of
*Prisoner of Chillon* (1816), the resemblance of 'Churchill's Grave'
(1816) to Southey's *English Eclogues*, and 'Darkness' (1816) and
'The Spell is Broke, the Charm is Flown' (1810) as recalling 'the
wild, unbridled, and fiery imagination of Coleridge'.[22] For Jeffrey, it
is Canto III of *Childe Harold* in particular that 'seemed to lean rather
too kindly to the peculiarities of the Lake school'.[23] He isolates the
passage running from stanza 72 to 88 as particularly resonant of
Laker sentiment. When Byron declaims that '[h]igh mountains are a
feeling, but the hum / Of human cities torture' (*Childe Harold* III, ll.
682–3), and rhetorically questions his metaphysical status ('Are not
the mountains, waves, and skies, a part / Of me and of my soul, as I
of them?' *Childe Harold* III, ll. 707–8), the 'peculiarities' of Wordsworth and Coleridge are none too difficult to discern. That Byron is
indulging 'rather too kindly' in these Lake School idiosyncrasies is
regarded rather less kindly by Jeffrey: 'These are mystical enough, we
think; but what follows is nearly as unintelligible as some of the sublimities of Wordsworth himself.'[24] What follows is Byron's agonised
– and peculiarly Romantic – outcry of thwarted poetic expression:
'Could I embody and unbosom now / That which is most within
me, – could I wreak / My thoughts upon expression' (*Childe Harold*
III, ll. 905–7). Gallingly for Byron, he had already written on unintelligibility as the primary Wordsworthian sin. He writes to Leigh
Hunt a year previous to Jeffrey's review: 'there is undoubtedly much
natural talent spilt over "the Excursion" but it is rain upon rocks
where it stands & stagnates – or rain upon sands where it falls without fertilising – who can understand him?' (*BLJ*, vol. 4, pp. 324–5).
This sentiment is recast to echo Jeffrey's terms remarkably closely in
the parody of the Lake Poets in the first Canto of *Don Juan* (1819):
'Unless, like Wordsworth, they prove unintelligible' (*Don Juan* I, l.
720). Reading *Childe Harold* with this parallel in mind yields surprising instances of Wordsworthian contemplation:

> To sit on rocks, to muse o'er flood and fell,
> To slowly trace the forest's shady scene,
> Where things that own not man's dominion dwell,
> And mortal foot hath ne'er, or rarely been;
> To climb the trackless mountain all unseen,
> With the wild flock that never needs a fold;
> Alone o'er steeps and foaming falls to lean;
> This is not solitude; 'tis but to hold
> Converse with Nature's charms, and view her stores unroll'd.
> (*Childe Harold* II, ll. 217–25)

With the benefit of hindsight, it is difficult not to call to mind Juan's 'lonely walks and lengthening reveries' (*Don Juan* I, l. 769), conjured by Byron ten years after he drafted the stanza above. Considered alongside the Romanticism of *Childe Harold*, the parody of the Lakers in the first Canto of *Don Juan* begins to look like self-parody. Yet it is when he began to reach beyond the all-too familiar margins of popular Romance, to the mode we now deem Romantic, that some of Byron's most exciting and unexpected poetic affiliations emerge.

Moments of lyric stasis that facilitate ontological, existential and metaphysical contemplation can be seen at once to characterise Wordsworth's and Byron's long poems. Yet it is not merely *Childe Harold*'s tendency towards reflection and description that Jeffrey identifies as what we now term 'Romantic', but also the uncertain line drawn between protagonist and narrator. For Jeffrey, it is the conflation of speaker and subject in *Childe Harold* that most closely aligns it with Wordsworth's verse narratives, being 'substantially a contemplative and ethical work, diversified with fine description, and adorned or overshaded by one emphatic person, who is sometimes the author, and sometimes the object of the reflections on which the interest is chiefly rested'.[25] Indeed, anachronistic speculation might regard such a description as equally apposite of *The Prelude*, not published until 1850 and so at this point unknown to Jeffrey. As such, we can extend Curran's assessment of Keats's *Endymion* (1818) to suggest that Romantic versions of the Romance find narrative impulse in 'the quest for the poetic identity of its singer'.[26] The coalescence of self and hero – of voice and subject – offers a further parallel that aligns Wordsworthian Romanticism with Byronic Romance: the poetic rendering of autobiography. *Childe Harold* is, famously, an autobiographical poem, the line that distinguished hero from poet being notoriously difficult to perceive. By the publication of the third Canto of *Childe Harold*, Scott, for one, admitted defeat: 'The works before us contain so many direct allusions to the author's personal feelings and private history, that it becomes impossible for us to divide Lord Byron from his poetry.'[27] That Byron saw greater Romance in the events of his own life than in anything imaginable in verse or prose is evident. Byron's Turkish Tales, too, relied on autobiographical event. He writes in his journal, having finished *The Bride of Abydos* (1813):

This afternoon I have burnt the scenes of my commenced comedy. I have some idea of expectorating a romance, or rather a tale in prose; – but what romance could equal the events – "quæque ipse . . . vidi, et quorum pars magna fui".[28] (*BLJ*, vol. 3, p. 205)

Byron's allusion to Virgil recalls the compositional circumstances of *The Giaour* (1813), the horrific background to which was based on an event in which Byron bore no small part. A version of these is given in a letter by the Marquis of Sligo. In summary, while in Athens in 1811, Byron witnessed an incident of a girl accused of adultery who, by order of the New Governor 'unaccustomed to have the intercourse with Christians which his predecessor had, had of course the barbarous Turkish Ideas with regard to Women', was sewn into a sack and to be drowned. Byron allegedly intervened and 'succeeded partly by personal threats & partly by bribery & entreaty, to procure her pardon on condition of her leaving Athens'. Alert to the advantages of the intrigue surrounding *The Giaour*, Byron was aware that 'the circumstances which are the groundwork make it' (*BLJ*, vol. 3, p. 208) – and, indeed, which sold it. The autobiographical intrigue that formed the basis of *Childe Harold* and at least two of the Turkish Tales became a poetical policy in *Beppo* (1818) and *Don Juan*, in which he reformulates his journalistic allusion to Virgil, life itself being equal to the events of any poetic Romance:

> If in the course of such a life as was
> At once adventurous and contemplative,
> Men who partake all passions as they pass,
> Acquire the deep and bitter power to give
> Their images again as in a glass,
> And in such colours that they seem to live;
> You may do right forbidding them to show 'em,
> But spoil (I think) a very pretty poem. (*Don Juan* IV, ll. 849–56)

These lines find their counterpart in Byron's prose explanation of his creative process, the collision of recollection and fabrication being again suggested by his work on *The Bride of Abydos*:

> I am much more indebted to the tale than I can ever be to the most partial reader; as it wrung my thoughts from reality to imagination – from selfish regrets to vivid recollections – and recalled me to a country replete with the *brightest* and *darkest*, but always most *lively* colours of my memory. (*BLJ*, vol. 3, pp. 230–1)

To insist that the adventure and contemplation of poetic life is held at arm's length from lived reality is to limit creative endeavour. As Byron scribbled defensively to Douglas Kinnaird of *Don Juan*, 'it may be profligate – but is it not *life*, is it not *the thing*? – Could any man have written it – who has not lived in the world?' (*BLJ*, vol. 4, p. 232).

Byron had an evident fascination for the productive relationship between experience and fantasy, and it is a fascination that becomes fundamental to his participation in what Godwin termed 'the reality of romance'.[29] Famously hating 'things *all fiction*' (*BLJ*, vol. 5, p. 203), Byron had combatted lustily for what he saw as the fundamental *believability* of poetic landscape more generally, and it is an aspect of his poetry that he felt fundamentally different from the Lake School. His irritation with Wordsworth and Southey surfaces when their poetry does not adhere to material truths. We can take Byron's opinion of Southey's Madoc to be reflective of his opinion of Southey himself, that he '[t]ells us strange tales, as other travellers do, / More old than Mandeville's, and not so true' (*English Bards and Scotch Reviewers* (1809), ll. 223–4). In a letter to Hunt (the very same that accuses Wordsworth of unintelligibility), Byron corrects what he regards as factual inaccuracies in Wordsworth's *Excursion*:

> He says of Greece in the body of his book – that it is a land of '*rivers – fertile* plains – & *sounding* shores
> Under a cope of *variegated* sky'
> The rivers are dry half the year – the plains are barren – and the shores *still* & *tideless* as the Mediterranean can make them – the Sky is anything but variegated – being for months & months – but "darkly – deeply – beautifully blue"' [. . .]. (*BLJ*, vol. 4, pp. 324–6)

The letter, dated 30 October 1815, was written whilst Byron was finishing his draft of the *Siege of Corinth* (1816). The poem's Mediterranean setting offered Byron the opportunity to correct Wordsworth's error in verse: 'There shrinks no ebb in that tideless sea' (*The Siege of Corinth*, l. 426). To ensure the point is not lost, Byron annotates '[t]he reader need hardly be reminded that there are no perceptible tides in the Mediterranean'. These are the very points of correctness that Byron had previously insisted he would 'combat lustily' (*BLJ*, vol. 3, p. 165); indeed, Byron's concern with the construction of a realist poetics remains constant throughout his career. *Don Juan* provides a meta-commentary concerning the importance of factual accuracy:

> But then the fact's a fact – and 'tis the part
> Of a true poet to escape from fiction
> Whene'er he can; for there is little art
> In leaving verse more free from the restriction
> Of truth than prose, unless to suit the mart
> For what is sometimes called poetic diction,
> And that outrageous appetite for lies
> Which Satan angles with, for souls, like flies. (*Don Juan* VIII, ll. 681–8)

Byron's use of 'fact' in the poem is remarkable; there are fifty-three instances within the main body of the poem, and it occurs at least once in each Canto, with the exception of the unfinished seventeenth Canto. There is nothing facetious in Byron's later claim that 'my Muse by no means deals in fiction: / She gathers a repertory of facts' (*Don Juan* XIV, ll. 97–8). Byron's syntactical play on the definition of a 'true poet' is revealing of what he sees as the function, or requirement, of greater art. Here Byron anticipates Robert Louis Stevenson's claim that '[t]rue romantic art [. . .] makes a romance of all things. It reaches into the highest abstraction of the ideal; it does not refuse the most pedestrian realism.'[30] Yet for Byron it is not simply that Romance does not refute reality, but that it should be held accountable to the facts. The assumed poetic licence, where poets are sanctioned by their chosen literary medium to indulge 'that outrageous appetite for lies', is for Byron exactly that – an outrage. Byron invokes more traditional Christian rhetoric to illustrate his point: poetic fabrications are the work of the Devil, an artful satanic sport to hook credulous readers.

It is the way in which history and fantasy coalesce that energises Byron's own Romances, which constantly take their origins from the uncertain margins of fact and fiction. In this process, his version of the genre is distinguishable from Keats's more overt participation in the aesthetics of the contemporary Medieval Revival, which, steeped in the nostalgic sepia tones of Romance, 'unmoors itself from history'.[31] In this way, Byron's Romances appear to align with Scott's concept of the Romance genre as embellished historical record, whose content is an artificially and artfully managed inheritance of past event.[32] Scott's declaration that 'Romance and real history [. . .] form a mixed class between them; and may be termed either romantic histories, or historical romances, according to the proportion in which their truth is debased by fiction, or their fiction mingled with truth' was a prevailing sentiment in other contemporary writings on the genre.[33] In a close echo of Scott's terms, Godwin announces that 'Romance then, strictly considered, may be pronounced to be one of the species of history.'[34] Byron's Romances, whilst insisting on factual correctness, demand that such 'facticity'[35] mingle fiction with truth. He is not interested in replicating reality, but in constructing an alternative *poetic* reality, and in doing so can be seen to engage with Romanticism's wider concern with the relation between the two states. As Schiller writes, 'Every person, indeed, expects from the arts of imagination a certain liberation from the bounds of the real world; he wants to take pleasure in what is possible and give room to his own fantasy,'[36] or, as Byron declared in his journal, '[t]o withdraw *myself* from *myself* (oh that cursed self-ishness!) has ever been my sole, my entire, my sincere motive in scribbling at all' (*BLJ*, vol. 3, p. 225). What Byron's Romances do, then, is rather more complex than Northrop Frye's general claim that '[i]t looks, therefore, as though romance were simply replacing the world of ordinary experience by a dream world'.[37] For Byron, the interplay of fact and fiction is not a question of displacement, but of constructive amalgamation.

Byron's Romances are products of the poetic collusion between fact and fiction, history and poetry, the public and the personal.[38] So far this chapter has indicated the ways in which Byron's poetry in general, and *Childe Harold* in particular, are caught between two dominant Romantic modes, standing as they do in the margins of Wordsworthian lyricism and Scottean historicism. Both the auto-biographical lyric and the historical Romance are poetic instances of the intersection of public history and private memory.[39] Indeed, we might read both of these models as versions of poetic memory. Scott's historical Romances offer a form of poetic memorial or commemoration, whilst Wordsworth's lyric is famously the product of tranquil recollection. Aristotle's distinction between memory and recollection is important here. While memory is imprecise and can function without a 'determinate time-notion' (i.e. one can remember a fact or event without certainty of the exact time or place when it transpired), recollection is 'a sort of investigation' and the result of deliberation.[40] Recollection is to recall, or call to mind, and in so doing to curate (and create) images and sensations deliberately. It is a commonplace critical assertion that the failures and triumphs of recollection dominate Romantic lyric. Most famous, perhaps, are Coleridge's efforts in the preface to 'Kubla Khan' (1816), thwarted by the person from Porlock, and his charting of the efforts of memory in the resulting poem: 'Could I revive within me / Her symphony and song' (ll. 42–3).[41] Yet recollection can equally be seen as the driving force of Romantic verse narratives. Coleridge's 'Ancient Mariner' (1798) – who exists himself as a figure in the margins – offers the paramount example. The Mariner, never able to forget, is bereft in a perpetual state of retelling. As with lyric, the tension in Romance is between the triumph of memory in recollection and its utter failure in forgetfulness. We might consider forgetfulness as the inevitable consequence of poetic remembrance, or, in Kierkegaard's words, '[t]he more poetically one remembers, the more easily one forgets, for to remember poetically is actually only an expression of forgetting'.[42] Frye's dominant reading of Romance as identifiable through inherent polarities is useful here.⁴³ Romantic versions of Romance can be understood to function in the margins, between opposite extremes: immortalisation on the one hand and oblivion on the other.

Romance is the literary mode that comes closest to history, its composition being (at least purportedly) to commemorate past acts and to ensure the transmission of story from past actions to future readers. It is also a mode that is critically marginalised as relying on distraction and delusion. While the opening cantos of *Childe Harold* can be read as adhering to the poetic realism of the travelogue genre, Byron's poem appears to offer the kind of diversionary poetics we anticipate from Romance. Diversion for the reader is provided not only by the promise of exotic adventure but also, more significantly, by immersion in Byromania. Byron's poeticisation of personal experience mediates between autobiography as historical record and as a means of achieving lasting notoriety. How far Byron managed the former is perhaps less relevant than the fact that, following the publication of *Childe Harold* I and II, Byron awoke to find himself famous. Part of the posturing that engendered such success was the very Romantic idea that the poem did not provide distraction solely for the benefit of the audience. At the same time as the audience is diverted from their present by entering the timeless realm of Romance, the poet too is diverted from his present by the narration of his past. In writing *Childe Harold*, Byron is seeking to be at a remove from reality. The possibilities of poetic abstraction emerge within the opening canto. At this point of the poem, the division between poet and protagonist is put into effect by distance: Harold is in Spain, whilst the narrator is in Delphi:

> Oh, thou Parnassus! whom I now survey,
> Not in the phrenzy of a dreamer's eye,
> Not in the fabled landscape of a lay,
> But soaring snow-clad through thy native sky,
> In the wild pomp of mountain majesty! (*Childe Harold* I, ll. 612–16)

The poet–narrator emphasises his geographic and temporal proximity to the dwelling place of the Muses – he surveys the sacred Mount Parnassus with his own eyes, '*now*'. Byron's distraction here is an affectation. Such literal closeness to the Muses implies figurative distance from his literary contemporaries. It proves an affectation from which a characteristic Byronic irony can be wrought. In so admiring the fountainhead of poetic inspiration, he neglects his own verse: 'Ev'n amidst my strain / I turn'd aside to pay my homage here; / Forgot the land, the sons, the maids of Spain' (*Childe Harold* I, ll. 639–41). The poetic symptom of distraction is the very Byronic quality of digression. Yet while such absent-mindedness may be poetically fecund, it is equally the hallmark of the indulgences of youth. The necessity of abstraction from his present emerges more forcefully in Canto III, by which point the travel-weary narrator *requires* poetically induced amnesia to obliterate the agonies of his present state of mind:

> Yet, though a dreary strain, to this I cling;
> So that it wean me from the weary dream
> Of selfish grief or gladness – so it fling
> Forgetfulness around me – it shall seem
> To me, though to none else, a not ungrateful theme. (*Childe Harold* III, ll. 32–6)

Writing poetry is therapeutic. Yet this is no talking cure: this poetic panacea is not the cathartic articulation of repressed memory, but rather the cloaking of personal grief with 'dreary strain'. Such oblivion can only ever be temporary. The impossibility of lasting relief is implied by the futile desperation of clinging to the insubstantial 'strain'. Paul de Man writes of forgetfulness in Shelley as 'an unbearable condition of indetermination which [. . .] necessarily hovers between a state of knowing and not-knowing, like the symptom of a disease which recurs at the precise moment that one remembers its absence'.[44] Likewise, for Byron, the indeterminacy of this state – poetically induced and poetically remedied – is suggested by the contrasting actions of 'wean' and 'fling'. Forgetfulness begins as a gradual process of accustomed withdrawal, before enveloping the poet in violent haste. The double negative in the final line, however, returns us inexorably to the selfsame selfishness the narrator purports to relinquish. Rather than being synonymous with gratitude, 'not ungrateful' indicates something pleasant, agreeable or tasteful. That no one other than himself would regard his 'dreary strain' as such suggests a poem written for the sole benefit of the poet – some distant remove from the promise of shared distraction with which the poem began. In attending to personal recollection, then, Byron's engagement in the art of forgetting appears to find its logical termination in escapist indulgence. While the Lethean indulgence of personal recollection occupies a significant portion of Byron's poem, we equally find *Childe Harold* to be a poem not merely reluctant to forget but also actively desirous of remembrance. In the commemoration of the dead – the most marginal figures of all – *Childe Harold* is revealed to be a Romance simultaneously alert to the demands of historical and personal recollection.

Writing to his friend, John Cam Hobhouse, Byron declared 'I love to remember the dead' (*BLJ*, vol. 2, p. 83). *Childe Harold* bears testimony to this love of remembrance. Alongside personal friends like John Wingfield and Charles Skinner Matthews,[45] the poem also commemorates numerous public figures: for instance, the Maid of Saragossa (*Childe Harold* I, ll. 54–8), Napoleon (*Childe Harold* III, ll. 36–41), Julia Alpinula (*Childe Harold* III, l. 66), Rousseau (*Childe Harold* III, ll. 77–81) and Caecilia Metella (*Childe Harold* III, ll. 99–103). The note to the stanza on Julia Alpinula reveals Byron's belief – and faith – in poetic commemoration:

> I know of no human composition so affecting as this [i.e. Julia's epitaph], nor a history of deeper interest. These are the names and actions which ought not to perish, and to which we turn with a true and healthy tenderness, from the wretched and glittering detail of a confused mass of conquests and battles, with which the mind is roused for a time to a false and feverish sympathy, from whence it recurs at length with all the nausea consequent on such intoxication. (*CPW*, p. 308)

As if to ensure the remembrance of his own words, this note reaffirms the versified rendition of this same sentiment in Canto III: 'these are deeds which should not pass away, / And names that must not wither' (*Childe Harold* III, ll. 635–6). This poetic rendition of memorial itself recalls a turn of phrase from earlier in the canto: 'And this is much, and all which will not pass away' (*Childe Harold* III, l. 315). Indeed, the listing of the dead of Canto III begins to suggest the poem has ossified into epitaph, these lines of remembrance resembling the inscription of a funeral monument. It is the fourth Canto, however, that attends most closely to the stony relics of the dead. Most notably in the stanza on the memorials of the famous dead in the Basilica di Santa Croce in Florence, notable not so much for its commemoration of Michelangelo, Alfieri, Galileo and Machiavelli ('Ashes which make it holier, dust which is / Even in itself an immortality', *Childe Harold* IV, ll. 479–80), but rather for the note which glosses it:

> This name will recall the memory, not only of those whose tombs have raised the Santa Croce into the centre of pilgrimage, the Mecca of Italy, but of her whose eloquence was poured over the illustrious ashes, and whose voice is now as mute as those she sung. (*CPW*, p. 235)

We are required to make a commemorative leap from the ashes of artists and thinkers interred at Santa Croce to the recently deceased Madame de Staël. Herself entombed at Coppet, de Staël provides a connection that is at once symbolic and allusive. In *Corinne, or Italy* (1807), the Santa Croce stands as a repository of true knowledge and the antithesis of neglect:

> Side by side with the city's uproar stands this church which would teach men the secret of everything if they wished, but they walk by without coming in, and the marvelous illusion of forgetfulness keeps the world turning.[46]

Byron's stanza refutes the illusion of forgetfulness offered by the bustle of Florence, choosing rather to commemorate the final silencing of her who sung of those long silent.[47] Equally, this moment of remembrance conflates public memorial with personal recollection; the death of a famous figure remembered by a friend witnesses the collusion of history with autobiography.

When Curran asserts that *Childe Harold* is '*the* romance for an age that had lost all its fictions',[48] the implication is that the poem triumphs through disenchantment with its own generic possibilities. Or, as O'Neill writes, the poem 'may consort with its own self-ironizing shadow'.[49] Whilst it is both possible and plausible to read *Childe Harold's Pilgrimage: A Romaunt* as a poem that self-marginalises by courting the ruin of its own mode, we might equally read its challenge to the accepted identity of Romance as expansive: both of our understanding of Romance itself and, specifically, of its relation to Romanticism. Rather than relegating himself to the margins of each, Byron's negotiation between Scottean historicism and Wordsworthian lyricism questions not only the identity of Romance but also the parameters of Romanticism, forcing us to extend our notions of the 'Romantic' and of the tonal possibilities of Romanticism itself.

## Notes

1. See, for example, the inclusion of the songs 'Adieu, adieu! my native shore', which is situated between stanzas xiii and xiv in Canto I of *Childe Harold*, and also 'The Isles of Greece', which forms an interlude between stanzas lxxxvi and lxxxvii of Canto III of *Don Juan*.
2. Cf. St Clair, *The Reading Nation in the Romantic Period*, p. 212, n. 10, for a thorough delineation of the critical history of 'romance' and 'Romantic' as applied to Wordsworth as against Scott and Byron.

3. Ibid., p. 211.
4. Curran, *Poetic Form and British Romanticism*, p. 129: 'The etymological root of Romanticism, it is easy to forget, is romance.'
5. O'Neill, 'Poetry of the Romantic Period: Coleridge and Keats', p. 306.
6. Saglia, 'Ending the Romance: Women Poets and the Romantic Verse Tale', p. 154.
7. Perry, 'Romanticism: The Brief History of a Concept', p. 3.
8. Cf. Curran, *Poetic Form*, p. 133, for a lengthy (though not exhaustive) list of publications of this sort.
9. Ibid.: 'The first decade of the nineteenth century found its actual center in the revival of romance, both as a scholarly and creative endeavor.'
10. Scott, 'To the Rev. George Crabbe', in: *The Letters of Sir Walter Scott: 1811–1814*, p. 282.
11. Cf. Table 12.1 of St Clair, *The Reading Nation*, p. 217.
12. Ibid., p. 219.
13. Saintsbury, *A Short History of English Literature*, p. 653.
14. For a full account of the subtitle 'A Romaunt', cf. St Clair, *The Reading Nation*, p. 212.
15. Kucich, *Keats, Shelley, and Romantic Spenserianism*, p. 92. For further discussion of Spenserian imitations of the eighteenth century and their influence of the Romantics, cf. his opening chapter, 'Spenser in the Eighteenth Century', pp. 11–64.
16. Hill, 'W. W. to Catherine Grace Godwin', in: *The Letters of William and Dorothy Wordsworth*, vol. 5, p. 58.
17. Kucich, *Keats, Shelley, and Romantic Spenserianism*, p. 115. For an extensive discussion of Byron's 'method', see pp. 113–33.
18. [Anon.], 'Childe Harold's Pilgrimage', *Anti-Jacobin Review*, in: Reiman, *The Romantics Reviewed: Part B: Byron and Regency Society Poets*, vols 1–5, p. 10.
19. Whilst Thomas Warton's 'Saracenic Theory' determined Spain as the birthplace of Romance (see his first volume of the *History of English Poetry*, specifically 'On the Origin of Romantic Fiction in Europe'), Walter Scott was sceptical. In his 'Essay on Romance' (1823), Scott challenges assumptions that Spain was 'the very cradle of romantic fiction', being 'among the last nations in Europe with whom Romance became popular' and possessing no examples of Spanish Metrical Romance, 'unless the poems describing the adventures of the Cid should be supposed to have any affinity to that class of composition'; cf. Scott, 'Essay on Romance', in: *The Miscellaneous Prose Works of Sir Walter Scott: Essays on Chivalry, Romance, and the Drama*, vol. 6, p. 196.
20. Saglia, *Poetic Castles in Spain: British Romanticism and Figurations of Iberia*, Amsterdam: Rodopi, p. 53.
21. In all five of the editions published in 1812 the notes to the poem were appended to the main body-text, collected after the conclusion of the

second Canto. This has set the trend for all later editions, including McGann's *CPW*. This collation of notes as external commentary differs from Byron's notational practice in the Turkish Tales, where early editions print Byron's notes at the foot of each page, suggesting a greater collusion between fact and fiction.

22. Scott, '*Childe Harold's Pilgrimage*, Canto III', pp. 172–208, in: Reiman, *The Romantics Reviewed*, pp. 2044–5.
23. Jeffrey, '*Childe Harold's Pilgrimage, Canto the Third* and *The Prisoner of Chillon, and other Poems*', pp. 277–310, in: Reiman, *The Romantics Reviewed*, p. 878.
24. Ibid., p. 878.
25. Ibid., p. 872.
26. Curran, *Poetic Form*, p. 150.
27. Scott in: Reiman, *The Romantics Reviewed*, p. 2030.
28. Marchand's translation reads: 'Virgil, *Aeneid*, II, l. 5. "I myself saw these things in all their horror, and I bore great part in them"' (*BLJ*, vol. 3, p. 205n).
29. Godwin, 'Of History and Romance', in: *Political and Philosophical Writings of William Godwin: Educational and Literary Writings*, vol. 5, p. 300.
30. Stevenson, 'A Gossip on Romance', p. 60.
31. O'Neill, 'Poetry of the Romantic Period', p. 318.
32. Scott, 'Essay on Romance', in: *The Miscellaneous Prose Works of Sir Walter Scott*, vol. 6, p. 136.
33. Scott, 'Essay on Romance', p. 134.
34. Godwin, 'Of History and Romance', p. 299.
35. The term is Carl Thompson's, whose remarks on the 'facticity' of the Travel Narrative can be extended to the Romance genre that influenced such narratives; Thompson, *The Suffering Traveller and the Romantic Imagination*, p. 14.
36. Schiller, 'On the Employment of the Chorus in Tragedy', p. 61.
37. Frye, *The Secular Scripture: A Study of the Structure of Romance in The Secular Scripture and Other Writings on Critical Theory, 1976–1991*, p. 38.
38. See also Sandy, *Romanticism, Memory, and Mourning*. Sandy comments on similarly 'complex, and complicating' binaries in his examination of Byron and mourning: 'Those boundaries between private grief and monumental historical loss were, for Byron, readily dissolvable', pp. 79, 82.
39. Kucich, 'Romanticism and the Re-engendering of Historical Memory', p. 15: 'History and memory intersect in various, complicated ways throughout the nineteenth century, especially in the rise of autobiographical discourses.'
40. Aristotle, 'On Memory', in: *The Complete Works of Aristotle*, vol. 1, p. 720.

41. Coleridge, 'Kubla Khan: or, a Vision in a Dream', in: *The Collected Works of Samuel Taylor Coleridge: Poetical Works*, p. 514.
42. Kierkegaard, 'The Rotation Method', p. 289.
43. See Northrop Frye's influential study *The Secular Scripture*; the Romance is initially divided into the naïve and sentimental, and Frye reads the latter as driven by the polarised representation of light and dark heroes, the idyllic world with the world of nightmare, and narrative patterns of descent and ascent.
44. De Man, *The Rhetoric of Romanticism*, p. 105.
45. See note to I, 927 and also *BLJ*, vol. 2, p. 84.
46. De Staël, *Corinne, or Italy*, Book XVIII, ch. III, pp. 366–7.
47. For further discussion on Byron, de Staël and the Santa Croce, see Wilkes, *Lord Byron and Madame de Staël: Born for Opposition*.
48. Curran, *Poetic Form*, p. 157.
49. O'Neill, 'Poetry of the Romantic Period', p. 305.

## Works cited

Aristotle (1984), *The Complete Works of Aristotle*, ed. Jonathan Barnes, trans. J. I. Beare, vol. 1, Princeton: Princeton University Press.

Coleridge, Samuel Taylor (2001), *The Collected Works of Samuel Taylor Coleridge: Poetical Works*, Part 1 Poems (Reading Text), ed. J. C. C. Mays, Princeton: Princeton University Press.

Curran, Stuart (1986), *Poetic Form and British Romanticism*, Oxford: Oxford University Press.

de Man, Paul (1984), *The Rhetoric of Romanticism*, New York: Columbia University Press.

de Staël, Madame (2008), *Corinne, or Italy*, trans. Sylvia Raphael, Oxford: Oxford University Press.

Frye, Northrop (2006), *The Secular Scripture: A Study of the Structure of Romance in The Secular Scripture and Other Writings on Critical Theory, 1976–1991*, vol. 18, ed. Joseph Adamson and Jean Wilson, Toronto: University of Toronto Press, pp. 3–124.

Godwin, William (1993), *Political and Philosophical Writings of William Godwin: Educational and Literary Writings*, ed. Pamela Clemit, vol. 5, London: Pickering & Chatto.

Hill, Alan G. (1979), *The Letters of William and Dorothy Wordsworth*, vol. 5, Oxford: Clarendon Press.

Kierkegaard, Søren (1959), 'The Rotation Method', in: Howard A. Johnson (ed.), *Either / Or*, vol. 1, trans. David F. Swenson and Liliane Marvin Swenson, Princeton: Princeton University Press.

Kucich, Greg (1991), *Keats, Shelley, and Romantic Spenserianism*, University Park, PA: Pennsylvania State University Press.

— (2000), 'Romanticism and the Re-engendering of Historical Memory', in: Matthew Campbell, Jacqueline Labbe and Sally Shuttleworth (eds), *Memory and Memorials 1789–1914: Literary and Cultural Perspectives*, London / New York: Routledge, pp. 15–29.

O'Neill, Michael (2007), 'Poetry of the Romantic Period: Coleridge and Keats', in: Corinne Saunders (ed.), *A Companion to Romance: From Classical to Contemporary*, Oxford: Blackwell, pp. 305–20.

Perry, Seamus (1999), 'Romanticism: The Brief History of a Concept', in: Duncan Wu (ed.), *A Companion to Romanticism*, Oxford: Blackwell, pp. 3–11.

Reiman, Donald H. (1972), *The Romantics Reviewed: Contemporary Reviews of British Romantic Writers: Part B: Byron and Regency Society Poets*, vols 1–5. New York / London: Garland.

Saglia, Diego (2000), 'Ending the Romance: Women Poets and the Romantic Verse Tale', in: Cecilia Pietropoli (ed.), *Romantic Women Poets: Genre and Gender*, Amsterdam: Rodopi, pp. 153–68.

— (2000), *Poetic Castles in Spain: British Romanticism and Figurations of Iberia*, Amsterdam: Rodopi.

St Clair, William (2004), *The Reading Nation in the Romantic Period*, Cambridge: Cambridge University Press.

Saintsbury, George (1922), *A Short History of English Literature*, London: Macmillan.

Sandy, Mark (2013), *Romanticism, Memory, and Mourning*, Farnham: Ashgate.

Schiller, Friedrich ([1803] 1993), 'On the Employment of the Chorus in Tragedy', trans. George Gregory, in: *Fidelio*, 2, pp. 60–4.

Scott, Sir Walter (1834), *The Miscellaneous Prose Works of Sir Walter Scott: Essays on Chivalry, Romance, and the Drama*, ed. James Ballantyne, vol. 6, Edinburgh: Robert Cadell.

— (1932), *The Letters of Sir Walter Scott: 1811–1814*, ed. Herbert J. C. Grierson, vol. 3, London: Constable & Co.

Stevenson, Robert Louis (1999), 'A Gossip on Romance', in: Glenda Norquay (ed.), *R. L. Stevenson on Fiction: An Anthology of Literary and Critical Essays*, Edinburgh: Edinburgh University Press, pp. 51–64.

Thompson, Carl (2007), *The Suffering Traveller and the Romantic Imagination*, Oxford: Oxford University Press.

Wilkes, Joanne (1999), *Lord Byron and Madame de Staël: Born for Opposition*, Aldershot: Ashgate.

Chapter 10

# The Margins of Genius: Byron, Nationalism and the Periodical Reviews

*Josefina Tuominen-Pope*

The dichotomy of respectable art and popular entertainment is a significant element in the hierarchy of professional authorship.[1] This dichotomy can be traced back to the late eighteenth and the early nineteenth centuries, when writers for the first time encountered a potential mass audience due to the increase in both literacy and printed material,[2] leading to an economic incentive for authors to reach as many readers as possible. These developments coincided with the heightening of public interest in artistic genius[3] along with the belief that true genius was misunderstood by the public. This, in turn, created a juxtaposition between the authors' ambitions of reaching as vast a readership as possible and the idea that writers with true genius cared little for the contemporary response. A debate arose around the question of whether or not a work could be considered the product of genius if it was also popular among the mass audience. A related question was whether or not it was acceptable for a genius author to seek contemporary popularity in addition to, or even instead of, posthumous fame.

In what follows I present a case study on the treatment of Lord Byron as a man of genius in the early nineteenth-century media. Byron was branded a genius from early on in his career as a poet, but he was also seen as someone who openly pursued contemporary popularity. He occupied a space at the margins of genius and the crossing point between high and popular culture, and this brought criticism from several contributors to the periodical press. What was seen as particularly problematic was Byron's perceived wasting of his genius on works designed to garner favour among the mass readership. Another theme that often comes up in the early nineteenth-century writing on genius is the relationship between genius and the nation that has produced it, and I suggest that there is a link between the discourse on national genius and the critics' dismay at Byron's profligate employment of his talent. I propose that one reason for the often hostile treatment of Byron in the Romantic media is that genius was perceived to be something that did not belong solely to the artist but rather to the nation that had produced him or her. This meant that Byron's genius was not his to throw away, and by wasting it in pursuit of fame he was injuring not only his own posthumous reputation but also Britain's national property.

As critics such as Mark Parker and David Higgins, among others, have noted, magazines and other periodicals were the leading literary form in the early decades of the nineteenth century.[4] Due to the high price of books, many members of the reading public relied predominantly, or even exclusively, on magazines and reviews for knowledge about the latest novels, poems and other literary productions. With their characteristically long excerpts from the works being discussed, periodicals such as the *Edinburgh Review*, the *Quarterly Review*, *Blackwood's Edinburgh Magazine* and the *London Magazine* were able to provide access to literature in a way that made reading the full-length work seemingly unnecessary. Having the time and the money to buy and read the latest work of Byron or Walter Scott was an indicator of social class that was now being blurred by the new reading culture of the periodical press. This loss of cultural capital caused anxiety and annoyance among people like Wordsworth, who complained that '[t]hese people, in the senseless hurry of their idle lives, do not *read* books, they merely snatch a glance at them, that they may talk about them'.[5] In addition to this, periodicals played an important role in creating cultural awareness of new fashions, important events and notable people, and they had a significant impact on their audiences when it came to making judgements of taste. It was also through the periodical press that authors and other public figures would gain fame and exposure, which in the Romantic period was for the first time becoming recognised as a goal that artists strived to achieve. Thus the power of the periodical press over public perception was considerable.

The concept of genius is central to all discussion of literature in the early nineteenth-century media. In his book *Romantic Genius and the Literary Magazine*, Higgins describes the portrayal of genius in the Romantic periodical press, and remarks that 'it was through [literary magazines] that, in Britain at least, genius first became widely discussed and represented'.[6] As he shows, the vast interest in genius – partly created by the magazines themselves – led to the practice of publishing biographies and other information about individuals perceived to possess genius. This interest in the personalities of authors contributed to the rise of celebrity culture in the Romantic period, as it led to artists like Byron being known for their lives and personalities as much as for their work. The periodical press is therefore a vital source in understanding the public image of Byron in his lifetime as both a genius and a celebrity – an image the periodicals themselves played a key role in shaping.

Genius is constantly evoked in the literary magazines of the period, yet the precise definition of the term remains unclear. Andrew Elfenbein has aptly characterised Romantic genius as 'a loose term of praise' that is used in all areas of culture, whose meaning 'was taken to be self-evident' and whose 'power came partly from its vagueness'.[7] The vagueness of the meaning did not go unnoticed by contemporary critics, and occasionally caused exasperation among them. John Gibson Lockhart expresses his frustration by complaining in *Blackwood's* that '[t]hat one word *genius* has done more harm than anything in the vocabulary. It has been prostituted till it has lost all meaning.'[8] This vagueness also presents a challenge for the analysis of early nineteenth-century discourse on genius, for it is often difficult to ascertain to what extent the various commentators mean the same thing when using the word 'genius' in their writing. In addition to the lack of a clear definition of poetic genius associated with writers' talents and abilities, one often finds references to genius in its original meaning of 'spirit' or 'disposition',[9] which further complicates the matter.

However, one defining feature that strongly characterises early nineteenth-century writing about genius is the dichotomy of high and popular culture. While the price of new books published by popular contemporary authors was very high, more and more cheaper reading material became available to the literate of lesser means. With the rapid increase in the publishing of books designed for quick mass-market consumption rather than any kind of permanent place in the annals of literature, a strong sense of resentment towards what Richard Altick refers to as 'the notorious twopenny trash'[10] was cultivated among the literati. Samuel Egerton Brydges writes in his autobiography that

> [i]t is a vile evil that literature is become so much a trade all over Europe. Nothing has gone so far to nurture a corrupt taste, and to give the unintellectual the power over the intellectual. Merit is now universally estimated by the multitude of readers that an author can attract.[11]

(Good) taste had become one of the ways in which the élite was able to differentiate itself from those with new wealth combined with a labouring-class background, a new faction of society that had emerged through the opportunities for financial improvement offered by industrialisation. As Altick notes, the emphasis placed on social class was on the rise throughout the nineteenth century,[12] and one consequence of this was the alarm Brydges expresses over the expansion of the literary marketplace.

A central element of this conflict was the notion that writers who possessed genius had to endure neglect and unappreciation during their lives, and would find a sympathetic audience only in future generations – apart from those particularly enlightened individuals who were capable of recognising genius in their contemporaries.[13] This figure of the neglected genius offered a way of drawing a distinction between high and popular culture, as it implied that works that were popular among the masses were not creations of genius and belonged to a lower order of literature. The idea that a mark of genius was being neglected by the mass audience is perhaps most famously put forward by William Wordsworth in his 'Essay, Supplementary to the Preface' (1815), where he argues that due to the originality of genius it is inevitable that the reading public, attracted by human nature to what is familiar, is at first repelled by works of genius.[14] The implication of this, of course, is that anything that is instantly popular cannot be the product of highly original genius.

Allusions to the neglect suffered by genius authors can also be found in the Romantic periodical press. An anonymous letter published in the *Imperial Magazine* in 1821 laments the 'fate which too commonly attends those great men', which is to live their lives 'in obscurity and contempt'.[15] Another writer for the same periodical states in the same year that

> [c]ould we by any possible means take a retrospective glance at the genius of every man who has lived within the last century, we should find that few, very few indeed, have met with the encouragement they deserved or expected.[16]

Not being appreciated by one's contemporaries is so strongly embedded in the tradition of genius that even today it can still be said to impact on our understanding of the relationship between talent and popularity.[17]

However, while the figure of the neglected genius was very much a part of the discourse on genius in publications such as the *Imperial Magazine*, the notion that the contemporary audience could not understand genius was becoming increasingly challenged in other periodicals. Some years after Byron's death, a writer for the *London Magazine* addresses the issue directly. He asserts that

> nothing ever really and permanently excellent was not popular, [. . .] no one who ever lived through many ages as a poet, could have built that reputation upon the applause of a few dreaming enthusiasts, who would hand down his merits as a sort of freemasonry secret [. . .] .[18]

This writer rejects Wordsworth's assertion that neglect is a sign of genius and instead argues the exact opposite. This argument reflects the stance taken by the popular magazines of the time, primarily the *London Magazine* and *Blackwood's Edinburgh Magazine* – at least as far as these publications can be said to have taken a unified stance at all. The critics writing for these periodicals acknowledged the aspiration to gain renown as a common quality of authors; as John Wilson remarks in *Blackwood's*, the 'pleasure of communicating to others what fills our own breast, impels youth to write'.[19] Critics also sought ways to reconcile the somewhat base pursuit for recognition with the lofty image of genius. A letter published in *Blackwood's* in 1820 and signed by Samuel Taylor Coleridge discusses the value of literary praise and argues for its importance for the flourishing of genius. Without praise, Coleridge writes, 'the hopes and purposes of genius sink back on the heart, like a sigh on the tightened chest of a sick man'.[20] This argument is directly related to the concept of the neglected genius, and it further emphasises the necessity of feeling loved for genius to thrive. This makes the pursuit of popularity not only normal but also vital for any writer with genius, and in accordance with Coleridge, *Blackwood's* declares that 'love of fame' is 'the universal passion, the stimulus, and the exciting cause' that drives artists of every kind to pursue excellence.[21] Similarly, the *London Magazine* argues that it is most natural to be fearful of the idea of being forgotten after death, remarking, 'This horror of oblivion was not planted in our souls only to sadden us, it being, perhaps, the most powerful and permanent of all motives to useful and honourable action.'[22] In other words, hunger for prestige can be a stronger motivator to do good than anything else. While this comment appears sarcastic in tone, it can be read to reflect some degree of honesty: the most compelling reason to do good is the desire to be thought of as a good person, just as the strongest incentive to strive to produce great art is to be remembered as a great artist. While such motives may not appear noble in themselves, desire for acclaim is needed for the creation of works of genius. One might suggest that the magazine writers are keen to justify hunger for fame and to argue that it can be a quality associated with genius because they themselves were openly pursuing as large an audience as possible, but at the same time wanted to align themselves with genius and high culture. By maintaining that the aspiration to gain maximum popularity was in keeping with the mind of a genius, they were effectively elevating their own profession.

An article published in *Blackwood's* in 1818 and titled 'On the Influence of the Love of Fame on Genius' conducts an analysis of the relationship between genius and desire for public acclaim in more detail, exploring the complex network of ideals that allows for the seemingly conflicting combination of motives. The article begins with the assumption that genius and desire for celebrity are mutually incompatible: 'In our reverent admiration of genius, the love of fame finds no place.'[23] The reason for this is that most ordinary people feel the hunger for public attention, and one of the functions of genius is to elevate the minds of its audience from such base cravings into a higher state of being. Therefore, the article argues, it is inconceivable that the genius author himself is troubled by the same lowly aspirations:

> How can we imagine that mind, in the very act of conceiving and embodying those creations which lift us up out of our ordinary life, [. . .] how can we imagine that such a mind should yet be occupied at the very time by the working of the passions from which it delivers us?[24]

The answer to this dilemma is that the passion for fame felt by writers of true genius is motivated by an urge to let others benefit from the fruits of their genius. Genius authors 'passionately desire that their thoughts may not pass away from the earth, but that they may live as powerful, as full a life, as glowing as in the first conception, during endless ages'.[25] This desire is altruistic; it is 'not for themselves; but that it may be an enduring power among the spirits of other men and other generations'.[26] The writer concludes the argument by stating that 'there are powerful and honourable causes for a deep impassioned interest in fame'.[27]

What these commentaries reflect is that the view that popularity and genius were mutually exclusive was not by any means held by all cultural commentators in the Romantic period. At the same time, they also reveal the anxiety still attached to the issue. The writer of the *Blackwood's* article quoted above states that genius authors receive from contemporary fame the assurance that 'what they have felt and known they have given to be felt and known for ever'[28]; in other words, appreciation from one's contemporaries implies posthumous fame, and for this reason love of fame is a 'noble feeling'.[29] This shows that the distinction between contemporary and posthumous fame was thought to be significant even by those who saw the former as an acceptable target of pursuit.

While Byron is not named anywhere in the *Blackwood's* article on genius and love of fame, he in many ways personifies the problematic balance between the demands of genius and the desire for fame that the article addresses. The word 'genius' is applied to Byron somewhat systematically in discussions of his works in the various periodicals of the early nineteenth century. He is called 'a poetical genius of a very high order'[30] and 'the personification of genius',[31] and even when his works are being criticised, they are more often than not acknowledged to display the marks of the mind of a genius.[32] However, a complaint frequently voiced by the early nineteenth-century critics was that, along with his mighty genius, Byron exhibited equally strong signs of an excessive thirst for renown. In *The Spirit of the Age* (1825), William Hazlitt states that, contrary to Byron's assertion that he wrote only for himself, his sole motivation was to garner attention. 'He would never write another page, if it were not to court popular applause, or to affect superiority over it,' Hazlitt argues.[33] The *London Magazine* refers to Byron's 'morbid and voracious appetite for fame',[34] and after his death a writer for *Blackwood's* reflects, 'Think what such a man might have been, had only better qualities of his heart been cherished, and his passion for fame fostered by the discipline of virtue!'[35] Lady Blessington also confirms this in *Conversations of Lord Byron*, where she states that

> Byron had so unquenchable a thirst for celebrity, that no means were left untried that might attain it [. . .]. There was no sort of celebrity that he did not, at some point or other, condescend to seek, and he was not over nice in the means, provided he obtained the end.[36]

Byron's desperation for fame is noted by several commentators with varying degrees of disapproval. However, since the same magazines that expressed such disdain had argued that it was acceptable, even noble, for a genius author to pursue popularity, and that love of fame was a 'universal passion', what prompted these responses must have been something beyond the mere fact that Byron was thought to be actively seeking recognition among his contemporaries. A key issue, I suggest, is that Byron was perceived to have made too great a sacrifice on the altar of fame. The *Blackwood's* article quoted above goes on to note that love of fame is a noble feeling only as long as it takes a secondary position in the mind of the genius. '[W]oe to him', the writer proclaims, 'in whom it precedes genius, or bears an undue proportion to its power.'[37] What may follow, according to the writer, is that the author may end up misusing his genius or 'compelling his genius to work for purposes not its own'.[38] This is what was thought to have befallen Byron. What made Byron's quest for popularity reprehensible in the eyes of the critics was that in their minds he was compromising his genius in the process. He was not merely a genius author who also wanted recognition from his contemporaries, but rather was seen as a gifted writer who would willingly waste his talent on works that were enjoyed by the ignorant masses ready to worship him, but that were beneath his higher abilities.

This allegation is voiced by a writer for *Ladies' Monthly Museum*, who complains that with his tales of pirates and faraway adventures Byron 'feeds the vulgar mind which delights in mystery'.[39] This, according to the writer, makes him 'like an actor who debases himself by playing to the gallery'.[40] In other words, by writing works that were aimed primarily at pleasing the masses, Byron was putting himself in a state of disgrace and dishonour. A similar statement is made by a writer for *The Champion*, who professes his confidence that if Byron were to abandon his 'paltry affectations and childish fondnesses for such things as giants and gigantic achievements', his poetic talent would entitle him to 'the praises of the wise, as well as the stupid admiration of the vulgar and unthinking'.[41] Eight years later, in 1822, the *Quarterly Review* discusses its reaction to Byron's three new plays – *Marino Faliero*, *Sardanapalus* and *Cain* (all 1821). The writer remarks that it is with 'deep regret and disappointment' that he has witnessed 'the systematic and increasing prostitution of those splendid talents to the expression of feelings, and the promulgation of opinions, which as Christians, as Englishmen, and even as men, we were constrained to regard with abhorrence'.[42] What all these comments reveal is a strong irritation and disappointment with Byron's choice of subject matter and the direction of his career as a poet.

I suggest there is a strong link between this expression of irritation and the rather emotional rhetoric used in the writing about genius. In an article published in the *London Magazine* in 1822, Peter G. Patmore reflects on the feelings brought on by the genius of others:

> I can scarcely conceive of a nobler and more inspiring sight than that of a man of genius in the solitude of his closet, conscious of his powers, and warmed by the fire of his conceptions – pouring forth those treasures of imagination and intellect which are to enrich, exalt, and delight future ages.[43]

There is a pride that comes across in these words, as if the writer felt ownership of sorts of the product of the genius he describes. I suggest this is due to an idea of genius as something that is produced by, and therefore belongs to, the nation as a whole, and in which all members of that nation can therefore take pride. Following the Napoleonic Wars, there was a rise of nationalist feeling all over Europe, manifested in newfound interest in past glory and emphasising emotional ties to the nation.[44] Seeing genius as a unifying force for the nation certainly fits in with this mindset.

References to the idea of national genius can be found in analyses of genius in the Romantic media. An article published in *Blackwood's* in 1819 discusses genius in relation to nationality, and the writer begins by noting that '[g]enius, among different nations, has found different means of giving expression to its inward power, and communicating itself to men'.[45] According to the writer, '[o]f all the arts of imagination, that which England has carried to the highest pitch is undoubtedly Poetry, as its annals will witness from the time of Chaucer to our own day'.[46] Genius is discussed here as an entity that can 'communicate itself to men' as opposed to a property of an individual poet, and as such belongs to the country that has 'carried it to the highest pitch'. It is England, or Britain, as a whole that is responsible for the development of its poetical genius, and therefore it is for the country as a whole to take pride in the products of its genius, or as in the case of Byron, feel wronged when that genius is misused or wasted.

Writing for *Blackwood's*, John Wilson draws attention to the connection between genius and its country of origin. He argues that it is 'the state of the mind of the whole nation that must determine the character of its literature'.[47] In other words, the entire nation can be held accountable for the state of its literature. Wilson goes on to say that if the country's state of mind is 'sound, strong, aspiring, and enlightened', then its literature will be safe from 'weakness, taint, or degradation'.[48] This puts the responsibility of producing high-quality literature on the shoulders of the entire country and not just the author, but at the same time it lays claim to the prestige given to such literature. The entire nation must put effort into making sure the atmosphere of the country is conducive to the growth of genius. If it succeeds in doing so, the entire nation can take some credit for the works of genius that are produced within its realm.

Wilson discusses the issue of national genius on more than one occasion. In another article in *Blackwood's* titled 'On the Analogy Between the Growth of Individual and National Genius' he states that 'there is a very general and deep-felt admiration of those works of genius in every kind, which bear impressed on them the character of the people among whom they have arisen, and which seem native, as it were, to their soil'.[49] Here, again, the idea of genius as something that is born out of a nation is strengthened through emphasising the invisible bond that ties the audience to works produced by domestic genius. Later in the same article, Wilson asks 'shall genius, by intellectual pride, separate itself from the lot of its people, refuse the bounty of nature, and imagine to itself sources of power opened up to it in its own bosom alone?'[50] This is stating rather directly the idea that genius belongs to the entire nation. For a man of genius to imagine that the power of that genius can be traced back 'to his bosom alone', instead of the community responsible for cultivating an environment that has nurtured the genius, is foolish. This point is made even clearer by the answer Wilson provides to his own question: genius 'cannot shake off the nature in which it lives; it cannot hold its power in independence of the bounty that nourished it up'.[51]

The greater the genius – and the fame – of an author, the more expectations were attached to his or her work. A writer for *Blackwood's* draws a direct link between Byron's genius and that of Britain when he says, 'The writings of Byron alone [. . .] are sufficient to carry down, to remotest posterity, a powerful impression of the genius of the age that produced them.'[52] In other words, what Byron has written will bring glory to all his contemporaries in the eyes of future readers. This gives the genius writers great responsibility, for they hold the reputation of the entire society in their hands. This responsibility was allocated to others as well, as Byron was not the only celebrity author whose genius was thought to belong to his country. In 1820, John Scott argues in the *London Magazine* that Walter Scott belongs to his country as well:

If Sir Walter Scott has been elevated to a situation of perfectly unexampled celebrity and influence, by the unanimous applauses of all who are in any way concerned in the distribution of the honours of intellect, and in awarding literary fame, he must be content, along with what is pleasant and profitable in this distinction, to bear its responsibility. His name has become national property; his conduct, therefore, may have an immediate and direct influence on his nation's interests and reputation.[53]

The argument put forward here is that the arrangement between an author and the audience is something like a contract that binds both parties. The author has been awarded celebrity by those 'who are in any way concerned in the distribution of the honours of intellect' – a phrase that seems to imply that allocating fame is done with great consideration by a body of experts with the power to give and take away renown. In return the author must act in a way that advances these benefactors. The last sentence of the excerpt could not be any clearer: Walter Scott (or any author to whom fame has been awarded) is 'national property' and his priority must be 'his nation's interests and reputation'.

As the above quotation shows, genius was felt to be something that belonged to the nation, and those in possession of it had the responsibility to use it correctly. This comes across in the criticism of the ways in which Byron chose to employ his skills. As the *Imperial Magazine* states in an article on Byron, '[t]he more powerful the genius of a man may be, if those powers are employed in the cause of vice and in the promotion of evil, the more they call for a louder denunciation against them'.[54] The reviewer of the first two Cantos of *Don Juan* (1819) in *Blackwood's* also connects his disappointment in Byron's use of his genius to the poet's relationship with his homeland. According to the writer, knowing this offensive poem is written 'by one of the most powerful intellects our island ever has produced, lends intensity a thousand fold to the bitterness of our indignation'.[55] The words chosen by the writer, which describe Byron as an 'intellect' Britain 'has produced', again underline the idea that the whole nation has had its hand in the creation of genius. Similarly, the *British Review* reflects on previous commentaries on Byron's (and others') work in the journal by remarking that 'we have spoken out very decidedly on the scandalous objects to which some of the best efforts of the British Muse have been devoted'.[56] Here the national genius is personified in the 'British Muse' that has been violated by the offending authors.

A letter published in the *Imperial Magazine* in 1821 adds another dimension to the discussion on national genius and its advancement. The writer makes the argument that it is everyone's duty to support, financially and otherwise, those artists who possess genius when the need arises. This, according to the writer, is doing a service to one's country: 'The benefit they render to the individual is great; the benefit they render their country is greater.'[57] In other words, it is the duty of the entire nation to look after its genius, which in practice means providing financial assistance and patronage. This, then, would suggest that the nation can expect something in return from the genius it fosters. Indeed, while Byron never received any such patronage from his countrymen, it was still expected of him that he use his genius for the good of his country. The *British Review* professes to find it difficult to believe that 'Lord Byron, an English nobleman, an English husband, and an English father', is the author of the offensive *Beppo* (1818),[58] and the *Imperial Magazine* accuses Byron of abandoning his country in a time of need and failing to use his genius to its benefit. The writer asks, 'While his country was engaged in a desperate conflict, did he wield the sword – did he devote his own powerful genius in her behalf? No; rambling in a foreign land, he turned the powers he possessed against her [. . .].'[59] The writer does not say what he would have expected Byron to do for his country instead of 'rambling in a foreign land', but his message is clearly that Byron had neglected to use his 'powerful genius' to benefit his country.

The demand that Byron serve his country better is also connected to his status as a peer of the realm, a position that would have allowed him to apply his genius to the benefit of his country even more directly, and as Nicholas Mason notes, the dichotomy of the roles of a poet and a peer caused Byron anxiety throughout his career.[60] The implications of the combined personas were also noted by contemporaries such as William Hazlitt, who remarks that 'Lord Byron has been twice as much talked of as he would have been, had he not been Lord Byron.'[61] Hazlitt argues that Byron's combination of nobility and genius is what makes him so interesting in the eyes of the public, stating that '[h]is rank and genius have been happily placed "each other's beams to share", and both together, by their mutually reflected splendour, may be said to have melted the public interest into the very wantonness of praise'.[62] If, as Hazlitt argues, Byron owes his celebrity not only to his genius but also to his aristocracy, then the call on him to dedicate his efforts to the advancement of his country is even stronger than on other men of genius.

The writing on national genius shows great enthusiasm on the part of the critics. William Carey, for instance, declares in the *New Monthly Magazine* in 1819 that it is his 'sincere and constant effort' to 'create a national pride in British genius, and a national love of British art'.[63] The other side of this earnestness is the outrage with which Byron's indiscretions are met. The feelings of violation are often expressed with much anger and bitterness. *Blackwood's* calls Byron's comments on Robert Southey in the notes to *The Two Foscari* (1821) 'shocking wilful degradation of majestic genius',[64] and in another issue of *Blackwood's* a writer comments on Cantos VI to VIII of *Don Juan* by lamenting the fact that 'one so gifted [. . .] should descend to the composition of heartless, heavy, dull, anti-British garbage'.[65] There are, of course, other significant reasons why many of the critics were offended by these works, but the fact that they were written by a man in possession of British genius appears to make the insult even more impactful. In a letter published in *Blackwood's* shortly after Byron's death, Robert Southey states that his own personal animosity towards Byron was due to the way the latter 'had brought a stigma upon English literature',[66] which, I would argue, is a key reason for the vehemence displayed by the other critics as well. As one contributor to the *London Magazine* states, addressing Byron directly, 'You are a man of genius, my Lord, and as such an honour to your country: – but, Sir, it were better for our fame that you never had been born amongst us.'[67]

We have no way of knowing how Byron himself would have reacted to the notion that the genius manifested in him belonged to his country and not to him alone. He never expressed any response to or even awareness of the arguments put forward by the commentators mentioned here, though he claimed to have little interest in what people thought of either him or his poetry. Discussing the reception of *Don Juan* in an 1819 letter to John Murray, Byron retorts, 'As for the Estimation of the English which you talk of [. . .] I have not written for their pleasure.'[68] He also did not display a great amount of respect for the literary periodicals and their views on poets and their work, referring in *Don Juan* to the varying lists of the 'greatest living poets' printed in 'every paltry magazine' (*Don Juan* XI, l. 54) and calling them 'the literary *lower* empire' (*Don Juan* XI, l. 62). It was, of course, common among authors to hold the periodical reviews in low regard.

What I have attempted to do in this chapter is to present one aspect of the treatment of genius in the early nineteenth-century media. In the time Byron wrote and published his work, the relationship between art and mass culture was only beginning to form, and this was reflected in the writing on genius, particularly in relation to popularity. Seeking contemporary fame and popularity was becoming acceptable even for writers with genius, but the matter was by no means unproblematic. Byron was operating in a new cultural territory at the margins of genius where high and popular culture intersect, but in the eyes of many critics he did not show due reverence for his own genius, and abused and wasted it in his pursuit of fame. This was taken as a personal insult by writers who felt a shared ownership of the national genius manifested in Byron. It may have been acceptable, occasionally even noble, for someone with genius to seek fame, but only as long as the building of the author's image did not interfere with the building of the nation's reputation.

There is something oddly circular about the juxtaposing of personal fame and genius in this way. It was demanded of Byron that he put his genius ahead of his desire for fame, and the justification for that demand came from the view that the genius Byron was wasting did not belong to him alone but to the entire nation. But in order for genius to be the product of a nationwide effort in a meaningful way, that nation must be aware of its accomplishment, which means being aware of the genius manifested in the works of an author. And what else is fame but public awareness of an individual? It may be that the will to protect national genius was more closely related to the 'stupid admiration of the vulgar and unthinking' than the critics were willing to admit. Only for them the admiration had turned into possession.

## Notes

1. Joe Moran argues in his extensive study on literary stardom that celebrity authors face a uniquely strong pressure to maintain a balance between the integrity of their art and the pursuit of financial gains from their work; see Moran, *Star Authors: Literary Celebrity in America*, p. 53.
2. Mole, *Byron's Romantic Celebrity: Industrial Culture and the Hermeneutic of Intimacy*, p. 10.
3. Higgins, *Romantic Genius and the Literary Magazine: Biography, Celebrity, Politics*, p. 1.
4. Parker, *Literary Magazines and British Romanticism*, p. 1; Higgins, *Romantic Genius*, p. 6.
5. Selincourt, ed., *The Letters of William and Dorothy Wordsworth: The Middle Years*, vol. 1, p. 150.
6. Higgins, *Romantic Genius*, p. 150.
7. Elfenbein, *Romantic Genius: The Prehistory of a Homosexual Role*, p. 28.
8. Lockhart, 'Sir Egerton Brydges's Recollections', pp. 505–67.
9. For example, when William Hazlitt states that '[t]he English genius excludes sententious and sentimental declamations on the passions', he appears to be referring above all to the spirit of the nation; Hazlitt, 'The Periodical Press', p. 354.
10. Altick, *The English Common Reader: A Social History of the Mass Reading Public, 1800–1900*, p. 271.
11. Brydges, *The Autobiography, Times, Opinions, and Contemporaries of Sir Egerton Brydges, Bart*, vol. 2, p. 202.
12. Altick, *The English Common Reader*, p. 85.
13. Higgins notes that literary magazines would often flatter their readers by implying that they were the only ones capable of recognising and appreciating contemporary genius; Higgins, *Romantic Genius*, p. 4.

14. Owen and Smyser, eds, *The Prose Works of William Wordsworth*, vol. 3, p. 64.
15. [P. G. J.], 'On the Neglect of Genius', p. 938.
16. [M. M.], 'On the Neglect of Genius', p. 1075.
17. As Wenche Ommundsen notes in an essay on twenty-first-century celebrity authors, a 'writer [. . .] has no business courting celebrity: in order to serve the cause of literature he must maintain a position separate from the grubby practices of politics or commercialized culture'; Ommundsen, 'From the Altar to the Market-place and Back Again: Understanding Literary Celebrity', p. 245.
18. [Anon.], 'The Editor's Room No VII', p. 428.
19. Wilson, 'On Literary Censorship', p. 176.
20. Coleridge, 'Letter to Peter Morris, M.D. on the Sorts and Uses of Literary Praise', p. 629.
21. [D. M.], 'On Critics and Criticism', p. 138.
22. [R. A.], 'On Fame and Monuments', p. 37.
23. [N.], 'On the Influence of the Love of Fame on Genius', p. 702.
24. Ibid., pp. 702–3.
25. Ibid., p. 703.
26. Ibid., p. 703.
27. Ibid., p. 704.
28. Ibid., p. 703.
29. Ibid., p. 703.
30. [C.], 'Lord Byron', p. 45
31. [Anon.], 'The Augustan Age in England', p. 205.
32. For example, Wilson or Lockhart, 'Remarks on *Don Juan*', pp. 512–18.
33. Howe, ed., *The Complete Works of William Hazlitt*, vol. 11, p. 76.
34. Southern, 'Personal Character of Lord Byron', p. 338.
35. Galt and Harness, 'Lord Byron's Conversations', p. 531.
36. Lovell, ed., *Lady Blessington's Conversations of Lord Byron*, p. 222.
37. [N.], 'On the Influence of the Love of Fame on Genius', p. 705.
38. Ibid., p. 704.
39. [R.], 'Portraits of Modern Poets. No II. Lord Byron', p. 88.
40. Ibid., p. 88.
41. Barnes, 'Portraits of Authors: Mr. Byron', p. 118.
42. Heber, 'Lord Byron's Dramas', p. 476.
43. Patmore [P.], 'On Magazine Writers', p. 21.
44. For example, Baycroft, *Nationalism in Europe 1789–1945*, p. 24.
45. [Anon.], 'On the Study of Language, as Essential to the Successful Cultivation of Literature', p. 55.
46. Ibid., p. 55.
47. Wilson, 'On Literary Censorship', p. 176.
48. Ibid., p. 176.
49. Wilson, 'On the Analogy Between the Growth of Individual and National Genius', p. 375.

50. Ibid., p. 380.
51. Ibid., p. 380.
52. [Anon.], 'Remarks on the Diversity of Genius', p. 677.
53. Scott, 'Blackwood's Magazine', p. 518.
54. Milner [G. M.], 'On the Genius and Writings of Lord Byron', p. 254.
55. Wilson or Lockhart, 'Remarks on *Don Juan*', p. 514.
56. Roberts, *'Beppo, a Venetian Story'*, p. 331.
57. [M. M.], 'On the Neglect of Genius', p. 1079.
58. Roberts, *'Beppo, A Venetian Story'*, p. 329.
59. Milner [G. M.], 'On the Genius and Writings of Lord Byron', p. 255.
60. Mason, 'Building Brand Byron: Early-Nineteenth-Century Advertising and the Marketing of *Childe Harold's Pilgrimage*', p. 427.
61. Hazlitt, 'Pope, Lord Byron, and Mr. Bowles', p. 594.
62. Ibid., p. 594.
63. Carey, 'Fine Arts', p. 52.
64. Lockhart, 'Lord Byron's Three New Tragedies', p. 92.
65. Maginn [T. T.], 'Letters of Timothy Tickler, Esq. No VII: On the New Cantos of *Don Juan*', p. 88.
66. Southey, 'Southey and Byron', p. 714.
67. Darley, 'A Fifth Letter to the Dramatists of the Day', p. 536.
68. *BLJ*, vol. 7, pp. 105–6.

## Works cited

Altick, Richard D. (1998), *The English Common Reader: A Social History of the Mass Reading Public, 1800–1900*, Columbus: Ohio State University Press.
[Anon.] (1819), 'On the Study of Language, as Essential to the Successful Cultivation of Literature', *Blackwood's Edinburgh Magazine*, 5, pp. 55–9.
— (1820), 'Remarks on the Diversity of Genius', *Blackwood's Edinburgh Magazine*, 6, pp. 674–8.
— (1822), 'The Augustan Age in England', *The Album*, 2, pp. 203–34.
— (1828), 'The Editor's Room No VII', *London Magazine*, 3rd series, vol. 2, pp. 422–30.
— [C.] (1822), 'Lord Byron', *Brighton Magazine*, 7, pp. 45–51.
— [D. M.] (1820), 'On Critics and Criticism', *Blackwood's Edinburgh Magazine*, 8, pp. 138–41.
— [M. M.] (1821), 'On the Neglect of Genius', *Imperial Magazine*, 3, pp. 1075–9.
— [N.] (1818), 'On the Influence of the Love of Fame on Genius', *Blackwood's Edinburgh Magazine*, 3, pp. 701–5.
— [P. G. J.] (1821), 'On the Neglect of Genius', *Imperial Magazine*, 3, pp. 938–9.

— [R.] (1822), 'Portraits of Modern Poets. No II. Lord Byron', *Ladies' Monthly Museum,* 3rd series, issue 15, pp. 86–91.

— [R. A.] (1823), 'On Fame and Monuments', *London Magazine,* 8, pp. 37–43.

Barnes, Thomas (1814), 'Portraits of Authors: Mr. Byron', *The Champion,* 7 May, p. 118.

Baycroft, Timothy (1998), *Nationalism in Europe 1789–1945,* Cambridge: Cambridge University Press.

Brydges, Samuel Egerton (1834), *The Autobiography, Times, Opinions, and Contemporaries of Sir Egerton Brydges, Bart,* 2 vols, London.

Carey, William [W. C.] (1819), 'Fine Arts', *New Monthly Magazine and Universal Register,* 11, pp. 50–3.

Coleridge, Samuel Taylor (1820), 'Letter to Peter Morris, M.D. on the Sorts and Uses of Literary Praise', *Blackwood's Edinburgh Magazine,* 7, pp. 629–31.

Darley, George [John Lacy] (1823), 'A Fifth Letter to the Dramatists of the Day', *London Magazine,* 8, pp. 535–8.

Elfenbein, Andrew (1999), *Romantic Genius: The Prehistory of a Homosexual Role,* New York: Columbia University Press.

Galt, John and William Harness [Harroviensis] (1824), 'Lord Byron's Conversations', *Blackwood's Edinburgh Magazine,* 16, pp. 530–40.

Hazlitt, William (1821), 'Pope, Lord Byron, and Mr. Bowles', *London Magazine,* 3, pp. 593–607.

— (1823), 'The Periodical Press', *Edinburgh Review,* 38, pp. 349–78.

Heber, Reginald (1822), 'Lord Byron's Dramas', *Quarterly Review,* 27, pp. 476–524.

Higgins, David (2005), *Romantic Genius and the Literary Magazine: Biography, Celebrity, Politics,* London / New York: Routledge.

Howe, P. P., ed. (1930–4), *The Complete Works of William Hazlitt,* 21 vols, London: Dent.

Lockhart, John Gibson (1822), 'Lord Byron's Three New Tragedies', *Blackwood's Edinburgh Magazine,* 11, pp. 90–4.

— (1825), 'Sir Egerton Brydges's Recollections', *Blackwood's Edinburgh Magazine,* 17, pp. 505–67.

Lovell, Ernest J., Jr, ed. (1969), *Lady Blessington's Conversations of Lord Byron,* Princeton: Princeton University Press.

Maginn, William [T. T.] (1823), 'Letters of Timothy Tickler, Esq. No VII: On the New Cantos of *Don Juan*', *Blackwood's Edinburgh Magazine,* 14, pp. 88–92.

Mason, Nicholas (2002), 'Building Brand Byron: Early-Nineteenth-Century Advertising and the Marketing of *Childe Harold's Pilgrimage*', *Modern Language Quarterly,* 63, pp. 411–40.

Milner, George [G. M.] (1821), 'On the Genius and Writings of Lord Byron', *Imperial Magazine,* 3, pp. 254–7.

Mole, Tom (2007), *Byron's Romantic Celebrity: Industrial Culture and the Hermeneutic of Intimacy*, Basingstoke / New York: Palgrave Macmillan.

Moran, Joe (2000), *Star Authors: Literary Celebrity in America*, London: Pluto Press.

Ommundsen, Wenche (2006), 'From the Altar to the Market-place and Back Again: Understanding Literary Celebrity', in: Sean Redmond and Su Holmes (eds), *Stardom and Celebrity: A Reader*, London: Routledge, pp. 244–56.

Owen, W. J. B. and Jane Worthington Smyser, eds (1974), *The Prose Works of William Wordsworth*, 3 vols, Oxford: Clarendon Press.

Parker, Mark (2000), *Literary Magazines and British Romanticism*, Cambridge: Cambridge University Press.

Patmore, Peter G. [P.] (1822), 'On Magazine Writers', *London Magazine*, 6, pp. 21–7.

Roberts, William (1818), '*Beppo, a Venetian Story*', *British Review and London Critical Journal*, 11, pp. 327–33.

Scott, John (1820), 'Blackwood's Magazine', *London Magazine*, 2, pp. 509–21.

Selincourt, Ernest de, rev. Mary Moorman and Alan G. Hill, eds (1969–70), *The Letters of William and Dorothy Wordsworth: The Middle Years*, 2 vols, Oxford: Clarendon Press.

Southern, Henry [R. N.] (1824), 'Personal Character of Lord Byron', *London Magazine*, 10, pp. 337–47.

Southey, Robert (1824), 'Southey and Byron', *Blackwood's Edinburgh Magazine*, 16, pp. 711–15.

Wilson, John (1818), 'On Literary Censorship', *Blackwood's Edinburgh Magazine*, 4, pp. 176–8.

— or John Gibson Lockhart (1819), 'Remarks on *Don Juan*', *Blackwood's Edinburgh Magazine*, 5, pp. 512–18.

— (1820), 'On the Analogy Between the Growth of Individual and National Genius', *Blackwood's Edinburgh Magazine*, 6, pp. 375–81.

# IV. On the Provocative Margins of Taste

# Chapter 11

# 'Stand not on that brink!': Byron, Gender and Romantic Suicide

## Caroline Franklin

> whatsoe'er thine ill,
> It must be borne.
>
> (*Manfred* II, i, 40–1)

> No; not despair precisely. When we know
> All that can come, and how to meet it, our
> Resolves, if firm, may merit a more noble
> Word than this is to give it utterance.
>
> (*Sardanapalus* V, i, 223–6)

It is surprising that Byron's obsession with suicide in his poetry does not seem to have been the subject of sustained critical attention. Caricatured by Peacock as Mr Cypress in *Nightmare Abbey* (1818), Byron's melancholy was notorious.

> Count o'er the joys thine hours have seen,
> Count o'er thy days from anguish free,
> And know, whatever thou hast been,
> 'Tis something better not to be.

These are lines 33–6 of Byron's lyric 'Euthanasia' – not Cypress's parody. In the 1844 second edition and second volume of *The World as Will and Representation* (1818), Schopenhauer quoted the poem with approval, for it encapsulated his own view that life should be seen from the perspective of one's mortality as a meaningless temporary reprieve, overshadowed from the beginning by death, towards which all are irresistibly impelled.[1] In many of his works, Byron gave serious consideration to suicide as an act of free will, which at least offered the individual control over the time, place and manner of death.

Suicide has been proved to be socially contagious and, in *Persuasion* (1817), Jane Austen accused Byron's early poetry of spreading the contamination of suicidal thoughts to impressionable young men. As Byron turned to comedy in *Don Juan* the same year, some critics have assumed his *Weltschmerz* was a youthful phase. He habitually used black humour to mock his own suicidal thoughts, especially after the failure of his marriage and his separation from his daughter and beloved half-sister: 'I should many a good day have blown my brains out, but for the recollection that it would have given pleasure to my mother-in-law' (*BLJ*, vol. 3, p. 165).[2] To Lady Blessington: 'I should possibly have destroyed myself but I guessed that ----- [Thomas Moore?] or ----- [John Cam Hobhouse?] would write my life and with this fear before my eyes I have lived on.'[3] Yet he confided seriously in his 'Epistle to Augusta': 'And I at times have found the struggle hard / And thought of shaking off my bonds of clay' ('Epistle to Augusta', ll. 29–30).[4] Far from abandoning the viewpoint expressed in 'Euthanasia', Byron went on to debate in several of his major works whether suicide or the renunciation of suicide was the greater act of will.

The Victorians were horrified to observe that Byron's letters and verse were saturated with references to self-murder. In his magisterial monograph *Eight Historical Dissertations in Suicide* (1856), Henry Gabriel Migault pronounced: 'that the influence, direct or indirect, of his [Byron's] poetry has really led many to self-destruction, I doubt not'.[5] They were concerned that the suicide rate had risen markedly: presumably because Enlightenment rationalism had weakened both religious orthodoxy and traditional fatalism. The Christian taboo against suicide had been breached in the eighteenth century when *philosophes* such as Montesquieu and Hume argued that the act could be a rational response to certain circumstances. What startled nineteenth-century commentators was that then, as now, at least twice as many men committed suicide as women.[6] Was Byron a masculine role model for them?

Johann Wolfgang von Goethe had been the first Romantic writer to be attacked for supposedly generating a wave of suicides amongst idealistic young men unsuccessful in love with *The Sorrows of Young Werther* (1774).[7] As Michelle Faubert has pointed out, Goethe had been inspired by Rousseau to question whether the act of self-murder signified human freedom (and self-ownership) on the one hand or – if for love - irresponsible sentimentality on the other.[8] Romantic writers were even more inclined to view the act in terms of individual liberty after the revolutionaries in France revived the Roman martial code for theatrical displays of suicide as a gesture of non-compliance with tyrannical power. In 1792, Beaurepaire, the Commander of Verdun, was buried in the Panthéon with the inscription 'He preferred suicide to surrender to tyrants.'[9] Not everyone believed that self-murder was ever rational. As early as 1733, George Cheyne had written *The English Malady* to explain the increase in suicide in Britain in medical and psychological terms. Suicide was also sympathetically portrayed in the story of Thomas Chatterton's self-destruction, exemplifying the morbid sensitivity of artistic genius.[10] Nevertheless, self-slaughter was increasingly viewed as evidence of insanity rather than respected as an act of will. The humanitarian poetry of Wordsworth, Coleridge and Clare responded by emphasising the social context, dramatising the extreme suffering experienced by the poor, dispossessed and outcasts from society, which led them to wish for death.

However, it was Byron who seemed most fully to inhabit the degenerate death wish. In 1840, Thomas Carlyle specifically dubbed him the über-Werther of the Romantic movement: '[their] Sentimentalist and Power Man, the strongest of his kind in Europe; the wildest, the gloomiest and it may be hoped the last'.[11] Byron was the very worst (in other words, the best) of a bad bunch of gloomy graveyard poets, decadent Gothic and sentimental European novelists and playwrights who (melo)dramatised the prospect of self-annihilation. In repudiating Byron, the Victorians hoped to draw a definite margin between themselves and the unhealthy morbidity of dark Romanticism, as a particular product of the revolutionary period and the raffish Regency. The purpose of this essay is to question this demarcation.

The darkness of Byron's verse, whether in the form of melancholic lyricism or splenetic black humour, certainly marked it off from the Victorians' selective Romantic canon, which would stress the importance of being earnest.[12] Byron's comic masterpiece *Don Juan* (1819–24) 'admits its frivolity or lack of authenticity'[13] in order to mock the stance of sincerity adopted by Wordsworth and Coleridge in their intimate Romantic lyrics. The dandy aesthetic he drew on, with its pseudo-aristocratic disdain for the work ethic, was no period piece, but lasted at least until Oscar Wilde. The Victorians therefore defined themselves against Byron, so that it was Wordsworth who became central to the syllabus of English literature in their new state schools and redbrick universities, his own moral realism and his fictional peasants' uncomplaining endurance of poverty and failure exemplifying English anti-Jacobinism.[14] Byronic Romanticism was, by contrast, influential in continental Europe, and inspired Baudelaire's attempted assaults on the bourgeois reader's sensibilities in *Les Fleurs du mal* (1857).[15] Baudelaire went on to form a 'suicide club' to show his contempt for modern society, though none of its members actually killed themselves, while André Breton's inspiration, Jacques Vaché, encapsulated Surrealism in 1919 with the ultimate sick joke of artistically arranging his own suicide along with the murder of two friends.[16] The dandy display of a foppish life of ostentatious idleness had itself constituted a theatrical protest against utilitarianism and contemporary loosening of the social hierarchy: to waste one's life – or end it – carelessly was surely the ultimate refusal of social duty.

Wordsworthian Romanticism was a product of modernity: an idealist protest against crass materialism, which was nostalgic for a simpler pre-capitalist past and – most of all – belief in the afterlife.[17] However, Byron and Shelley – as aristocrats necessarily out of step with the bourgeois present and as expatriates literally and figuratively beyond the pale of respectable publishing – were in a privileged position to challenge modernity's strongest taboo, death. The anatomist Marie François Xavier Bichat (1771–1802), the inspirer of Michel Foucault's *Birth of the Clinic* ([1963] 1989) had, even before Schopenhauer, adopted the universal limits imposed by death as a marker defining life itself 'as those sets of functions which resist death'.[18] Byron and the Shelleys accessed such new scientific and medical discourses, as they imagined individuals demonstrating extraordinary self-will by choosing the time and place of their own demise in order to tame and aestheticise death.

Suicide was thus a preoccupation of their coterie when they revivified the Gothic. Mary Shelley's *Frankenstein* (1818) and John Polidori's *The Vampyre* (1819) reimagined the ghoul of folktale: an undead soul who had committed a mortal sin too great to allow him to join the community of the dead or even the damned (this was usually suicide or blasphemy) and who would – if not staked – wander through the universe for all time. Suicide had first been made a mortal sin by St Augustine, even though it is not explicitly condemned in the Bible, and there had sometimes been a degree of ambiguity between death-seeking behaviour and Christian martyrdom. A stigma attached to the act because, according to Matthew's gospel, Judas hanged himself when he realised he had caused the crucifixion of Jesus. However, the taboo, which probably had pagan origins, became firmly embedded into Christian culture only in the early modern period.[19] Communal repugnance for the suicide seems to have been exacerbated by Protestantism (with its removal of the concept of purgatory) and the scientific viewpoint of the Enlightenment, which further eroded the comfort of the afterlife.[20] Until the first quarter of the nineteenth century, those found guilty of self-destruction were interred at midnight under the supervision of church wardens at a crossroads, naked and often staked through the heart. The survival of the taboo into modernity inspired Romantic Gothic writers to reimagine folkloric outcasts from the Christian community of the living and the dead, such as the Wandering Jew, Cain and other ostracised figures in works like Coleridge's 'Rime of the Ancient Mariner' (1798), Charles Maturin's *Melmoth the Wanderer* (1820) and Byron's own *Cain* (1821). James Hogg drama-tised the misuse of religion itself as producing abnormal psychic states in *The Private Memoirs and Confessions of a Justified Sinner* (1824), which was reissued in 1828 under the title *The Suicide's Grave*.

In their dramatic verse, too, Byron's coterie specifically explored the psychology of suicidal thoughts and acts: Byron's *Manfred* (1817), in which the protagonist's suicide is prevented by the chamois hunter; Percy Shelley's *The Cenci* (1819), whose villain Cenci and his daughter Beatrice both consider suicide; and John Polidori's *Ximenes* (1819), whose eponymous protagonist takes poison after having goaded his enemy into stabbing himself – shockingly declar-ing 'God forced me on to this.'[21] In Mary Shelley's unpublished 1819 novella, *Mathilda*, the heroine proposes a suicide pact to her male friend and they discuss whether the deed should be seen as a protest against death separating them from their loved ones or as an antiso-cial act. These works all asked how far is self-murder honourable? How far might it be motivated by self-indulgent individualism? How far is it gendered?

Robert Southey labelled Byron's coterie 'the Satanic School' in 1821 – for Byron's Don Juan and Manfred, and Mary Shelley's Victor Frankenstein were over-reachers who set themselves up to challenge divine punishment. The gibe may have also alluded to the works stag-ing suicidal acts cited above. In Christian tradition, self-murder was literally demonic: suicidal thoughts were temptation by the Devil and the self-slayer had been possessed by the Devil. Not only did such liter-ary works corrupt the young but also the authors themselves set a bad example: Dr John Polidori swallowed prussic acid on 24 August 1821 while Percy Shelley, who could not swim, deliberately courted danger while sailing, and was drowned in 1822. But it was the female suicides who were perceived as particular victims of the Godwin / Byron cote-ries' irreligion and libertinism. Mary's mother, Mary Wollstonecraft, had been described as 'a female Werther' in the biography her husband, William Godwin, wrote after her death. Of her second unsuccessful sui-cide attempt in 1795 after her desertion by Gilbert Imlay, she herself had written, 'Nor will I allow that to be a frantic attempt which was one of the calmest acts of reason.'[22] This provoked Richard Polwhele's satire, *The Unsex'd Females* (1798), which labelled her 'The dire apostate, the fell suicide'.[23] Then in 1816, following the elopement of her daughter Mary with the married Percy Shelley to the continent, Mary's half-sister Fanny Imlay and Percy's first wife Harriet both committed suicide, aged 22 and 21, respectively.[24] Mary wrote in her journal that she considered she was being punished for Harriet's fate when she went on to lose all but one of her children as well as her husband within the next six years.[25]

The representation of female suicide had been pioneered by the two most important women writers of the Romantic period who wrote on gender: Mary Wollstonecraft, who had planned to fictionalise her own suicide attempt in her unfinished novel *The Wrongs of Woman* (posthumously published in 1798), and Madame de Staël, who praised suicide as 'cette grande route du bonheur' in *De l'influence des passions* (1797). De Staël then depicted her first novel's heroine, Delphine (1802), taking poison as a self-affirmative protest against an oppressive society.[26] This paradoxically combined feminism with feminine self-abnegation.

Byron deliberately infuriated de Staël by publicly lecturing her that the novel was *hors de question* 'very dangerous' and immoral. This was especially annoying, as he himself was considered an immoral writer, because he was echoing Bonaparte's similar criticism[27] and also because de Staël had changed her mind on the issue, for in *Réflexions sur le suicide* (1813)[28] she rejected Wertherism. Byron knew this perfectly well when he teased her, as he had commented to Moore in a letter on 8 July 1813: 'Madame de Staël hath published an Essay against Suicide, which, I presume, will make somebody shoot himself' (*BLJ*, vol. 3, p. 73). De Staël now argued that being crossed in love was 'no adequate motive for committing suicide' (p. 24); stoic resignation was morally superior. That suicide was known as the English disease throughout Europe she astutely attributed less to the northern climate than to the 'extreme importance attached to public opinion' and 'horror of censure' in England (p. 75) for, in modern society, it was 'ruin and disgrace' and 'loss of the rank we occupied in the world' (p. 24) that prompt suicide – not love and unrecognised genius. This sociological explanation would be echoed by de Staël's contemporary, the French psychiatrist Jean-Pierre Falret, who, in *De l'hypochondrie et du suicide* (1822), would argue against the prevailing nineteenth-century view that suicide was almost always a symptom of madness.

Despite her retraction, de Staël had set a trend. The critic Margaret Higonnet has written that in late nineteenth-century art female suicide became a 'cultural obsession', instancing Madame Butterfly, Emma Bovary, Anna Karenina, Hedda Gabler, Miss Julie and paintings of the death of Ophelia.[29] The paradox was that, although it was men who were turning to suicide in greater numbers in the real world, art preferred to depict women victims. Such representations feminised and sentimentalised the deed, which was sometimes pejoratively perceived as linked to fragility or moral weakness. Poe had famously declared the death of a beautiful woman to be the most poetical topic in the world. He was doubtless inspired by Byron's heroines – Zuleika in *The Bride of Abydos* (1813), Medora in *The Corsair* (1814) and Haidée of *Don Juan* – who are even more passive than later Victorian suicides, as they simply expire in grief at the loss of their lovers: an involuntary and therefore blameless dissolution of the self, exaggerating their feminine passivity and delicacy.

Myrrha in *Sardanapalus* (1821) wants her suicide to be seen as willed and not merely complicit with social pressures: 'And dost thou think / A Greek girl dare not do for love that which / An Indian widow braves for custom?' (*Sardanapalus* V, i, 465–8). The execution of the non-protesting Leila in *The Giaour* (1813), however, exhibits willed self-surrender to overwhelming patriarchal codes. The fisherman observes Leila's body, so motionless during her death by drowning that the water is not disturbed:

> I watch'd it as it sank, methought
> Some motion from the current caught
> Bestirr'd it more, – 'twas but the beam
> That checker'd o'er the living stream [. . .]. (*The Giaour*, ll. 376–9)

Byronic heroes themselves exhibit compliance with fate, such as the Giaour, who endures a long self-imposed retreat in a monastery waiting for death to release him, or with patriarchal power: for example, Conrad, resigned to imprisonment and impalement by his Turkish enemy, or the prisoner of Chillon, who has outlived two of his brothers.

> It might be months, or years, or days,
> I keep no count – I took no note,
> I had no hope my eyes to raise,
> And clear them of their dreary mote;
> At last men came to set me free,

> I asked not why, and reck'd not where,
> It was at length the same to me,
> Fettered or fetterless to be,
> I learned to love despair. (*The Prisoner of Chillon*, ll. 366–74)

All exemplify a stoic, passive endurance by men of their own lack of autonomy in the face of overwhelming social forces.

I argue in this essay that, by the time he wrote *Manfred*, Byron decided specifically to depict suicide as a feminine act and to make an emphatic contrast with true masculinity, which he associates with heroic endurance of suffering. Both Christopher Marlowe and Goethe, in their versions of the Faust legend, had shown the learned protagonist fleetingly contemplating suicide before rejecting the urge, but Byron put the question right at the centre of his drama. At the same time, he omitted the notion of a pact with the Devil, so emphasising the putative deed as an act of individual will rather than succumbing to temptation or manipulation. Manfred feels his life is too long already (*Manfred* I, i, 170) but is cursed to a 'trial' of the strength of his endurance of suffering, being condemned 'Not to slumber, nor to die' (*Manfred* I, i, 254) but to 'live – and live for ever' (*Manfred* II, ii, 149). His suicidal thoughts are linked in the play with grief and guilt: his feelings of responsibility for his sister's demise (*Manfred* I, ii, 87). Having 'the fierce thirst of death' (*Manfred* II, i, 48), he admits, 'I sunk before my vain despair, and knelt / To my own desolation' (*Manfred* II, iv, 41–2). The egoism of this melancholy state is such that it replaces consciousness of a higher being. This could be compared to what Kierkegaard calls 'the most dialectical frontier between despair and sin [. . .] what could be called a poet-existence'. The individual 'does have a conception of God or is before God [. . .] yet loves the anguish and will not give it up'.[30] Yet Manfred desires the obliteration of the torment of selfhood, exclaiming:

> Oh that I were
> The viewless spirit of a lovely sound,
> A living voice, a breathing harmony,
> A bodiless enjoyment – born and dying
> With the blest tone which made me! (*Manfred* I, ii, 52–6)

Manfred wants 'Oblivion, self-oblivion!' (*Manfred* I, i, 144), yet to commit suicide would be an act of violence; it might, anyway, not achieve the forgetfulness he seeks. When he asks the spirits if death will bestow oblivion, they answer: 'We are immortal, and do not forget; / We are eternal; and to us the past / Is, as the future, present' (*Manfred* I, i, 149–50). He stands upon the extreme edge of the Jungfrau, at first unable either to leap or to retreat, wishing an avalanche would overwhelm him. In order to dramatise the common idea that higher-class and highly educated geniuses were more likely to commit suicide than peasants, Byron has the aristocratic Manfred seized by the chamois hunter, the epitome of the Wordsworthian common man, at the very moment of casting himself on to the rocks below. His rescuer regards Manfred as a madman (*Manfred* I, ii, 110; II, i, 59): 'whate'er / Thy dread and sufferance be, there's comfort yet – / The aid of holy men, and heavenly patience' (*Manfred* II, i, 32–4). Manfred cannot identify with 'brutes of burthen' who subscribe to such fatalism (*Manfred* II, i, 36). He denies he is mad, for his desolation is equivalent to the extremity of his transgression: 'actions are our epochs: mine / Have made my days and nights imperishable' (*Manfred* II, i, 52). We are told repeatedly that Manfred is not insane and shown he is not possessed by evil spirits, for he refuses to kneel to the satanic Arimanes and defies the demons when they come for him at the hour of death. Conceding the effeminacy associated with both aristocrats and intellectuals, Byron has a peasant showing the would-be self-slayer the way to masculine stoicism and physical courage, counselling him, 'whatsoe'er thine ill, / It must be borne' (*Manfred* II, i, 40–1). To underline the point, while Manfred learns to endure, it is his feminine counterpart, his twin sister Astarte, who apparently *has* committed suicide over their incestuous love, for he states, 'I have shed / Blood, but not hers – and yet her blood was shed – / I saw – and could not stanch it' (*Manfred* II, ii, 119–21). She is therefore 'one without a tomb' (*Manfred* II, iv, 82), and when she is made to rise from the dead he dreads to look on her changed face: 'What is she now? [. . .] A thing I dare not think upon' (*Manfred* II, ii, 196–8). Yet Byron boldly demonstrates that the evil spirits have no power over Astarte, despite her having committed a mortal sin according to Christian theology. Nemesis admits, 'She is not of our order, but belongs / To the other powers' (*Manfred* II, iv, 115–16). Byron therefore went even further than Goethe, whose Gretchen in *Faust* also seemed to have been saved, despite having apparently committed infanticide, perhaps when mentally unbalanced through grief and guilt.

Manfred breaks the curse over both brother and sister when he petitions Astarte: 'that I do bear / This punishment for both – that thou wilt be / One of the blessed – and that I shall die' (*Manfred* II, iv, 125–7), for though they are equal in all their powers, Astarte was 'gentler' with 'Pity, and smiles, and tears – which I had not; / And tenderness', says

Manfred (*Manfred* II, ii, 113–16). These are Christian virtues in contrast to the pagan stoicism Manfred now exemplifies when he bids farewell to the sun and moon. Christianity is effeminised by these binaries. Though the play controversially implies that this female suicide will go to heaven, it also aligns her act with feminine lack of stamina in the face of shame. It is the male twin who has strength to accept responsibility for their sins and to live on alone with no forgiveness or hope of meeting again, suffering:

> [. . .] the innate tortures of that deep despair,
> Which is remorse without the fear of hell,
> But all in all sufficient to itself
> Would make a hell of heaven. (*Manfred* III, i, 70–3)

When Manfred is allowed to die at the end of the play, this is not shown as suicide, as the time of death is announced by Astarte and not chosen by himself. Mark Canuel, however, argues that there is some ambiguity, as, at the close of the tragedy, Manfred claims to be his own 'destroyer', not the 'dupe' or 'prey' of the satanic spirit who comes to claim him.[31] However, it is clear from the context that Manfred means moral self-destruction here rather than physical suicide. The Abbot's plea, 'die not thus', does not refer to self-slaughter either, but to Manfred's refusal to pray for salvation on his deathbed. Manfred is shown welcoming the calmness that knowing of his impending end has brought him. He certainly wishes to die, even comparing himself to Nero, who rejected help from a soldier for a self-inflicted wound (*Manfred* III, i, 88–90). Nevertheless, as Canuel remarks, his declaration 'the hand of death is on me' (*Manfred* III, iv, 141) externalises his demise. The details of his white lips, heaving breast, gasping throat and death rattle (*Manfred* III, iv, 141–4) suggest a natural death.

The Giaour also had prided himself on endurance and on not ending his own life:

> My spirit shrunk not to sustain
> The searching throes of ceaseless pain;
> Nor sought the self-accorded grave
> Of ancient fool, and modern knave. (*The Giaour*, ll. 1004–7)

Admittedly, he is ironically perceived through the multiple viewpoints and framing of the tale. Suicide is also described as 'a selfish death' (*Prisoner of Chillon*, l. 230) by the narrator in *The Prisoner of Chillon* (1816), written just before *Manfred*. But in *Manfred* the poet emphatically deployed identical twins specifically to feminise and to abjure suicide, even while immensely sympathetic to the hero's desire for self-destruction.

The ethical dimension of suicide was crucial not only to Byron's own personal drama but to contemporary politics. In April 1814, when Napoleon had abdicated for the first time, Byron had felt very differently about it. His anonymously published 'Ode to Napoleon Buonaparte' (1814) had berated his fallen idol for not falling on his sword in the Roman manner instead of abdicating:

> So abject – yet alive!
> Is this the man of thousand thrones,
> Who strew'd our Earth with hostile bones,
> And can he thus survive? ('Ode to Napoleon Buonaparte', ll. 4–7)[32]

His epigraph was 'Expende Annibalem – quot libras in duce summo Invenies?' ('Put Hannibal in the scales; how much weight will you find in that greatest of commanders?'; Juvenal, *Satires*, x [147–8]). This compared the French Emperor unfavourably with Hannibal, the enemy of Rome, who had chosen self-inflicted death over dishonour in defeat. Had Byron but known it, the Emperor had indeed attempted suicide by taking poison.[33] As a young man in 1786, Napoleon had written an essay on his suicidal feelings because his native Corsica was enslaved, and had eagerly taken the opportunity to discuss the plot of Werther with Goethe in 1808. The *Critical Review* mocked Byron as an out-of-date émigré aristocrat, in drawing upon his male classical education to justify suicide in the Ode:

> The unqualified manner it is taken for granted that a violent death would have added to the character and consistency of Buonaparte. [. . .] The disposition to connect heroism with voluntary death at this time of day, we conceive to be a remnant of classical barbarity, a relique of school sentiment.[34]

Actually, the last stanza of the Ode – as Simon Bainbridge points out – suddenly introduces the possibility of heroising Promethean endurance:[35]

> Or like the thief of fire from heaven,
> Wilt thou withstand the shock?
> And share with him, the unforgiven,
> His vulture and his rock! ('Ode to Napoleon Buonaparte', ll. 136–9)

It was this alternative hero from Classical mythology, who stole from the Gods for humanity's sake, with whom Napoleon could be justly compared on his rock of Elba: a model of masculine stoicism.

It was surely only because of his reassessment of Romantic suicide that Byron chose to take the ultimate historical example of self-destruction as an effeminised, pagan and Oriental act as the basis of one of his most ambitious tragedies: *Sardanapalus* (1821). In his immense 1790 treatise on suicide, Charles Moore had described the self-immolation of the monarch of Nineveh as 'a magnificent and luxurious mode of self-murder, worthy of the extravagance and dissoluteness of his former life'.[36] William Dean Brewer comments that the heaping up of possessions and women is 'the most emphatically negative act that a man can commit – not only meant to destroy oneself but to disinherit one's children or dispossess one's enemies'. Brewer notes that, as he read Percy Shelley's *The Cenci* before composing his own play, Byron may have been influenced by the passage where Cenci imagines his self-destruction:

> I will pile up my silver and my gold
> My costly robes, paintings and tapestries;
> My parchments and all records of my wealth,
> And make a bonfire in my joy and leave
> Of my possessions nothing but my name. (*The Cenci* IV, i, 52–6)[37]

Byron prepared for writing the play by reading Seneca, for whom suicide was *the* act *par excellence* that was the simplest way to achieve wisdom.[38] On the other hand, he also consulted modern literature representing female suicide for transgressive or unfulfilled love. In 1819, he had been convulsed by tears during a production of Alfieri's *Mirra* (1788), whose heroine commits suicide; in 1821, he was reading an Italian translation of Grillparzer's *Sappho* (1819).

Perhaps it is not a coincidence that Byron dedicated this particular play expressing his ambivalence over the association between suicide and masculine honour to 'the illustrious Goethe', author of *Werther*. Yet the play presents Sardanapalus sympathetically as well as contentiously. Byron has his monarch espousing Christian pacifism together with pagan pleasure, loving his wife yet enjoying his harem. A contemporary reviewer commented contemptuously that Byron's dandy monarch was 'no Antony: he shewed himself in no way superior to Cleopatra'.[39] Sardanapalus's effeminacy and sloth are pointed out contemptuously by his brother-in-law Salemenes (*Sardanapalus* I, i, 9) and rival Arbaces (*Sardanapalus* II, i, 48). His female slave also supports his eventual adoption of conventional masculinity, for when he eventually takes up arms, Myrrha honours him (*Sardanapalus* III, i, 108) and joins him in battle. Gerard Cohen-Vrignaud comments that Sardanapalus is thus goaded to abandon his Eastern fatalism, which had liberated him from regretting the past and fearing the future. Instead he must (albeit temporarily) become the active manager of his empire and adopt bourgeois-liberal norms.[40]

Byron was, of course, using traditional republican discourse in having Sardanapalus epitomise aristocratic and monarchical culture through his effeminacy. In order not to detract from this political association, Byron omits the historical character's homosexuality.[41] As Susan Wolfson comments, he also transforms Sardanapalus's eventual adoption of martial masculinity into outright chivalry, as he carefully ensures the safety of his family and harem instead of incorporating them into the funeral pyre.[42] As the last ruler of a 1,300-year empire, which fell to the Medes in 612 BC, Sardanapalus's effeminacy might be interpreted by the modern audience as a hereditary effect of aristocratic in-breeding, as well as cultural difference from modern Western models of masculinity.

It is fitting that, on his defeat, Sardanapalus adopts a feminised death by his own hand. Earlier we saw him ask the Greek slave girl to sing 'a song of Sappho' (*Sardanapalus* III, i, 67). Myrrha had herself been contemplating suicide, but not for love like the poet; she procured a vial of poison to free her from life as a captive (*Sardanapalus* III, i, 187). As a Greek patriot, she feels dishonoured by her 'monstrous love for a barbarian' (*Sardanapalus* III, i, 183). Sardanapalus's staging of his death comprises the voluntary destruction of his inheritance, treasure, abode and 'sacred relics / Of arms, and records and spoils' of the kingdom (*Sardanapalus* V, i, 430–1), but not of his slaves, other than Myrrha who joins him voluntarily. As Cohen-Vrignaud notes, this conflagration 'rejects death-deferral and moderate expenditure', and thus in his self-slaughter Sardanapalus rejects Western modernity and returns to his pagan fatalist model of behaviour of embracing the present moment to the full.[43] It is highly ironic when he adopts suicide as an honourable death in defeat, and theatrically ignites his own funeral pyre: 'a light / To lesson ages' (*Sardanapalus* V, i, 441). The last of his kind, Sardanapalus functions for the modern audience as a representative of an odious monarchical regime, as well as a well-intentioned individual, when he orders: 'Let the throne form the *core* of it' (*Sardanapalus* V, i, 361). Byron put himself, as well as George IV, into the portrait of the King of Nineveh; we have sympathy for the character trapped in an inherited social role, whose model of masculine behaviour offers an uninviting choice of either imposing sex slavery or imperial warfare on others. Despite his capacity for transformation, Sardanapalus's suicide shows him returning to the exotic otherness of his way of life in his way of death.[44]

In *The Deformed Transformed* (1824), Byron experimented further in reversing the gender roles with regard to suicide. The deformed Arnold contemplates committing suicide for effeminate reasons – because he is unloved and unattractive.

> And shall I live on,
> A burthen to the earth, myself, and shame
> Unto what brought me into life? Thou blood,
> Which flowest so freely from a scratch, let me
> Try if thou wilt not in a fuller stream
> Pour forth my woes for ever with thyself
> On earth, to which I will restore at once
> This hateful compound of her atoms, and
> Resolve back to her elements, and take
> The shape of any reptile save myself,
> And make a world for myriads of new worms! (*The Deformed Transformed* I, i, 52–62)

Placing his knife in the ground in order to fall upon it activates the taboo against suicide. Arnold's intent to destroy himself causes a fountain to ripple, out of which appears a satanic stranger. Rather than encouraging the act, however, the spirit prevents it by enabling him to adopt the beautiful outer shape of Achilles while he himself dons Arnold's unwanted body. In the guise of the greatest warrior hero portrayed by Homer, Arnold outwardly appears the model of masculinity – but does not possess honour in the chivalric sense.

Olimpia (whose name alludes to Greek values) *does* attempt to commit suicide by heroically throwing herself off the high altar. This is not merely to save her inferior female 'honour' or virginity, as she has thrown a massive crucifix at the head of an attempted rapist and killed him, and Arnold had subsequently saved her from the other soldiers' revenge. Byron portrays her adopting the heroism attached to the suicidal act by classical cultures, when defeated by an invading army. She seeks death in order to preserve her patriotic honour during the Bourbons' sack of Rome, by refusing to live a captive. She defies Arnold:

> I see thee purple with the blood of Rome;
> Take mine, 'tis all thou e'er shalt have of me!
> And here, upon the marble of this temple,

Where the baptismal font baptised me God's,
I offer him a blood less holy
But not less pure (pure as it left me then,
A redeemed infant) than the holy water
The saints have sanctified! (*The Deformed Transformed* II, ii,
124–31)

Charles Robinson has convincingly worked out, from studying
Byron's sources for the fragment, that, had Byron completed the
play, Olimpia would have survived her suicide attempt, only to be
later murdered by Arnold – jealous that Olimpia was more charmed
by the hunchback's bitter humour and intelligence than his own new
exterior beauty.[45] The reversal of gender roles shows that, in staging
suicide, women can be heroic patriots and men vain and effeminate,
that men and women are not confined to stereotypes but equally
strive for honour or are driven by libido.

In *Don Juan*, the confessional Byronic narrator uses black humour
knowingly – confiding in the reader in order to catch him or her out
in admitting that we have all been attracted at some time or another
by the taboo of suicide:

A sleep without dreams, after a rough day
Of toil is what we covet most; and yet
How clay shrinks back from more quiescent clay!
The very Suicide that pays his debt
At once without instalments (an old way
Of paying debts, which creditors regret)
Lets out impatiently his rushing breath,
Less from disgust of life than dread of death.

'Tis round him, near him, here, there, every where,
And there's a courage which grows out of fear;
Perhaps of all most desperate, which will dare
The worst to *know* it; – when the mountains rear
Their peaks beneath your human foot, and there
You look down o'er the precipice, drear
The gulf of rock yawns, – you can't gaze a minute,
Without an awful wish to plunge within it.

'Tis true you don't, but pale and struck with terror,
Retire; but look into your past impression!
And you will find, though shuddering at the mirror
Of your own thoughts; in all their self-confession,
The lurking bias, be it truth or error,

> To the *unknown*; a secret prepossession
> To plunge with all your fears – but where? You know not,
> And that's the reason why you do – or do not. (*Don Juan* XIV, ll. 25–48)

Here the last lines express the desire of the suicidal individual (like Manfred or his author) to shape the story of their lives, by choosing an ending, without fear of the unknown postscript – which might, for all he knows, be the last judgement.

Having stepped back from the brink, himself, Byron actually 'led the English into the Victorian period, drawing Europe out of the era of romantic suicide' – as Barbara Gates has suggested.[46] Despite pronouncements like Thomas Carlyle's, based on his melancholic early verse, Byron had portrayed stoic suffering of life's torments as the main characteristic of his Byronic heroes and in some major works linked suicide to effeminacy. He even occasionally donned the mask of religious orthodoxy in *Don Juan* – alluding to hell in the stanza describing the suicide of some of the shipwrecked mariners (*Don Juan* II, ll. 801–32); and depicting cannibalism as being aligned with madness and suicide. The narrator also adopts the righteous tone of the bourgeoisie, in order to impugn the manhood of personal enemies who had committed suicide. Sir Samuel Romilly, though a fellow Whig, had offended him by agreeing to represent Lady Byron in their separation – despite having received Byron's retainer. Romilly had killed himself on 2 November 1818 after the death of his wife.

> An all-in-all-sufficient self-director,
> Like the lamented late Sir Samuel Romilly,
> The Law's expounder, and the State's corrector,
> Whose suicide was almost an anomaly –
> One sad example more, that 'all is vanity' –
> (The Jury brought their verdict in 'Insanity'.) (*Don Juan* I, ll. 115–20)

Here Byron implies effeminacy by making a direct comparison between the reader of conduct books, Donna Inez (Annabella), and the lawyer who was a 'self-director' in his act of self-destruction. He brings out the double standard applied to a politician who had broken the law, yet escaped being branded *felo de se* (a felon of himself).

From Tudor times until 1870, all the suicide's property was confiscated by the Crown if the coroner's jury found *felo de se*, and the act or attempted act continued to be a crime in Britain until 1961. Punishment of self-destruction was formalised and enforced in Britain in the sixteenth and early seventeenth centuries, as a direct result of the rise of the modern state with its national Protestant church under the Tudors – bolstered by a modern legal system and local government.[47] It was then that the harshest penalties were exacted on perpetrators and, despite the protests of medical and liberal writers during the eighteenth and nineteenth centuries, religious conservatives blocked reform. Therefore, suicides were refused Christian burial in Britain right up until 1917.

Romilly was the leading campaigner for legal reform and a hero of Polidori, who had himself written a pamphlet against the death penalty,[48] so, deploying his satire for purely personal abuse, Byron paradoxically uses conservative legal discourse to brand this recently departed fellow liberal a felon or lunatic or both, and adopts anti-sentimental ridicule of the would-be Wertherism of a conjugal 'Sexagenary Suicide' (*BLJ*, vol. 6, p. 80).[49] He was here prepared to put himself on a spectrum with the conservative press, which denounced Unitarian minister Thomas Belsham's palliation of suicidal sin in his funeral oration on Romilly.[50]

In contrast, Byron's brutal treatment of 'carotid-artery-cutting Castlereagh!' (*Don Juan* X, l. 468) in his epigrams in *The Liberal* is undertaken for the particular delight of the radicals. He uses mock heroic to cut the late penknife wielder down to size by comparing him to Cato:

> Oh, Castlereagh! thou art a patriot now;
> Cato died for his country, so did'st thou;
> He perish'd rather than see Rome enslav'd,
> Thou cut'st thy throat, that Britain may be saved.
>
> So Castlereagh has cut his throat! – the worst
> Of this is – that his own was not the first.
>
> So *He* has cut his throat at last! – He? Who?
> The Man who cut his country's long ago. ('Epigrams')

In his 1822 preface to Cantos VI, VII and VIII of *Don Juan*, Byron asserts his attack is purely political. Indeed, in pointing out the double standard with which suicide was treated, Byron undoubtedly accorded with popular outrage in the newspapers at the burial of the Foreign Secretary in Westminster Abbey with all honours, despite the harsh legal and religious penalties:[51]

> Of the manner of his death little need be said, except that if a poor radical, such as Waddington or Watson had cut his throat, he would have been buried in a cross-road with the usual appurtenances of the stake and mallet. (*CPW*, vol. 5, p. 715)

Byron's satire deems the act to be effeminate and its coverage in the papers to be sentimental when he mocks Castlereagh as an 'elegant lunatic – a sentimental suicide' and as 'the Werther of politics!!!'.[52] The storm over the double standard operating in respect of Castlereagh's suicide reactivated a campaign to reform the suicide laws. Ironically, this had actually been part of Samuel Romilly's own proposals for reforming the penal code. By the nineteenth century, despair and depression were perceived less as sinfulness and more as a form of madness, though a stigma persisted. Juries were becoming more likely to medicalise the act of suicide by declaring temporary insanity, and increasingly reluctant to find *felo de se*, when the Crown deprived the widows and children of the family property.

Byron's black bile of melancholic spleen both looks back to Swiftian satire and yet anticipates the dandified posing of twentieth-century Surrealism. However, it is apparent that the theme of suicide in his works was at the same time closely related to a very particular legal issue of his lifetime. While his coterie's works of Romantic Gothic confronted the Christian taboo surrounding suicide, Byron in particular questioned how far the act was masculine and whether, in modern society, it could be considered the heroic and honourable way to acknowledge failure. He thus anticipated and addressed the question of the imbalance in the suicide rates of men and women, which would puzzle Victorian sociologists and inspire a debate that continues to this very day.[53] It is no wonder that suicide was a prevalent theme in Byron's poetry, considering the controversy raging in the years leading up to the first reform of the suicide laws in 1823. On the death of Sir Samuel Romilly, it was Byron's and de Staël's friend Sir James Mackintosh who led the campaign, prompting some religious opponents to cite Reverend Charles Moore's declaration that suicide was an offence against God.

On 21 May 1823, while Byron was preparing to sail for Greece, Mackintosh was arguing in Parliament that '[t]he punishment inflicted in a case of suicide was rather an act of malignant and brutal folly [. . .] useless as regarded the dead and only tortured the living'.[54] He declared he had not brought forward the measure earlier only on account of events 'which might mix the question with matters of a political nature' – presumably the death of Castlereagh. But now Mackintosh proposed to abolish the forfeiture of goods and chattels in cases of suicide, arguing that the law aggravated the suicide's own selfishness in reducing the fatherless to beggary. He stressed the double standard: 'verdicts of insanity were almost always found in the cases of persons in *the higher stations of life*; where self-slayers were humble, there *felo de se* was usually returned'. Mackintosh, like de Staël, connected the act with 'false pride' and 'wounded shame' – in other words, masculine and aristocratic codes of honour. There is real substance to this claim even today. He also compared the indignities visited on the corpses of suicides with the barbarity of cannibalism. Mackintosh failed in this attempt to abolish both the religious and the secular punishments for suicide – but the reforming Member of Parliament Thomas Barrett Leonard (1788–1856) took up the cause and succeeded in having the law changed, so that suicides would no longer be staked or buried at a crossroads, though they still had to be interred in unconsecrated ground and their property was still confiscated by the Crown.

Byron doubtless supported Mackintosh's proposed reforms, as he was a liberal and as politically engaged a writer as Shelley, despite his mercurial black humour. At this very time, he had consecrated his energies and money to the cause of Greek independence. In his last lyrics, the broken dandy – no longer beautiful, beloved or cool – counsels himself to adopt stoic endurance of death. Like a second Hamlet, the speaker seeks death at another's hands rather than actively taking his own life, hoping the act will be endowed with an aura of heroism.[55] By forgoing the narcissistic staging of one's suicide and choosing a death with social meaning, Byron hopes to endorse the notion of masculine, aristocratic honour.

> Seek out – less often sought than found –
> A Soldier's Grave, for thee the best;
> Then look around, and choose thy ground,
> And take thy Rest! ('On this Day I Complete My Thirty-Sixth
> Year', ll. 37–40)

## Notes

1. See Jacquette, *The Philosophy of Schopenhauer*, p. 126.
2. In the context of money worries, the twenty-year-old had once written to his lawyer: 'I suppose it will end in my marrying a *Golden Dolly* or blowing my brains out, it does not much matter which, the Remedies are nearly alike' (*BLJ*, vol. 1, p. 181). Compare his journal entry for 10 December 1813: 'I am ennuyé beyond my usual tense of that yawning verb, which I am always conjugating; and I don't find that society much mends the matter. *I am too lazy to shoot myself* – and it would annoy Augusta, and perhaps**; but it would be a good thing for George, on the other side, and no bad one for me; but I won't be tempted' (*BLJ*, vol. 3, p. 236).

3. Blessington, *Lady Blessington's Conversations of Lord Byron*, p. 42.
4. He wrote in a personal letter on 29 June 1819, when his mistress was ill, 'I do not know what I should do – if She died – but *I ought to blow my brains out –*' (*BLJ*, vol. 6, p. 168).
5. Migault, *Eight Historical Dissertations in Suicide, Chiefly in Reference to Philosophy, Theology and Legislation*, p. 94.
6. According to official figures, the male suicide rate in the UK during 2012 was three and a half times that of women. In 2013, there was a further 4 per cent increase in deaths by suicide, 78 per cent of which were of men (*The Guardian*, 19 February 2015). The Samaritans' studies have found middle-aged men of low socio-economic status to be most at risk.
7. In 1814–16, Thomas Rowlandson's series of comical prints *The English Dance of Death*, accompanied by the verses of William Combe, ironically included suicide among various sudden deaths striking down people of fashion.
8. Faubert, 'Romantic Suicide, Contagion and Rousseau's *Julie*', pp. 38–53.
9. The Stoic concept of rational suicide, but also the notion of sacrificing oneself for love, infused the opera of the period with the romanticisation of self-slaughter. See Bartley, 'The New Repertory at the Opéra during the Reign of Terror: Revolutionary Rhetoric and Operatic Consequences', pp. 107–56.
10. Wordsworth, Coleridge, Southey, Mary Robinson, Keats and Shelley all made reference to the death of Chatterton in their works, which then became the subject of Henry Wallis's painting (1855–6).
11. Carlyle, *The Works of Thomas Carlyle*, p. 218.
12. Even in the twentieth century, Byron was perceived as 'an odd, if not distinctly marginal writer, as opposed to, for example, the centrality, especially in the Romantic frame of reference, of say Keats or Wordsworth', as Jerome McGann comments in *Byron and Romanticism*, pp. 134–5.
13. Yu, *Nothing to Admire: The Politics of Poetic Satire from Dryden to Merrill*, p. 94.
14. See Gardiner, *The Constitution of English Literature: The State, the Nation and the Canon*, p. 45; Beatty, 'Wordsworth's and Byron's Links with British and French Decadence', pp. 43–58; Elfenbein, *Byron and the Victorians*.
15. McGann, *Byron and Romanticism*, p. 93. See Baudelaire, *The Essence of Laughter*.
16. See Wells, *The Twilight of Romanticism: Lives and Literature in French Bohemian Culture and the Beat Generation*, p. xii.
17. See for example, Lowy and Sayre, *Romanticism Against the Tide of Modernity*, p. 20.
18. See Deleuze, *Foucault*, p. 77.
19. Enlightenment philosophers Rousseau and Voltaire questioned whether self-murder should be judged morally wrong in all circumstances. The

first outright defence of the individual's right to take his or her own life, David Hume's *Essay on Suicide* (1783), was considered too radical to be published until after the author's death. It took a long time for a secular rational view of suicide to gain acceptance. See Retterstol, *Suicide: A European Perspective*, p. 19.

20. The influential thesis of Philippe Ariès suggests that the semi-public ritual that surrounded the dying tamed the fear of death, whereas the modern medical focus encourages denial. See Ariès, *Western Attitudes Toward Death: From the Middle Ages to the Present*.

21. On *Frankenstein* and suicide, see Sanderson, 'Glutting the Maw of Death: Suicide and Procreation in *Frankenstein*', pp. 49–64; and Koretsky, '"Unhallowed arts": *Frankenstein* and the Poetics of Suicide', pp. 241–60.

22. Wollstonecraft, *Memoirs and Posthumous Works of Mary Wollstonecraft Godwin, Author of A Vindication of the Rights of Woman*, vol. 1, p. 246.

23. Polewhele [sic], *The Unsex'd Females; a Poem addressed to the Author of The Pursuits of Literature*, p. 37.

24. Class differences and money dictated whether the severest penalties were exacted. Though Fanny was found in the Swansea inn where she killed herself with a bottle of laudanum and a suicide note (printed in the local paper without her name, which had been torn off), she was apparently not condemned by the coroner's court, perhaps because the corpse was well dressed. It is possible that Percy bribed officials to have her buried secretly when Godwin refused to identify the body out of fear of scandal. Shortly afterwards, in Swansea, a former sailor who had hanged himself was pronounced *felo de se* and buried at the crossroads at dawn. See Todd, *Death and the Maidens: Fanny Wollstonecraft and the Shelley Circle*, p. 236.

25. 'To whose sad fate I attribute so many of my own heavy sorrows as the atonement claimed by fate for her death', Wollstonecraft Shelley, *The Journals of Mary Shelley*, vol. 1, p. 560.

26. De Staël did rewrite the novel so that Delphine merely dies of a broken heart but she never had this version published in her lifetime; it was brought out by her son only posthumously. For critical views on the two versions, see Pascoe, *Revolutionary Love in Eighteenth-century and Early Nineteenth-century France*, p. 122.

27. Blessington, *Lady Blessington's Conversations of Lord Byron*, p. 32. Napoleon also described it as antisocial. See Goodden, *Madame de Staël: The Dangerous Exile*, p. 123.

28. De Staël, *Reflections on Suicide*, page numbers of quotations in parenthesis in the text.

29. Higonnet, 'Speaking Silences: Women's Suicide', pp. 68–83. See also MacDonald and Murphy, *Sleepless Souls: Suicide in Early Modern England*.

30. Kierkegaard, *The Sickness unto Death: Kierkegaard's Writings*, p. 77.

31. Canuel, *Justice, Dissent and the Sublime*, p. 54.

32. Byron commented to the musician Isaac Nathan: '"Napoleon would have ranked higher in future history, had he, even like your venerable ancestor Saul, on Mount Gilboa, or like a second Cato, fallen on his own sword, and finished his mortal career at Waterloo." His lordship here gave me a significant look as if reading my abhorrence of anything like self-destruction, and said "bear in mind, Nathan, that I do not wish by any means to become the patron of suicide."' Nathan, *Fugitive Pieces and Reminiscences of Lord Byron*, p. 40.

33. Healey, *The Literary Culture of Napoleon*, p. 160; Lieberman, *Leaving You: The Cultural Meaning of Suicide*, p. 24.

34. [Anon.], 'Lord Byron's "Ode to Buonaparte"', p. 529.

35. Bainbridge, *Napoleon and English Romanticism*, p. 149.

36. Moore, *A Full Enquiry into the Subject of Suicide*, vol. 1, p. 273.

37. Quoted by Brewer, *The Shelley–Byron Conversation*, p. 89.

38. See Veyne, *Seneca, the Life of a Stoic*, p. 113.

39. *Scots Edinburgh Magazine*, p. 103, cited in: Wolfson, *Borderlines: The Shiftings of Gender in British Romanticism*, p. 260.

40. Cohen-Vrignaud, *Radical Orientalism: Rights, Reform and Romanticism*, p. 147.

41. Byron did, however, add a footnote alluding to the Roman Emperor Otho's homosexuality and transvestism (and suicide), which is mentioned in Juvenal, *Satires* II, ll. 99–103. See *CPW*, vol. 6, p. 620.

42. Wolfson, *Borderlines*, p. 160.

43. Cohen-Vrignaud, *Radical Orientalism*, p. 155.

44. Daniel P. Watkins comments that it is not merely personal failings that bring about Nineveh's destruction: Sardanapalus's 'sins arise from the kind of world he has inherited [. . .] Nineveh itself cannot resolve the conflict between social glory and vicious conquest', Watkins, *A Materialist Critique of English Romantic Drama*, p. 166.

45. Robinson, 'The Devil as Doppelganger in *The Deformed Transformed*', pp. 321–46.

46. Gates, *Victorian Suicide: Mad Crimes and Sad Histories*, p. 24.

47. MacDonald and Murphy, *Sleepless Souls*, p. 5.

48. Dr Polidori had written in his 'Essay on the Punishment of Death': 'All must agree that our being here originating from God it is not allowable to take into our own hands our own dismissal.' See Polidori, 'Essay on the Punishment of Death', p. 132.

49. See also his remorseless hatred for the lawyer even by 1819: 'When that felon, or Lunatic – (take your choice – he must be one and might be both) was doing his worst to uproot my whole family tree, branch and blossoms; when after taking my retainer he went over to them – when he was bringing desolation on my hearth – and destruction on my household Gods – did he think that in less than three years a natural event – a severe domestic – but an expected and common domestic calamity – would lay his Carcase in a Cross road or stamp his name in a Verdict of Lunacy?' (*BLJ*, vol. 6, p. 150). On the political debate

over Romilly's suicide, see Andrew, 'The Suicide of Sir Samuel Romilly: Apotheosis or Outrage', pp. 175–88.

50. Andrew, 'The Suicide of Sir Samuel Romilly', p. 186.
51. See Brown, *The Art of Suicide*, p. 68, who takes this as a marker of the perception of suicide as feminine. For contemporary fascination with Castlereagh's suicide, see, for example, Fitzgerald, *The Political and Private Life of the Marquess of Londonderry including Most Important and Authentic Particulars of his Last Moments and Death*.
52. There is a distant but unlikely possibility of an allusion to gossip over Castlereagh having gone with a transvestite man to a brothel some years before his death.
53. The rates were exceptionally high for young men in the middle of the nineteenth century and much higher than average for older men by the end of it. See Anderson, *Suicide in Victorian and Edwardian England*, pp. 41–73. Modern scholars argue that economic liberalism creates unstable conditions for workers and businesses in capitalism, and unemployment or failure to fulfil a role in society puts particular pressures on men attempting to live up to patriarchal codes of masculine honour. Inability to fulfil the traditional role of head of the family brings shame.
54. See Hansard, *The Parliamentary Debates*, n.s. vol. 9, pp. 397–420.
55. Ron Brown comments that, in contrast, 'Ophelia's self-chosen death [. . .] stems from loss, frailty, and the disintegration of reason, which demeans the act and diminishes her from the heroic to the pathetic.' Brown, *Art of Suicide*, p. 2. Ophelia's death was the subject of mid-Victorian paintings by John Everett Millais and Arthur Hughes.

## Works cited

Anderson, Olive (1987), *Suicide in Victorian and Edwardian England*, Oxford: Oxford University Press.

Andrew, Donna T. (2004), 'The Suicide of Sir Samuel Romilly: Apotheosis or Outrage', in: Jeffrey Rodgers Watt (ed.), *From Sin to Insanity: Suicide in Early Modern Europe*, Ithaca, NY: Cornell University Press, pp. 175–88.

[Anon.] (1814), 'Lord Byron's "Ode to Buonaparte"', *Critical Review*, 5, pp. 524–79.

Ariès, Philippe (1974), *Western Attitudes Toward Death: From the Middle Ages to the Present*, trans. Patricia M. Ranum, Baltimore: Johns Hopkins University Press.

Bainbridge, Simon (1997), *Napoleon and English Romanticism*, Cambridge: Cambridge University Press.

Bartley, M. Elizabeth C. (1992), 'The New Repertory at the Opéra during the Reign of Terror: Revolutionary Rhetoric and Operatic Consequences', in: Malcolm Boyd (ed.), *Music and the French Revolution*, Cambridge: Cambridge University Press, pp. 107–56.

Baudelaire, Charles (1956), *The Essence of Laughter: And Other Essays, Journals and Letters*, ed. Peter Quennell, London: Meridian.

Beatty, Bernard (2015), 'Wordsworth's and Byron's Links with British and French Decadence', in: Mark Sandy and Kostas Boyiopoulos (eds), *Decadent Romanticism 1780–1914*, Farnham: Ashgate.

Blessington, Marguerite, Countess of (1969), *Lady Blessington's Conversations of Lord Byron*, ed. Ernest J. Lovell, Jr, Princeton: Princeton University Press.

Brewer, William Dean (1994), *The Shelley–Byron Conversation*, Gainesville: University of Florida Press.

Brown, Ron (2001, repr. 2004), *The Art of Suicide*, London: Reaktion Books.

Canuel, Mark (2012), *Justice, Dissent and the Sublime*, Baltimore: Johns Hopkins University Press.

Carlyle, Thomas ([1899] 2010), *The Works of Thomas Carlyle*, ed. Henry Duff Traill, Cambridge: Cambridge University Press.

Cohen-Vrignaud, Gerard (2015), *Radical Orientalism: Rights, Reform and Romanticism*, Cambridge: Cambridge University Press.

Deleuze, Gilles (2006), *Foucault*, trans. and ed. Seán Hand, London / New York: Continuum.

De Staël, Anne Louise Germaine (1813), *Reflections on Suicide*, London: Longman / Hurst et al.

Elfenbein, Andrew (1995), *Byron and the Victorians*, Cambridge: Cambridge University Press.

Faubert, Michelle (2015), 'Romantic Suicide, Contagion, and Rousseau's *Julie*', in: Angela Esterhammer, Diane Piccitto and Patrick Vincent (eds), *Romanticism, Rousseau, Switzerland: New Prospects*, Basingstoke and New York: Palgrave.

Fitzgerald, T. P. (1822), *The Political and Private Life of the Marquess of Londonderry including Most Important and Authentic Particulars of his Last Moments and Death*, Dublin: O'Neil.

Gardiner, Michael (2013), *The Constitution of English Literature: The State, the Nation and the Canon*, London: Bloomsbury.

Gates, Barbara (1988), *Victorian Suicide: Mad Crimes and Sad Histories*, Princeton: Princeton University Press.

Goodden, Angelica (2008), *Madame de Staël: The Dangerous Exile*, Oxford: Oxford University Press.

Hansard, T. C., ed. (1824), *The Parliamentary Debates*, vol. 9, London: Hansard.

Healey, F. G. (1959), *The Literary Culture of Napoleon*, Paris / Geneva: Librairie Droz / Librairie Minard.

Higonnet, Margaret (1986), 'Speaking Silences: Women's Suicide', in: Susan Rubin Suleiman (ed.), *The Female Body in Western Culture: Contemporary Perspectives*, Cambridge, MA: Harvard University Press, pp. 68–83.

Jacquette, Dale (2005, repr. 2014), *The Philosophy of Schopenhauer*, London / New York: Routledge.

Kierkegaard, Søren (1983), *The Sickness unto Death: Kierkegaard's Writings*, Princeton: Princeton University Press.

Koretsky, Deanna P. (2015), '"Unhallowed arts": *Frankenstein* and the Poetics of Suicide', *European Romantic Review*, 26, pp. 241–60.

Lieberman, Lisa (2003), *Leaving You: The Cultural Meaning of Suicide*, Chicago: Ivan R. Dee.

Lowy, Michael and Robert Sayre (2002), *Romanticism Against the Tide of Modernity*, Durham, NC: Duke University Press.

MacDonald, Michael and Terence R. Murphy (1990), *Sleepless Souls: Suicide in Early Modern England*, Oxford: Clarendon Press.

McGann, Jerome J. (2002), *Byron and Romanticism*, ed. James Søderholm, Cambridge: Cambridge University Press.

Migault, Henry Gabriel (1856), *Eight Historical Dissertations in Suicide, Chiefly in Reference to Philosophy, Theology and Legislation*, Heidelberg: printed for the author by G. Mohr.

Moore, Charles (1790), *A Full Enquiry into the Subject of Suicide*, 2 vols, London: J. F. / C. Rivington.

Nathan, Isaac (1829), *Fugitive Pieces and Reminiscences of Lord Byron*, London: Whittaker, Treacher and Co.

Pascoe, Allan H. (2009), *Revolutionary Love in Eighteenth-century and Early Nineteenth-century France*, Aldershot: Ashgate.

Polewhele, Revd Richard [sic] (1798, repr.1800), *The Unsex'd Females; a Poem addressed to the Author of The Pursuits of Literature*, New York: republished by Wm Cobbett.

Polidori, John (1866), 'Essay on the Punishment of Death', *Notes & Queries*, 10, p. 132.

Retterstol, Nils (1993), *Suicide: A European Perspective*, Cambridge: Cambridge University Press.

Robinson, Charles E. (1997), 'The Devil as Doppelganger in *The Deformed Transformed*: The Sources and Meaning of Byron's Unfinished Drama', in: Robert F. Gleckner and Bernard Beatty (eds), *The Plays of Lord Byron: Critical Essays*, Liverpool: Liverpool University Press, pp. 321–46.

Sanderson, Richard K. (1992), 'Glutting the Maw of Death: Suicide and Procreation in *Frankenstein*', *South Central Review*, 9, pp. 49–64.

Todd, Janet (2007, repr. 2013), *Death and the Maidens: Fanny Wollstonecraft and the Shelley Circle*, London: Bloomsbury.

Veyne, Paul (2003), *Seneca, the Life of a Stoic*, trans. David Sullivan, New York / London: Routledge.

Watkins, Daniel P. (1993), *A Materialist Critique of English Romantic Drama*, Gainesville: University Press of Florida.

Wells, John David (2008), *The Twilight of Romanticism: Lives and Literature in French Bohemian Culture and the Beat Generation*, New York / Bloomington: iUniverse.

Wolfson, Susan (2006), *Borderlines: The Shiftings of Gender in British Romanticism*, Stanford: Stanford University Press.

Wollstonecraft, Mary (1798), *Memoirs and Posthumous Works of Mary Wollstonecraft Godwin, Author of A Vindication of the Rights of Woman*, 2 vols, Dublin: Thomas Burnside.

Wollstonecraft Shelley, Mary ([1814–44] 1987), *The Journals of Mary Shelley*, ed. Paula Feldman and Diana Scott-Kilvert, 2 vols, Oxford: Clarendon Press.

Yu, Christopher (2003), *Nothing to Admire: The Politics of Poetic Satire from Dryden to Merrill*, Oxford: Oxford University Press.

# Chapter 12

# Byron and the Good Death

*Tom Mole*

When Byron's corpse arrived back in England in 1824, immersed in spirits and encased in a double coffin, his long-serving and long-suffering valet Fletcher accompanied it. Fletcher was reunited with his wife, whom he had not seen since 1816, and also with his wife's employer, Lady Byron, who wanted to know about her ex-husband's final hours. In particular, she implored Fletcher to recall his master's last words.[1] But Byron – delirious with fever and weakened by the repeated and misguided bleedings administered by his doctors – did not leave a resonant final statement to posterity. His last words were 'I want to sleep now.'[2] Perhaps Lady Byron was moved by what Byron had called 'the late remorse of love' (*Childe Harold* IV, l. 137), but she was also responding to an ideology of the good death that was widely shared by her contemporaries. Several people tried to influence how Byron faced his death, or left accounts of his final hours. James Kennedy sent Byron a tract that recounted Rochester's death-bed conversion.[3] But Julius Millingen recorded, 'with infinite regret', that, while he 'seldom left Lord Byron's pillow during the latter part of his illness, [he] did not hear him make any, even the smallest, mention of religion'.[4] Edward John Trelawny claimed to have written an account of Byron's death, from Fletcher's dictation, resting his paper on Byron's coffin.[5] They all shared Annabella's belief that the final hours were particularly revealing.

Byron repeatedly returned to this idea in his poetry, reflecting and interrogating the Romantic ideology of the good death. This ideology was formed out of both Classical and Christian traditions of thinking about death, which sometimes coexisted uneasily. The Classical tradition emphasised facing one's death with equanimity, surrounded by one's friends. Philosophy would free one from the fear of death, and even allow one to welcome it as the end of earthly ills. In Plato's *Phaedo*, Socrates approaches his death squarely and rationally, without distress or regret, talking philosophically with his friends to the end. Phaedo reports that 'the man appeared happy in both manner and words as he died nobly and without fear'.[6] This tradition of facing death with nobility extended into Stoic thought, and was condensed into Cicero's dictum that 'to philosophize is to learn how to die'. In 1776, Adam Smith held up David Hume as an example of someone who died a good death in this tradition. He emphasised that Hume remained cheerful and sociable to the last, reconciling himself to death by reading classical works such as Lucian's *Dialogues of the Dead*, and even joking about his coming end.[7]

But if the way Hume approached his death revealed his virtues, Smith's account was controversial because they were certainly not Christian virtues. By the eighteenth century, the Classical ideal of the good death was entwined with a Christian ideal that was quite different. The Christian tradition emphasised facing death piously, trusting that, through God's grace, the soul would find repose and reward in heaven, where the individual would be reunited with loved ones who had gone before. This tradition encouraged people to cast off the concerns of the world as they approached death, and turn their eyes to the hereafter. From the fifteenth-century *ars moriendi*, through Jeremy Taylor's *Holy Dying* (1651), the doctrine was widely preached that only faith in God's saving grace allowed one to die in tranquillity. Edward Young's *Conjectures on Original Composition* (1759) included a long discussion of how Joseph Addison met his death. Addison sent for his wayward stepson, saying to him 'see in what peace a Christian can die'.[8] Robert Southey tried to weaponise this Christian tradition of the good death in his attack on the 'Satanic School', where he argued that '[w]hatever remorse of conscience' the writer of a 'lascivious book' may feel 'when his hour comes (and come it must!) [it] will be of no avail'.[9] 'What Mr. S.'s sensations or ours may be in the awful moment of leaving this state of existence,' Byron retorted, 'neither he nor we can pretend to decide' (Appendix to *The Two Foscari*, 1821).

Hume and Addison died very different deaths, but in both cases it seemed to their contemporaries that their deaths revealed something important about their lives and their characters. Hume's death purportedly showed his scepticism to be a firmly held belief capable of sustaining him in extremity, while Addison's revealed the deep-rooted nature of his religious convictions. Philippe Ariès, in his well-known history of Western attitudes towards death, describes a modern understanding of death, emerging in the twelfth century and stretching up to the end of the eighteenth. This modern attitude shaped 'a series of new phenomena which introduced a concern for the individuality of each person into the old idea of the collective destiny of the species'.[10] It individualised death, seeing it not as our common fate, but as an occurrence that retrospectively gave meaning to the biography it concluded: 'In the mirror of his own death each man would discover the secret of his individuality.'[11] Ariès's chronology, which draws largely on evidence from Catholic Europe, has been disputed by other historians, but his terms remain useful.[12] By the Romantic period, the moment of death was scrutinised not so much for clues about the fate of the deceased person's soul hereafter, as for a revelation of the character traits that had shaped his or her life heretofore. At a point when all feigning seemed redundant, a person's authentic character revealed itself. Death offered a life's denouement in the final chapter.

This attitude, combining Classical and Christian influences, underpinned a masculine, militaristic ideology of the good death, reflected in representations of heroic deaths in battle. General Wolfe's death at the moment of victory at the Battle of Québec in 1759 was widely received as a glorious patriotic sacrifice. It was commemorated not only in the famous painting by Benjamin West (1770) – which presents a dramatised and idealised version of Wolfe's death, depicting him with Christ-like iconography and surrounding him with men who were not actually there – but also in a host of other reports and representations, written and visual.[13] Lord Nelson's death at the Battle of Trafalgar in 1805 was similarly held up as an exemplary military sacrifice, painted by Arthur William Devis (1807) and described at length in Robert Southey's popular biography (1813), which concludes, 'if the chariot and the horses of fire had been vouchsafed for Nelson's translation, he could scarcely have departed in a brighter blaze of glory'.[14] This understanding of the moment of death as one that revealed a person's character was so powerful that it led people to shape and stage their own final moments in conformity with it. Especially for upper-class men, their final thoughts were often about how their final thoughts would be recorded. William Pitt the Younger reportedly expired in 1806 with the words 'Oh, my country! How I love my country!' General Sir John Moore, dying at the Battle of Corunna in 1809, piously said 'I hope the people of England will be satisfied.'[15] The moment of death had taken on what Ariès calls 'a dramatic and personal meaning'; it was privileged as a uniquely revealing instant in which, beyond all dissembling, an individual's fundamental traits and values flashed out.[16]

Byron reiterated this understanding. In a poem written when he was 18, he cited Pitt the Elder as a pattern of the good death, writing '[f]or the life of a Fox, of a Chatham the death / What censure, what danger, what woe would I brave!'('Lines to the Rev. J. T. Becher', ll. 17–18). Pitt, who became Earl of Chatham in 1766, continued to attend the House of Lords until he was 69, when, rising to make a speech, he clutched his chest and collapsed. He died less than a month later. Dying in harness after a distinguished political career, Pitt's death was of a piece with his exemplary public service, and stood as a shorthand for Byron's patrician ambitions. Pitt's death reflected back lustre on his life. Fifteen years later, Byron's response to Viscount Castlereagh's death started from the same assumptions but came to the opposite judgement. Like Pitt's death, Castlereagh's revealed something important about his character; in this case, Byron found Castlereagh as contemptible in death as he had been in life. Byron's comment in *Don Juan* (1819–24) was not 'quietly facetious', as he had promised to be about everything, but audibly enraged. 'Of the manner of his death', he wrote, 'little need be said':

> [T]he minister was an elegant lunatic, a sentimental suicide; he merely cut the 'carotid artery' (blessings on their learning), and lo! the pageant and the Abbey! and 'the syllables of dolour yelled forth' by the newspapers, and the harangue of the coroner in an eulogy over the bleeding body of the deceased (an Anthony worthy of such a Caesar), and the nauseous and atrocious cant of a degraded crew of conspirators against all that is sincere or honourable. In his death he was necessarily one of two things by the law – a felon or a madman – and in either case no great subject for panegyric. ('Preface' to *Don Juan* Cantos VI–VIII, *CPW*, vol. 5, p. 296)

If Byron knew the details of Castlereagh's suicide, he did not let them move him to sympathy. Wracked with overwork and increasingly paranoid and unstable, Castlereagh thought he detected a conspiracy against him and said before he died that he feared exposure as a sodomite, possibly following an encounter with a transvestite prostitute staged by blackmailers trying to entrap him.[17] Byron understood Castlereagh's death not as a response to these circumstances, but as the clinching summation of his life, which brought with it the obloquy his policies had always deserved. He drove the point home in his epigram, 'So he has cut his throat at last! He? Who? / The man who cut his country's long ago' ('Epigrams', ll. 7–8). Whether he was writing about a man he admired, such as Pitt, or one he despised, such as Castlereagh, Byron regarded their deaths as what Ariès describes as a kind of final test.[18]

This understanding of the moment of death as one with uniquely revealing potential led Byron to draw particular attention to how his characters meet, or prepare to meet, their deaths. When the ship-wrecked crew in *Don Juan* '[t]hought it would be becoming to die drunk' (*Don Juan* II, l. 280), Juan objects:

> 'Tis true that death awaits both you and me,
> But let us die like men, not sink below
> Like brutes. (*Don Juan* II, ll. 283–5)

Dying 'like men' means facing death squarely, courageously, and without the help of palliatives, sedatives or intoxicants. (Millingen reported that Byron declined to pray before dying, saying 'Come, come, no weakness! let's be a man to the last.'[19]) Juan's servants fail this test by dying drunk (*Don Juan* II, ll. 56–7). In love, Juan is content to be swept along by the stream; he is famously more acted upon than acting. But when he faces death, as he does repeatedly in the poem, he always tries to take control of the situation. On Lambro's island, he is 'resolved to die' (*Don Juan* IV, l. 39); at the siege of Ismail he 'rushe[s] where the thickest fire announced most foes' (*Don Juan* VIII, l. 32); faced with highwaymen on Shooters' Hill, he becomes 'choleric and sudden', killing one of them with his pistol (*Don Juan* XI, l. 33). In every case, Juan attempts not just to avoid death but also, if necessary, to meet it unflinchingly and on his own terms, in accordance with the ideology of the good death that Byron inherited.

That ideology required not only a certain way of facing death but also a certain way of representing one's death. It was not enough to die courageously: one also had to be observed doing so, and then the moment of death had to be reported or represented as exemplary. The moment of death therefore became a flashpoint for contesting understandings of an individual's life. According to another report, Pitt the Younger's last words were not 'Oh, my country! How I love my country!', but 'I could just do with one of Bellamy's meat pies.'[20] Byron dwelt on Castlereagh's suicide precisely because he thought it was being misrepresented in his eulogies; the battle over how to understand Castlereagh's death was the first battle in the war to determine his legacy. In *The Corsair* (1814), the worst of woes that await Conrad in prison is to be left

> With not a friend to animate, and tell
> To other ears that death became thee well:
> Around thee foes to forge the ready lie,
> And blot life's latest scene with calumny [. . .]. (*The Corsair* III,
> ll. 228–31)

His final indignity would be not simply dying in captivity, but also losing control over how his death was represented. Seyd and his men can still harm Conrad after they have killed him, by misrepresenting his final hours. The assumption underlying that fear is that the final scene is a particularly revealing one, with the power to amend our estimation of what went before. 'There is something of pride in the perilous hour, / Whatever the shape in which death may lower,' Byron wrote in *The Siege of Corinth* (1816), '[f]or Fame is there to say who bleeds, / And Honour's eye on daring deeds' (*The Siege of Corinth*, ll. 440–3). The question of who would represent the moment of death, and how they would do so, was therefore an important one.

Many of Byron's heroes, like Juan in moments of danger, try to exert control over their deaths. They refuse to accept consolation from others if doing so means sacrificing that control. The Giaour makes it clear that his dying confession to the Monk is neither an act of submission nor a rite of repentance:

> But talk no more of penitence;
> Thou see'st I soon shall part from hence:
> And if thy holy tale were true,
> The deed that's done canst *thou* undo?
> Think me not thankless – but this grief
> Looks not to priesthood for relief. (*The Giaour*, ll. 1202–7)

Rather than becoming incorporated in a religious narrative of sin, repentance and salvation, the Giaour's death clinches the narrative that he tells of his own life. Manfred likewise rejects the Abbot's attempt to impose a doctrinal apparatus on his final moments. 'Give thy prayers to Heaven', the Abbot exhorts, '[p]ray – albeit in thought, – but die not thus.' Manfred refuses to expire on any terms but his own, saying 'Old man! 'tis not so difficult to die' (*Manfred*, III, iv, ll. 144–51). They both insist, like Juan, on controlling their own final hours and meeting death on their own terms.

Hugo, alone among Byron's heroes, accepts religious consolation before his death. We see him '[k]neeling at the Friar's knee' (*Parisina*, l. 397), where he confesses his sins (*Parisina*, l. 413) and says the rosary (*Parisina*, l. 432). Hugo dies 'as erring man should die' (*Parisina*, l. 462), 'not disdaining priestly aid, / Nor desperate of all hope on high' (*Parisina*, ll. 465–6). But, like Manfred's, his final words are defiant:

> [']Strike:' – and as the word he said,
> Upon the block he bow'd his head;

These the last accents Hugo spoke:
'Strike' – and flashing fell the stroke[.] (*Parisina*, ll. 452–5)

With the repeated imperative 'Strike', Byron reasserts Hugo's will at the last possible moment. Hugo's instruction to his executioners makes him once again an agent, not simply a victim. He symbolically usurps Azo's right to command by appropriating the death sentence and pronouncing it against himself. By choosing the death that will come in any case, Hugo manages a minimal reassertion of agency, a final restatement of subjective control in the face of the subject's dissolution. Brought by circumstances to the threshold of death, several of Byron's characters actively choose to cross it. The dying gladiator in *Childe Harold* Canto IV '[c]onsents to death, but conquers agony' (*Childe Harold* IV, l. 140). Minotti in *The Siege of Corinth* chooses to die in the explosion he sets off rather than be captured in battle. By contrast, Byron criticised Napoleon for failing to choose death instead of exile; he had not 'died as honour dies' ('Ode to Napoleon Buonaparte', l. 95). In 'Elegiac Stanzas on the Death of Sir Peter Parker' (1814), Byron distinguishes a group called 'the brave' ('Elegiac Stanzas', l. 4), asking rhetorically, 'Who would not share their glorious lot? / Who would not die the death they chose?' ('Elegiac Stanzas', ll. 19–20). While others find it thrust upon them, the brave *choose* death, and so epitomise their exemplary lives and ensure their posthumous reputation. Byron seems to have envisaged a similar choice for the end of his own life. He told Millingen that he wanted to die 'rushing, sword in hand, on a body of Turks, and fighting like one weary of existence', and advised himself to 'choose thy ground, / And take thy rest' ('On This Day I Complete My Thirty-Sixth Year', ll. 39–40).[21] To die well, on this account, was to choose death, not to succumb to it. Lady Blessington remembered that Byron 'dreamt more than once' of dying in Greece, and 'continually entertained a presentiment' that he would never come back. 'Then why go?' she asked. Byron replied: 'Precisely because I yield myself to the dictates of irrevocable fate.'[22] Rejecting palliatives or easy consolations in your final hours, and actively embracing a death that you cannot avoid, are key virtues in Byron's account of the good death.

These virtues are not available to everyone equally, but are primarily reserved for men (and, among men, are more available to aristocrats or those exhibiting inner nobility than to lower-class men). Women in Byron's poetry are often passive in the face of death. Insofar as their deaths reveal their characters, it is because those characters are defined in relation to their lovers. Leila is condemned to death for her love of the Giaour, but unlike Hugo has no opportunity to recover agency in her final moments. Zuleika in *The Bride of Abydos* (1813) dies of grief when she realises Selim is doomed. Medora, in *The Corsair*, dies offstage; although her corpse looks peaceful, the poem gives no account of how she met her death, only of Conrad's response to it. Kaled becomes deranged after Lara's death, and falls into a decline. Haidée wastes away after Juan is sold into slavery. While Byron does not condemn any of these characters for how they face their deaths, the masculine good death is apparently not available to them. Myrrha in *Sardanapalus* (1821) is the exception to this rule. By the standards implied in Byron's other poems, she makes an exemplary masculine good death, which is a counterweight to Sardanapalus's feminisation. She refuses to escape when she has the opportunity and, when her death is inevitable, she takes matters into her own hands, lighting the funeral pyre and choosing death on it.

Byron's understanding of the good death involved not only facing one's own death with courage but also scrutinising the dying moments of others. This scrutiny would provide evidence of their characters, but would also foster or reflect one's own moral fortitude in the face of death. What Byron and his characters seek in these passages is not a way of holy dying, in which mortifying the flesh or contemplating mortality cultivates detachment from the world and fixes attention on the hereafter. Rather, the Byronic hero seeks truly to know the fact of his own mortality by fixing his attention on others at the moment of their deaths. Male characters in Byron's poems repeatedly claim to have witnessed the deaths of others, often with particular attention. Having killed his enemy Hassan, the Giaour reports that 'I gazed upon him as he lay, / And watch'd his spirit ebb away' (*The Giaour*, ll. 1085–6). Bonnivard in *The Prisoner of Chillon* (1816) has a whole catalogue of eye-witness encounters with death:

> Oh, God! it is a fearful thing
> To see the human soul take wing
> In any shape, in any mood: –
> I've seen it rushing forth in blood,
> I've seen it on the breaking ocean
> Strive with swoln convulsive motion,
> I've seen the sick and ghastly bed
> Of Sin delirious in its dread [. . .]. (*The Prisoner of Chillon*, ll. 176–83)

Cain, who lives in a world where death is known to be coming but where no one has yet experienced it, also seeks to look death in the face. When Lucifer asks him if '[t]hou seekest to behold death, and dead things?', he replies 'I seek it not; but as I know there are / Such [. . .] I would behold at once, what I / Must one day see perforce' (*Cain*, II, i, 191–5). The Giaour, Bonnivard and Cain all exhibit their moral fortitude in the face of death not only by facing their own deaths with courage but also by looking unflinchingly at the deaths of others, or wishing to do so.

Byron himself scrutinised the deaths of others too. He hinted at his familiarity with death in a note to *The Giaour*, glossing the passage where he images Greece as a recently deceased corpse:

> I trust that few of my readers have ever had an opportunity of witnessing what is here attempted in description, but those who have will probably retain a painful remembrance of that singular beauty which pervades, with few exceptions, the features of the dead, a few hours, and but for a few hours, after 'the spirit is not there'. (*The Giaour*, p. 89n)

Here, as part of Byron's characteristic claim to the authority of experience, he gives the impression that he has witnessed several violent deaths.[23] He is even a connoisseur of death, who goes on in the note to distinguish between the appearance of corpses shot or stabbed to death. *Don Juan*'s narrator notes, 'I have seen many corpses' (*Don Juan* V, l. 35). Byron went to see executions by hanging in England and by the guillotine in Italy. In both cases, he was not content simply to attend, but insisted on scrutinising the proceedings closely. In England he rented a window opposite the gallows to get a good view, and in Italy he took his opera glass, 'as one should see every thing once – with attention' (*BLJ*, vol. 5, p. 229).[24] These excursions not only offered a *frisson* of excitement, but they also responded to, and helped to shape, a coherent set of attitudes towards death. Byron undertook them, I suggest, partly as a kind of personal test of nerve or moral fibre, in an effort to face the death of others as a form of preparation for his own.

But more than this, Byron sought out opportunities to scrutinise the moment of death not only for what it would reveal about the dying individual, but also for what he could learn about the nature of death itself. Rather than primarily thinking about death in existential or eschatological terms, Byron was fascinated by what we might call the phenomenology of death. He repeatedly returned to descriptions of dying characters in his poetry in order to explore intellectually questions about what it was like to die. In seeking a phenomenology of death, Byron was seeking what a long philosophical tradition had declared to be impossible. Death, this tradition insists, is a non-phenomenon. It is not experienced because the subject who would experience it is extinguished by death. Death cannot be the object of experience because it is the dissolution of the experiencing subject. For this reason, I can never coincide with my own death, which will always remain ungraspable to me. I can experience the events that lead up to my death, but death itself is not among those experiences. This tradition stretches back to Epicurus, who explains that you cannot find yourself in the state of death during your existence, nor in the state of existence once you are dead. From this insight, he famously argues that death is 'nothing to us, since so long as we exist, death is not with us; but when death comes, then we do not exist'.[25] For Epicurus, it is therefore irrational to fear death. A long philosophical tradition has agreed with Epicurus that death cannot be the object of experience. Wittgenstein, for example, says that 'death is not an event of life: we do not live to experience death'.[26] Epicurus begins from the postulate that death is the end of existence, but even for philosophers who leave open the possibility of existence after death, the moment of death itself remains beyond experience for the individual who is on this side of the border. As Bernard Schumacher puts it, 'the philosopher finds himself obliged to turn back once he reaches the insuperable threshold of death's door'.[27]

Imagination does not help here. When I try to imagine what it is like to die or to be dead, I quickly run up against a hard limit. My imaginings necessarily include a self who is doing the imagining, whereas death is precisely the moment at which this self cannot be present. I can imagine different scenarios of dying: what it would be like to be terminally ill, or to commit suicide, or to be sentenced to death. I can imagine the effect my death will have on others, or what the world will be like after my death. I can imagine what my corpse will look like. But all these cases imply an imagining subject. I cannot imagine the moment of my death 'from the inside'. In 1811, soon after Byron was struck by the triple blow inflicted by the deaths of his mother and of his two Cambridge friends, the brilliant homosexual undergraduate Charles Skinner Matthews, and John Edleston, the chorister to whom Byron was passionately attached, the poet wrote, 'There is to me something so incomprehensible in death, that I can neither speak nor think on the subject' (BLJ, vol. 2, p. 69). This response expresses Byron's numbed state of shock, but also his understanding of the epistemological complexity of death. Kant observes that 'the thought *I am not* simply cannot exist: for if I am not, then I cannot be conscious that I am not'.[28] If imagination involves extrapolating from experience, it cannot encompass something that, by definition, constitutes the limit of experience. To say that you cannot think on the subject is therefore not to confess your intellectual inadequacy but to recognise something important about the nature of death.

For the same reasons, death cannot be observed in others. An onlooker can regard someone dying and can examine their corpse once they are dead. Byron's heroes do this repeatedly, as he claimed to have done himself. But these observations do not provide any information about what the moment of death is like 'from the inside' or about the state of being dead. 'The relation with the death of the other', Emmanuel Levinas asserts, 'is not a *knowledge* [*savoir*] about the death of the other, nor the experience of that death in its particular way of annihilating being (if, as is commonly thought, the event of this death is reducible to this annihilation).'[29] The death of others retreats from perception, no matter how closely I scrutinise their dying or their corpse. Observing their final moments can tell me something about how they face their deaths, but nothing about what death itself is like, or what it is like to be dead. In sum, neither the moment of death nor the state of being dead can be experienced, imagined or observed. Byron therefore faces an intellectual problem. Insofar as his repeated scrutiny of the moment of death is a search, not for information about dying, but for knowledge of death itself, he is attempting to scrutinise something that resists scrutiny and retreats from experience.

The difficulties inherent in making death into an object of knowledge mean that it is often defined negatively, by saying what it is not. This habit of speech is not just evasive but also reflects the epistemological difficulty of grasping death as a phenomenon. An example of this negative definition is provided by a medical textbook published in the same year as *Don Juan* III, IV and V:

> If we are aware of what *indicates* life, which everyone may be supposed to know, though perhaps no one can say that he truly and clearly understands what *constitutes* it, we at once arrive at the discrimination of death. It is the cessation of the phenomena with which we are so especially familiar – the phenomena of life.[30]

The author ties himself in knots syntactically as he tries to come to terms with that fact that he can define death only in opposition to life, which in turn can be defined only by appealing to the reader's sense of its indefinable attributes. When Byron writes that he cannot speak on the subject of death, he is registering the same difficulty. Lucifer, in *Cain* (1821), says that death 'has no shape' (*Cain* I, i, 259). Describing a character's death, Byron often resorts to negative diction that registers the impossibility of representing the moment of death: 'the man was gone', 'the spirit is not there', he 'ceased to breathe', his heart 'beats no more', he is 'already with the slain'. This phrasing is not simply euphemistic. It suggests how representing death becomes an artistic problem as well as an intellectual one in Byron's poetry, where he finds himself committed to representing something that cannot be experienced or expressed except through negation.

Byron employs two poetic resources to address this problem: elision and aposiopesis. Despite his dedication to scrutinising the moment of death in his poetry, he repeatedly elides that moment, using a dash in his manuscripts again and again to mark the moment when experience reaches its limit. Hugo's death, already quoted, disappears into the dash that separates his last word from the action that ends his life: '"Strike" – and flashing fell the stroke'. Events before and after death are visible but death itself vanishes into a rhetorical ellipsis. When one of his brothers dies, Bonnivard, chained to a pillar out of sight of his brother, misses the moment of death, which Byron again elides into a dash:

> I call'd, and thought I heard a sound –
> I burst my chain with one strong bound,
> And rush'd to him: – I found him not [. . .]. (*The Prisoner of Chillon*, ll. 209–11)

Here the moment of death is, significantly, difficult to locate. It could be in the moment of time marked by the first dash or the second. Ten lines later, Byron connects the dash with death again, when Bonnivard says, 'My brothers – both had ceased to breathe' (*The Prisoner of Chillon*, l. 220). In *Lara* (1814), Byron employs a dash at the end of a line to allow the moment of the hero's death to disappear into the texture of the verse: 'He press'd the hand he held upon his heart – / It beats no more' (*Lara* II, ll. 494–5). In *The Siege of Corinth*, the moment of Alp's death is also signalled by a dash at the end of the line (he is shot by a sniper). Minotti goads Alp to attack, but '[t]hat challenge is in vain – / Alp's already with the slain!' (*The Siege of Corinth*, ll. 820–1). In *Cain*, Byron uses the dash specifically to mark the frustration of Cain's desire to scrutinise death. Cain, thinking of death as 'a being' (*Cain* I, i, 262), 'watch'd for what I thought his coming: for / With fear rose longing in my heart to know / What 'twas which shook us all – but nothing came' (*Cain* I, i, 272–4). In every case, a small piece of punctuation is made to bear a lot of weight. As an unvoiced mark, the dash serves Byron as a way to register the limit of what can be said, signalling the moment of death that so fascinates him while also testifying to its unknowability.

Any argument about Byron's punctuation is complicated by the publication history of his poems. Byron expected his manuscripts to be edited before they appeared in print, and in particular his punctuation. He asked Murray, 'Do you know any body who can stop – I mean point-commas, and so forth? for I am, I hear, a sad hand at your punctuation' (*BLJ*, vol. 3, p. 100). Byron punctuated his manuscripts freely and expressively, and used dashes for a wide variety of purposes, from marking parenthetical asides, to connecting clauses parataxically, to pointing out sexual innuendo. Like Emily Dickinson, he also used dashes of different lengths and weights. His punctuation was sometimes altered by his amanuenses and by his publisher's editors. On occasion they introduced dashes, but more often they removed them in the name of regularising Byron's eccentric punctuation. In the process, they sometimes obscured Byron's association of the dash with the moment of death. In *Manfred*, for example, Byron placed a dash at the moment of Manfred's death in the manuscript. 'Old Man! 'tis not so difficult to die. –' was followed by the stage direction '(Manfred expires. –)'.[31] As in other examples, the moment of death is significantly difficult to locate, but both possible moments are marked in the manuscript with dashes that follow full stops. While the full stop marks an end, the dash opens up a space to wonder if it really is the end. The line-end dash produces a moment of silence of indefinite duration in which to consider the recalcitrant nature of death, its resistance to understanding. Manfred's final line was omitted entirely in the first edition and restored in the second and subsequent editions, but neither of these dashes appeared in print.

The rhetorical device of aposiopesis – breaking off as though unwilling or unable to continue – also serves Byron as a way of handling the difficulty of scrutinising death. Aposiopesis often involves the speaker being apparently overcome with emotion, or desisting out of tact, but Jonathon Shears argues that Byron uses this rhetorical device at 'moments when discourse breaks down to reveal the limits of the creative artist'.[32] The moment of death is such a moment, *par excellence*. When his first brother dies, Bonnivard breaks off a description of his character with the words 'But why delay the truth? – he died' (*The Prisoner of Chillon*, l. 144). Byron's verse elides the moment of death, offering no description of it but offering instead an aposiopesis – a rhetorical break that, by telling us the worst at once, spares the speaker from dwelling on his brother's death and the reader from a gruesome description. Again the moment is marked with a dash. In *Don Juan*, Byron uses a similar rhetorical move in describing the death of the Commandant in Canto V: 'But why should I add / More circumstances? Vain was every care; / The man was gone' (*Don Juan* V, l. 34). In these examples, Byron's speaker refuses to indulge in any periphrasis that would delay or obscure the knowledge of death. The poems break off from circumstantial detail to give it to us straight. This repeats at the level of style the virtue of facing death unflinchingly, as cultivated by Byron's heroes at the level of characterisation.

Byron on several occasions attempts to represent the experience of death, 'from the inside'. In *The Siege of Corinth*, he tries to stay with Alp's dying consciousness until the last possible moment. 'A flash like fire within his eyes / Blazed, as he bent no more to rise, / And then eternal darkness sunk' (*The Siege of Corinth*, ll. 834–6). Byron scrutinises the dying body, which is 'quivering', without a pulse, but these lines also attend to the consciousness that is suddenly snuffed out: 'Ere his very thought could pray, / Unaneled he passed away' (*The Siege of Corinth*, ll. 848–9). The tight focus here on the moment when the subject is extinguished, timing the poem's description to the speed of thought, reflects Byron's goal of making representation coincide with the non-phenomenon of death. The tendency to fall back on conventional expressions, such as 'eternal darkness' and 'passed away', reflects the impossibility of attaining that goal.

In other poems, Byron stretches out the process of dying into a kind of living death, where the character is as close as possible to the state of death while still being representable as an experiencing subject. Bonnivard, in a poem haunted by the difficulty of representing death, enters this condition of living death. His description – couched in negative terms, striated with dashes – is marked by the difficulties of approaching the limits of representation:

> What next befell me then and there
> I know not well – I never knew –
> First came the loss of light, and air,
> And then of darkness too:
> I had no thought, no feeling – none –
> Among the stones I stood a stone [. . .]. (*The Prisoner of Chillon*, ll. 231–6)

Left with only 'silence, and a stirless breath / Which neither was of life nor death', Bonnivard's death-in-life is mysterious even to himself (*The Prisoner of Chillon*, ll. 257–8). Haidée enters a similar state of death-in-life – 'Like one life could not hold, nor death destroy' – during her long demise in *Don Juan* Canto IV (*Don Juan* IV, l. 59). Anne Barton suggests that this condition of death-like stasis almost brought the poem to a standstill, given the narrator's 'profound reluctance [. . .] to bring Haidée's story to its inevitable tragic end'.[33] Although Haidée shows no sign of life, yet 'death seem'd absent still' (*Don Juan* IV, l. 60). The canto narrates her demise in detail, but despite its extended scrutiny, the moment of death remains mysterious, '[a]nd they who watch'd her nearest could not know / The very instant' (*Don Juan* IV, l. 69).

But if death itself can never be the object of experience – and therefore cannot be the object of representation – death none the less stalks experience and is, at some level, continuously present. While the instant of death necessarily remains elusive to the experiencing subject, the fact of mortality presses on all the subject's experiences.[34] Death, which is never with us, is always with us. A *memento mori* serves to recall that fact; Byron kept no less than four skulls in his study at Newstead Abbey (*BLJ*, vol. 2, pp. 69, 70) and drank from a skull-cup inscribed 'Quaff while thou canst' ('Lines Inscribed on a Cup Formed from a Skull', l. 17). The constant shadow of death leads him to an intensified version of *carpe diem*:

> My time has been passed viciously and agreeably – at thirty-one so few years months days hours or minutes remain that 'Carpe diem' is not enough – I have been obliged to crop even the seconds – for who can trust *tomorrow*? *tomorrow* quotha? *to-hour – to-minute –* – I can *not* repent me (I try very often) so much of any thing I have done – as of any thing I have left undone – alas! (*BLJ*, vol. 6, p. 211)

Here the Horatian prescription for the good life takes on a frantic edge, as the immanence of death accelerates the experience of life. 'Few men can live faster than I did. I am, literally speaking, a young old man,' Byron told Millingen, which recalls his poetic comment 'in short I / Have squandered my whole summer while 'twas May' (*Don Juan* I, l. 213).[35] If Byron's effort to scrutinise death in his poetry is bound to fail, then, he none the less cannot abandon it because of the insistent pressure exerted on experience by mortality.

Many of the aspects of Byron's approach to death and dying come together in the passage in *Don Juan* V describing the death of the military Commandant. This episode erupts into the poem as a digression from a digression from the story of Juan being sold as a slave. It narrates the assassination of the military Commandant Del Pinto, in the street outside Byron's house in Ravenna, on 8 December 1820. Byron had already described the event in several letters written soon afterwards (*BLJ*, vol. 7, pp. 245–52). When he incorporated it into his poem, he made it the occasion for a meditation on death that acts as a summation of several concerns he explored elsewhere in his poetry. The Commandant's death is received as a revelation of his character. Although he does not choose his death in the manner of a Byronic hero, his 'calm' demeanour in death reveals his fortitude in facing extinction unperturbedly (*Don Juan* V, l. 35). As with Conrad's death in *The Corsair*, Byron draws attention to the way this death is witnessed and represented. The Commandant's death is witnessed by his men, who '[w]ith their rough faces throng'd about the bed' (*Don Juan* V, l. 37), and Byron draws attention to the authenticity of his own representation, writing that 'this is a fact and no poetic fable' (*Don Juan* V, l. 33).

As on other occasions, Byron scrutinises the moment of death, repeating that he 'gazed upon him' (*Don Juan* V, l. 35), 'gazed on him', 'gazed (as oft I have gazed the same)' (*Don Juan* V. l. 38), and that the soldiers gathered to 'gaze once more' (*Don Juan* V, l. 37). But, again as it does on other occasions, the moment of death retreats from scrutiny and eludes representation. As in *The Prisoner of Chillon*, or *Manfred*, or Haidée's death in the previous canto, the moment of death is not easy to locate. The Commandant is alive in stanza 33 ('able scarce to pant') but the poem says 'they had slain him with five slugs' in the next stanza; 'slain' replaced the manuscript's cancelled word 'killed' and it must mean 'fatally wounded', as he is left to 'perish on the pavement' (*Don Juan* V, l. 34). By the end of the stanza 'The man was gone' (*Don Juan* V, l. 34), though in the next stanza 'you could scarcely tell [. . .] that he was dead' (*Don Juan* V, l. 35).

Byron looks to the Commandant's corpse for some revelation about the nature of death. 'Can this be death?' he asks, 'then what is life or death?' (*Don Juan* V, l. 36). But, as elsewhere, he employs elision and aposiopesis to register the unrepresentable nature of the moment of death. In a dash-filled letter describing the event in breathless paratactic prose, the Commandant's death is marked with a dash: '[I] had the Commandant carried up Stairs to my own quarters. – But he was quite gone. –' (*BLJ*, vol. 7, p. 247). In the poem, repeated dashes mark both the moment of death and the narrator's response to it. The Commandant was 'stripp'd and look'd to, – But why should

I add / More circumstances? vain was every care; / The man was gone' (*Don Juan* V, l. 34). In the manuscript, these lines had another dash after the question mark. Dashes are used at the end of lines in stanzas 36 (twice), 37 and 38, as well as in the middle of a line in stanza 39 ('Here we are, / And there we go: – but *where?*') to mark the imponderable nature of death and register the limits of knowledge and representation. Byron again employs aposiopesis, breaking off as if unwilling to protract his description, writing 'let me quit this theme' (*Don Juan* V, l. 38) and 'No more' (*Don Juan* V, l. 39).

The Commandant's death introduces a new word into Byron's account of death and dying: 'mystery'. This word both reflects a long-standing element of Byron's poetic handling of death and suggests a new departure:

> I gazed (as oft I have gazed the same)
> To try if I could wrench aught out of death
> Which should confirm or shake or make a faith;
> But it was all a mystery. (*Don Juan* V, ll. 38–9)

This is not an admission of defeat, but an effort to bring a new set of conceptual tools to bear upon a long-standing problem. Identifying death as a mystery does not produce any new information about it, or allow it to be experienced, imagined or observed, but it does offer a new element in Byron's ethos of facing death. Coleridge, in *Aids to Reflection* (1825), provides an apposite definition of a mystery. It is 'a Fact, which we see, but cannot explain; [. . .] which we apprehend, but can neither comprehend nor communicate'.[36] We should read Byron's use of the word in this sense. The series of unanswered questions that conclude the Commandant passage indicates that Byron has not solved any of the problems posed by death's unknowable nature, but he has produced a new iteration of the effort to face death. Whereas in earlier comments having scrutinised the deaths of others provided a test of nerve or a proof of moral fortitude, describing death as a mystery requires a discipline of contemplation. This entails returning repeatedly to the moment of death, and the fact of mortality, without getting any closer to perceiving, understanding or representing it satisfactorily.

Byron worries that 'such things claim / Perhaps even more attention than is due / from me' (*Don Juan* V, l. 38). *Fraser's Magazine* would complain about his recurrent concern with the scene of death in 1876, noting that 'it is to Byron one must turn to find death *in its physical circumstances displayed* and dwelt upon over and over again' (italics in the original). The critic responded to Byron's intense scrutiny of the moment of death but complained that he did not link the scene of death to any promise of redemption.

> After the horrors of description, he has nothing to say to us but this – always the same reflection – See! a moment ago this was a human being, full of pain, pleasure, passion, agitation; now it is a piece of clay, food for worms.[37]

*Fraser's* understood Byron's ethos of the good death, even as it condemned it. He returned to 'the same reflection' again and again because his approach to death reflected the limits of what can be known about something that – as a long philosophical tradition explained – cannot be experienced, imagined or observed. Alongside his attempt to grapple with the limits of how death could be represented or understood, he also developed an ethos of dying that valued facing the death of others head on, rejecting palliatives or easy consolations in your final hours, and actively embracing a death that you cannot avoid. In his most profound meditation on death, in the Commandant passage of *Don Juan*, his description of death as 'all a mystery' is not just a way of throwing his hands up in frustration at how little we can know of death, even if the frustration is palpable. It is also a sceptical response that values iterated contemplation of death without looking for a solution to the problem of understanding it.

## Notes

1. Marchand, *Byron: A Biography*, vol. 3, p. 1258.
2. Ibid., p. 1228.
3. *CCB*, p. 456.
4. Ibid., p. 591.
5. Trelawny, *Recollections of the Last Days of Shelley and Byron*, p. 228.
6. Plato, *Complete Works*, p. 51.
7. Smith, 'Letter to William Strahan, 9 November 1776', in: *The Glasgow Edition of the Works and Correspondence of Adam Smith*, pp. 217–21.
8. Young, *Conjectures on Original Composition, in a Letter to the Author of Sir Charles Grandison*, pp. 103–4.
9. Southey, *A Vision of Judgement*, pp. xviii–xix.
10. Ariès, *Western Attitudes Toward Death from the Middle Ages to the Present*, p. 28.
11. Ibid., pp. 51–2.

12. See Gittings, *Death, Burial and the Individual in Early Modern England*; Jupp and Gittings, *Death in England*.

13. McNairn, *Behold the Hero: General Wolfe and the Arts in the Eighteenth Century*; Schama, *Dead Certainties: Unwarranted Speculations*, pp. 3–70.

14. Southey, *The Life of Horatio, Lord Nelson*, vol. 2, p. 280.

15. Pitt's and Moore's dying words are quoted by Linda Colley in the course of a helpful discussion of the period's 'ideal of patrician valour and self-sacrifice' (p. 196). Colley, *Britons: Forging the Nation*, pp. 193–7.

16. Ariès, *Western Attitudes Toward Death*, p. 27.

17. Bew, *Castlereagh: The Biography of a Statesman*, pp. 537–44, 552–7.

18. Ariès, *Western Attitudes Toward Death*, p. 36.

19. *CCB*, p. 591.

20. Cited in Colley, *Britons: Forging the Nation*, p. 195.

21. *CCB*, p. 529.

22. Ibid., p. 367.

23. The phrase 'the spirit is not there' is probably drawn from Robert Southey's poem 'The Dead Friend' (1799), and perhaps hints at the difference between Southey's circumscribed experience of dead bodies and Byron's more extensive knowledge.

24. For the hanging in England, see *CCB*, p. 53.

25. Epicurus, 'Letter to Menoeceus §125', in: *Epicurus: The Extant Remains*, p. 85.

26. Wittgenstein, *Tractatus Logico-Philosophicus*, §6.4311, p. 87.

27. Schumacher, *Death and Mortality in Contemporary Philosophy*, p. 145.

28. Kant, 'Anthropology from a Pragmatic Point of View §27', cited in: Schumacher, *Death and Mortality in Contemporary Philosophy*, p. 129.

29. Levinas, *God, Death and Time*, p. 16.

30. Smith, *Principles of Forensic Medicine, Systematically Arranged and Applied to British Practice*, p. 16.

31. See Cochran, *Manfred: An Edition of Byron's Manuscripts and a Collection of Essays*, p. 123.

32. Shears, 'Byron's Aposiopesis', pp. 183–95, at p. 184.

33. Barton, *Byron: Don Juan*, p. 37.

34. Schumacher observes that 'While it is invisible in the sense of phenomenon nonperception, death is nevertheless present somehow at every moment of human existence, and it belongs, in a certain way, to the phenomenal world,' in: *Death and Mortality in Contemporary Philosophy*, p. 121.

35. *CCB*, p. 529.

36. Coleridge, 'Aids to Reflection', in: *The Collected Works of Samuel Taylor Coleridge*, vol. 9, p. 288.

37. [Anon.], 'The Proposed Byron Memorial', pp. 246–60, at p. 255.

## Works cited

[Anon.] (1876), 'The Proposed Byron Memorial', *Fraser's Magazine*, 13, pp. 246–60.

Ariès, Philippe (1974), *Western Attitudes Toward Death from the Middle Ages to the Present*, trans. Patricia M. Ranum, Baltimore: Johns Hopkins University Press.

Barton, Anne (1992), *Byron: Don Juan*, Cambridge: Cambridge University Press.

Bew, John (2011), *Castlereagh: The Biography of a Statesman*, London: Quercus.

Cochran, Peter (2015), *Manfred: An Edition of Byron's Manuscripts and a Collection of Essays*, Newcastle: Cambridge Scholars Press.

Coleridge, Samuel Taylor (1993), *Aids to Reflection*, ed. John Beer, *The Collected Works of Samuel Taylor Coleridge*, vol. 9, Princeton: Princeton University Press.

Colley, Linda (1996), *Britons: Forging the Nation, 1707–1837*, London: Vintage.

Epicurus (1926), *The Extant Remains*, ed. and trans. Cyril Bailey, Oxford: Clarendon Press.

Gittings, Claire (1984), *Death, Burial and the Individual in Early Modern England*, London: Croom Helm.

Jupp, Peter and Clare Gittings, eds (1999), *Death in England*, Manchester: Manchester University Press.

Levinas, Emmanuel (2000), *God, Death and Time*, trans. Bettina Bergo, Stanford: Stanford University Press.

McNairn, Alan (1997), *Behold the Hero: General Wolfe and the Arts in the Eighteenth Century*, Montreal: McGill–Queen's University Press.

Marchand, Leslie (1957), *Byron: A Biography*, London: John Murray.

Plato (1997), *Complete Works*, ed. John M. Cooper, Indianapolis: Hackett.

Schama, Simon (1991), *Dead Certainties: Unwarranted Speculations*, New York: Alfred A. Knopf.

Schumacher, Bernard (2010), *Death and Mortality in Contemporary Philosophy*, trans. Michael J. Miller, Cambridge: Cambridge University Press.

Shears, Jonathon (2008), 'Byron's Aposiopesis', *Romanticism*, 14, pp. 183–95.

Smith, Adam (1987), 'Correspondence', in *The Glasgow Edition of the Works and Correspondence of Adam Smith*, vol. 6, ed. Ernest Campbell Mossner and Ian Simpson Ross, Oxford: Oxford University Press.

Smith, John Gordon (1821), *Principles of Forensic Medicine, Systematically Arranged and Applied to British Practice*, London: Thomas and George Underwood.

Southey, Robert (1814), *The Life of Horatio, Lord Nelson*, 2 vols, London: John Murray.

— (1821), *A Vision of Judgement*, London: Longman.

Trelawny, Edward John (1858), *Recollections of the Last Days of Shelley and Byron*, London: Edward Moxon.

Wittgenstein, Ludwig (2001), *Tractatus Logico-Philosophicus*, trans. D. F. Pears and B. F. McGuinness, London: Routledge.

Young, Edward (1759), *Conjectures on Original Composition, in a Letter to the Author of Sir Charles Grandison*, London: A. Millar and R. and J. Dodsley.

# Chapter 13

# At the Margins of Romanticism: The Women of *Don Juan's* English Cantos

*Drummond Bone*

It was a cliché of early and mid-twentieth-century criticism to see Byron's late *ottava rima* poems as leaving the Romantic in a turn backwards to the Neoclassicism and mock-heroic of Pope. Later descriptions, including my own, preferred to characterise the shift as a forward step into the instability of Romantic Irony and the world of Sterne, Clough, Melville and Joyce.[1] In this essay, born from, and retaining something of the informality of, a lecture – and probably my valedictory wave to the poem, at least in print – I am not concerned with the taxonomy *per se*, but in its use heuristically. I will argue that a better way of accounting for the experience of reading *Don Juan* (1819–24) is to think of an inconstant fluctuation between satire assuming a stable world view (looking towards Pope), and irony that dissolves any such possibility of stability, further troubled by a nostalgia for a something more transcendent (looking towards the Romantic), and almost its exact opposite, an insistent blockish physicality. Another way of putting that is to say that the unstable ironic world, created with immersion and gusto, includes nevertheless a nostalgia for a stable world either Classically civilised or Romantically transcendent – but that is not quite accurate, for inside the experience it is not nostalgia but reality. Is a better characterisation a sense of the elegiac – not nostalgia for time past, but the awareness of our human time passing against the solidity of the material, yet without devaluing the present or the evanescent emotion? The three central female figures of the English Cantos are taken as a key part of this shadow-play.

That meaning for Byron at least in his later years resides not in nature but in art, not in an objective world but in a world created by ourselves, is most pointedly expressed in the letters of the Bowles controversy, and is thus often linked with his admiration for Pope and with satire.² But aside from his typical energy in the Bowles letters we must distinguish his more extreme view of the artificial from Pope's. From *Manfred* onwards, it is art – 'stories' in the sense of *Beppo's* (1818) concluding stanza – that gives life value. This may look like Neoclassicism dealing satirically with the sophisticated civilised world, but it can be thought of as virtually the opposite. Civilisation and art are not an attempt to return humans to God's Nature, but a fiction made up to protect us from the void. Though Byron typically is not consistent, this view can also be found *passim* explicitly in *Don Juan*, for example:

> No more – no more – Oh! never more on me
> The freshness of the heart can fall like dew,
> Which out of all the lovely things we see
> Extracts emotions beautiful and new,
> Hived in our bosoms like the bag o' the bee:
> Think'st thou the honey with those objects grew?
> Alas! 'twas not in them, but in thy power
> To double even the sweetness of a flower. (*Don Juan* I, ll. 1705–12)

We need to be careful of what happens to Pope in the Bowles letters – mimesis of the natural God-given order by civilisation in Pope has turned into the human given precedence over the natural. So the Pope obsession is not quite what it seems. The Neoclassical world view and the dramatic unities do not represent (re-present in its fullest sense) for Byron some absolute, but rather are a humanly created artifice. *Ottava rima* is like a carefully built interlocking brick wall, but it is not a rock. If the Romantic ideal is the structureless whiteness of Shelley's Mont Blanc,³ the step further into Romantic irony is the realisation, firstly that that whiteness may not be all-colour but none at all, and secondly that that brick wall not only can be, but will be, continually knocked down and rebuilt.

In poetic practice, as in life, this inversion of Pope is not necessarily experienced as an inversion; what is read, what is experienced, *is* the present moment, may well be stable, though the experience of a sequence is an experience of instability. The famous mobility note is an account of this exactly in terms of Byron's own psychology:

> Commentary to line 820 of Canto XVI: In French, 'mobilité'. I am not sure that mobility is English, but it is expressive of a quality which rather belongs to other climates, though it is sometimes seen to a great

extent in our own. It may be defined as an excessive susceptibility of immediate impressions – at the same time without *losing* the past; and is, though sometimes apparently useful to the possessor, a most painful and unhappy attribute. ('Note to *Don Juan* XVI, l. 820', *CPW*, vol. 5, pp. 649, 769)

It is of course associated with Adeline,[4] which leads us to the women – at last, but only for a passing moment. It is made almost explicit that Adeline and absolutely explicit that Aurora are developed replays in a different context of Julia and Haidée.[5] What is implicit is that the third term, unbalancing this di-pole, Fitz-Fulke, is a kind of replay too, of her aristocratic forebears Gulbayez and Catherine. The sophisticated but self-unknowing, the innocent and the sexually predatory are brought together in these English Cantos. It is perhaps revealing to gloss these characters in slightly different ways – the apparently ordered but at the same time deeply unstable (Adeline), the Romanticised natural (Aurora) and the unintellectualised physical (Fitz-Fulke). If this was a piece of music, you might feel that the themes of three preceding movements were being woven together – which might signify an ending, if not necessarily a resolution.

But before we consider the women in detail, let us consider the background texture against which, or rather out of which, they are realised.[6] At the very beginning of the English country-house episode in Canto XIII Neoclassical satire is set up against the Romantic Sublime:

> I now mean to be serious; – it is time,
> Since laughter now-a-days is deemed too serious.
> A jest at Vice by Virtue's called a crime,
> And critically held as deleterious:
> Besides, the sad's a source of the sublime,
> Although when long a little apt to weary us;
> And therefore shall my lay soar high and solemn
> As an old temple dwindled to a column. (*Don Juan* XIII, ll. 1–8)

But note too in passing the little personal elegiac note at the beginning of stanza 2:

> The Lady Adeline Amundeville –
> ('Tis an old Norman name, and to be found
> In pedigrees by those who wander still
> Along the last fields of that Gothic ground) – (*Don Juan* XIII,
> ll. 9–12)

This is no casual juxtaposition of the Neoclassical and the Romantic. It sets the scene for a kaleidoscope of shape-shifting Classical and Romantic reference and character, where neither is quite what it might at first seem.[7] The Cantos are, of course, replete with classical and Neoclassical quotations – nothing new for *Don Juan* – but unlike the Classical world of his contemporaries – think Keats – these are usually signalled as quotations: that is, they are there overt as language-form as well as content. Here are some examples: Addison's Cato – "Tis not in mortals to command success; / But *do you more*, Sempronius – *don't* deserve it' (*Don Juan* XIII, ll. 137–8); 'Perhaps from Horace: his "Nil admirari" / Was what he called the "Art of Happiness," / An art on which the artists greatly vary' (*Don Juan* XIII, ll. 273–5). He often plays with the reader's knowledge of the text – thus:

> I'm 'at my old Lunes' – digression, and forget
> The Lady Adeline Amundeville;
> The fair most fatal Juan ever met,
> Although she was not evil, nor meant ill;
> But Destiny and Passion spread the net,
> (Fate is a good excuse for our own will)
> And caught them; – what do they *not* catch, methinks?
> But I'm not Oedipus, and life's a Sphinx.

> I tell the tale as it is told, nor dare,
> To venture a solution: '*Davus sum*!'
> And now I will proceed upon the pair.
> Sweet Adeline, amidst the gay world's hum,
> Was the Queen-Bee, the glass of all that's fair;
> Whose charms made all men speak, and women dumb.
> The last's a miracle, and such was reckoned,
> And since that time there has not been a second. (*Don Juan* XIII, ll. 89–104)

'I'm not Oedipus' comes from Terence's *Andria* 'Davus sum, non Oedipus', but the 'clue' is held back. The pervading intertextuality of *Don Juan* is of course destabilising, shifting literary 'givens' to show they are not at all 'givens', but at the mercy of time and context. However, the wealth of Classical and Neoclassical quotations, and the games he plays with them would, to Byron's chosen readers, also be a construction of fellow feeling – author and reader complicit in the context of their shared Classical education. If irony is destabilising, we have to remember that in shared understanding it also builds a community; we wink at each other's understanding of the joke, so we are building at the same moment as ironising.

And what is true of the quotations is also true of the lists. The most famous may be the menu from Achilles' feast in Canto XV or the Russians as the Greek heroes in Canto VII, but they are everywhere. Canto XV (ll. 313–36) lists Juan's possible wives, leading into the omission of Aurora from the list; or Canto XVI (ll. 521–8), the lists of those in audience on Lord Henry, a passage that leads into that on a genuinely marginalised woman, a different case from Fitz-Fulke of the unignorable physical – the pregnant girl:

> But this poor girl was left in the great hall,
> While Scout, the parish guardian of the frail,
> Discussed (he hated beer yclept the 'small')
> A mighty mug of *moral* double ale:
> She waited until Justice could recall
> Its kind attentions to their proper pale,
> To name a thing in nomenclature rather
> Perplexing for most virgins – a child's father. (*Don Juan* XVI,
> ll. 577–84)

Are the lists an allusion to Homer or 'life's infinite variety' (*Don Juan* XV, l. 146)? – in mock-heroic epic satire the Homeric allusion would work by contrasting the contemporary with the epic – but is that what is happening here (one might ask the same question actually of some accepted satirical epic lists)? There is a delight in the listing that seems to overwhelm the critical, and a delight in contorting the allusion that is almost Promethean. Byron cannot resist a list, and the complicit laugh at the Classical underpinning can become a more hysterical giggle when the exuberance of the material takes over. But let us return to Canto XIII:

> Before the mansion lay a lucid lake,
> Broad as transparent, deep, and freshly fed
> By a river, which its soften'd way did take
> In currents through the calmer water spread
> Around: the wild fowl nestled in the brake
> And sedges, brooding in their liquid bed:
> The woods sloped downwards to its brink, and stood
> With their green faces fix'd upon the flood.
>
> Its outlet dash'd into a steep cascade,
> Sparkling with foam, until again subsiding
> Its shriller echoes – like an infant made

Quiet – sank into softer ripples, gliding
Into a rivulet; and thus allay'd
Pursued its course, now gleaming, now hiding
Its windings through the woods; now clear, now blue,
According as the skies their shadows threw.

A glorious remnant of the Gothic pile,
(While yet the church was Rome's) stood half apart [. . .]. (*Don Juan*
XIII, ll. 449–66)

Where are we? Lac Leman, Italy? No, Newstead Abbey. There is an extraordinary nine stanzas from 55 of Canto XIII onwards without a joke, describing the architecture and setting of Newstead in palpably sublime terms, with a touch of Arcadia admittedly thrown in, and they do not do much, if anything, to rewrite Byron's early Romantic view of Newstead. Compare this with the following introduction to Aurora:

Early in years, and yet more infantine
In figure, she had something of sublime
In eyes which sadly shone, as seraphs' shine.
All youth – but with an aspect beyond time;
Radiant and grave – as pitying man's decline;
Mournful – but mournful of another's crime,
She look'd as if she sat by Eden's door,
And grieved for those who could return no more.

She was a Catholic too, sincere, austere,
As far as her own gentle heart allow'd,
And deem'd that fallen worship far more dear
Perhaps because 'twas fallen: her sires were proud
Of deeds and days when they had fill'd the ear
Of nations, and had never bent or bow'd
To novel power; and as she was the last,
She held their old faith and old feelings fast. (*Don Juan* XV, ll.
353–68)

The mood is very similar to the Newstead passage, which ends with another list – of paintings and painters this time, moving us from the Romantic definitively into a celebration not of art but of 'infinite variety':

But ever and anon, to soothe your vision,
Fatigued with these hereditary glories,
There rose a Carlo Dolce or a Titian,
Or wilder groupe of savage Salvatore's:

> Here danced Albano's boys, and here the sea shone
> In Vernet's ocean lights; and there the stories
> Of martyrs awed, as Spagnoletto tainted
> His brush with all the blood of all the sainted.
>
> Here sweetly spread a landscape of Lorraine;
> There Rembrandt made his darkness equal light,
> Or gloomy Caravaggio's gloomier stain
> Bronzed o'er some lean and stoic Anchorite: –
> But lo! a Teniers woos, and not in vain,
> Your eyes to revel in a livelier sight:
> His bell-mouthed goblet makes me feel quite Danish
> Or Dutch with thirst – What ho! a flask of Rhenish. (*Don Juan* XIII,
> ll. 561–76)

The civilised world of 'art' can thus switch easily into its mirror opposite, no longer the stable in opposition to the perhaps vacuous Romantic sublime, but the ironised world of the protean 'infinite variety'.

Among those in the list awaiting Lord Amundeville are two 'wits', and they make the Classical/Romantic/ironic tension we are discussing pretty explicit:[8]

> There also were two wits by acclamation,
> Longbow from Ireland, Strongbow from the Tweed,
> Both lawyers and both men of education;
> But Strongbow's wit was of more polish'd breed:
> Longbow was rich in an imagination,
> As beautiful and bounding as a steed,
> But sometimes stumbling over a potatoe, -
> While Strongbow's best things might have come from Cato.
> (*Don Juan* XIII, ll. 729–36)

Strongbow is our Neoclassicist, Longbow the Romantic, the couplet the irony. And, in this mix of the classical, sublime and Romantic-ironic, the crux is the opposition of Adeline and Aurora, with *tracasserie* and *agaçerie*, the Fitz-Fulke, waiting in the wings. The passage that brings them together follows from Canto XVI, stanza 44:

> In Babylon's bravuras – as the home
> Heart-ballads of Green Erin or Grey Highlands,
> That bring Lochaber back to eyes that roam
> O'er far Atlantic continents or islands,
> The calentures of music which o'ercome
> All mountaineers with dreams that they are nigh lands,

No more to be beheld but in such visions, –
Was Adeline well versed, as compositions.

She also had a twilight tinge of '*Blue*',
Could write rhymes, and compose more than she wrote;
Made epigrams occasionally too
Upon her friends, as every body ought.
But still from that sublimer azure hue,
So much the present dye, she was remote,
Was weak enough to deem Pope a great poet,
And what was worse, was not ashamed to show it. (*Don Juan* XVI,
ll. 409–24)

Now Adeline is here being identified pretty clearly with Byron, as
she is in the mobility stanzas with their note – here she has sung the
*Hebrew Melodies* (1815), Moore's *Irish Melodies* (1808–34), Byron's
Scottish juvenilia, and likes Pope: that is, she is Byron's present without losing his past. Adeline has both a hollow at her core, covered by
her civilised propriety (or her mobility? – not at all the same thing):

Our gentle Adeline had one defect –
Her heart was vacant, though a splendid mansion;
Her conduct had been perfectly correct,
As she had seen nought claiming its expansion.
A wavering spirit may be easier wreck'd,
Because 'tis frailer, doubtless, than a staunch one;
But when the latter works its own undoing,
Its inner crash is like an Earthquake's ruin. (*Don Juan* XIV, ll.
673–80)

*and* also of course a concentrated sexual energy:

But Adeline was not indifferent: for
(*Now* for a common place!) beneath the snow,
As a Volcano holds the lava more
Within – *et cetera*. Shall I go on? – No!
I hate to hunt down a tired metaphor:
So let the often used volcano go.
Poor thing! How frequently, by me and others,
It hath been stirred up till its smoke quite smothers.

I'll have another figure in a trice: –
What say you to a bottle of champagne?
Frozen into a very vinous ice,

> Which leaves few drops of that immortal rain,
> Yet in the very centre, past all price,
> About a liquid glassful will remain;
> And this is stronger than the strongest grape
> Could e'er express in its expanded shape:
>
> 'Tis the whole spirit brought to a quintessence;
> And thus the chilliest aspects may concentre
> A hidden nectar under a cold presence.
> And such are many – though I only meant her,
> From whom I now deduce these moral lessons,
> On which the Muse has always sought to enter: –
> And your cold people are beyond all price,
> When once you have broken their confounded ice. (*Don Juan* XIII,
> ll. 281–304)

This comparison is dressed in Romantic-ironic reflexiveness (*Don Juan* XIII, ll. 536–44) and *double entendre*, backs away from the Romantic-Nature cliché of the volcano and takes up the 'civilised', highly wrought figure of the champagne. On the one hand, this creates Adeline's character in terms of the world of her mobility, though, on the other, we need to remember that irony and *double entendre* destabilise language but create community between the text and the reader. The overall effect may be as much about the relationship of the reader to the text as a whole as it is to his or her relationship to the character of Adeline.

Aurora, however, is Shakespearean and, for Byron, Shakespeare's 'native woodnotes wild' place him, at least in the context of Pope and the Italian dramatists, in the camp of the Romanticists.[9] And we have, remember, seen her close to Byron's Newstead mood:

> Aurora – since we are touching upon taste,
> Which now-a-days is the thermometer
> By whose degrees all characters are classed –
> Was more Shakespearian, if I do not err.
> The worlds beyond this world's perplexing waste
> Had more of her existence, for in her
> There was a depth of feeling to embrace
> Thoughts, boundless, deep, but silent too as Space. (*Don Juan*
> XVI, ll. 425–32)

This silence has a visual analogy in the second stanza of Canto XV:

> But, more or less, the whole's a syncopé,
> Or a singultus – emblems of Emotion,

> The grand Anthithesis to great Ennui,
> Wherewith we break our bubbles on the ocean,
> That Watery Outline of Eternity,
> Or miniature at least, as is my notion,
> Which ministers unto the soul's delight,
> In seeing matters which are out of sight. (*Don Juan* XV, ll. 9–16)

Do we read the 'matters which are out of sight' as there, but unseen, or not there at all?

Those thoughts of Aurora's, as Romantically silent as can be, are maybe *all*, or maybe *nothing*. Aurora is not exactly Haidée, because she exists not on an island but in a civilised context, here that of 'taste'; if she is Nature, she is Nature Romanticised.[10] She belongs to Nature post Rousseau, nature as already a cultural idea, and very much post Byron's own earlier conception of the Romantic Sublime as co-existing with loss (compare the final line of stanza 59 of Canto XIII quoted above: 'while yet the Church was Rome's').

The third member of the crowd, however, is Nature very much in the raw. It is not at all surprising that she is 'associated' with the ghost – (*Don Juan* XVI, ll. 1025–32) – we cannot escape the flesh, and the flesh cannot escape death. The three are brought together again in *Don Juan* XVI, ll. 777–848:

> But what was bad, she [Aurora] did not blush in turn,
> Nor seemed embarrassed – quite the contrary;
> Her aspect was as usual, still – *not* stern –
> And she withdrew, but cast not down, her eye,
> Yet grew a little pale – with what? concern?
> I know not; but her colour ne'er was high –
> Though sometimes faintly flushed – and always clear,
> As deep seas in a Sunny Atmosphere.
>
> But Adeline was occupied by fame
> This day; and watching, witching, condescending
> To the consumers of fish, fowl and game,
> And dignity with courtesy so blending,
> As all must blend whose part it is to aim
> (Especially as the sixth year is ending)
> At their lord's, son's or similar connection's
> Safe conduct through the rocks of re-elections. (*Don Juan* XVI,
> ll. 793–808)
>
> While Adeline dispensed her airs and graces,
> The fair Fitz-Fulke seemed very much at ease;
> Though too well bred to quiz men to their faces,

> Her laughing blue eyes with a glance could seize
> The ridicules of people in all places –
> That honey of your fashionable bees –
> And store it up for mischievous enjoyment;
> And this at present was her kind employment. (*Don Juan* XVI,
> ll. 841–8)

Aurora is a notably blank canvas, and is almost as much defined by what she does not seem to express as by what she does, and again the 'depth' metaphor with all its ambiguity of all or nothing reappears. In Adeline's case are we to read her behaviour as a satire on the reasons behind apparently civilised good manners or as Romantic-ironic mobility? Take the passage in isolation and you might say the former; place particular weight on the first four lines rather than the last four of stanza 95 and on the general characterisation of Adeline, and you might think the latter. If Aurora is a pitch at the transcendent unpindownable, Adeline is a queasy mixture of irony used as satire, and irony used as an expression of existential instability. Fitz-Fulke's civilised manner is, in the true sense, perverse – the key words are 'blue eyes', that little physical detail, and 'kind employment'.

If Adeline resists both flesh and emptiness through Classical good manners and is satirised for it, she also expresses the poem's involvement with mobility as the condition of life's 'infinite variety'. She is the embodiment of the poem's uneasy relationship with Byron's admiration of the Neoclassical – satirical mock-epic keeps metamorphosing into 'human' epic,[11] as he characterised it to Murray, with no stable beginning or end in sight. If the 'plot' of the English Cantos is effectively Adeline's, to distract Juan from Aurora, the outturn, at least as we have it when the poem breaks off, can only be described as an ironic success. Canto XVII, such as it is, is full of life's instabilities, the necessity of singing its trivialities, and Juan's very physical encounter with the bulk of Fitz-Fulke. Adeline's control of herself and of the plot is illusory. Viewed as a vehicle for satire, that is exactly what one would expect. Viewed from the perspective of an unstable world, 'mobility' is a necessary but a 'painful and unhappy' attribute.

Aurora exists as a type of Romanticism but inside a poem that can create that transcendence only in a nostalgic medium. The texture of the poem includes that medium, and that 'mobility'-like texture is not lost but is forced to be interwoven with, on the one hand, a Neoclassical-like moral realism and, on the other, a radical ironic instability.

Fitz-Fulke is the Goneril and Regan of the daughters, Nature decivilised, sex returned to death. She is what happens, so to speak, when the music stops; she is the kicked stone that disproves Berkeley. Odd, of course, that it is with her that the poem does indeed stop. The reader, like Bernard Beatty and myself, is clearly being set up to choose between the two 'A's, or rather we assume Juan is. But the experience of reading the poem gives us only that rich but kaleidoscopic patterning. It slips and slides from satire to existential irony to Romanticism, recognisable, if not as Wordsworthian, at least as Byron's own early mode with perhaps a touch too of his friend Shelley's more transcendental notes. It slips and slides within Adeline and between Adeline and Aurora, and pauses on a collision with Fitz-Fulke.

The experience of reading *Don Juan* is often elegiac, a sense of loss infused with a paradoxical sense of life, trivia redeemed, meaning saved by a thread from absurdity, a rhyme miraculously found for the unrhymable. *Ottava rima*, order, rewritten on the edge of disorder. A Neoclassical world rewritten where Romanticism has already dissolved into irony.

I had thought of ending there but such expression is too leaden-footed. In the following from Canto XVII we have in Byron's own gossamer film the unknowability of life, Classical allusion and Neoclassical balance in the release of tension in the fresh light of day, the moral importance of life's trivialities as they bind us together, a sense of things gone by unvalued, and the whole carried in self-reflexive irony. The only thing missing from 'our conundrum of a dish' (*Don Juan* XV, l. 168) is maybe the Romantic, but possibly it is there in the self-assured mastery of the verse. I then discovered to my amused horror that I have ended discussions of *Don Juan* in this way not once, but twice. Nevertheless, and for a final time:

> I leave the thing a problem, like all things: –
> The morning came – and breakfast, tea and toast,
> Of which most men partake, but no one sings. (*Don Juan* XVII, ll. 97–9)

## Notes

1. Examples can be found in Rutherford, ed., *Byron: Augustan and Romantic*; and Bone, 'A Sense of Endings: Some Romantic and Postmodern Comparisons'. My own pilgrimage towards this essay can be traced in a gradually changing position from Bone, *Byron*, for example p. 60, and on through Bone, ed., *The Cambridge Companion to Byron*, pp. 156–70. The fact that this essay and the previous two end on the same quotation (!) might, with luck and a kind reader, be seen as an attempt to get it right at last.

2. *CMP*, pp. 120–83. As interesting as the anti-Lakeland pro-Pope 'Art is *not* inferior to Nature for poetical purposes' drift is his frequent insistence on the importance, inclusion and accuracy of physical detail: 'peculiarly *white* sails (the Levant sails not being of "coarse canvas" but of white cotton) . . . our 44's *teak* timbers (she was built in India) [. . .]'.

3. Mont Blanc's whiteness is emptied, or at the least made hopelessly unreadable, by a certain mid-century whale. See below the problem of Aurora's silence.

4. So well she acted, all and every part
   By turns – with that vivacious versatility,
   Which many people take for want of heart.
   They err – 'tis merely what is called mobility,
   A thing of temperament and not of art,
   Though seeming so, from its supposed facility;
   And false – though true; for surely they're sincerest,
   Who are strongly acted on by what is nearest. (*Don Juan* XVI, ll. 817–24)

5. The context in which they exist is crucially different:

   Juan knew nought of such a character –
   High, yet resembling not his lost Haidée;
   Yet each was radiant in her proper sphere;
   The Island girl, bred up by the lone sea,
   More warm, as lovely, and not less sincere,
   Was Nature's all: Aurora could not be
   Nor would be thus; - the difference in them
   Was such as lies between a flower and gem. (*Don Juan* XV, ll. 457–64)

   The movement from 'flower' to 'gem' parallels that from 'volcano' to 'champagne' in the figure describing Adeline's sexuality discussed above, but is notably simpler (we might almost think of an uncut gemstone).

6. In Beatty, *Byron's Don Juan*, Aurora is seen as the 'end-point' of the poem, in a way that I have previously seen Adeline. Neither 'answer' now seems satisfactory.

7. And in the following the reflexivity becomes explicit – the Classical underpinnings and allusions are used to undercut continuity, not create it – things change:

   Dan Phoebus takes me for an auctioneer.
   That Poets were so from their earliest date,
   By Homer's 'Catalogue of Ships', is clear;
   But a mere modern must be moderate –
   I spare you then the furniture and plate. (*Don Juan* XIII, ll. 588–92)

8. Byron's own attitude to the very word Romantic, leave aside his distaste for the Lakers, did not vary much from his anti-system approach to the Schlegels' and Madame de Staël's usage to a philologically reasonable identification of 'romantic', 'romance' and nonsense – he rhymes 'romantic' four times with 'frantic' in the course of *Don Juan*. In a note intended for *Marino Faliero* (1821) but published in the end with *Sardanapalus* (1821), he wrote: 'I perceive that in Germany as well as in Italy there is a great struggle about what they call *"Classical* and *Romantic"* terms which were not subjects of Classification in England – at least when I left it four or five years ago' (*CPW*, vol. 4, p. 546).

9. Pope may be the 'best of poets' in the Ravenna Journal (*BLJ*, vol. 8, pp. 19–20), contemporaneous with the Bowles letters, but in these letters however, contrary as ever, Byron gives Shakespeare the laurels: 'I shall not presume to say that Pope is as high a poet as Shakespeare and Milton', *CMP*, pp. 149–50. In a letter to Murray a little later, on 14 July 1821, he writes that Shakespeare is 'the worst of models – though the most extraordinary of writers' (*BLJ*, vol. 8, p. 152). It is more difficult to see that balanced view in his discussions of his own and Italian dramas. See Barton, 'Byron and Shakespeare', pp. 224–35. For the most extended discussion of Byron and Pope see Gayle, *Byron and the Best of Poets*.

10. See above, n. 5

11. With reference to *Childe Harold*, see Byron's 'Letter to Murray, 6 April 1819': 'you have so many *'divine'* poems, is it nothing to have written a *Human* one [. . .] since you want length you shall have enough of Juan for I'll make 50 cantos' (*BLJ*, vol. 6, p. 105).


## Works cited

Barton, Anne (2004), 'Byron and Shakespeare', in: Drummond Bone (ed.), *The Cambridge Companion to Byron*, Cambridge: Cambridge University Press, pp. 224–35.

Beatty, Bernard (1985), *Byron's Don Juan*, New Jersey: Barnes and Noble.

Bone, Drummond (1999), 'A Sense of Endings: Some Romantic and Postmodern Comparisons', in: Edward Larissey (ed.), *Romanticism and Postmodernism*, Cambridge: Cambridge University Press, pp. 73–85.

— (2000), *Byron*, London: Northcote House.

—, ed. (2004), *The Cambridge Companion to Byron*, Cambridge: Cambridge University Press.

Gayle, Nicholas (2016), *Byron and the Best of Poets*, Newcastle upon Tyne: Cambridge Scholars Publishing.

Rutherford, Andrew, ed. (1990), *Byron: Augustan and Romantic*, London: Macmillan.

# V. Marginal Affairs – Visual and Paratextual Aspects in Byron

# Chapter 14

# A Marginal Interest? Byron and the Fine Arts

*Richard Lansdown*

What is it about art that we find intellectually so elusive? Is it because it takes the form of colour, shape, and pattern in two or three dimensions, rather than words, themselves the instruments of reflection and analysis? Why is it that Keats is so right to say of his Grecian urn that it can 'express / A flowery tale more *sweetly* than our rhyme'[1]: to suggest that art is a *sweeter* medium than literature? Is it because paintings make such an (apparently) immediate impact on our senses, in a rush and in one go, whereas literature is condemned to operate at one remove from the throne of truth by the ploddingly sequential and syntactic medium it exploits (that it 'pours ideas into our minds', as Jonathan Richardson wrote in his *The Theory of Painting* in 1715, whereas 'words only drop them. The whole scene opens at one view, whereas the other way lifts up the curtain by little and little'[2])? What are the varying relations between form and content in the two forms of creative communication? Perhaps an amateur of genius, like Lord Byron, can shed some light on these perplexing questions.

1.

Byron's indifference to painting is well attested to, not least by himself. Three examples are representative. On 6 March 1814, he wrote to Thomas Phillips, who had painted no fewer than three portraits of the poet in recent months:

> Dear Sir/ – I regret troubling you – but my friend H[obhouse] who saw the pictures today suggests to me that the *nose* of the smaller portrait is too much turned *up* – if you recollect I thought so too – but as one never can tell the truth of one's own features – I should

have said no more on the subject but for this remark of a friend whom I have known so long that he must at least be aware of the length of that *nose* by which I am so easily led. – Perhaps you will have the goodness to retouch it – as it is a feature of some importance [. . .]. (*BLJ*, vol. 4, p. 79)

In the same year, John Knowles recorded a conversation between Byron and the Swiss artist, Henry Fuseli:

'I have been looking in vain, Mr. Fuseli, for some months, in the poets and historians of Italy, for the subject of your picture of Ezzelin: pray where is it to be found?' 'Only in my brain, my Lord,' was the answer, 'for I invented it'.[3]

Finally, in January 1821, seven years after the event, Byron recollected a social engagement he and Thomas Moore had attended:

the same evening, I met Lawrence the painter, and heard one of Lord Grey's daughters (a fine, tall, spirit-looking girl, with much of the patrician, thoroughbred look of her father, which I dote upon) play on the harp, so modestly and ingenuously, that she *looked* music. Well, I would rather have had my talk with Lawrence (who talked delightfully) and heard the girl, than have had all the fame of Moore and me put together. (*BLJ*, vol. 8, p. 28)

In short, Byron would appear to have been an egregious philistine. He was firmly of the belief that a sitter had the right to correct his own portrait by dictation; he could not believe that a painter might imagine a historical subject; and he valued the greatest English portrait painter of his age, Thomas Lawrence, more for his conversation than his artistic output.

The American painter William Edward West made portraits of Byron and his mistress Teresa Guiccioli in Montenero, between June and July 1822, and recorded Byron's diffident attitude to art:

At different stages of my picture of the Guiccioli, he appeared to think that I had made her too handsome: on one of which occasions I told him that, in the eyes of a painter, no picture could be so beautiful as the object for which it was meant. He seemed a little surprised at the observation, and said, 'Do *I* not then see with a painter's eye?' Nevertheless, he did not pretend to be much of a judge of painting, for he felt no great passion for it, and had never made it his study [. . .].[4]

In 1823 his visitor in Italy, Lady Blessington, recorded that 'he declared that he never believed people serious in their admiration of pictures, statues, &c., and that those who expressed the most admiration were "Amatori senza Amore, and Conoscitori senza Cognizione"'.[5]

On the few occasions when he did discuss art, furthermore, Byron was given to doing so in conventional terms. 'Art, Glory, Freedom fail', he wrote in the second Canto of *Childe Harold's Pilgrimage* (1812), 'but Nature still is fair' (*Childe Harold* II, l. 827), as if art's inferiority to nature involves some kind of clearly accessible standard, against which it fails by measurement. 'My writings, indeed, tend to exalt the [female] sex; and my imagination has always delighted in giving them a *beau idéal* likeness,' he told Thomas Medwin in 1822,[6] 'but I only drew them as a painter or statuary would do, – as they should be,' which suggests that art naturally or inherently idealises its subjects in a laudable (or perhaps suspect) way. Or he could lapse into an *ut pictura poesis* analogy with little intellectual rigour behind it: 'Like paintings,' he said, 'poems may be too highly finished. The great art is effect, no matter how produced.'[7] Finally, a search of his letters and journals reveals that Byron made not one single substantial comment about painting in them – portrait commissions and miniatures aside – before leaving England for good as a 28-year-old in 1816. Once abroad, he often demonstrated a self-conscious irritation with the whole notion of cultural tourism and 'seeing the sights' – what he called 'that time-tax of travel' (*BLJ*, vol. 5, p. 123) – or the 'intolerably tedious' 'farce of visiting antiquities' (*BLJ*, vol. 6, p. 154). He was almost immune to the Roman and Gothic sublimities at Verona, for example, admitting that 'The Gothic monuments of the Scaligers pleased me,' before concluding, 'but "a poor virtuoso am I"' (*BLJ*, vol. 5, p. 126). Even the Uffizi exhausted his patience: 'Too many visitors to allow me to *feel* anything properly,' he recorded in his journal, the 'crowd of jostling starers & travelling talkers' making an aesthetic experience practically impossible (*BLJ*, vol. 9, p. 50). In early 1821 his landlord in Ravenna – the very Count Guiccioli whom he was cuckolding – had some frescos designed and installed, and Byron dropped in one afternoon to look them over: 'The painter has not copied badly the prints from Titian, &c.,' he blandly commented, 'considering all things' (*BLJ*, vol. 8, p. 19). This was hardly the reaction of an enthusiast. 'Depend upon it,' he wrote to his publisher in April 1817, 'of all the arts it is the most artificial & unnatural – & that by which the nonsense of mankind is the most imposed upon' (*BLJ*, vol. 5, p. 213). This seems to be a marginal interest, indeed.

2.

But that is not the end of the story. We know that Byron encouraged his friend William Bankes to buy a *Judgment of Solomon* from the Marescalchi collection in Bologna in February 1820 for his estate at Kingston Lacy, Dorset, where it still hangs. (Byron and Bankes thought the work was by Giorgione, but it was ascribed to Sebastiano del Piombo by Bernard Berenson in 1903. Giorgione or not, it is a remarkable picture, however incomplete.[8]) 'The real mother is beautiful, exquisitely beautiful,' he told Bankes. 'Buy her, by all means, if you can, and take her home with you: put her in safety: for be assured there are troublous times brewing for Italy' (*BLJ*, vol. 7, p. 45). In Milan in 1816, Byron told his sister he knew nothing of galleries like the Brera, 'except as far as liking one picture out of a thousand' (*BLJ*, vol. 5, p. 114), which he spoke of repeatedly. 'Of painting I know nothing – but I like the Guercino – a picture of Abraham putting away Hagar' (*BLJ*, vol. 5, p. 116). Stendhal said Guercino's painting 'electrified' Byron,[9] and Thomas Moore substantiates that comment in recounting a conversation at La Mira from October 1819, three years later:

> As we were conversing one day after dinner about the various collections I had visited that morning, on my saying that fearful as I was, at all times, of praising any picture, lest I should draw upon myself the connoisseur's sneer for my pains, I would yet, to him, venture to own that I had seen a picture at Milan which – 'The Hagar!' he exclaimed, eagerly interrupting me.[10]

'It was with no small degree of pride and pleasure', Moore concluded, 'I now discovered that my noble friend had felt equally with myself the affecting mixture of sorrow and reproach with which the woman's eyes tell the whole story in that picture.'[11]

In Milan in 1816, Stendhal described 'the astonishing effect produced on Lord Byron by the view of a fine painting by Daniel[e] Crespi':

> The subject was taken from the well-known story of a monk supposed to have died in the odour of sanctity; and who, whilst his brethren were chanting the service of the dead around the bier in the church at midnight, was said to have suddenly lifted the funeral pall, and quitted his coffin, exclaiming, 'Justo judicio Dei damnatus sum!' [I am damned and the judgement of God is just.] We were unable to wrest Byron from the contemplation of this picture, which produced on his mind a sensation amounting to horror.[12]

Stendhal was a habitual embroiderer of the truth where his brief acquaintance with Byron is concerned but this anecdote appears to be true. The episode he describes is from the life of St Bruno of Cologne, painted by Crespi in a cycle of paintings at the church of Santa Maria Assunta at the Certosa di Garegnano in Milan. The particular painting is *Raimond Diocrès annuncia la sua condonna*, and it is a grisly affair, with the haggard and cadaverous departed monk rearing up from his catafalque in severe foreshortening.[13] It appears the poet and the future novelist must have visited the Charterhouse at some time between their first meeting on 23 October 1816 and Byron's departure from Milan on 3 November, though there is no reference to such a visit in any biography of Byron that I know.

The Brera and the Garegnano Charterhouse were not the only Italian artistic sites that Byron visited. At Bologna in April 1817, he saw Guido Reni's *Massacre of the Innocents* – removed from the city by the French in 1796 and returned only in 1815 – which brought a characteristically literal-minded response from him: 'What a superb face there in Guido's innocents in the Gallery!' he told Hobhouse: 'not the *shrieking* mother – but the *kneeling* one – it is the image of Lady Ponsonby – who is as beautiful as Thought' (*BLJ*, vol. 5, p. 216). I assume he has in mind Mary Elizabeth Ponsonby, Countess Grey (1776–1861), wife of the future Prime Minister, and mother of the harp-player he had appreciated in 1814. (Byron was given to making unexpected, indeed eccentric, identifications of this kind: he told Thomas Moore after his visit to Florence that 'The Apollo Belvedere is the image of Lady Adelaide Forbes – I think I never saw such a likeness' (*BLJ*, vol. 5, p. 227).)

The story of French Revolutionary and Napoleonic art theft and restitution – which Wellington and foreign minister Castlereagh insisted on in the second Treaty of Paris, thus laying the groundwork for modern law surrounding the repatriation of cultural heritage – is part of the background to Byron's experience as a tourist after Waterloo (though he makes no reference to it), and is yet to be told in full.[14] Such thefts caused disruption to the whereabouts and provenance of hundreds of works, and half of the looted material was never in fact returned. (British art collecting also moved many paintings during the period, especially out of Italy, as William Bankes's purchases demonstrate, but at least with consent.) 'Napoleon's soldiers cut paintings out of their frames in churches' in Italy, according to Margaret Miles,[15] 'emptied private collections, and sent what they did not destroy in a series of convoys pulled by water buffalo and oxen. The crates were then shipped to Marseilles,' before making their way to the Louvre, then renamed the

*Musée Napoléon*. 'Les fruits de nos victoires' was the label hung over the galleries augmented in this fashion.[16] In 1808, a ten-year-old boy, Eugène Delacroix by name, was inspired to become a painter, standing in front of Veronese's *Wedding Feast at Cana* at the Louvre, stolen from San Giorgio Maggiore in Venice and never returned. As Miles goes on to say, Wellington could very well himself have packed up the four horses from St Mark's, the Laocoön, the Apollo Belvedere, the Medici Venus and the Dying Gaul for the British Museum – and thrown in some French works from the collection to boot, on the principle of 'to the victor the spoils'. (Indeed, the Prince Regent dropped some hints.) 'The scale of the British generosity, based on principle, to Italy was unprecedented,' she writes,[17] 'but the restraint from plundering the French was extraordinary.' Interestingly, the French resisted the process of restitution on some of the same grounds that the British Museum now employs to justify the retention of the Parthenon Marbles: that such works were best understood in an encyclopaedic collection in a central European capital, and so forth.

Guido Reni, alongside Giorgione – or paintings erroneously ascribed to Giorgione, like Bankes's purchase – should probably be called Byron's favourite painter. The poet revisited the Pinacoteca in Bologna in June 1819, from where he told his publisher John Murray, 'I have been picture-gazing this morning at the famous Domenichino and Guido – both of which are superlative' (*BLJ*, vol. 6, p. 146). (Being a Bolognese like Reni, Domenichino is well represented in the Pinacoteca, by his *Madonna of the Rosary*, the *Martyrdom of St Agnes* and the *Martyrdom of St Peter Martyr*. Which one of these Byron meant I do not know, but I would propose the Madonna as the most likely candidate: he did not incline to the dramatic or sadistic end of Catholic art.) As long ago as 1813, he had written a sonnet 'To Genevra' (that is, to Lady Frances Wedderburn Webster), comparing her to the 'Magdalen of Guido', from the artist's 'beauty-breathing pencil born' ('Sonnet – To Genevra', ll. 10–12), now in the National Gallery in London. (Perhaps Byron was thinking more of Lady Frances's moral resemblance to Mary Magdalene than her physical one; they had escaped an affair with each other by a hair's breadth in 1813.) More significantly, Byron drops a rare clue as to Don Juan's physical appearance, where he is seen dancing 'like a personified Bolero':

> Or, like a flying Hour before Aurora
> In Guido's famous fresco, which alone
> Is worth a tour to Rome [. . .]. (*Don Juan* XIV, ll. 313–15)

This is Reni's fresco of 1612, *Apollo in his Chariot, Preceded by the Dawn*, in the Casino dell'Aurora in the Borghese Palazzo Pallavicini-Rospigliosi, which Byron saw in May 1817. It is a surprise to find that Byron envisaged his Spanish hero as this strawberry-blond *amoretto*, representing Phosphorus, the morning star. (The theme was one Reni handled earlier in his career, in an oil fresco for the Palazzo Zani in Bologna: *Dawn Separating Day from Night*. In 1840 it was removed from the ceiling there and transferred to canvas – to be bought by Byron's old friend William Bankes, by then in exile on the continent after being charged with homosexual activity with a guardsman. It, too, remains at Kingston Lacy.)

The Bologna gallery was not the only one Byron visited. In one day in Florence, 22 April 1817, he visited both the Uffizi and the Pitti Palace, from which, he told Murray,

> one returns drunk with beauty – the Venus is more for admiration than love – but there are sculpture and painting – which for the first time at all gave me an idea of what people mean by their *cant* [. . .] about those two most artificial of the arts. – What struck me most were the Mistress of Raphael a portrait [the so-called *La Fornarina*, now ascribed to del Piombo] – the mistress of Titian a portrait – a Venus of Titian in the Medici gallery [that is, the Venus of Urbino] – *the* Venus [that is, the Medici Venus] – Canova's Venus also in the other gallery – Titian's mistress is also in the other gallery [. . .] the Parcae of Michel Angelo a picture [now ascribed to Francesco Salviati], – and the Antinous – the Alexander – & one or two not very decent groups in marble. (*BLJ*, vol. 5, p. 218)

This is a substantial list of works to see and to remember – and Byron's comparison of his Turkish sultana, Gulbeyaz, in the fifth Canto of *Don Juan*, to Venus 'r[ising] from the wave' (*Don Juan* V, l. 762) suggests he cast an eye over the legendary Botticelli at the Uffizi, too.

Byron rattled around Rome at a similar pace: 'As for the Coliseum, Pantheon, St. Peter's, the Vatican, Palatine, &c. &c.,' he told Thomas Moore in May 1817, 'vide Guidebook' (*BLJ*, vol. 5, p. 227). But he must have seen Michelangelo's Sistine frescos and his statue of Moses in San Pietro in Vincoli because both are mentioned in the fourth Canto of *The Prophecy of Dante* (1821) (*The Prophecy of Dante* IV, ll. 57–66). More unexpectedly, he also told Murray – who had just issued a life of Raphael – 'that a set of German artists here allow their hair to grow and trim it in his fashion'. '[I]f they would cut their hair & convert it into brushes & paint like him,' he went on, 'it would be more "German to the matter"' (*BLJ*, vol. 5, p. 221). How he came across the Nazarenes we do not know, but it is true that they occupied the monastery of Sant Isidro (closed by Napoleon) on the Pincio, not far from Byron's lodgings in the Piazza di Spagna – if that is where he stayed.[18]

These are hardly the writings and comments of a man insensible to art, but it remains true that, left to his own devices, Byron was by no means a gallery-haunter. John Cam Hobhouse, on the other hand, was every inch what the English call a culture-vulture, and dragged him around Rome *ad nauseam*. Another acquaintance performed a similar role, not once but twice: Byron's unfortunate doctor and tra-velling companion between April and September 1816, John William Polidori, whom the poet re-encountered both in Milan in October of the same year and in Venice in April 1817.

From the moment Byron and Polidori arrived in Belgium from Dover in late April 1816 the doctor proved an insatiable connoisseur of the arts, as his diary reveals. In Ghent and Antwerp in particular, Polidori led Byron to all the notable sights. At the Cathedral of St Bavo in the former city on 27 April the pair went to see 'paintings that were by the hand of masters', as Polidori describes them[19] – above all the early fifteenth-century Van Eyck altarpiece, but also a Rubens – and climbed the steeple. ('At Ghent we stared at pictures', Byron reported to Hobhouse, '& climbed up a steeple 450 steps in altitude – from which I had a good view of these "paese bassi"' (*BLJ*, vol. 5, p. 73).) From the cathedral they went to the Royal Ecole de Des-sin, 'where we found a well-provided gallery of paintings', Polidori noted,[20] including 'a *chef d'œuvre* of Rubens, *St. Roch amongst the Sick of the Plague*'. I assume that this is the great altarpiece from St Martin's in Aalst, looted by Napoleon and returned from France the year before Byron's visit, in temporary storage at the Royal School until its re-establishment in the church. (Polidori was irritated that a student had parked his easel directly in front of the painting.) There were also two Van Eycks in the Royal School; a Teniers on a favou-rite theme of his, the temptation of St Anthony (perhaps the one now in the Royal Museum of Fine Arts in Brussels); and another *Judg-ment of Solomon*, which Polidori attributed to a now obscure artist named Kruger,[21] but which I think must be the painting of that title by Frans Floris (now in the Royal Museum of Fine Arts in Antwerp), 'where the child was painted dead with most perfect nature', accord-ing to Polidori:[22] 'so much so that my companion, who is a father, could not bear its sight'.

By 29 April the travellers were in Antwerp, where Byron had a decisive confrontation with Rubens, firstly in St James's Church, where he is buried, and secondly at the recently opened Royal Museum of Fine Arts, where his *Descent from the Cross* (looted by the French Revolutionary government in 1794, and now in the Cathedral of Our Lady) was displayed. '[A]s for Rubens,' Byron told Hobhouse,

> I was glad to see his tomb on account of that ridiculous description (in Smollett's P[eregrine] Pickle) of Pallet's absurdity at his monument – but as for his works – and his superb 'tableaux' – he seems to me (who by the way know nothing of the matter) the most glaring – flaring – staring – harlotry imposter that ever passed a trick upon the senses of mankind – it is not nature – it is not art – with the exception of some linen (which hangs over the cross in one of his pictures [that is, the *Descent*]) which to do it justice looked like a very handsome table cloth – I never saw such an assemblage of florid night-mares as his canvas contains – his portraits seem clothed in pulpit cushions. (*BLJ*, vol. 5, p. 73)

(Mr Pallet is a painter and dilettante in Tobias Smollett's *Peregrine Pickle* (1751). In Chapter 57 he falls to his knees at Rubens's tomb 'and worshipped with such appearance of devotion, that the attendant, scandalised at his superstition, pulled him up; observing [. . .] that the person buried in that place was no saint, but as great a sinner as himself'.) Polidori concurred as regards the *Descent*, 'the effect of the white sheet is wonderfully beautiful', he noted; 'but there are defects'.[23] Yet more Rubens was on display in St Augustine's Church, where Polidori noted 'A Vandyck near him is much superior.'[24] Byron chimed in in a letter to his sister, 'I think Rubens a very great dauber', he wrote, 'and prefer Vandyke a hundred times over' (*BLJ*, vol. 5, p. 74). Who was leading whose eye in these artistic judgements it is impossible to say. Byron was dragged to one more Rubens by Polidori, the *Crucifixion of St Peter* at St Peter's Church in Cologne (his last major work, also looted by the French), on the way to Switzerland, before being able to say good riddance to him, but years later, in 1823, he continued to recall his disapprobation. 'When I say I object to delicate women', he told Lady Blessington,[25] 'I don't mean to say that I like coarse, fat ladies, *à la Rubens*, whose minds must be impenetrable, from the mass of matter in which they are incased.' Again, Byron's habit was to concentrate on the subject – Rubens's 'coarse, fat ladies' – rather than the means by which the subject was portrayed.

3.

The Flemish School was a disappointment, therefore, but on 13 April 1817 Polidori made up for his failure as a Belgian cicisbeo by taking Byron to the most famous private collection of art in Venice. This had been built up by the wealthy tobacco plantation owner and trades-man, Girolamo Manfrin, who, as Francis Haskell records,[26] 'had already established himself as one of the most important patrons and collectors in Venice' by the mid-1780s.[27] His collection – of more than 400 paintings by the time of his death in 1802 – was a some-what patchy affair, despite its aim 'to have some of the definitive sta-tus of a national institution' and 'to be a tribute to the achievement of Venetian painting' in particular.[28] Be that as it may, the Palazzo Manfrin was on every tourist's itinerary after the turn of the century – including the banker–poet Samuel Rogers, who visited in 1814, and William Hazlitt, who went through in 1825. Typically, Byron, who had settled in Venice in November 1816, had not visited by April of the following year, but when he did he was impressed. Amongst the paintings, he told Murray,

> there is a Portrait of *Ariosto* by *Titian* surpassing all my anticipation of the power of painting – or human expression – it is the poetry of por-trait – & the portrait of poetry. – There was also one of some learned lady – centuries old whose name I forget – & it is forgotten – but whose features must always be remembered – I never saw greater beauty – or sweetness or wisdom – it is the kind of face to go mad for – because it cannot walk out of its frame. – There is also a famous dead Christ & live apostles – for which Buonaparte offered in vain five thousand Louis – & of which though it is a capo d'opera of Titian – as I am no connoisseur I say little – & thought less except of one figure in it. – There are ten thousand others – & some very fine Giorgiones amongst them, &c. &c. – There is an Original Laura & Petrarch – very hideous both – Petrarch has not only the dress – but the features & air of an old woman – & Laura looks by no means like a young one, – or a pretty one. – What struck me most in the general collection was the extreme resemblance of the style of the female faces in the mass of pictures – so many centuries and generations old – to those you see & meet every day amongst the existing Italians. – The queen of Cyprus & Giorgione's wife – particularly the latter – are Venetians as it were of yesterday – the same eyes and expression – & to my mind there is none finer.

'You must recollect however', Byron concluded, 'that I know nothing of painting – & that I detest it – unless it reminds me of something I have seen or think it possible to see' – before returning to his dislike of Rubens and his indifference to the works by Velázquez and Murillo that he had seen in Spain in 1810 (*BLJ*, vol. 5, p. 213).

This description of the Manfrin Collection is by far Byron's most vivid evocation of art – in prose, at any rate. It would be wonderful to be able to trace each of the seven paintings he responded to here: the portrait of Ariosto, the 'learned lady', the 'famous dead Christ & live apostles', the 'Original Laura & Petrarch' (a pair of portraits), the 'queen of Cyprus' and the wife of Giorgione. Five of them we can identify – and I have been greatly assisted in my efforts to do so by Professor Linda Borean of the University of Udine.[29] The Ariosto is now generally referred to as a *Ritratto maschile*; what Byron saw was an antique copy (or perhaps a variant) of the famous purple-sleeved Titian in the National Gallery in London, and is in a private collection in Italy ('Sharp-featured and tawny-coloured,' Hazlitt reported, 'with a light Morisco look').[30] The dead Christ is the *Deposizione di Cristo nel sepolcro*, by a follower of Titian, now at the Borgogna Museum in Vercelli (which figure in it Byron preferred I cannot say). According to a manuscript catalogue in the National Gallery in London, the Manfrin Collection contained a *Ritratto di Laura del Petrarca* and a *Ritratto del Petrarca*, both said to be by Giovanni Bellini. A *Ritratto di Laura* and a *Ritratto del Petrarca* are both listed by Fritz Heinemann,[31] but he ascribes the first (now in the Vienna Kunsthistorisches Museum) to Andrea Previtali, and the second as a lost copy of an original by Gentile Bellini, itself lost in Berlin in the 1930s. The Vienna Previtali is certainly not a winsome depiction of Petrarch's legendary love. Byron's 'Queen of Cyprus' is, in fact, the painting by Carpaccio now known (for no very good reason, it seems) as *Saint Ursula Taking Leave of Her Father*, in the National Gallery in London, but earlier known as *The Landing of Caterina Cornaro at Cyprus* – the rarest and finest of nine works by Italian old masters that the National Gallery acquired from the Manfrin Collection after his grandchildren began to break it up in the late 1840s (acquisitions including works by Bramantino, Busati, Jacometto, Mansueti, Marco D'Oggiono, Previtali and Vivarini).[32]

The painting Byron calls 'Giorgione's wife' made a deeper impression and came back in his verse in *Beppo*, written exactly six months after his visit to the Manfrin Collection, where he made the same point about the similar appearance of women in old master paintings and those 'amongst the existing Italians':

> They've pretty faces yet, those same Venetians,
> Black-eyes, arch'd brows, and sweet expressions still,
> Such as of old were copied from the Grecians,

In ancient arts by moderns mimick'd ill;
And like so many Venuses of Titian's
(The best's at Florence – see it, if ye will)
They look when leaning over the balcony,
Or stepp'd from out a picture by Giorgione,

Whose tints are truth and beauty at their best;
And when you to Manfrini's palace go,
That picture (howsoever fine the rest)
Is loveliest to my mind of all the show;
It may perhaps be also to *your* zest,
And that's the cause I rhyme upon it so:
'Tis but a portrait of his son, and wife,
And self; but *such* a woman! love in life!

Love in full life, not love ideal,
No, nor ideal beauty, that fine name,
But something better still, so very real,
That the sweet model must have been the same;
A thing that you would purchase, beg, or steal,
Wer't not impossible, besides a shame:
The face recalls some face, as 'twere with pain,
You once have seen, but ne'er will see again;

One of those forms which flit by us, when we
Are young, and fix our eyes on every face;
And, oh! the loveliness at times we see
In momentary gliding, the soft grace,
The youth, the bloom, the beauty which agree,
In many a nameless being we retrace,
Whose course, and home we knew not, nor shall know,
Like the lost Pleiad seen no more below. (*Beppo*, ll. 81–112)

For many years Byron's reference to this 'portrait of his son, and wife, / And self' was taken to be to Giorgione's masterpiece, *La tempesta* (once indeed known as *Sua famiglia*), now at the Venice Accademia, and once in the Manfrin Collection – where, ironically, it was inspected by agents of the National Gallery in 1851, who thought that it was overrated due to its mistaken association with Byron's verses, and valued it at only £100 (so Byron is to be blamed for the British people never coming by one of the pearls of the Accademia, and at a knock-down price). The painting Byron *did* intend, which the National Gallery's agents thought far superior to the Giorgione and valued at no less than £2,500, is the *Triple Portrait* by a follower of Titian, 'now forgotten by all but the most assiduous art lovers', according to Francis Haskell,[33] and in the collection of the Duke of Northumberland at Alnwick Castle.[34]

The last picture Byron noted at the Palazzo Manfrin – the fascinating 'learned lady [. . .] centuries old', with the 'kind of face to go mad for – because it cannot walk out of its frame' (reminiscent of the 'face [. . .] / You once have seen, but ne'er will see again' in *Beppo*) – remains elusive, mainly because of 'the cavalier fashion in which paintings in the collection were attributed',[35] and the secretive way in which it was disposed of by its inheritors. Leaving Madonnas and saints to one side, catalogues of the Manfrin Collection list any number of *teste* and *ritratti* of women, young and old. There are some tempting possibilities in these lists: *donne* by Bordone, Veneto and Palma Vecchio, to name but three; the *Sibilla Libica* by Benedetto Gennari, now in a private collection; and an *Artemisia*. This last, as an icon of wifely loyalty, might well have caught Byron's eye. Would that I could suggest the Boltraffio *Artemisia* now in the Mattioli Collection in Milan, which fits Byron's description to perfection; in fact, the Manfrin *Artemisia* is clearly listed as by the German 'Giovanni' (that is, Johann or Hans) Rottenhammer (1564–1625) – and that, too, has disappeared.

In fact, we can make an educated guess as to what Byron's 'learned lady' looked like. Byron was wrong to say, as he did to Murray, that he 'knew nothing of painting'. None of us is in that parlous condition: you do not need to know anything about art, as the old saying goes, to know what you like – and it would not be a cliché unless it contained a truth. In an important sense, however, he was correct to say to Edward West that he was not a '*judge* of painting', that he 'felt no great *passion* for it' and 'had never made it his *study*'. It is an embarrassing fact to record that Byron's response to painting is hardly an *aesthetic* one at all: it is the subject, not its treatment, that catches his eye. And that subject is, mostly, images of women: images themselves betraying that 'extreme resemblance of the style of the female faces' he had noted in the Manfrin Collection. The real mother in the *Judgment of Solomon*, Hagar in the Guercino, the kneeling mother in Reni's *Massacre of the Innocents*, the Reni *Magdalene*, del Piombo's *Fornarina*, Titian's 'mistress' and Venus of Urbino, the 'wife' in the *Triple Portrait*: these images compositely come to form a sort of feminine ideal, whether embodied 'in the mass of pictures' at the Palazzo Manfrin or leaning in the flesh over a balcony in Venice. Most of all, one would have to say, 'the style of the female faces' he appreciated in art bear more than a passing resemblance to his mistress, Teresa Guiccioli, *whom he had not met before seeing the pictures that resemble her*. It is not so much a matter of some paintings resembling Byron's mistress, then, as his mistress resembling some paintings. Life imitates art, indeed. (Some images of Teresa hardly fit Byron's Italian composite,[36] but West's portrait of her (at the Miami University Art Museum in Oxford, Ohio) certainly does.)

### 4.

Byron's letter to Murray of 14 April 1817 is his most vivid evocation of painting in prose, but his poetry outdoes it. Readers of *Don Juan* will remember the gallery of pictures at Norman Abbey, in the thirteenth Canto of the poem, written in February 1823 and thus close to the end of his poetic career. There is a survey of English country house portraits in stanzas 68–70, itself a miraculous evocation of time and change in Tudor and Stuart England: 'Steel Barons, molten the next generation', as Byron puts it, 'To silken rows of gay and garter'd Earls'; 'Also some beauties of Sir Peter Lely, / Whose drapery hints we may admire them freely' (*Don Juan* XIII, ll. 537–8, 543–4). But the Amundevilles have a Continental collection, too:

> But ever and anon, to soothe your vision,
> Fatigued with these hereditary glories,
> There rose a Carlo Dolce or a Titian,
> Or a wilder groupe of savage Salvatore's:
> Here danced Albano's boys, and here the sea shone
> In Vernet's ocean lights; and there the stories
> Of martyrs awed, as Spagnoletto tainted
> His brush with all the blood of all the sainted.
>
> Here sweetly spread a landscape of Lorraine;
> There Rembrandt made his darkness equal light,
> Or gloomy Caravaggio's gloomier stain
> Bronzed o'er some lean and stoic Anchorite: –
> But lo! a Teniers woos, and not in vain,
> Your eyes to revel in a livelier sight:
> His bell-mouthed goblet makes me feel quite Danish
> Or Dutch with thirst – What ho! a flask of Rhenish. (*Don Juan*
> XIII, ll. 561–76)

It is apparently a simple passage but it could not have been written by someone unappreciative of painting – in both its art-historical and aesthetic dimensions. That 'lean and stoic Anchorite' of Caravaggio's, for example: is it the St Jerome in the Villa Borghese or the one in Valetta – either of which Byron might have seen, bronzed out of the gloom? How true is it of Rembrandt, as opposed to Caravaggio, that his darkness *equals* light – or is equal *to* light? Is not 'sweet' exactly the word to use of Claude's landscapes? There was 'a fine Portrait of himself' by Rembrandt in the Manfrin Collection, and of the other painters Byron lists, many were represented there, as a near-contemporary guidebook for English visitors attests: 'Gamblers, by Caravaggio', 'St Cecilia and a Magdalen by Carlo Dolce', 'Astronomy, Chemistry, by Salvator Rosa' and 'A small marine piece, by Vernet'.[37] George Hume Weatherhead's *Pedestrian Tour*, which takes visitors through the Manfrin Collection, does not mention either Francesco Albani or Jusepe de Ribera, better known as Spagnoletto: but the former's *Danza degli amorini* was there for Byron to see at the Brera Gallery in Milan, and if the Brera did not possess any of Spagnoletto's splashier martyrdoms, it certainly has a *St Jerome in Meditation*. There were 'two fine Teniers' at the Manfrin Collection, and we might remember the Teniers *Temptation of St Anthony* in the Ecole de Dessin at Ghent. Teniers painted many pictures on that theme – but there is a *Temptation* now in the Royal Museum at Antwerp that certainly features a 'bell-mouthed goblet' of the kind Byron describes in his Norman Abbey catalogue.

## 5.

Perhaps I have said enough to suggest that painting is not quite the marginal interest it seems in Byron's life and work. The passage from Canto XIII of *Don Juan* gives us some idea of his prodigious visual memory, which again and again suggests the perfect epithet for an eclectic range of European painters, from north and south. The Italian collections, on the other hand, suggest to us that just as *Don Juan* presents an astonishing gallery of female portraits, so the women painted by the old masters of Italy came for Byron to compose a particular type, and that his interest in that type transcended the aesthetic altogether – or, rather, blended the aesthetic with the sexual, since these two categories clearly overlap in our experience. 'Taste, however capricious,' as Francis Haskell says, 'always depends on more than taste.'[38] Byron wanted these subjects to walk out of the frame, or at least to remind him of something he had seen, or thought it possible to see: 'something so very *real*', as he said in *Beppo*. 'I never yet saw the picture – or the statue – which came within a league of my conception or expectation', he wrote; 'but I have seen many mountains &

Seas – & Rivers and views – & two or three women – who went as far beyond it – besides some horses; and a Lion [. . .] in the Morea & a tiger at supper in Exeter change' (*BLJ*, vol. 5, pp. 213–14). We shall never be able to distinguish entirely between the subjects of art and the way an artist treats them in pictures that we appreciate, nor do we find it easy to appreciate paintings where the subject is repellent to us, like one of Chaïm Soutine's rotten chickens. Byron reminds us of that ancient dilemma, and whereas it is true that he fails to resolve it, no one else has convincingly done so, either.

## Notes

1. Keats, *Complete Poems*, p. 344.
2. Richardson, *The Works of Jonathan Richardson*, p. 6.
3. *CCB*, p. 81.
4. Ibid., p. 299.
5. Blessington, *Conversations of Lord Byron*, p. 32.
6. Medwin, *Conversations of Lord Byron*, p. 73.
7. Ibid., p. 114.
8. Bankes's biographer records, 'According to an entry in [William's sister] Frances Bankes' diary for 8 February: "A letter from William (who is at Bologna) has horrified his Father, having drawn five hundred pounds to pay for unfinished pictures of masters he does not fancy."' Sebba, *The Exiled Collector: William Bankes and the Making of an English Country House*, p. 109. The story of the Marescalchi collection and its dispersal is told in Preti Hamard, *Ferdinando Marescalchi, 1754–1816: Un collezionista Italiano nella Parigi Napoleonica*. Bankes bought the Titian portrait of Nicolò Zen (also at Kingston Lacy) from the Marescalchi collection at the same time.
9. *CCB*, p. 198.
10. Moore, *Letters, Journals and Other Prose Writings of Lord Byron*, vol. 2, pp. 175–6.
11. *CCB*, p. 236.
12. Ibid., p. 205.
13. Neilson, *Daniele Crespi*, p. 164.
14. But see Gould, *Trophy of Conquest: The Musée Napoléon and the Creation of the Louvre*; McClellan, *Inventing the Louvre: Art, Politics, and the Origins of the Modern Museum in Eighteenth-century Paris*; Greenfield, *The Return of Cultural Treasures*, pp. 111–12; Miles, *Art as Plunder: The Ancient Origins of Debate about Cultural Property*, ch. 5; and Goodwin, 'Mapping the Limits of Repatriable Cultural Heritage: A Case Study of Stolen Flemish Art in French Museums', pp. 673–705. Byron's schoolfellow at Aberdeen Grammar, John Scott, published *Paris Revisited in 1815* the year after his visit: it contains a four-page list of

returned works, including sixty-five works of sculpture, eight Raphaels and eighteen Peruginos, among others: 'a small portion of the restorations', as he said. Scott, *Paris Revisited in 1815*, p. 366.

15. Miles, *Art as Plunder*, p. 321.
16. Uglow, *In These Times: Living in Britain Through Napoleon's Wars, 1793–1815*, p. 293.
17. Miles, *Art as Plunder*, p. 330.
18. 'There is no record of where Byron resided while in Rome,' Leslie Marchand records 'but according to one local tradition it was in the vicinity of the Piazza di Spagna.' Marchand, *Byron: A Biography*, p. 691 and note.
19. Polidori, *The Diary of Dr John William Polidori, 1816, Relating to Byron, Shelley, Etc.*, p. 38.
20. Ibid., p. 39.
21. Polidori noted 'Kruger has many here in honour of Charles the Vth. Amongst the others, one rather . . . satirical: Charles, landing, takes hold of Dame Africa, who quietly points to a lion at her feet. Query – to drive him away?' Polidori, *The Diary of Dr John William Polidori*, p. 40. Charles V did indeed land at Tunis in 1535, and Frans Floris painted a triumphal arch on behalf of the Genoese inhabitants of Antwerp for his imperial entry into the city in 1549. Such structures were ephemeral but perhaps some sketches or drawings by Floris remained in the Royal School. (An etching by Floris based on one of these decorations, *Victory Surrounded by the Defeated and Trophies*, of 1552, is at the Hunterian Museum in Glasgow.) Polidori perhaps misinterpreted what he saw: a similar triumphal image at Lille in the same year shows Charles releasing 'a fettered [Christian] damsel who had been guarded by demons and Turks' in Tunis. See Pinson, 'Imperial Ideology in the Triumphal Entry into Lille of Charles V and the Crown Prince (1549)', p. 208.
22. Polidori, *The Diary of Dr John William Polidori*, p. 40.
23. Ibid., pp. 52–3.
24. Ibid., p. 51; this would be Van Dyck's *St Augustine in Ecstasy*.
25. Blessington, *Conversations of Lord Byron*, p. 162.
26. Haskell, *Patrons and Painters: A Study in Relations between Italian Art and Society in the Age of the Baroque*, p. 379.
27. Manfrin was evidently a colourful figure: 'a nouveau-riche business man, who through sheer unscrupulous Balzacian energy and talent achieved a high position in a society where such achievements were despised in favour of the more gracious attributes of life'. Haskell, *Patrons and Painters*, p. 379.
28. Ibid., p. 380.
29. See Borean, 'Il caso Manfrin', pp. 192–216; Borean and Sones, 'Drawings of the Installation of a Nineteenth-Century Picture Gallery', pp. 169–76; and Borean (18 April 2014), personal communication. I would also like to thank Ceri Brough, librarian at the National Gallery in London, who has been exceptionally helpful in handling enquiries about the Manfrin Collection.

30. Hazlitt, *Collected Works*, vol. 10, p. 270.
31. Heinemann, *Bellini e i Belliniani*, pp. 146, 224.
32. See Davies, *The Earlier Italian Schools*. By 1856, the National Gallery's agent and its first Keeper, Sir Charles Locke Eastlake, reported that 'The Manfrini Gallery is now stripped of some of its best works, and exorbitant prices are asked for the inferior works remaining.' Robertson, *Sir Charles Eastlake and the Victorian Art World*, p. 317.
33. Haskell, *Rediscoveries in Art: Some Aspects of Taste, Fashion, and Collecting in England and France*, p. 22.
34. For the identification see Gatti, 'Byron and Giorgione's Wife', pp. 237–43; for the National Gallery agents and other details on the Gallery and the Manfrin collection see Hauptman, 'Some New Nineteenth-century References to Giorgione's "Tempesta"', pp. 78–82. Giorgione or Titian, all visitors to the Palazzo Manfrin were shown the second picture: Titian's mistress, according to Hazlitt, 'introduced into a composition with a gay cavalier and a page'. Hazlitt, *Collected Works*, vol. 10, p. 270. 'Saw in the Casa Manfrini a multitude of pictures,' Samuel Rogers recorded, 'some good particularly a groupe of three heads ascribed to Giorgione, but the woman's appeared to be that of Titian's Mistress. In the evening eat ice in the Caffé.' Hale, ed., *The Italian Journal of Samuel Rogers*, p. 178.
35. Hauptman, 'Some New Nineteenth-century References to Giorgione's "Tempesta"', p. 82.
36. See Marchand, *Byron: A Biography*, p. 991, for an example.
37. See Weatherhead, *A Pedestrian Tour through France and Italy*, pp. 439–41: 'Paintings in the Palace Manfrin (Open to Strangers on Mondays and Thursdays)'.
38. Haskell, *Rediscoveries in Art*, p. 23.

## Works cited

Blessington, Marguerite (1969), *Conversations of Lord Byron*, ed. Ernest J. Lovell, Jr, Princeton: Princeton University Press,

Borean, Linda (2009), 'Il caso Manfrin', in: Linda Borean and Stefania Mason (eds), *Il collezione d'arte a Venezia: Il Settecento*, Venice: Marsilio, pp. 192–216.

— and Anna Cera Sones (2010), 'Drawings of the Installation of a Nineteenth-century Picture Gallery: A Study of the Display of Art in Venice', *Getty Research Journal*, 2, pp. 169–76.

Davies, Martin (1961), *The Earlier Italian Schools*, London: National Gallery.

Gatti, Hilary (1984), 'Byron and Giorgione's Wife', *Studies in Romanticism*, 23, pp. 237–43.

Goodwin, Paige S. (2008), 'Mapping the Limits of Repatriable Cultural Heritage: A Case Study of Stolen Flemish Art in French Museums', *University of Pennsylvania Law Review*, 157, pp. 673–705.

Gould, Cecil (1965), *Trophy of Conquest: The Musée Napoléon and the Creation of the Louvre*, London: Faber and Faber.

Greenfield, Jeanette (2007), *The Return of Cultural Treasures*, Cambridge: Cambridge University Press.

Hale, J. R., ed. (1956), *The Italian Journal of Samuel Rogers*, London: Faber and Faber.

Haskell, Francis (1980), *Patrons and Painters: A Study in Relations between Italian Art and Society in the Age of the Baroque*, New Haven: Yale University Press.

— (1980), *Rediscoveries in Art: Some Aspects of Taste, Fashion, and Collecting in England and France*, Oxford: Phaidon.

Hauptman, William (1994), 'Some New Nineteenth-century References to Giorgione's "Tempesta"', *Burlington Magazine*, 1091, pp. 78–82.

Hazlitt, William (1934), *Collected Works*, 21 vols, ed. P. P. Howe, London: J. M. Dent.

Heinemann, Fritz (1962), *Bellini e i Belliniani*, Venice: Neri Pozza.

Keats, John (1976), *Complete Poems*, ed. John Barnard, Harmondsworth: Penguin.

McClellan, Andrew (1994), *Inventing the Louvre: Art, Politics, and the Origins of the Modern Museum in Eighteenth-century Paris*, Cambridge: Cambridge University Press.

Marchand, Leslie A. (1957), *Byron: A Biography*, London: John Murray.

Medwin, Thomas, *Conversations of Lord Byron*, ed. Ernest J. Lovell, Jr, Princeton: Princeton University Press.

Miles, Margaret (2008), *Art as Plunder: The Ancient Origins of Debate about Cultural Property*, Cambridge: Cambridge University Press.

Moore, Thomas (1831), *Letters, Journals and Other Prose Writings of Lord Byron*, 2 vols, New York: J. J. Harper.

Neilson, Nancy Ward (1996), *Daniele Crespi*, Soncino: Edizione dei Soncino.

Pinson, Yona (2001), 'Imperial Ideology in the Triumphal Entry into Lille of Charles V and the Crown Prince (1549)', *Assaph: Studies in Art History*, 6, pp. 205–33.

Polidori, John (1911), *The Diary of Dr John William Polidori, 1816, Relating to Byron, Shelley, Etc.*, ed. William Michael Rossetti, London: Elkin Matthews.

Preti Hamard, Monica (2005), *Ferdinando Marescalchi, 1754–1816: Un collezionista Italiano nella Parigi Napoleonica*, Bologna: Minerva.

Richardson, Jonathan (1792), *The Works of Jonathan Richardson*, London: Strawberry Hill.

Robertson, David (1978), *Sir Charles Eastlake and the Victorian Art World*, Princeton: Princeton University Press.

Scott, John (1816), *Paris Revisited in 1815*, London: Longman / Hurst / Rees / Orme / Brown.

Sebba, Anne (2004), *The Exiled Collector: William Bankes and the Making of an English Country House*, London: John Murray.

Uglow, Jenny (2014), *In These Times: Living in Britain Through Napoleon's Wars, 1793–1815*, London: Faber and Faber.

Weatherhead, George Hume (1834), *A Pedestrian Tour through France and Italy*, London: Simpkin and Marshall.

# Chapter 15

# 'I ask his pardon for a postscript': Byron's Epistolary Afterthoughts

## Jonathon Shears

It is arguable that Byron's letters and journals have never really been on the fringes or margins of our responses to the poet. Those published, albeit in censored form, in Thomas Moore's *Letters and Journals of Lord Byron* as early as 1830 made an immediate impression on the reading public.[1] Nevertheless, the two most important twentieth-century critics of Byron's correspondence felt the need to make a case for seeing it as something greater than what Gérard Genette termed an 'epitext' – a marginal or supplementary discourse – to the literary works.[2] Leslie Marchand, in the general introduction to his priceless twelve-volume edition of Byron's letters and journals, hoped that his endeavours would prove 'why Byron's literary reputation will at last rest as much on them as on his poetry' (*BLJ*, vol. 1, p. 18). John Jump believed Byron's letters had claim 'to the kind of attention we normally reserve for more deliberate literary works'.[3] That claim, not one that I wish to dispute here, derives from a series of frequently attested qualities that include Byron's wit, emotional and intellectual frankness, an ability to shift deftly tone and idiom, capriciousness, sincerity and the capacity to entertain or outrage his correspondent. Byron's letters actually fit rather well within Romanticism – and this might be said to make them central, rather than marginal, to it – for the sense of excessive, boundless energy that they often display, even when Byron professes to his correspondent, as he sometimes did, laziness and lassitude, a kind of Romantic overflow of powerful feeling. To this end, Marchand noted the 'free-flowing and on-rushing style of composition' (*BLJ*, vol. 2, p. 6), and Jump the fact that Byron's handwriting – the poet termed it his 'detestable scrawl' (*BLJ*, vol. 4, p. 95)[4] – indicated that he wrote quickly, 'what comes uppermost at the moment' (*BLJ*, vol. 10, p. 33) (sometimes as many as five letters in half an hour, he claimed in a journal entry (*BLJ*, vol. 8, p. 12)).

These interventions, along with others by Andrew Nicholson, Nina Diakonova and Richard Lansdown, have contributed to the established view that the most attractive quality of Byron's epistolary prose is its spontaneity.[5] More specifically, the apparently careless composition denotes an appealing kind of self-assertion, uncompromised by the views of others – he was 'short and savage' to his 'rascally correspondents' (*BLJ*, vol. 8, p. 12) – which provides an accurate 'self-portrait' of the poet because 'less self-conscious than his verse' (*BLJ*, vol. 1, p. 1). The impression of an absence of caution led Jump to observe that 'never, we feel, can written utterance have been less premeditated, less rehearsed, less inhibited, less controlled'.[6] How else could we characterise Byron's famous abruptness, which could lead him to write to Murray, in a fit of pique about the publisher's frequent excisions from his work, '[y]ou sometimes take the liberty of *omitting* what I send for publication: if you do so in this instance I will never speak to you again as long as I breathe' (*BLJ*, vol. 7, p. 173). (Byron's frankness was not always an appealing quality, as Andrew Stauffer has argued at length.[7]) As he wrote to Lady Melbourne about his reputation for calculation, 'when they give me a character for "Art" it is surely most mistaken – no one was ever more heedless' (*BLJ*, vol. 4, p. 21). 'I write in the greatest haste', he explained on another occasion to Douglas Kinnaird, 'with a *girl* in waiting' (*BLJ*, vol. 8, p. 58). Byron writes as he behaves: in haste and with his guard down.

Such observations, from Byron and later critics, cannot of course represent the entirety of a body of work as varied as the correspondence. When Jump made his analysis he could not, for example, have been thinking of some of Byron's letters to Annabella Milbanke, composed during the period in which his proposals of marriage were rejected in 1814, which are deliberate, cagey and rather wooden in the formality of some of their diction, punctuated by modesty formulations and carefully considered caveats. As Alan Rawes has recently argued, Byron's love letters as a group are actually disappointingly conventional.[8] It would be wrong to assert that it is always the case that the more indecisive Byron is on a subject, the more formal and inflexible his diction becomes, but there is no doubt that, to take as an example the letter in which he entertains his doubts about Annabella's acceptance of another proposal of marriage, his style becomes more than a little circumspect:

> [T]he fact is that I am even now apprehensive of having misunderstood you and of appearing presumptuous when I am only happy – in the hope that you will not repent having made me more so than I ever thought to have been again. (*BLJ*, vol. 4, p. 176).[9]

The awkward self-consciousness of Austen's Edward Ferrars comes to mind: as others have observed, it is important to remember that context – particularly social and political – and his standing in regard to his addressee could inhibit even Byron's customary expressiveness. (Examples of letters written to the Duke of Portland (*BLJ*, vol. 1, pp. 177–8), Lord Holland (*BLJ*, vol. 2, p. 165) and even his mother (*BLJ*, vol. 1, pp. 218–20) could be cited as further evidence on this theme.)

There are exceptions to every rule, but while the letter to Annabella may be atypical in one sense, in another – which initially appears to contradict most of Jump's praise and to which the majority of the present essay will be devoted – it is curiously representative. The formality and evident care taken in composition, something endorsed by the solemn and apparently moderate pace, are not unusual in Byron (even allowing for the fact that he is usually writing at high speed). Here they can be explained by the fact that the marriage stakes were so high, and are revealed in Byron's confession that Annabella's letter of acceptance has 'shaken' (*BLJ*, vol. 4, p. 176) him out of his ordinary composure. (His idiom, which breaks down into near inarticulacy, is noticeably more discomposed than in the letters he wrote on the earlier occasions of having been rejected by Annabella, which are full of facetiousness and fun (*BLJ*, vol. 4, p. 79).) The act of writing, as he acknowledges, has curiously betrayed a failure to assert his intentions – 'I have written – yet hardly a word that I intended to say' – when occasion most required it.

If we were looking for other evidence of Byron's heightened awareness of, and precision in dealing with, tone and idiom, it can be found in the admission that he would sometimes burn letters and begin them afresh, as on the occasion of 7 July 1815, when he revealed that his first attempt of the day to write to Moore was consigned to the fire because it contained too much 'buffoonery' that, on reflection, might have offended (*BLJ*, vol. 4, p. 301). In a world where inferences are easily misconstrued – a phenomenon that is perhaps at its most perceptible in his corresponding relationship with Lady Melbourne about the liaisons with Augusta, Lady Frances Webster and Annabella – it is unsurprising to find that there is much more of an interplay between heedlessness and self-consciousness, or even restraint, in Byron's letters than has usually been observed.[10] Indeed, as L. M. Findlay remarks, Byron exhibits a high level of 'stylistic self-consciousness' in his epistolary prose – writing very much with his *guard up*, we might say – easily equal at times to that of his published poetry.[11] As in the case of the letter to Moore, he is particularly concerned to establish what Findlay terms the 'rules of relation' to his addressee.[12] Any sense that Byron has breached or mistaken decorum – 'excuse the freedom of my Remarks' (*BLJ*, vol. 1, p. 118), 'forgive my levity' (*BLJ*, vol. 1, p. 52), 'excuse the phrase which is neither diplomatic nor decorous' (*BLJ*, vol. 9, p. 144) and other similar formulations are common – causes anxiety. Setting formal parameters was, on occasion, important too: 'My last was an Epistle "*entre nous*" [Byron's usual expression of intimacy] *this is a Letter of Business*' (*BLJ*, vol. 1, p. 116), he wrote to Hanson in April 1807.[13]

Squaring the two impressions – of carelessness and great care – that reading Byron's letters fosters, rather than setting them at variance, is no easy matter. Yet this, along with a better understanding of those quintessential 'rules of relation' and stylistic self-consciousness noted by Findlay, can, I believe, be achieved by examination of one particularly common formal property of Byron's epistolary writing, which up until now has not been considered worthy of much attention. The feature in question is the postscript, a specific type of paratext or marginal utterance, usually appended to the foot of a letter, of which Byron was a liberal user. The postscript has a number of connotations that impinge directly on the interplay of the assertion and relinquishment of self-control, evident in Byron's epistolary prose as much as his verse, that make it a peculiarly suitable site on which to focus our analysis.

In its basic function the postscript would at first seem to be, along with evidence derived from the state of Byron's handwriting, the most reliable indicator of haste, the absence of forethought and, potentially, the accompanying loss of self-control or inhibition promoted by Jump's more general reading of Byron's correspondence.[14] A postscript is unplanned and extraneous: a thought left out, or occurring later, that suggests more careful initial thought would have seen its inclusion in the main text. The postscript contributes to the impression, noted above, of excessive sentiment – it is an overspilling of text. Postscripts that promote such an impression in Byron's letters are legion; notable examples that might be cited include those in the correspondence to John Hanson concerning the protracted sale of Newstead Abbey in 1814, when Byron could barely contain his wrath and when one postscript often spilled over into two. The threat made to Murray – 'I will never speak to you again' – also comes in a postscript; combining with the sentiment, this suggests a sudden, unguarded outburst of anger, stirred by the main subject of the letter, which concerns the publication of Byron's response to the 'cursed and impudent' author of *Sketches Descriptive of Italy*, who claimed to once have snubbed an invitation to meet Byron in Venice.[15] Discomposed by the subject matter, in the postscript Byron's aggression spills over into a supplementary attack on Murray, which, to follow this logic through, would have been included in the main text if Byron's anger had not been so consuming. The necessity of the postscript – its very facticity – endorses the impression of a loss of composure (even if that postscript itself exhibits agitation rather than cool).

For the *Oxford English Dictionary* (*OED*), the postscript is a special case of paratext or marginal text, defined as 'a paragraph or passage written at the end of a letter, after the signature, containing an afterthought or additional matter', 'something added on or happening later' and 'an additional or conclusory remark or action, an afterthought'. Later happenings are certainly relevant to reading Byron's postscripts: Byron often opened his letters to add a postscript due to some later event the same, or following, day, particularly whilst travelling abroad, when dispatch of letters was less frequent and paper scarce. It is another feature that contributes to the impression of spontaneity, a personal equivalent of the journalistic cry 'stop the press'. That aspect of the *OED*'s definition of a postscript is of less concern to me, however, than are those other facets that involve the nature of an afterthought or the ability to draw a conclusion on a topic. Specifically, it seems important to address the way that the postscript's existence is apparently predicated on – in the view of its author – the feeling that something has been missed: that the main body of an epistolary utterance is incomplete and requires supplementation or further commentary, seemingly due to its hastiness.

This sits well with what we already know of Byron's writing habits. Despite the velocity of his poetic composition, for example, he 'was always sending in "after thoughts" for all his publications', which comprised amendments, excisions and additions (*BLJ*, vol. 4, p. 11, n. 1). His mind in composition was accretive as much as architectonic, working through numerous tangents and second thoughts, despite his well-known reluctance to revise his verse, and it is surely relevant that much of the comedy of *Don Juan* is achieved through exaggerating this habit of mind. The concluding couplet in *ottava rima* – the stanza in which Byron is often said to have truly 'found his voice'[16] – famously appends a supplementary thought to the 'body' of the stanza that ironically subverts what has gone before. The effect of spontaneity was, of course, achieved through, and becomes a sign of, careful planning. In recent years, Timothy Webb and Ourania Chatsiou have made similar arguments about Byron's use of paratext in his verse, analysing the notes attached to poems such as *Childe Harold's Pilgrimage* and *Don Juan* (1819–24), often purporting to be the 'key to the charismatic author's "real" voice', but still largely providing evidence of his ability to shift readers into unexpected ironic contexts in relation to the opinions expressed in the main body of the text (one function of paratext noted by Genette).[17] It is tempting to align Byron's use of postscripts with this predominantly comic theme, and he could certainly be highly face-tious in postscripts or use them for comic vignettes, writing, for exam-ple, to Lady Melbourne about his romantic prospects in September 1812, 'I am sadly out of practice lately, except for a few sighs to a Gentlewoman at supper who was too much occupied with ye. *fourth* wing of her *second* chicken to mind anything that was not material' (*BLJ*, vol. 2, p. 219).[18] Byron also undoubtedly exhibited sufficient self-awareness that his literary afterthoughts could try the patience of his publishers or agents, humorously threatening Dallas in a post-script following a series of emendations he made to the first edition of *English Bards and Scotch Reviewers*, 'P. S. Print soon or I shall overflow with more rhyme' (*BLJ*, vol. 1, p. 194). Marchand's only comment, to my knowledge, on Byron's use of postscripts similarly points out their inevitability and contradictory nature, part of Byron's 'habit of giving an ironical or cynical ending to a serious statement' (*BLJ*, vol. 1, p. 6).

If there is comic possibility in flaunting the absence of fore-thought, or his own heedlessness, through the use of postscripts (not unrelated to the *ottava rima* model), we should remember that another common Byronic juxtaposition is the facetious delivery of a serious thought.[19] The postscript to Dallas *is* an apology, albeit one that is ironically dressed, but it serves a more calculated pur-pose, taking us closer to being able to analyse the twin impressions of spontaneity and reflection that the use of a postscript demon-strates. It allows Byron to regain control of a situation that threatens to break the rules of relation to his correspondent due to his earlier inattention and uninhibitedness. Byron makes a joke out of trying Dallas's patience: a joke, delivered carelessly in a postscript, and so apparently downgraded in relation to the body of the letter (where the serious business is contained), it is actually the most important feature in ensuring an ongoing relationship that Byron had no desire to jeopardise. What seems throwaway, or marginal, is of the essence in understanding Byron's intentions and adroit manipulation of his addressee: by drawing attention to his self-awareness about his loss of control, Byron is able to reassert it.

As John Wisdom notes, in his comments on the difference between 'showing' and 'stating' facts in Wittgenstein's *Tractatus*, there is always a verbal sleight of hand at work in claiming or expressing haste (which is not equally pertinent to what the condition of one's handwriting suggests):

> If I write a letter in haste I may either let the letter show my haste – by the scrawliness of the writing – or add a postscript stating my haste. But was I in haste when I wrote the postscript? This the postscript (so they say) cannot state. If I want to state that I was in haste when writing the postscript I must add a postscript to the postscript.[20]

Considered in this way, the supplementary postscript partakes of Derridean *différance*, failing to summon forth what it means because its explicatory function implicates further verbal explanation. But the effect of a Byronic postscript is not really to throw out the establishment of meaning, so much as to complicate its operation. When Byron states in, for example, a postscript added to a letter to Hobhouse of 22 April 1820, 'P.S. – I have written in great haste' and 'I have hardly had time to be commonsensible but never mind' (*BLJ*, vol. 7, p. 82), he is dually acknowledging his relinquishment of composure but also affirming it is a temporary relinquishment of which he is entirely aware and so otherwise in control.[21] Likewise, the postscript to Dallas, far from being a mere afterthought signalling negligence, plays a significant role in revealing how the implicit rules of relation operate within the letter, which works to Byron's advantage. In other words, alerting his addressee to his inattentiveness – even when accompanied by a strong sense of Byron's indifference to that fact – is itself an act of attentiveness.

I would argue that the postscript to Dallas is an indicative example of the genre: this postscript demonstrates that, far from being a simple indicator of his impulsive nature, Byron's self-assertion is usually highly, and stylistically, self-regulated, whatever the impression of speed. There is also an impression that, as with the notes appended to *Childe Harold*, this is the key to the charismatic author's real voice. Of course, many of Byron's postscripts, after the general fashion of the early nineteenth-century epistle, involve straightforward expressions of courtesy and politesse, another sort of stylistic self-consciousness. Enquiries about the health of family members, the desire to be remembered or general compliments – 'P.S. My Compts. To Mrs. H. and the whole Corps' (*BLJ*, vol. 1, p. 143), 'P.S. I hope you are quite *recovered*!,' and 'P.S. Do not forget me to your father & mother' (*BLJ*, vol. 4, p. 176) – are especially common in letters to correspondents with whom Byron had enjoyed significant periods of domesticity, such as the Hansons and the Melbournes. During his time spent periodically in London during the period 1812 to 1815, the postscripts to his rapidly dispatched letters were frequently used simply to arrange, or excuse himself from, social engagements: 'P.S. An you will, I will call for you at half-past six, or any time of your own dial' (*BLJ*, vol. 4, p. 115). Specific concerns with appropriate epistolary style and decorum, however, bring us closer to understanding the proximity of care and abandon that characterises the singular experience of reading Byron's letters. Indeed, second thoughts, concerned with tone and misjudging the rules of relation, feature from the outset.

Byron's very first extant letter was an epistle written to his aunt, Charlotte Augusta Parker, on behalf of his mother, on the mundane subjects of a pony, some potatoes and a rabbit – a 'humdrum epistle' according to Findlay; in it, we see Byron's stylistic self-consciousness at work.[22] Appended to the letter, the postscript pleads for his aunt's patience due to his apprentice status as correspondent: 'I hope you will excuse all blunders as it is the first letter I ever wrote' (*BLJ*, vol. 1, p. 39). What effect is the *post hoc* addition of this sentiment designed to have on its reader? Firstly, it is a perceptive utterance, primarily demonstrating an anxiety to please, or at least to avoid social embarrassment: a modesty formulation (despite also having the slight whiff of a boast). But secondly, and more importantly, its reflective nature is, as we will see more extensively in other examples, an acknowledgement that writing a letter means taking on a formal role or persona and adopting a manner or idiom. Byron breaks the rules of relation he has established in the letter – bringing what is implicit out into the open – in order to impress the terms of those rules with greater clarity. If the general function of a postscript is to redress the writer's perceived inability to express himself adequately first time around – and, in so doing, encourage the association of spontaneity with the original thought to which it relates – the sentiment undermines that function. It instead points up the care taken in composition, and specifically in adopting the persona of a correspondent, courteously tailored to the individual reader.

Commonly, it is Byron's awareness of his tendency to exaggerate his melancholy that prompts such supplementary reflections. While becalmed on the *Volage* frigate on his return journey to England in 1811, for example, Byron was bleak and peppered his epistles liberally with passages of black humour. On 19 June 1811 he wrote a long letter to Hobhouse in this mode, in which he dramatised his sense of foreboding and gloom at returning to England. Noticeably, the tone of the letter is uneven – perhaps desultory would be a better word – shifting between bad jokes, such as the famous one about passing through the 'Gut' of Gibraltar like an 'oil Glyster', and amplified seriousness – 'I am now going to patrole the melancholy deck.' Levity, of an almost giddy sort, mixes with confessions of depression. Perhaps sensing that his departing salvo to Hobhouse has left the wrong impression, Byron shifts gear in his postscript, introducing a short nautical song, which clears his own problems from the scene through the establishment of a new mode of low, comic diction, a 'reversion to commonplace vocabulary' that Diakonova has argued is typical of Byron's epistolary style:[23]

> P. S. – Take a mouthful of Salt-water poetry by a tar on the late Lissa Victory. –
>> "If I had an Ediation [sic]
>> "I'd sing your praise *more large*,
>> "But I'm only a common foremast Jack
>> "On Board of *the Le Volage*!!!!! (*BLJ*, vol. 2, pp. 48–51)

What I want to stress here is that the postscript is not so much a change of subject – it partly qualifies as this, though is really a variation on the main theme of the body of the letter – as a shift in tone that suggests stylistic self-consciousness prompted by a feeling of incompletion. In fact, the tone is much more like that which Byron adopted repeatedly in his jolly and enthusiastic letters as he first sailed from England in 1808 (*BLJ*, vol. 1, pp. 210–18). The postscript is in essence concerned with establishing tone – one which Byron has used previously and revisits, perhaps, due to its happier connotations – rather than denoting meaning.

The same motif, whereby apparent uncertainty in his rules of relation prompts Byron into the inclusion of a self-conscious afterthought, can be found in a letter to Murray of 20 January 1821 on the subject of *Marino Faliero* (Byron was alternately eager and hesitant about its production at Drury Lane). Prompted by reading in an Italian newspaper that 'Ld. B. has a tragedy coming out,' Byron's concerns spill into his postscript, where his comparison of *Marino Faliero* to 'the Prometheus of Aeschylus' impels him to check his manner. 'I speak of course humbly', he announces, retreating from a rash thought, 'and with the greatest sense of the distance of time and merit between the two performances' (*BLJ*, vol. 8, p. 67). Impetuosity is reined in through an afterthought. Byron's idiom, as much as his real indignation, has momentarily jeopardised his composure. And the same impression is left by the opposite effect. One of Byron's most famous and lengthy postscripts, appended to a letter to Hobhouse and dated 5 December, relates the episode of the Mainnotes, from whom Byron and his party escaped at Cape Colonna: 'We were all armed (about 12 with our attendants),' narrates Byron. 'The Albanians, my Turkish bandy legged Cook, a servant of Lusieri's & myself had guns and pistols [. . .] but how we should have carried out the war is very doubtful.' That self-effacement does not underplay the degree of risk in the situation, however, in which Byron revels in 'free-flowing and on-rushing style'. It is one of those moments of later happening, which helps reflect immediacy and impact – 'I open my letter to mention an escape' – imbuing urgency in a way that a separate letter would not. The act of reopening the letter is partly the key to this, but the stylistic affect lies primarily in juxtaposition with the body of an epistle in which Byron has wearily reflected on his lack of news and general indolence: 'my life has, with the exception of a very few moments, never been anything but a *yawn*' (*BLJ*, vol. 2, pp. 27–31). Letter and postscript give entirely contrary impressions – both characterised by Byron writing what comes 'uppermost', of course – but so tonally distinct as to suggest that Byron's afterthought is designed to correct the impression given earlier as one unrepresentative of his character and mood. Far from being disconnected – by the threshold of Byron's signature and the passage of over a week (the original letter is dated 26 November) – there is a dialogue of sorts between text and para-text, which has to do with style and pitch.

All of these examples work through at length the stylistic anxieties brought on by haste. Byron would even at times address these openly in his postscripts, as when he writes to Hobhouse about not having time to be 'commonsensible' or, as in a letter to Murray of 1 March 1821, again citing haste as the excuse for his uninhibitedness, 'I am in a polemical humour' (*BLJ*, vol. 8, p. 88). These are in one sense, to quote Genette, 'genre indications', aimed at reasserting Byron's control over his original thoughts.[24] Byron's postscripts of this sort, like the concluding couplet of the *ottava rima* stanza, serve the double function, then, of signalling spontaneity and artfulness, heedlessness and caution. The impression of haste can, in this model, be just as much an indicator of attention to detail and stylistic self-consciousness as it can be of impulsiveness.

It was not uncommon for Byron to include a postscript that was longer than his original letter, and one such example to Hobhouse on the subject of Byron's refusal to sell Newstead Abbey reveals the complexity of his stylistic manœuvrings in his attempt to assert control through highlighting its apparent relinquishment. I will analyse this letter in full in bringing this essay to a conclusion, as it seems to me to be exemplary of the argument I am making:

> Dear Hobhouse, – I wrote to you to apprise Mr. Hanson (as I have done in a letter, but wish you to repeat my refusal) that I will *not* sell Newstead according to his suggestion. – I shall enter into no details but state the sum total, viz, that I am ruined. – For further particulars enquire at No. 6. – My compts to Matthews and Davies, send Mrs. Pigot a copy of your miscellany, and believe me
>
> > yours very truly
> > BYRON
>
> P.S. – I beg you will repeat very seriously for me, that let the consequence be as it may, ruin to myself and all connected with me (D. and the old women inclusive) I will not sell Newstead, *No, oXi, yok, yeo* (Albanesico) *Noa* (Nottinghamshirico) [*Ναω*?], μή, ούκ, Christ, Mahomet, Confucius and Zoroaster to witness my sincerity and Cam Hobhouse to make it manifest to the ears and eyes of men, and I further ask his pardon for a long postscript to a short letter.
>
> P. S. 2d. – If any body is savage and wants satisfaction for my satire, write, that I may return, and give it. – (*BLJ*, vol. 2, p. 26)

The main text could not communicate more successfully the impression of speed. Byron negates Hanson's suggestion by confirming, in a version of the declaration of haste we have already examined, that he will 'enter into no details': giving short shrift to them, in fact. But the perfunctory nature of the comment – communicating Byron's desire to keep things brief – leads him into a comic dismissiveness of a serious subject, a juxtaposition that he often felt free to adopt in his correspondence with an intimate friend: 'For further particulars enquire at No. 6.' Byron's facetiousness and melodramatic strategy come to the fore ('viz, that I am ruined'). The full meaning of the text can be sourced elsewhere (if Hobhouse is interested enough to enquire). Byron's incautious self-assertion is designed to leave the impression of his lack of truck with Hanson – he strikes a haughty pose – but his stylistic self-consciousness is immediately indicated by his return to the subject in the postscript, where he commands Hobhouse to repeat 'very *seriously*' what, in the main body of the letter, the comic tone may have misrepresented. The effectiveness of haste – its brevity 'without verbosity' leading to 'a climax of clarity and emphasis' (*BLJ*, vol. 1, p. 2) – is simultaneously the quality that might undo its success.

Far from bringing clarity or closure to the matter, Byron's abruptness instead requires a postscript, and a lengthy one at that, to serve that function, and what a wonderful comic study of Byron's own deepest anxieties that postscript is. Far from correct, it amplifies levity, becoming, through the parade of the many languages in which Byron felt he could say 'No', a comic parody of the brevity that he seeks and fails to assert: '*No*, *oXi*, *yok*, *yeo* (Albanesico) *Noa* (Nottinghamshirico) [*Naw?*], μή, οὐκ'. 'No' is English; 'Oxi' means 'no' in Greek; 'yok' is Turkish; 'yeo' Albanian; 'Noa' an approximation of an East Midlands accent; 'Naw' a variant of no associated with Northern England but probably indicating Scotland in this instance; μή and οὐκ' are, of course, Ancient Greek. This tour of domestic linguistic possibilities – added to those of the Levant – is abetted by the hyperbole of Byron's invocation of a series of figures of major world religions and his plea that Hobhouse make manifest his 'sincerity'. The word 'sincerity', as with declarations of haste (but particularly given the context of its usage here in prophetic mode), invites ironic scrutiny, and yet Byron felt utterly in earnest about resisting the sale of Newstead. He self-consciously draws attention to his tone or style even in haste, which indicates – and perhaps we could even say is enacting or performing – his frustration. Writing hastily leads to second thoughts. The second postscript, on the subject of *English Bards and Scotch Reviewers* (1809), also needs to be accommodated. It is not just the addition of a subject Byron forgot to mention – a thought left out that again corroborates haste – but a further reassertion, if there was any doubt, that he is in feisty mood.[25]

A long postscript to a short letter reveals, if nothing else, the ways in which Byron's epistolary afterthoughts complicate the familiar attribution of unselfconsciousness and disregard for his rules of relation (at least relative to his high regard for rules and form – often seen as contrasting a general movement away from strict adherence to form and genre in the Romantic period – in his published work). It also indicates, chiming with a theme that has often struck Byron scholars as significant, a related anxiety about the ability to achieve closure, or provide the conclusory statement that the *OED*'s definition of the postscript also incorporates. Paul Elledge has considered the subject of valediction in relation to the most famous example of a letter in Byron's verse, which is the one that Donna Julia composes to Juan at the end of Canto I, which runs over six stanzas. As Elledge observes, the act of closing and sending a letter is a difficult one (*Don Juan* I, ll. 1577–84) because it entails the acknowledgement of a severance: 'hers the anxiety of every writer about to abandon an imagined audience by suspending address to it (in order, of course, to establish contact with it)'.[26] Establishing contact – closing, sealing, franking and dispatching a letter – entails all the ceremony of leave-taking, the relinquishment of personal control on its subject, and it is not difficult to sense an equivalent anxiety in Byron here (he was genuinely unsettled by his financial predicament, whatever his bravado may suggest) and in many of his other postscripts. Byron could certainly overplay his valedictions, ornamenting and lingering over them, as in the example of a letter to William Harness: 'But all this will be dull enough for you and so, good night, to end my chapter or rather homily in an orthodox manner, "as it was in the beginning, is now & ever shall be" believe me my dear H. yours most affectly. BYRON' (*BLJ*, vol. 1, p. 198). More than this, the postscript signals what Findlay called the 'ambiguities of Byronic affirmation', where tone belies content and vice versa. We might add to this the ambiguities of Byronic indifference, which often turns out to be anything but.

Rebecca Earle has argued that letter-writers are often concerned with defining the status of their non-literary, 'ephemeral epistolary selves', largely because letters lack the closure and authority provided by publication.[27] This is a type of self-consciousness. Writing what comes uppermost at the moment, Byron frequently acknowledges the provisional status of his epistolary self and, as has been often written of Byron, this involves his ability to perform a *volte-face* on a subject at any moment. A postscript is useful for this, as it can generate juxtaposition. And even though codicils do not necessarily point to a change of mind, they usually imply doubt of some kind, whether a given postscript ironically subverts, superintends, supplements, glosses or reinscribes the sentiment of the main body of the letter (and Byron's do all of these things at different times). Doubt also lies in valediction, on which subject the postscript, having the privileged status of providing the last word, also speaks. Elledge argues that '[d]ecisive physical and verbal disengagements are difficult Byronic acts', but curiously they are often made even more so, as in the long postscript to a short letter to Hobhouse, for the very appearance of decisiveness.[28] For Findlay, 'the prospect of imminent closure is as unnerving to [Byron] in prose as in poetry, because he wishes always to make a clearing for himself to secure escape from the thickets of his own affirmations'.[29] I have argued that the postscript, that most marginal of texts, plays a central role in Byron's correspondence in placing those Byronic affirmations in doubt, in indicating a circumspection that often cannot be allowed to intrude into the main body of a letter. The postscript seems to be one of those very 'obstacles' that, according to Findlay, Byron uses to hedge around his affirmations, indicating that something has been left out. We should not be surprised at the glut of Byronic postscripts, given that afterthoughts are usually concomitant with spontaneous utterances. But while Byron could dismiss the extraneous details of publishing in a letter to Murray – 'I care nothing about types or margins' (*BLJ*, vol. 2, p. 100) – I believe the marginal text in the postscripts to his epistolary prose tells us something about the relational anxiety that is just as central to our reading of Byron's verbal self-fashioning as are his oft-remarked heedlessness and indifference.

## Notes

1. Moore, *Letters and Journals of Lord Byron*. As Elfenbein has argued, no book 'had a greater impact on Victorian perceptions of Byron'. Elfenbein, *Byron and the Victorians*, p. 78.
2. Genette defines an epitext as a type of text outside the main literary one under consideration: for example, 'newspapers and magazines, radio or television programs, lectures and colloquia [. . .]. Anywhere outside the book may also be the statements contained in an author's correspondence.' Genette, *Paratexts: Thresholds of Interpretation*, pp. 344–5. It is not my intention to engage with Genette at length in this essay, particularly as he has little to say about postscripts, rather to point out that reading postscripts involves similar manœuvres to considering Genette's other category of 'peritext' – any text appended to a literary work – which forms a threshold to the reading experience that we must self-consciously cross on exiting a letter.
3. Jump, 'Byron's Prose', p. 16.
4. Interestingly, this was a day on which Byron wrote at least six, rapidly composed letters.
5. Nicholson argues that 'one essential difference emerges between Byron the poet and Byron the prose-writer: self-consciousness'. Nicholson, 'Byron's Prose', p. 194. Diakonova distinguishes between the effects of spontaneity and incongruity in Byron's prose and verse, arguing that the 'innovations of Byron's prose style are enhanced [in the poetry] because they are emphasized by their contrast [. . .] to established rules'. Diakonova, 'Byron's Prose and Poetry', p. 558. It is my contention, departing from this reading, that, while they may have been less visible or coherent, Byron's epistolary prose still invoked rules of a literary kind, even as they were often being transgressed. See also Lansdown, 'The Letters and Journals', pp. 47–62.
6. Jump, 'Byron's Prose', p. 17.
7. See Stauffer, *Anger, Revolution and Romanticism*.
8. Rawes, 'Byron's Love Letters', pp. 1–14.

9. Further examples of Byron's use of very formal or ceremonial diction might include the postscript to his letter to Annabella on the subject of an earlier '*ambiguous* expression' (*BLJ*, vol. 4, p. 149), where he writes in the plainest terms imaginable. His earlier ambiguity leads to the need for later clarity, which fits with the dominant theme that I explore in his use of postscripts in this essay. On the subject of tone, Byron wrote to Hobhouse 'nothing like *Self* to make a man in earnest' (*BLJ*, vol. 4, p. 270), but if we really want to find earnestness in Byron's letters, then subjects such as the precedent for his swimming the Hellespont would be high on the list of examples. With a subject on which he can really hold forth – rather than his own mood – Byron's tone is utter earnestness in a postscript such as the one added to a letter to Murray of 21 February 1821 (*BLJ*, vol. 8, pp. 82–3).

10. At certain periods, including his residence in Ravenna in 1821, Byron was also on his guard, as he suspected his letters were being opened and read (see 'Letter to Murray, 26 April 1821', *BLJ*, vol. 8, p. 102).

11. Findlay, '"Perpetual Activity" in Byron's Prose', p. 32.

12. Ibid., p. 32.

13. For other examples, see the 'Letter to Lady Melbourne, 16 May 1814' (*BLJ*, vol. 4, p. 116) or the 'Letter to Kinnaird, 11 May 1817' (*BLJ*, vol. 5, p. 226).

14. Although Byron could write about his haste of composition and still proceed to append a postscript, suggesting he had found a little more time, as in the 'Letter to Augusta, 25 April 1805' (*BLJ*, vol. 1, p. 68).

15. This episode is particularly pertinent to the subject of the present essay, as it involves a further afterthought on Byron's part. Having discovered that the author of the book was a woman, Byron ordered Murray to cancel the note appended to *Marino Faliero* (*BLJ*, vol. 7, p. 173, n. 1).

16. Franklin, *Byron: Routledge Guides to Literature*, p. 17.

17. Chatsiou, 'Lord Byron: Paratext and Poetics', p. 642. See also Webb, '*Childe Harold's Pilgrimage*: Annotating the Second Canto', pp. 127–44; Genette, *Paratexts*, pp. 82–3.

18. Another example of a supplementary joke that I feel compelled to include here is the one made to Henry Drury immediately following his marriage to Annabella, in which Byron precipitately casts for himself the role of jaundiced spouse: 'P.S. – My Half – (or three quarters) receives & returns your compliments – she is a woman of Learning – which I have great hopes she means to keep to herself' (*BLJ*, vol. 4, p. 271). It is a gag that could come straight from Congreve and shows Byron writing in his buffooning mode. Comic tone and diction is no guarantee of comic mood however. On the eve of his marriage, Byron's postscript to Moore captures the bridegroom's anxiety much better than would an open admission: 'P.S. – I have just been composing an epistle to the archbishop for an especial licence. Oons! it looks serious [. . .]. Your new coat! – I wonder you like the colour, and don't go about, like Dives, in purple' (*BLJ*, vol. 4, p. 243).

19. In a similar vein, Gayle describes Byron dressing 'his most serious thoughts in flippancy', Gayle, 'Byron, the Matchless Lily and Aurora', pp. 15–25, at p. 22.
20. Wisdom, 'Logical Constructions (I)', p. 58.
21. Byron is not, of course, alone in invoking haste as an excuse for errors or misjudgements. Compare Walter Scott's 'Excuse this hasty scrawl' in a letter written to Byron in summer 1814. Grierson, ed., *The Letters of Sir Walter Scott 1815–17*, p. 4. Byron, however, develops the familiar entreaty into something of an art form.
22. Findlay, '"Perpetual Activity"', p. 32.
23. Diakonova, 'Byron's Prose and Poetry', p. 548.
24. Genette, *Paratexts*, p. 94.
25. It may also be the case that, concerned with the way he may appear to Hobhouse, he directs him 'as explicitly as he dares without sacrificing his ironic cover', as Findlay has argued of a different letter to Dallas. Findlay, '"Perpetual Activity"', p. 38.
26. Elledge, '"Breaking Up Is Hard to Do": Byron's Julia and the Instabilities of Valediction', pp. 52–3.
27. Earle, *Epistolary Selves: Letters and Letter-Writers, 1600–1945*, p. 3.
28. Elledge, 'Never Say(ing) Goodbye: Mediated Valediction in Byron's *Don Juan XI*', p. 18.
29. Findlay, '"Perpetual Activity"', p. 38.

## Works cited

Chatsiou, Ourania (2014), 'Lord Byron: Paratext and Poetics', *The Modern Language Review*, 109, pp. 640–62.

Diakonova, Nina (1976), 'Byron's Prose and Poetry', *Studies in English Literature, 1500–1900*, 16, pp. 547–61.

Earle, Rebecca (1999), *Epistolary Selves: Letters and Letter-Writers, 1600–1945*, Aldershot: Ashgate.

Elfenbein, Andrew (1995), *Byron and the Victorians*, Cambridge: Cambridge University Press.

Elledge, Paul (1991), '"Breaking Up Is Hard to Do": Byron's Julia and the Instabilities of Valediction', *South Atlantic Review*, 56, pp. 43–57.

— (1992), 'Never Say(ing) Goodbye: Mediated Valediction in Byron's *Don Juan XI*', *The Byron Journal*, 20, pp. 17–26.

Findlay, L. M. (1984), '"Perpetual Activity" in Byron's Prose', *The Byron Journal*, 12, pp. 31–47.

Franklin, Caroline (2007), *Byron: Routledge Guides to Literature*. London: Routledge.

Gayle, N. E. (2016), 'Byron, the Matchless Lily and Aurora', *The Byron Journal*, 44, pp. 15–26.

Genette, Gérard (1997), *Paratexts: Thresholds of Interpretation*, trans. Jane E. Lewin, Cambridge: Cambridge University Press.

Grierson, Herbert J. C., ed. (1932–7), *The Letters of Sir Walter Scott 1815–17*, London: Constable.

Jump, John D. (1975), 'Byron's Prose', in: John D. Jump (ed.), *Byron: A Symposium*, London and Basingstoke: Macmillan, pp. 16–34.

Lansdown, Richard (2004), 'The Letters and Journals', in: Drummond Bone (ed.), *The Cambridge Companion to Byron*, Cambridge: Cambridge University Press, pp. 47–62.

Moore, Thomas (1830), *Letters and Journals of Lord Byron*, New York: J. & J. Harper.

Nicholson, Andrew (2004), 'Byron's Prose', in: Drummond Bone (ed.), *The Cambridge Companion to Byron*, Cambridge: Cambridge University Press, pp. 186–206.

Rawes, Alan (2015), 'Byron's Love Letters', *The Byron Journal*, 43, pp. 1–14.

Stauffer, Andrew M. (2005), *Anger, Revolution and Romanticism*, Cambridge: Cambridge University Press.

Webb, Timothy (2013), '*Childe Harold's Pilgrimage*: Annotating the Second Canto', *Byron Journal*, 41, pp. 127–44.

Wisdom, John (1966, repr. 2006), 'Logical Constructions (I)', in: Irving M. Copi and Robert W. Beard (eds), *Essays on Wittgenstein's Tractatus*, Oxford: Routledge, pp. 39–66.

## List of Contributors

**Drummond Bone** was Professor of English Literature at the Universities of Glasgow and London. He has been Principal of Royal Holloway, University of London, Vice-Chancellor of the University of Liverpool and President of Universities UK, and is currently Master of Balliol College, Oxford, and Chair of the Arts and Humanities Research Council. He was the academic editor of the *Byron Journal* for ten years, was a founding editor and is now a Senior Advisory editor of the journal *Romanticism*, and has published much on Byron and the Romantics, including *Byron* for the Writers and their Work series (2000), and editing the *Cambridge Companion to Byron* (2004). He has also published the occasional short story.

**Anna Camilleri** currently holds a Career Development Fellowship in English at Christ Church, Oxford, where she teaches Literature from 1660 to the Present Day. Her primary research interests are on aspects of Romantic poetry, especially Byron, with a particular focus on gender, genre and form. She has published articles in *Essays in Criticism*, *The Byron Journal* and *The Charles Lamb Bulletin*, and is currently preparing her first book, *Byron, Gender, and the Heroic* for publication in the Oxford English Monograph series. Her second book, *Byron: The Man, the Myth, the Poet* is under contract with Harvard University Press.

**Caroline Franklin** is Professor of English at Swansea University. Her latest book is *The Female Romantics: Nineteenth-Century Women Novelists and Byronism* (2013). She leads an Arts and Humanities Research Council (AHRC)-funded project to publish a digital edition of the letters of the eighteenth-century Shakespearean critic, Elizabeth Montagu.

**Jonathan Gross** is the author of *Byron: The Erotic Liberal* (2000) and *The Life of Anne Damer: Portrait of a Regency Artist* (2013).

He has edited *Byron's 'Corbeau Blanc': The Life and Letters of Lady Melbourne* (1997) and the scrapbooks of Thomas Jefferson (2006). He is also the editor of *Emma, or the Unfortunate Attachment* (2004), *The Sylph* (2007) and *Belmour* (2011), and of novels by Georgiana, Duchess of Devonshire (1757–1806), and Anne Damer. In 2012, he produced a CD entitled *The Harlem Renaissance Remembered*, featured on the Duke Ellington webpage, and two other short works entitled 'Eye on the Sparrow: Afterlives of Ethel Waters and Bessie Smith' and 'Graffiti Kings', which have been performed at Stockton University in New Jersey and at the Old Town School of Folk Music. A Board Member of the Byron Society of America, he serves as Joint President of the International Association of Byron Societies.

**Ralf Haekel** teaches English Literature and Culture at the Georg-August-University Göttingen. In 2003 he received his PhD degree from the Freie Universität Berlin and in 2013 his Habilitation from Göttingen University. He has acted as substitute Chair at the universities of Frankfurt, Darmstadt and Hanover. His recent publications include *The Soul in British Romanticism: Negotiating Human Nature in Philosophy, Science and Poetry* (2014) and (with Sabine Blackmore) *Discovering the Human: Life Sciences and the Arts in the 18th and Early 19th Centuries* (2013). He is also editor of the *Handbook of British Romanticism: Text and Theory* (2017).

**Nicholas Halmi** is Professor of English and Comparative Literature at the University of Oxford and Margaret Canfield Fellow of University College, Oxford. He is the author of *The Genealogy of the Romantic Symbol* (2007) and the editor, most recently, of the Norton Critical Edition of *Wordsworth's Poetry and Prose* (2013). He was awarded a Leverhulme Trust Major Research Fellowship for 2015–17 to write a book on aesthetic historicism in the Romantic era.

**Richard Lansdown** teaches English Literature in Groningen, The Netherlands. He is the author of *Byron's Historical Dramas* (1992), *The Cambridge Introduction to Byron* (2012) and *Byron's Letters and Journals: A New Selection* (2015). He has also written *The Autonomy of Literature* (2001), *Strangers in the South Seas: The Idea of the Pacific in Western Thought* (2006) and *A New Scene of Thought: Studies in Romantic Realism* (2016), as well as articles on William Wordsworth, Jane Austen, Thomas Hardy, Henrik Ibsen, Bronislaw Malinowski and James Kelman.

**Norbert Lennartz** is Professor of English Literature at the University of Vechta in Germany. His teaching and research range from Shakespeare to Byron, from the Victorian Age to the early 20th century. Among his major publications are a book on the deconstruction of eroticism in seventeenth-century British poetry (2009), a collection of essays on representations of food (*The Pleasures and Horrors of Eating: The Cultural History of Eating in Anglophone Literature*, 2010, co-edited with Marion Gymnich) and two on new directions in Dickens criticism (*Dickens's Signs, Readers Designs*, 2012, with Francesca Orestano, and *Text, Contexts and Intertextuality: Dickens as a Reader*, 2014, with Dieter Koch). He is currently preparing for publication a monograph on bodily fluids and porous bodies, *Niobe's Siblings: A Cultural History of Tears, Fluids and Porous Bodies*, and a collection of essays on *The Lost Romantics*.

**Rolf Lessenich** is Professor Emeritus of English (and Comparative) Literature at Bonn University, Germany. Among his book publications are *Elements of Pulpit Oratory in Eighteenth-Century England 1660–1800* (1972), *Lord Byron and the Nature of Man* (1978), *Aspects of English Preromanticism* (1989) and *Neoclassical Satire and the Romantic School 1780–1830* (2012). His latest book on *Romantic Disillusionism and the Sceptical Tradition* has just been released with Bonn University Press (2017). His research interests are chiefly in literary history from the 17th to the 19th centuries. He is the author of about seventy periodical and *Festschrift* essays, contributions to books, dictionary articles on English and comparative literature from Shakespeare to Modernism, as well as the Classical tradition.

**Stephen Minta** is Senior Lecturer in the Department of English and Related Literature at the University of York. He is the author of books on French and Italian poetry, and on the Latin American novelist Gabriel García Márquez, as well as two travel books, *Aguirre, the Re-creation of a Sixteenth-century Journey Across South America*, which was a New York Times Notable Book for 1994, and *On a Voiceless Shore: Byron in Greece* (1998). He has written numerous articles on Byron, with particular reference to Byron's engagement with Greece and the politics of the Greek War of Independence.

**Tom Mole** is Reader in English Literature and Director of the Centre for the History of the Book at the University of Edinburgh. He specialises in literature and book history in the eighteenth and nineteenth centuries in Britain. He is the author of *Byron's Romantic Celebrity*

(2007) and the editor of *Romanticism and Celebrity Culture* (2009), *The Broadview Reader in Book History* (with Michelle Levy, 2014) and a volume of selections from *Blackwood's Edinburgh Magazine* (2006). His most recent works are *What the Victorians Made of Romanticism* (2017), *The Broadview Introduction to Book History* (with Michelle Levy, 2017) and *Interacting with Print* (with the Interacting with Print Collective, 2017).

**Michael O'Neill** is Professor of English at Durham University. His publications include, as sole author, books on Shelley, Romantic poetry and the twentieth-century legacy of Romantic poetry; as co-author, books on poets of the 1930s (with Gareth Reeves) and on poetic form (with Michael D. Hurley, 2012); as editor, *The Cambridge History of English Poetry* (2010); and, as co-editor, a selection of Shelley's poetry and prose (with Zachary Leader, 2003), volume 3 of the Johns Hopkins edition of Shelley's poetry (with various editors, 2012), *The Oxford Handbook of Percy Bysshe Shelley* (with Anthony Howe and with the assistance of Madeleine Callaghan, 2012), and *The Persistence of Beauty: Victorians to Moderns* (with Mark Sandy and Sarah Wootton, 2015). He has written a number of essays and chapters on Byron. His most recent volume of poems, *Gangs of Shadow*, appeared in 2014.

**Jonathon Shears** is a Senior Lecturer in English at Keele University who specialises in literature of the long nineteenth century. Since 2012 he has been editor of *The Byron Journal*. His major publications include *The Romantic Legacy of Paradise Lost* (2009), *Reading, Writing and the Influence of Harold Bloom* (co-edited with Alan Rawes, 2010), *Literary Bric-à-Brac and the Victorians* (co-edited with Jen Harrison, 2013) and *The Great Exhibition, 1851: A Sourcebook* (2016). He has recently edited a collection of essays with Bernard Beatty called *Byron's Temperament* (2016). He is currently writing a monograph, *The Hangover: A Cultural History, 1600–2000*, due for publication in 2018, and working on ideas for a book on Byron.

**Josefina Tuominen-Pope** is a doctoral student at the University of Zürich. She has an MA in English Language, Linguistics and English Literature from the University of Zürich and a BA in German Philology from the University of Helsinki.

**Friederike Wolfrum** has worked as a university assistant with the interdisciplinary doctorate programme 'Figuration Counterculture' of the Research Area 'Cultural Encounters – Cultural Conflicts' at the University of Innsbruck and as a research and teaching assistant at the University of Bonn. She read English Studies and Computer Science at the Universities of Bonn and Arizona, and is currently writing her doctoral thesis on the motif of nympholepsy as countercultural mythopoiesis in the writings of Late Romanticism. Her research interests include British Romanticism, cognitive poetics, countercultural writing practices, and ideological uses of mythology. She is currently publishing an edited volume *Counter | Culture: Literature, Language, Agency.*

# Index